Sociology of sport

THE DORSEY SERIES IN SOCIOLOGY

Editor   ROBIN M. WILLIAMS, JR.   *Cornell University*

Sociology of sport

HARRY EDWARDS
University of California, Berkeley

1973

THE DORSEY PRESS Homewood, Illinois 60430
Irwin-Dorsey International, Arundel, Sussex BN18 9AB
Irwin-Dorsey Limited, Georgetown, Ontario L7G 4B3

© THE DORSEY PRESS, 1973

First Printing, March 1973
Second Printing, August 1973
Third Printing, June 1974
Fourth Printing, May 1975
Fifth Printing, January 1975

ISBN 0–256–01415–9
Library of Congress Catalog Card No. 72–95401
Printed in the United States of America

To Jackie Robinson

Preface

Highly organized competitive sports in America have today become so enmeshed in the social turbulence of our times, so embroiled in economic struggles and the stresses of corporate expansionism, and so generally complex as social phenomena that the origins of many of these activities in the casual amusements and diversionary pastimes of 19th century Americans seem all but utterly irrelevent. Yet, despite the obvious interconnectedness of organized sports with other societal structures and processes, little writing has emerged of either an academic or nonacademic nature that even approaches a broad, analytical assessment of what has happened and is happening *in* and *to* American sport. The present book is aimed at closing this gap in our knowledge and understanding of what is, sociologically speaking, perhaps the most ignored of America's institutions.

This work tries to present a comprehensive analytical profile of the institution of sport in America, its development, the complexities of its contemporary functions for the individual and society, and its potential as a significant and influential factor in the future of what has come to be termed "the American way of life."

The book is divided into three parts:

Part I presents a brief introduction, a cursory survey of the significant writings on sport in sociology and psychology, a historical overview of the development of sport in America, and a chapter detailing the unique features of "sport" as opposed to "play," "games," "contests or matches," and "recreation" types of physical activity. At the conclusion of this chapter an operational definition of sport is developed and employed throughout the remainder of the work.

Part II constitutes the core chapters of the book. This section presents an analysis and discussion of the social, political, and economic complexities of sport. Particular emphasis is given to the analysis of the coaching role, the athlete role, and the role of the fan as these are influenced by the values regulating behavior in the sports institution. It is this system of values, referred to here as the "dominant American sports creed," which is demonstrated to be a key to the understanding of sport as an important institutional component of the American social system.

Part III is concerned with the significance of sport in relation to social change processes. The book concludes with a brief discussion of the soundness and utility of viewing the processes and stresses inside of the institution of sport as microcosmic manifestations of many forces influencing the contemporary situation and the future prospects of American society as a whole.

It would take another volume to acknowledge the contributions of all the people who aided in the production of this work. However, I must express my deep appreciation to the following individuals without whose help and interest this book could never have been completed. Drs. Gordon F. Streib, Robin M. Williams, Jr., and William F. Whyte of Cornell University rendered criticisms of the first draft of this manuscript and insightful suggestions for revisions that are greatly responsible for whatever scholarly attributes this final version might possess.

The published works of Drs. Jack Scott, Eldon Snyder, Norman R. Yetman, Stanley Eitzen, John W. Loy, Gerald S. Kenyon, Paul Weiss, Bruce C. Ogilvie, and Thomas A. Tutko were invaluable as resources in the production of this work.

The theory and ideas of Francis X. Sutton, Seymour E. Harris, Carl Kaysen, and James Tobin as expressed in their book *The American Business Creed* have provided the developmental format for this manuscript. To the extent that the present work represents a contribution to the study and sociological investigation of sport, it was possible largely because the author "stood on the shoulders of giants."

My thanks also to Willa Parrott and Janice Tanigawa who typed the manuscript. And, finally, I would like to express my appreciation for the understanding and moral support provided by my lovely wife, Sandra, who in our first two years of marriage has not known a day that I did not work on this manuscript.

February 1973   HARRY EDWARDS

Contents

The occupational milieu of the coach. The coaching role. Coach-athlete relations. The coach and the academic community. The head coach and his assistants. The black assistant coach. The black coach in professional sport. The coaching role and the utility of the dominant sports creed in the symbolic resolution of strain. Some exemplary strains in the coaching role and their resolution: *Self-interest versus norms of social responsibility. Self-interest personal goals versus normative demand for cooperation, flexibility, and unselfishness. Aggressiveness and violence versus societal and religious values prescribing altruism. Unquestioning obedience to authority versus values emphasizing superiority of democracy over autocracy. Deliberate physical risk and endangerment versus societal value emphasis on human safety and physical security. Intellectual achievement versus physical accomplishment.*

The athlete role in American sport. Role conflicts. Institutionalized powerlessness. The athlete in black and white. Black athletic superiority. Race-linked physical characteristics. Race-linked psychological factors. Racially specific historical occurrences. Occupational discrimination. Racism within sports. Psychological determinants. The IPAT: Results and some speculative interpretations. The Jackson and the Edwards tests: Results and interpretations. Racial stereotypes. The female athlete role in sport. Strain and the male athlete role.

Fan involvement: Two personal functions. The alumni. The sports reporter. Fan identification. Strains and fan enthusiasm.

Professional sports. Amateur sports. High-level amateur sports. Interscholastic sports. The future of sports.

Character: *Sports participation develops "good character." Sports participation develops a value on loyalty. Sports participation generates altruism.* Discipline: *Sports participation generates a value on social and/or self-control.* Competition: *Sports participation develops fortitude. Sports participation prepares the athlete for life. Sports provide opportunities for individual advancement.* Physical Fitness: *Sports participation generates physical fitness.* Mental fitness: *Sports participation generates mental alertness. Sports participation is supportive of educational achievement.* Other claimed attributes: *Religiosity. Nationalism.*

Part III
Sport in society

part one

The study of American sport

THIS SECTION deals with the definitions, academic history, and developmental background necessary to an understanding of sport in American society. After the introductory statements of chapter 1, there follows a brief discussion of the study of sport in psychology and sociology. Chapter 2 sketches a historical overview of the emergence of modern American sport from nineteenth-century leisure-time amusements and diversionary activities and gives an analysis of major social and technological forces influencing this development. The concern of chapter 3 is to develop operational definitions of "sport" and "sports activities" in contrast to those physical activities more appropriately designated "play," "games," "contests or matches," and "recreation."

1

1

Introduction

An EXTENSIVE SURVEY of the available literature on athletics reveals that there is literally no institution or stratum in modern American society which is not touched in some manner by sport.

In high political circles, athletics have been accorded a status of great significance, as witnessed by the efforts of the late President John F. Kennedy, former President Lyndon B. Johnson, the United States Congress, and the late General Douglas MacArthur to settle disputes between two competing athletic associations—the Amateur Athletic Union and the National Collegiate Athletic Association. President Richard M. Nixon, in one of his first official acts as president, presented a trophy to the University of Texas as the nation's number-one collegiate football power —much to the consternation of the supporters of Pennsylvania University (who pointed to a better record than that of Texas and to the fact that both Pennsylvania State and Texas had prestigious bowl games yet to play).

Sport also has its adherents within the ranks of traditional American religious denominations. In fact, the attitudes of these denominations toward sports have changed markedly since this country's early history, paralleling the general cultural transition from the puritanical ideals of hard work and no play, to highly supportive positions relative to the participation in, and enjoyment of, sports.

The field of medicine, too, offers a supportive and professional interest in athletics. One has only to read the pages of the nation's leading medical journals to ascertain the degree to which the medical profession

3

has accepted sports and even made "semiathletic" activity an integral part of its therapeutic and rehabilitative services. A medical speciality called "sport medicine," which is concerned with the physical and psychological welfare of the athlete and others directly involved in sports, has even developed.

And, of course, the most evident manifestation of Americans' pervasive interest in athletics is to be found in the yearly attendance figures for sporting events and the polls estimating the numbers of Americans viewing and listening to sports events over the electronic media.

More than a few foreign visitors to this country have puzzled over the fact that, despite America's proclamations to the world about its commitment to the capitalistic system, in virtually every newspaper in America—save perhaps the *Wall Street Journal*—the economic section of the paper, if there is one, takes a back seat to the sports pages. In a survey of twenty-five newspapers selected on random dates in 1969 from cities across the nation, I found that three papers had no economic section, five had economic sections less than two pages in length, but all twenty-five papers had sports sections. The average length of the sports sections was three and a half pages and in no case did the economic reports precede the sports sections of these papers. Most often, information on economic matters came after the horse-racing results and, not infrequently, shared a page with the obituaries.

In September of 1969, during the height of a heated mayoral election race in New York City which had attracted international publicity due to the failure of the Republican party to support its own incumbent mayoral candidate (John Lindsay), I carried out a simple survey in an attempt to discover the relative impact of sports as opposed to politics in America's largest city. Standing in front of my hotel at Fifty-fourth and Lexington in the heart of downtown Manhattan, I asked one question, without prompting or further explanation, to 150 people (men and women) who happened by, and then recorded their responses. The question was, "Who is going to win?" The results were as follows: thirteen, no relevant response; twenty-seven, Lindsay (for mayor); six, Proccacino (for mayor); one, Marchi (for mayor); 103, the Mets (for the world championship of professional baseball).

The results of this survey indicate that, during September of 1969, at any rate, the average person on the street in New York City was much more keenly attuned to the possible impending fate of the Mets baseball team than he was to the possible fate of New York City itself under the leadership of one or another of the three highly different political personalities vying for the mayor's job.

Most of this nation's local radio newscasts and news telecasts have special sections of time allotted for sports reporting. And, while it is true that economic matters are often part and parcel of regular news reporting, it is still rather curious that aside from the daily stock market averages—typically tacked on at the end of the regular newscast—the broadcast time specifically allotted to economic matters nowhere even approaches the time given to sports. Major sporting events capture the overwhelming majority of the viewing and listening audience.

In 1968, to avoid interrupting a professional football event with a scheduled third telecast from the vicinity of the moon by Apollo II astronauts, the CBS television network showed the Apollo materials by delayed broadcast, in deference to an anticipated deluge of calls from irate football fans over an interruption of viewing the game.

Even the word "fan," which is short for "fanatic," indicates the enthusiasm for sports in this country.

OBSTACLES TO RESEARCH

However, despite, or even, perhaps, because of, the overwhelming enthusiasm, the staggering amount of news time given to sports, and the increasingly more apparent fact that athletics in America are a good deal more than "fun and games," scholarly and analytical investigation of sport has not kept pace with its increasing significance as an important factor in modern life. Scholarly writings on sports come from many parts of the world and across the ages; they have been contributed by men as diverse in circumstances, interests, and life styles as ancient Greek philosophers and modern physiologists, social scientists, and physical educators. Unfortunately, most of these writings are buried beneath the accumulated daily avalanche of sports folklore, journalistic reports, and sports propaganda—all being produced and disseminated in ever greater volume by ever more efficient means. These phenomena—the tradition of the journalistic orientation to the institution of sport, the diversity of disciplines, interests, and concerns of the more serious scientific thinkers on sport as a social fact, and the fact that scholarly writings on the subject are relatively meager and greatly scattered—have all contributed to the development of a popularized or "folk" appreciation and understanding of the significance of sports. One of the primary effects of this perspective has been to dilute and further obscure the relatively minimal factual information which is available.

There are, however, other specific reasons why serious analytical writings have not kept pace with the development of widespread interest in athletics and the great significance of sports in American life. The following factors appear to be of major importance in this regard.

The first factor has to do with the nature of the academic training given those people most directly involved professionally in sports. Most of the coaching, administrative, and other staff positions in sports require a master's degree or less. Therefore, many of these people see no need to pursue any of the appropriate doctorate degrees which aim at the development of scientific research and analytical skills. (In a survey of the qualifications of 137 coaches affiliated with eighteen California state colleges and three private West Coast universities, it was found that, as of January, 1970, 78 percent had obtained master's degrees; 19 percent had obtained bachelor's degrees, and only 3 percent held the educational doctorate or the Ph.D.) Also, job descriptions and personnel qualification forms for coaching and administrative jobs in athletics seldom mention activities wherein a demonstrated skill in scholarly research or analysis assumes any degree of professional value. Thus, the lack of research training in athletics is reinforced by the traditional practical emphasis placed upon the demonstrated capacity to develop successful sports programs.

In 1969, thirty institutions of higher learning, through their respective departments of physical education, offered to prospective coaches, teachers, and administrators, undergraduate courses dealing with the relationship between athletics and other institutions of the society.[1] Not a single course had prerequisites in methodology or statistics, and only three had introductory sociology as a prerequisite. Further, if one judges course content by the descriptions in the catalogues, most of these courses entailed surveys of the ways athletic organizations have involved civic communities in organization-sponsored sports programs as financial contributors and in terms of fan support. Those which vary from this theme (again if one can believe the course descriptions) seemed to focus primarily upon extolling the virtues of sports in developing character and building citizenship. There was no mention of research as a means of exploring the relationships between athletics and other subsystems of the society.

Thus, one reason why scholarly investigation and writing has not kept pace with the growth of athletics relative to popular interest is that those who are professionally involved in the institution are not, for the most part, trained or oriented toward carrying our rigorous research and analyses. And no scientific research means no scientific reporting.

A second factor underlying the lack of a flourishing *sociologically* oriented research interest in athletics proportionate to its popular social significance is that disciplines outside of physical education have traditionally ignored sport as a realm of human behavior worthy of serious scholarly investigation.

In large part, American scholars' neglect of sport appears to stem from influences characteristic of Western academia as a whole. In essence, the slow emergence of the study of sport as a subdiscipline in the social sciences is attributable to the Western educational tradition of

---

[1] J. W. Loy, Jr., and G. S. Kenyon, *Sport, Culture and Society* (New York: Macmillan Co., 1969), p. 7.

emphasizing intellectual development as opposed to physical expression. Such a tradition demands the avoidance of any academic association with sport which, despite its complexities and significance, nonetheless maintains physical expression as its most dominant and obvious characteristic. This, perhaps, explains why the *International Encyclopedia of the Social Sciences* has no article on "Games," only on "Gambling" and "Game Theory"; no article on "Recreation" or "Sport" but rather cross references to other topics. Only "Leisure" is dignified by the presence of an article. And the American Sociological Association held its *first* section on the sociology of sport as recently as 1971.

Among sociologists, the meager scientific interest in sport has been particularly conspicuous. Along with the pervasive "antiphysical" bias affecting the thrust of Western scholarship, sociologists have in addition for decades harbored professional insecurities stemming from the designation of sociology as a "soft science" (in contrast to the "hard sciences" of physics, chemistry, medicine, engineering, and so forth). This has further heightened the desire to avoid involvement with anything that detracted from the intellectual credibility of the discipline. The avoidance of sport by sociologists has been particularly regrettable since the functioning of the interrelationships among the various components of social systems constitutes a major part of their legitimate scientific domain. Perhaps it is owing to this that nowhere in academia has the neglect of sports as a legitimate scientific concern been so conspicuous as in sociology.

In the humanities and arts, one finds manifestations of considerable interest in athletics. Literature, painting, sculpture, philosophy, and even ballet have all attempted to capture and interpret athletics in terms of their respective mediums. Anthropologists have for years studied the "games" played in particular societies, be they contemporary or extinct, in order to develop a more accurate appraisal of the values and the nature of life in these societies. Psychology has developed a burgeoning new field dubbed "sports psychology" which has dozens of professional practitioners. But, out of eighty schools rated by a University of Michigan study as the top institutions of higher learning, only three sociology-oriented departments offered graduate degrees in the "sociology of sports" or the "sociology of athletics."[2] And, in the judgment of one critic, "Not all who are teaching the sociology of sport today are as well prepared to teach it as they might be."[3] One must assume that at least one of the elements contributing to this lack of preparedness is insufficient sociological research and investigation into the subject.

A third element contributing to the dearth of scholarly writing on athletics has to do with the characteristics of the persons whose coopera-

---

[2] The three universities offering graduate degrees in the sociology of sport are the Universities of Illinois and Wisconsin and Michigan State University.

[3] Loy and Kenyon, p. 5.

tion is imperative if access to the intricacies of organized sport is to be gained. These people are, of course, coaches and administrators. Earlier, some brief statements were made regarding the lack of research and scientific orientation in the professional educational curricula from which most of these individuals emerge.

In light of statements from several psychologists at San Jose State College and at the University of California at Berkeley, it would seem that these professionals—like people in some other professions—have little patience or tolerance for potential "intrusions" into their field by "outsiders." They are seemingly not amenable to cooperation with research projects in which they see little value from the practical standpoint of improving athletic performances. Thus, in the words of Thomas Tutko, a sports psychologist at San Jose State College:

> Entry to the sports arena at the present time is all but completely closed to social scientists, except for those who they (coaches and athletic administrators) feel represent absolutely no threat to them or their notions of what sports is all about. This means no threat to them intellectually; no threat in terms of disrupting their orientations by pointing up needed change; no threat in terms of complicating their lives as coaches and administrators by demonstrating the intricacies and complexities of an institution that they see in very simplistic and intuitive terms.[4]

One important secondary effect of the lack of an emphasis upon scientific research and the development of analytical skills in the physical education curricula might be that the people who are graduated are not only unprepared themselves to carry out sorely needed research, but are also suspicious of those professionals from other disciplines who are so qualified. Thus, those "outsiders" who are granted access to the inner circles of the sport are likely to be only those who the coaches and administrators feel will carry out investigations that yield practical, usable results rather than merely "objective"—and, quite possibly, some unflattering—contributions to the knowledge and understanding of a significant social institution. Hence, the element of suspicion borne of a divergence in educational preparation and professional goals becomes a factor in precluding pursuit of the traditional scientific goal of objective research; and the lack of such research contributes to the already thick veil of ignorance concealing the complexities and significance of sport.

A fourth factor contributing to an insufficient volume of scientific knowledge about athletics is that many people have succumbed to the sports propagandist's theme that organized athletics is, for the most part, merely recreation. In short, throughout the social structure of America, people—laymen and professionals—have traditionally accepted the "fun-

---

[4] Taken from the text of an interview with Dr. Tutko at San jose State College on March 15, 1970.

and-games" image of sport to the almost total exclusion of any consideration regarding its more serious aspects.

Finally, the fifth limiting factor is a scarcity of research funds. In this regard, potential sociological research into athletics has probably fallen victim to more explosive social problems such as violence, race relations, overpopulation, pollution of the environment, and other generally more traditional concerns of those bodies that fund scientific research. And since approximately 75 percent of all research funds granted to both public and private research agencies come either directly or indirectly from some branch, level, or department of government, it is even more understandable why research into athletics—with its "happy-go-lucky" fun-and-games image—are presently of low priority.[5]

But the sports world, too, is entering a period of conflict, confrontation, and instability which poses serious problems for both sport and society. This new period will likely hasten research into this realm of human interaction, particularly as the significance of sport as a social institution becomes more evident.

In the main, analysis and references to the social importance of sport have appeared primarily in three fields of social science: sociology, psychology, and anthropology.

SPORT IN THE SOCIAL SCIENCES

Given the scattered nature of research on sport, it will be useful to present an overview of writings from the two disciplines which ultimately must intensify the scientific investigation of sport if we are to grasp its full social significance. Let us, accordingly, examine the major contributions of sociology and psychology toward the understanding of sport as an element of modern life.

Sociologists have, in the main, concerned themselves with the *functions* of sports. Those who have participated in laying a foundation for what is becoming known as the sociology of sport have done so primarily through their attempts to understand the intricacies of social organization. Some of the most prominent names in sociology and social psychology have incorporated into their work theoretical statements and propositions focusing upon the relevance and significance of athletics in social relationships. The roster of these personages includes Max Weber, Georg Simmel, William Sumner, George H. Mead, and Thorsten Veblen. Nevertheless, one still cannot help but be struck by the lack of empirical investigations offering either support or negation of the theoretical statements that do exist.

Psychology has made its contributions primarily in terms of the de-

---

[5] Ibid.

velopment of theoretical statements aimed at explaining the significance of sport as a factor in intrapersonal development. Unlike sociology, which has had as its central theoretical thrust an attempt to explain the function of sport in society, psychology has traditionally been oriented toward an understanding of the *motivations* determining the appeal of sport for those involved both directly and indirectly with it. But here too, until very recently, very little empirical evidence has been presented either in support or negation of such theories.

As is the case in sociology, theoretical statements concerning recreation and sport have been put forth over the years by psychologists and incorporated to some degree into their best-known theories. Among the prominent thinkers in the field who have put forth theoretical statements focusing upon sport are Sigmund Freud, Erik H. Erickson, and S. R. Slavson, as well as such specialists among contemporary psychologists as Bruce C. Ogilvie and Thomas A. Tutko.

Anthropologists have been concerned chiefly with the *content* of "games." This thrust in the field of anthropology developed from the knowledge that a society will often incorporate into its leisure-time and ceremonial activities key clusters of social rules and values. Particularly in cases where the society has been long extinct, anthropological analysis of the artifacts left from games has not infrequently been of great value in assessing the overall character of that society. Among the leading anthropologists who have utilized this method of investigation are Margaret Mead, Pearl Buck, and Florence Stumpf.

While scientists in each of the fields outlined above have, upon occasion, been concerned about all three aspects of athletic activity—*function, motivation,* and *content*—in general, the tendency has been to focus upon one or another of the three.

With these brief introductory statements in mind, more detailed reviews of the major theoretical and empirical work from sociology and psychology are presented below. Much of the anthropological work done in sport is of high quality and relatively extensive, but, since most of it is of only indirect relevance for present purposes, it will not be discussed.

SPORT IN SOCIOLOGY

The result of the limited and greatly scattered volume of serious writing primarily devoted to the investigation of sport is an increasingly more conspicuous gap in our theories of social organization. For, upon analysis, the various fragments of work comprising the emergent sub-discipline of sport sociology show that, in its broadest sense, this field should be concerned with the description and explanation of the interrelations between sport and other societal components. More specifically, these fragmentary writings have been concerned with the functions of athletics in relation to basic social institutions and processes. The unique feature of the sociological approach to sport, as distinct from that of psychology, has been a focus upon sport in its functions as a component of social organization, used here in the sense defined by Blau and Scott:

> Social organization refers to ways in which human conduct becomes organized, that is, to the observed regularities in the behavior of people that are due to the social conditions in which they find themselves, rather than to their physiological or psychological characteristics as individuals. The many social conditions that influence the conduct of people can be divided into two main types: the structure of social relations in a group or larger collectivity, and the shared beliefs and orientations that unite the members of the collectivity and guide their conduct.[6]

It is under this general rubric of social organization that most of the writings referred to below may be clustered.

Neither time nor space permit an exhaustive presentation of the historical development of sociological interest in sport. However, my review will point up the serious concerns of major sociological thinkers about the functions of sport in social systems.

Serious interest in the nature and functions of athletics by some sociologically oriented scholars has been evident since the 1870s. In the United States, for instance, statements have been made attesting to the role of sports in character formation, in cementing group solidarity, and in the development of fortitude for many years. Some writers have reflected upon their casual observations of athletics over the years, often within a theoretical framework. Others have carried out empirical studies using some rudiments of scientific inquiry. But there is little indication that these writers used a consistent set of conceptual schemas to describe the object of their interests. And even where different writers have used the same terms, the meanings were often inconsistent. Despite these difficulties, over the past 100 years three concepts have emerged to which most writers have addressed themselves: the concepts of "play," "game," and "sport."

In sociological literature, "play" apparently preceded the concepts of "game" and "sport" as a scientific concept. Moreover, the first attempts to utilize the concept of play in theoretical frameworks were more often in a sociopsychological vein than in a strict sociological usage.

Though buried deep within the context of larger bodies of work in which an interest in the sociological significance of play was only one component, some early theoretical statements have made valuable contributions in that they stimulated further inquiry. Both the sociology and the psychology of sport have common beginnings in the sociopsychologi-

---

[6] Peter M. Blau and W. Richard Scott, *Formal Organizations* (San Francisco: Chandler, 1962), p. 2.

cal and sociophilosophical works of writers such as Spencer (1873), who say play as the use of "accumulated energy in unused faculties";[7] Groos, who in 1898 proposed that play was "role practice for life";[8] G. Stanley Hall, whose recapitulation theory (1920) explained play as being due to the fact that "ontogeny repeats Phylogeny";[9] and McDougall, for whom play was the primitive expression of instincts.[10]

By the turn of the century, more sociologically inclined writers had already begun to acknowledge the complexities of leisure-time activities as they functioned as elements of social organization. In an effort to grasp these more complex qualities, these sociologists discarded the concept of play and all but replaced it with the term "game." The exact reasoning underlying the preference for "game" over "play" is somewhat unclear. None of the theorists who used "game" dealt at length with the concept itself. But, by contrasting the contexts in which the two words were used, one gets the impression that, to men such as Weber and Simmel, "game" denoted play in a more collective, goal-directed sense. To them "game" apparently meant social activity carried out within the context of a network of rules, roles, and relationships and guided by the desire to accomplish a defined goal. Thus, the conceptualization of the "game" added new dimensions to what Spencer, McDougall, Groos, and Hall had observed as "play" resulting from social instincts, unused faculties, and the like.

While Simmel suggested in his writings that games have the function of preparing people for adult roles, Weber was mostly concerned with the historical prevalence of games as social phenomena.[11]

Weber, however, was not alone in attempting to develop a partial theoretical framework to explain the traditional prevalence of games through the ages and across social strata. George H. Mead, writing in 1934, studied children at play and observed how games theoretically provided "a medium for the development of the self."[12]

More recent conceptualizations of game have been those of Erving Goffman and Eric Berne. For Goffman, the games were a "situated ac-

---

[7] H. Spencer, *The Principles of Psychology* (New York: D. Appleton and Co., 1873), cited by H. C. Lehman and P. A. Witty, *The Psychology of Play Activities* (New York: A. S. Barnes, 1927), p. 73.

[8] Karl Groos, *The Play of Animals* (New York: D. Appleton and Co., 1898), cited in Loy, Gerald Kenyon, p. 2.

[9] G. S. Hall, *Youth* (New York: D. Appleton and Co., 1920), p. 2.

[10] W. McDougall, *Social Psychology* (New York: J. W. Luce and Co., 1918), cited in Loy and Kenyon, p. 9.

[11] H. Wolff, *The Sociology of Georg Simmel* (New York: Free Press, 1964), pp. 49–50. R. Bendix, *Max Weber, an Intellectual Portrait* (New York: Doubleday, 1962), p. 364.

[12] G. H. Mead, *Self and Society* (Chicago: University of Chicago Press, 1934), p. 152.

tivity system" or "focused gathering" having rules for role playing and interaction for all participants.[13] For Berne, the various forms of human interaction were all considered within a "game situation," with all forms capable of being played in an "adult," "parent," or "child" context.[14] Thus, games, for Berne as for others, constituted vehicles of socialization and "models" of much adult interaction.

Of the three conceptualizations receiving primary sociological attention—play, game, and sport—"sport" has been the least used, partly because its meaning and its differences from play and game in the literature are unclear. Nevertheless, Veblen had made use of the term extensively as early as 1899. In his *Theory of the Leisure Class*, Veblen saw sport as a "reversion to barbarian culture." Whether engaged in by the leisure class or the working class, sport was a "mark of an arrested spiritual development."[15]

Compared with the caustic Veblen, other sociologically oriented early twentieth-century writers were more analytical and less harsh in their evaluations of sport. As early as 1906, William Graham Sumner devoted an entire chapter of his classic *Folkways* to sports, exhibitionism, and drama.[16] His usage of the term was also unclear and rather nebulous. However, he did see sport as one means of socializing children to the values of the society.

By the middle of the 1930s, cumulatively speaking, play, game, and sport had received a good deal of scattered, unorganized, but, nonetheless, important attention. By far the most consistent sociological analysis of the concepts had been achieved in Europe. Of the European writers, one of the most significant is Huizinga. In 1938, John Huizinga, a sociologically oriented Dutch historian, wrote *Homo Ludens*, in which he attempted to show the role of sport in nearly every aspect of social life from war to religion.[17] Although his work is referred to by members of a number of disciplines, no work of note has surfaced which pretends to test any of Huizinga's suppositions and hypotheses.

Roger Caillois, a French sociologist, going beyond Huizinga, classified games into four major types according to whether competition, fate, disguise, or "pursuit of vertigo" predominated. (Caillois labeled these categories "Agon," "Alea," "Mimicry," and "Ilinx," respectively.)[18] He en-

---

[13] Erving Goffman, *Encounters* (Indianapolis: Bobbs-Merril, 1961); *The Presentation of Self in Everyday Life* (New York: Doubleday and Co., 1959).

[14] Eric Berne, *Games People Play* (New York: Grove Press, 1964).

[15] Thorsten Veblen, *Theory of the Leisure Class* (New York: Modern Library, 1934), p. 253.

[16] W. G. Sumner, *Folkways* (Boston: Ginn and Co., 1906; 1940).

[17] John Huizinga, *Homo Ludens: A Study of the Play Element in Culture* (Boston: Beacon Press, 1938).

[18] Roger Caillois, *Man, Play and Games,* trans. Meyer Barash (New York: Free Press, 1961).

deavored to show the function of each type in society. But here again, no empirical research has emerged to either validate or negate his scheme.

Another writer, Peter McIntosh, speaking specifically of organized sports, outlined various dimensions of sport in contemporary society and drew heavily upon the work of Huizinga and Caillois.[19]

Several comprehensive books of readings have also emerged in the area of the sociology of sport: Natan's *Sport and Society* and G. Magnane's *Sociologie du Sport.*[20]

It should be apparent that, in Europe, where most of the serious sociological writing about sport has taken place, there is an abundance of theory, but, as is also the case in America, there still remains a tremendous need for empirical research on the subject. From a historical perspective then, the sociology of sport has not been a deliberately developed and pursued subdiscipline. Rather, it emerges mostly from widespread and divergent writings of scholars who touched upon the subject in some fashion. Few of the writers discussed above committed any significant portion of their scholarly careers to the study of interrelationships between sport and society.

On the contemporary scene, several sociologically oriented scholars have committed themselves to the investigation of sport on a full-time basis. Today one also finds that increasingly there are serious calls for the development of a sociology of sport. National and international organizations have emerged dedicated to the development of the field, though, for the most part, such groups are small, widely dispersed, and composed primarily of physical educators.

Perhaps the foremost effort thus far to bring order to the maze of contemporary writings potentially belonging to sport sociology is that of Loy and Kenyon in *Sport, Culture and Society.* Loy and Kenyon view the field today as having bifurcated into two distinct orientations—the normative orientation and the nonnormative orientation.[21]

Their contention, that there are, in fact, differing broad orientations extant within the field, seems valid. But their framework produces difficulties because of the dichotomous classification: any serious sociological writing on sport must, *ipso facto,* fall under either the normative *or* nonnormative typology. As in any case where the principle of the zero-sum game is employed in this manner, the authors thus run the risk of oversimplifying the thrusts of potentially significant writings.

Further, Loy and Kenyon, in using their classifications, of necessity

---

[19] Peter C. McIntosh, *Sport in Society* (London: C. A. Warrs Publishers, 1963).

[20] A. Natan, *Sport and Society* (London: Bowes and Bowes, 1958); G. Magnane, *Sociologie du Sport* (Paris, 1964).

[21] Loy and Kenyon, p. 9.

would have had to make decisions concerning the a priori assumptions of many writers on sport which are neither explicitly stated in their writings nor implicity discernable from the contents of their works.

And, finally, the evidence indicates that work in the field is much too scattered, the methodology much too underdeveloped and uncertain, and its concepts much too imprecise to warrant the imposition of a rigid typology at present. Much more data gathering and critical assessment of research must be done before any faith can be put in the reliability of such classifications. We are not yet sure of the scope of the field, much less the precise nature of the works in it.

However, despite the above objections, Loy and Kenyon's classifications do provide a framework with which to *begin* assessing some orienting threads running through writings in the sociology of sport.

By normatively oriented sport sociology, the authors refer to writings which assume that certain desirable social goals are *automatically* the end product of sports activities and that considerable consensus exists as to their nature. The writers who subscribe to this orientation are, according to Loy and Kenyon, divided into two camps. One may be described as the Western camp, composed of authors from the United States, England, and Western Europe; and the second, the Eastern camp, is composed of writers from the Soviet Union and Eastern Europe. (In other words, the normatively oriented writers in the field of sport sociology are divided along the political lines established by the Cold War.)

The prevailing attitude in the Western camp appears to be one which visualizes sport as a vehicle for character formation in the tradition of Judeo-Christian morality—to wit, "The battle of Waterloo was won on the playing fields of Eton."

In the Eastern camp, the Marxist-Leninist tradition prevails. These sociologists, too, presumably accept as established fact the assumed ends of sports activities, but they concern themselves primarily with the questions of how athletics may be organized and developed most efficiently to help meet the goals of socialism and facilitate the achievement of a communist society.

As an example of a writer in the normative Western camp, Loy and Kenyon discuss A. S. Daniels's article, "Sport as an Element of Culture."[22] Here Daniels writes in one instance about the potential use of sports as an index of "the quality of society" without first citing empirical evidence to support and establish the reliability of such an index. However, Daniels also argues enthusiastically for the development of rigorous scientific research methods in sport sociology (a characteristic of the non-normative orientation). Thus, the work defies any attempt to characterize it as exclusively normative in orientation as defined by Loy and Kenyon.

---

[22] Ibid., p. 13–22.

Much the same can be said regarding Loy and Kenyon's treatment of writings supposedly representing "normative-oriented" work among sport sociologists belonging to the Eastern camp. While many of these works do in fact contain heavy doses of Marxist-Leninist ideology, many of the authors also espouse the development of a highly rigorous scientific discipline which (without a more detailed explanation of their positions) one would have to assume would minimize the influence of ideological differences as it has in the more advanced physical and biological sciences.

By their nonnormative classification of writings in the literature on sports sociology, Loy and Kenyon refer to those which are more in conformity with the Western scholarly ideal of "value-neutral" scholarship. As self-proclaimed subscribers to this position, they use their own article, "Toward a Sociology of Sport," as one example of work emerging out of such a "value-neutral" orientation. However, upon analysis, it is evident that the article constitutes neither a statement of a theoretical position nor a report on the results of an empirical inquiry. Neither does it detail any methodologies aimed at objectifying inquiry into the field. Rather, it entails a somewhat benign and well-organized list of suggestions as to what a sociology of sport might include, a brief historical perspective, and a rather short list of suggested avenues for future inquiry.[23]

But the Loy and Kenyon book does bring together the works of many authors concerned with the sociological aspects of sport. As a book of readings, it is by far the most professional effort to be found in the literature to date in terms of the quality of the articles included and the breadth of genuinely sport-centered interests covered.

This brief survey of the evolving discipline of sport sociology shows that the yet amorphous field encompasses a large variety of diverse interests, all manifesting at least a general concern with some activity or phenomenon designated "sport" and its role as an element of society. Although much of the literature represents a low order of theoretical analysis and reflects little methodological sophistication, some of the work does suggest fruitful avenues for inquiry and provides a few hypotheses in sufficient operational form for empirical tests.

Although few writings of contemporary authors attempt to articulate sociology of sport with prior systematic theories, linkage of the field with such theories clearly is feasible. To take only one prominent example, there is the potentiality of useful linkage with a, perhaps modified, Parsonian functional analysis framework.

According to Parsons, every social system is confronted with the functional problems of adaptation to the external environment, attaining collective goals, assuring the continuity of the diverse elements existing within the system. The

---

[23] Ibid., pp. 36–43.

patterned mechanism for solving these problems are typically distributed among various sub-systems of the society; i.e., the economy is chiefly concerned with the adaptive function; goal attainment is in the hands of the polity; the educational institutions handle the pattern maintenance problem and the various primary groups are the first-line defenses against the emergence of integrative problems.[24]

It is clear that sport could be a component of each of these societal subsystems. Thus, consistent with the implicit aims of most serious sociological writers in the field, it could be profitable as an avenue of future inquiry to explicitly analyze the significance of sport in terms of its inputs and outputs relative to the functional problems of society. Of course, the quality of future contributions resulting from this or any other suggested avenue of inquiry into the field will depend upon the development of reliable empirical research based upon testable hypotheses.

SPORT IN PSYCHOLOGY

As shown in the last section, a scholarly concern with sport had its beginnings in sociophilosophical and sociopsychological works on play as manifest in the work of such men as Spencer, Groos, McDougall, and Hall. But whereas sociological interests led to an involvement with questions centering upon the *functions* of sport, play, and games as elements of social behavior—as evidenced in the writings of Simmel, Sumner, Weber, Veblen, and Goffman—psychological interests focused primarily upon questions concerning the *motivations* underlying interest and participation in "play." The fact that usage of the concept "play" predominates in the psychological literature is consistent with this concern with motivation. Psychologists traditionally have had only passing use for the more collective and social connotations of the concepts of "game" and "sport."

In 1901, Karl Groos wrote:

The effect of ordinary play is supported by social imitation. To do what others do and get the advantage of the stimulus which belongs to collective activity . . . to get out of the narrow circle of ones own desires and efforts— these the child learns with his playmates and the grown man (learns also) in athletic sports and in festive gatherings.[25]

He thus expanded upon a notion put forth in his *The Play of Animals* (cited earlier) and simultaneously gave impetus to what sociological interest there was in sports at that time. Unfortunately, Groos did not

---

[24] Talcott Parsons, "General Theory in Sociology" in R. K. Merton, *Sociology Today* (New York: Basic Books, 1959), pp. 3–38; cited in and adapted from Loy and Kenyon, pp. 85–86.

[25] Karl Groos, *The Play of Man* (New York: D. Appleton Co., 1901), p. 404.

fully develop his ideas on play as a factor in the socialization and integration processes in society. Rather, he embarked upon the development of an "instinct" theory of play in man—an unproductive extension of his interest in the play of animals. By 1918, Groos had teamed with William McDougall and postulated a theory which "emphasized man's need to have a prolonged period of play (in order) for his native endowments or instincts to become sufficiently developed to prepare him for life.[26]

It is with this "instinct" theory that Groos's name is identified.[27] Although the proposition that instincts play predominant roles in human behavior fell into almost total disrepute, Groos's total theoretical framework, when taken in combination with his ideas on play as "preparation for life," anticipated the emergence of psycho-analytic conceptions of play.

The key and lasting contributions of Groos to the psychology of sport were his efforts to order the broad range of activities which had been observed as play, thus providing extensive descriptive material in the field. And his critiques of other theories of play, even by today's standards, were very keen and insightful.[28]

There were a number of other influential early theories of play. Appleton centered her theory upon an explanation of play as an aspect of growth that involves the "developmental exercise of maturing faculties." This theory bore signs of the influence of Groos's work. Lehman and Witty interpreted Appleton's approach as follows: "[The author] sees growth, or the hunger for it, as the basic drive of play behavior. Play thus precedes the ability to function and gives use to it."[29]

This orientation was used extensively in explanation of play in children, but it was severely criticized for its shortcomings in explaining play in adults.

Several writers explained that play was a cathartic device, a safety valve for pent up emotions. By the tenets of this body of theory, "a pathological need for conflict and stormy struggle might be satisfied through aggressive play (thus) relieving the individual somewhat of these emotions."[30]

This theory, too, had obvious shortcomings. The most serious of these was the fact that it explicitly postulated the hazardous generalization that play by itself, through letting a person work out his aggressions

---

[26] R. A. Moore, *Sports and Mental Health* (Springfield, Ill.: C. C Thomas Publishing Co., 1966), p. 22.

[27] Charles A. Bucher, *Foundations of Physical Education* (St. Louis: C. V. Mosby Co., 1968), p. 561.

[28] Karl Groos, *The Play of Man*, p. 361.

[29] Lehman and Witty, *The Psychology of Play Activities*, p. 21.

[30] N. P. Miller and D. M. Robinson, *The Leisure Age* (Belmont: Wadsworth Publishing Co., 1963), p. 113.

and hostilities, would solve emotional problems. It was obvious to many psychologists even in the early 1900s that most emotional problems are considerably more involved than the cathartic approach to an understanding of play suggested.

As with other major developments in the discipline of psychology, significant advances were generated through the genius of Sigmund Freud. Although he did not write directly on the subject of play, Freud did concern himself with the psychology of group relations and suggested useful points of consideration for theorists interested in play. It was in large part through Freud's work on the impact of the group on individual psychological states that the psychology of sport was at long last liberated from the "individual-centered" theories of instinct, surplus energy, and other such approaches that had shackled advancement in the field for almost three decades.

In 1922, Freud formulated a concept of group psychology that severely criticized the views of Le Bon and other "mob psychologists" and that illuminated the shortcomings of individualistically oriented theories.[31] Le Bon's key notion was that an individual in a group is caught by the contagion and suggestibility of group emotional feelings, that he loses his inhibitions, his will, and his rational self-discipline, and further, that he takes refuge in the anonymity of the group. He therefore behaves irrationally and irresponsibly as he might never do if he were by himself.[32] In contrast, Freud argued that groups may be cruel, destructive, and extreme, but that they may also be influenced by suggestion to acts of high achievement and devotion to an idea, and resulting actions could have a positive influence on the individual: "The group mind is capable of genius in intellectual creation, as is shown . . . by language itself, as well as by folklore and the like. It remains an open question, moreover, how much the individual thinker, writer or player owes to the stimulation of the group in which he lives."[33]

Thus, Freud's argument opened serious debate among psychologists interested in play activities over the possibility that the motivation for such endeavors originates at least partly in group interaction processes rather than being solely a function of individual "instinct," "drives," or "needs."

All of Freud's contributions to play theory have not yet been fully delineated or evaluated, but later writers such as Erickson and Slavson drew much from Freud's views on the influence of collective psychological forces on leisure activities. These and other later students of play were led to analyze such activities in terms of their relation to the total

---

[31] Sigmund Freud, "Group Psychology and the Analysis of Ego," *International Psychoanalytic Library*, vol. 6 (New York: Liveright Publishing Corp., 1959), p. 24.

[32] Gustave Le Bon, *The Crowd* (London: Owen Press, 1917).

[33] Freud, "Group Psychology," p. 25.

mental, physical, and social "self" and to be concerned with play in relation to these aspects of human development.

Among modern writers, S. R. Slavson undertook one of the most searching analyses into the psychology of play, basing his analysis upon Freudian concepts and portraying the individual at play as a being functioning as a psycho-organic-social unit. Like others—E. L. Thorndike, for instance—he recognized that play was an important learning process for the child.

Play is the means by which the child, in fantasy, comes to know reality. The child psychologically scales down the world around him to simpler patterns that he can understand and master, gaining greater security and acquiring power as he does. The adult world to the child is threatening and forbidding, and in play he reduces its complexity to the level of his powers and understanding. As he grows and is able to deal with the world, his play activities gradually fuse with reality, until the latter becomes predominant.[34]

Play was thus visualized by Slavson as facilitating the development of important mental competencies necessary if the individual is to make a proper psychological adjustment to his total environment. One of Slavson's major contributions to the psychology of sport was his postulation of various types of play and the adjustment motives underlying each. Here he focused on psychic tensions generated by the frustrations of the individual's nonadjustment to the social demands of "competitive and insecure modern life."[35] His major thesis was that play is a vital means of meeting the adjustment needs pointed up by such strains.

A somewhat different analytical approach to the study of play was given by Eric Erickson in *Childhood and Society*. He explicitly combines sociology and psychoanalysis in his approach aimed at understanding the child's problem of growing up in any society. He too assigns to play an important role in the mental growth processes. "The play act [is] a function of the ego, an attempt to bring into sychronization bodily, mental and social processes of which one is a part."[36]

Erickson thus approached play from a therapeutic perspective. That is, he saw play as a vehicle of value in helping a child to understand himself and to obtain an adequate identity in the society through facilitating the learning of socially approved behavior and responses.

Following the acceptance of what was generally called physical education and sport as integral parts of the educational process and its legitimation by psychologists, it was inevitable that the complexities of such activities would raise new questions and bring to the fore new

---

[34] S. R. Slavson, *Recreation and the Total Personality* (New York: Association Press, 1948), p. 3.

[35] Ibid., p. 21.

[36] Erick Erickson, *Childhood and Society* (New York: W. W. Norton and Co., 1950), p. 184.

problems for those who organized and controlled these activities in schools and for psychologists themselves. It was the inclusion of sports, in particular, as components of the educational process that has stimulated most of the problem-centered psychological research which predominates in the field of sports psychology today.

Most of these problems have had to do with the character of organized sports or athletics, as opposed to the activity of play which has traditionally been the concern of psychologists. Representative of the kinds of investigations psychologists have undertaken in their explorations of some of these problems are the writings of Beisser and of Ogilvie and Tutko.

Arnold R. Beisser's chief concern in *The Madness in Sports* is with the motivations underlying an individual's choice of a particular game or sports activity and the psychological pressures associated with participation. His analysis is primarily one which stresses the abuses, or what he terms "the madness," in sports. Beisser's work indicates that the "fanaticism" in organized athletics does much more psychological damage to the individuals involved than could possibly be offset by the rewards to be gained. He attempts to support his contentions by way of presenting a series of psychiatric case studies. Of course, the primary shortcoming of his approach is that in using the case-study method, he is compelled to rely upon detailed discussions of single cases to support each of his contentions, and one case is seldom sufficient to establish the validity of one's argument.

Ogilvie and Tutko utilized a different approach. Rather than analyzing the various aspects of the sports institution for elements that may precipitate negative reactions in people, they attempted to identify various psychological states brought by individuals to the sporting situation that predispose them to be "problem athletes."

Their book, *Problem Athletes and How to Handle Them*, is based primarily upon data gathered by means of survey and interview techniques. The work is confined to discussions of "anomalies and pathological conditions" in athletes and makes little mention of stresses and inconsistencies in the athletic institution itself or detrimental pathologies among athletic practitioners. Although this problem-centered research is the predominating trend in sports psychology at the present time, the *perspectives* of some psychologists on the problems investigated have been subjected to searching criticism from several quarters.[37]

Criticisms notwithstanding, the end products of both Beisser's and Ogilvie and Tutko's approaches have tended to stimulate the development of sports psychology, for both have sparked new debate over the proper role of psychologists in investigating the sport institution. They

---

[37] See, for instance, Jack Scott, *Athletics for Athletes* (Berkeley, Calif.: Otherways Books, 1969), pp. 25–27.

have generated new questions about the methods employed by psychologists interested in sports and about the scope and boundaries of such interests. And, finally, the resulting arguments and debates have generated new interests in the field and precipitated new literature.

As might be apparent from the discussion of the histories and contemporary statuses of sports in sociology and psychology, there is a great deal of potentially productive overlap between the two fields of interest despite the differentiation in their focal concerns. This is to be expected given the complex nature of the subject matter. This complexity would seem to indicate the probability of the establishment of yet a third area of interest in sports—a social psychology of sport.

This approach would, of course, be neither purely sociological nor psychological; that is, it would be exclusively concerned with neither sport as an institution nor solely with sports activities as products of individual psychological attitudes, motivations, or needs. Rather, it would mesh the two approaches in order to gain a more complete understanding of sport as a social phenomenon. It is primarily in this vein that the present work is offered.

2

Historical overview

THE PROCESSES by which sport evolved as a significant component of modern American life are intricate, deserving of treatment that would result in several detailed volumes. Here, however, the effort is only to present the reader with a brief overview of some of the more significant factors contributing to these processes.

Most of the activities that are part of organized sport in America had their beginnings little more than 100 years ago. Sport's major developmental stages roughly parallel the growth of large-scale industrialization and resultant urbanization and the emergence of truly "mass" communication. These facts provide clues to the significant influences upon its development.

However, the roots of sport in America extend back into the colonial period when the British and other European immigrants to North America introduced the rudimentary forms of some of the activities we call sports today into what was for them a new land. The activities carried out during the colonial period were mostly recreational in character, though some, such as rowing and horse racing, were full-blown sports even at that time.[1]

During this period, America was primarily agrarian and its people were widely dispersed even in some of the most densely populated areas. Transportation was crude, not having undergone any essential change in form for centuries. Nine out of ten able-bodied people were engaged

---

[1] C. W. Hackensmith, *History of Physical Education* (New York: Harper and Row, 1966), p. 342.

directly or indirectly in agriculture. It was typical for most of these people to spend their entire lives and die within twenty-five miles of the spot where they were born.[2] Thus, sport had little opportunity to commence the development which has brought it to its present stage of complexity and organization.

It was not until the latter half of the nineteenth century, just prior to the Civil War, that the impetus and thrust toward the development of modern sport commenced. By this time, circa 1850, not only had industrialization begun to revolutionize the economic institutions of America and change radically the life styles of its people—particularly in the North—but also, earlier religious controls over leisure-time activities had loosened, thus opening the door for more secular use of new-found leisure time occasioned by industrialization.

The demand created by the Civil War for rifles, guns, ammunition, and other military supplies provided a running start for an industrial expansion that dwarfed the gains of previous years. New factories and heavy industries opened in the North, in particular, and people flocked from the farms and rural areas of this region to take advantage of new, more promising economic opportunities.

From 1860 to 1900, manufacturing businesses alone increased in number from 140,000 to 500,000. And, as people were drawn to these work places, towns and cities reached new heights of population density, newspapers flourished, and blocks of scheduled, predictable leisure time were available to the common man on a scale never before known. The average employee in one of the factories worked from ten to twelve hours a day, six days a week. Sunday was still a "day of rest" even under relaxed religious proscriptions.

But, unlike the rural areas of America, in the cities and urban areas recreation was not easily achievable or organized. Due to the phenomenal unplanned growth of the cities, slum districts predominated wherein both immigrants and the native born crowded within severely limited space in modest homes and multiple-unit dwellings. Not only was there a lack of the open space and fresh air to which many of these workers had been accustomed in rural settings, but also overall living conditions had worsened.

Due to factors such as the necessity of parents leaving children alone in the home in order to earn meager wages, the discontinuity between urban social culture and traditional rural values, mores, and folkways governing human and institutional relationships, and the drastic and instantaneous change for many families from a trade to a wholly money economy, crime and juvenile delinquency flourished. Sociocultural discontinuity also contributed to the perpetuation of other

---

[2] *Ibid.*, p. 343.

problems which were not simply social in nature or impact, such as increases in rates of venereal disease and problems of sanitation and waste disposal.

During America's agrarian era most recreation was centered in the family. It was closely related to tasks of dredging a living from the soil. But, with the shift from this rural life style to one of a more urban character, the recreational function of the family shifted, as did many other family functions, to secondary institutions.

The problems mentioned above spurred the development of recreation agencies which sought to organize the leisure time of adults and children who were unaccustomed to free time in an urban setting. Many recreational activities were organized through factory work groups, and modern team sports received its first developmental boost. Other activities, such as gymnastics and cycling, were organized in neighborhoods.

Given the competitive ethic endemic to American culture, perhaps it was to be expected that it would be only a short time before competition among groups of factory workers and among neighborhoods developed. As large-scale corporations, monopolies, and unregulated trade and labor practices flourished, there emerged an increased demand for cheap labor. The continued influx of workers provided a greater pool of athletic talent for competing factories and neighborhoods, and the inevitable soon came about. As the emphasis in recreational activities shifted from mere diversion from the rigors and pressures of daily life to a premium placed upon winning in competition, the number of persons who actually were able to represent various groups diminished; Sunday mornings were spent by a select few practicing for evening events, and role specialization in sport activities developed. As far as organized sport was concerned, the masses had already begun to move down the road to spectatorship.

This thrust toward the widespread development of full-blown sports was aided tremendously by veterans returning to both the North and South from the Civil War. During this episode in American history, for the first time, men were brought together from all walks of life and from all corners of the two regions of the country.

In the Civil War, as in every major conflict since the advent of recorded history, there were large blocks of time in which the actual conflict was at a lull. Weber, among others, saw "games" as one way such time was filled. Simultaneously, according to Weber, valuable training and discipline were provided that served to maintain both the soldiers' morale and their fighting edge or spirit for battle.

During the Civil War, games were also prevalent in battle zones. Chief among these was baseball. Though it was certainly not the sport we know today, it did have a set of rules, and the form and procedure of the activity would be recognizable today. Baseball among soldiers during the Civil War period was basically an impromptu affair and was played extensively by both sides. Given the estimated amount of time spent fighting or otherwise carrying out military duties as opposed to time given to monotonous waiting, one could justifiably speculate that the soldiers spent more time playing baseball than engaging in military activities. At any rate, veterans who returned to both the North and South had decided edges in talent over their civilian counterparts who had spent most of their time in sweatshop labor, with recreational activities being relegated to Sundays. With many of these returning veterans taking up factory jobs and the urban style of life, there was another input in talent which further heightened competition and specialization and brought baseball on the scene as a nationally appreciated sport.

By 1868, the sport had reached such a level of popularity and organization that admission was charged to spectators.[3] Popularity and profit encouraged several teams to organize themselves into a professional baseball league, the National League, in 1876. Other such leagues were soon formed—the American Association in 1882 and the American League in 1900.

But the story of baseball was only one aspect of the overall evolutionary process. Other sports had evolved from Civil War leisure activities also. Football had become accepted in its American style, and the first intercollegiate game was played between Princeton and Rutgers in 1869.

Other factors gave further impetus to the national appreciation of sport. The first unsupervised recreational facility in an urban area of America was established in 1876 at Washington Park in Chicago, thus affording both youths and adults the necessary space and equipment to carry out leisure activities. The first organized recreational camp for boys was started in 1880 in New Hampshire. Due to the tremendous increase in interest in baseball and football and the need to assure the standardization and impersonal supervision of the events, the Amateur Athletic Union was formed in 1888. In 1896, James Naismith popularized a game that would come to be known as basketball.

In 1894, a pioneering effort to establish recreational facilities across America was begun by Jane Addams with the formation of Hull House in Chicago. Because of the cramped quarters of such urban facilities, outdoor activities such as softball, volley ball, and outdoor basketball received a special stimulus.

By 1900, ten major cities in the United States had in their

---

[3] R. A. Moore, *Sports and Mental Health* (Springfield, Ill.: C. C Thomas Publishing Co.), p. 11.

municipal budgets some funds allocated for the maintenance of recreational and sport facilities. In 1903, the first public-school athletic league was established in New York City. The National Recreational Association was started in 1906 to set standards for and perpetuate interest in recreation as a professional interest and as an activity.

As a result of criticism of intercollegiate injuries and deaths in football and unethical recruitment practices for all college sports between 1895 and 1905, particularly for football, the Intercollegiate Athletic Association of the United States (later to become the National Collegiate Athletic Association) was formed in 1905. And, in 1915, intramural sports were formally introduced and funded as part of the extracurricular offerings of American colleges. The Olympic Games were revived in 1896 by Pierre De Culbertin. De Culbertin seems to have based his actions on the belief that British emphasis upon sport in education had been a major factor in influencing England's emergence as a world power rather than on any particular love of sport.

However, despite all of this growth and development toward modern sports, it remained again for wars to inject new vigor into the "movement." With the coming of World War I, sports in the educational institutions were to receive the most significant boost to that point in American history.

Team sports as an official and widespread component of some educational institutions had been evident for at least two decades by 1900. But these activities were still, for the most part, unique to only a few organizations and localities. Few members of the public residing in areas outside of the northeastern region of the country had viewed first-hand a collegiate football or baseball game. But this was all to change.

In 1909, W. P. Bowen of Michigan State University stated, "It is surprising that the leaders in America should have for two decades failed to grasp the value of [intercollegiate athletics] . . . "[4]

With this statement, the physical educator gave vent to an increasingly prevalent attitude among administrators of American colleges and universities. Both the publicity for their schools and the potential of generating badly needed funds from gate receipts helped to build support for such sentiments from academically inclined faculty members.

Thus began a massive move away from a recreational emphasis in college physical education toward programs emphasizing intercollegiate sports. This new emphasis was to be the forerunner of a trend that would cause many to view America as a spectator society wherein the masses would watch highly trained athletes carry out specialized roles in sports.

---

[4] W. P. Bowen, "The Evaluation of Athletic Evils," *American Physical Education Review* 14, no. 3 (March 1909): 156.

Though several justifications were offered to the public for the change in emphasis, none had any proven basis of validity beyond simple faith. Nonetheless, massive physical fitness efforts were de-emphasized in the colleges and universities, and sports were thrust to the fore.

Prior to 1900, baseball was the only sport which was truly organized at the national level; it was also the biggest money maker and the only professional sport. Football and basketball had remained, from a national perspective, relatively unstandardized games, carried out on local and intramural levels for the most part. The shift toward organized sports in colleges would soon change this as well as the nature of the role responsibilities of those persons directing athletic programs and activities. It was this change in role responsibilities which necessitated changes in training procedures for physical educators; and it was out of these revised training procedures that the coaching position as we know it today was developed. Given the centrality of the coaching position to the sport institution, let us look briefly at *how* it has emerged.

EMERGENCE OF THE COACH'S ROLE

In 1908, Thomas D. Stoney conducted a survey of the academic status and educational backgrounds of directors of physical education in colleges and universities.

Of forty institutions surveyed, 41 percent of the directors had medical degrees; 18 percent had master's degrees; and 30 percent had bachelor's degrees. The high representation of M.D.s was due to two factors. First, as was stated, the emphasis of college physical-activity programs had been on recreation for the masses and on the development of physical fitness among young people. Also, professional physical educators were still struggling for acceptance in the academic world and few schools would hire people possessing only credentials in physical education. But, due to the re-emphasis of sports in education from 1909 to 1912, this picture changed sharply.

In 1911, when Abraham Flexner conducted his pioneering and influential study of medical education for the Carnegie Foundation, he found that the M.D. degree was very superficial in the United States as compared with medical degrees in Europe. The result of this study was that medical training was upgraded and made more demanding. Many doctors returned to medical school for additional training. This exodus was particularly felt in the physical educational programs of colleges. Medical doctors were as much pushed out of physical education by the re-emphasis on sports as they were pulled out by their professional desire to upgrade their trade. As Hackensmith states, few medical men were willing to return to the "relatively unrenumerative position of physical education director."[5]

With the exodus of men with professional interest in physical fitness and health, the way was further cleared for the emergence of sports. The improved status of teacher training and the gradual acceptance of physical education as a legitimate department of the college or university encouraged the employment of the physical education director with an academic degree. His job was threefold—to coach, to teach, and to administer the general physical education program—in that order.[6]

The impact of this shift in emphasis was manifest in other ways. Between 1907 and 1915, the phenomenon of the "tramp athlete" reached a prevalence never before known in American academia. It was common practice for partisans of major educational institutions to make almost annual "raiding" campaigns aimed at drawing outstanding athletes away from smaller colleges.[7] This practice was facilitated by the fact that registration in a single course was allowable in the cases of "special students." Thus, the scene was set for the emergence of the "prima donna athlete-student." According to Moore:

The athlete on the campus became relatively untouchable in such matters as discipline and study; even worse, he was encouraged to develop an unrealistic picture of himself. He discovered that his varsity letter would have little impact on his potential for future success unless he was an unusual performer.[8]

Further, in many colleges and universities sports reached a prominence superior to scholarship.

The football and basketball coaches and their teams became more important than physics and physics teachers, more important than English teachers, more important than college presidents, and even more important than the better judgment of boards of trustees and directors who were constantly under pressure from the public.[9]

When the United States entered World War I, the exploits of American athletes on the gridiron were portrayed as demonstrative of Americans' national virility. Sports clubs were established and supported

---

[5] Hackensmith, p. 395.

[6] Ibid., pp. 396–97.

[7] Howard J. Savage, et al., "The Growth of American College Athletics," in *American College Athletics,* Carnegie Foundation for the Advancement of Teaching Bulletin no. 25 (New York, 1930).

[8] Moore, p. 15.

[9] Savage, p. 30.

by the federal government. It was during this period that public "participation" through identification with "the team" for the first time replaced mass recreational activities as the primary national pastime.[10]

Federal support of intercollegiate sports activities was justified on the grounds that these activities were essential to maintaining public morale. Funds spent on mass recreational and physical fitness programs were justified on another basis. Through the induction process, many young men of military age who resided in urban areas were discovered to be physically unfit for military service at the time of entry into the army. The educational world was shocked, as was the government. A deluge of funds poured into colleges and universities between 1915 and 1918 for the development and maintenance of physical education programs which were made a mandatory part of every student's educational matriculation.

In December of 1917, the provost marshal confirmed what many people already believed. A report was released which showed that of over three million men drafted into the armed forces, one-third were physically unfit for service. Those who were accepted had to be taught the most rudimentary exercises and physical activities.[11]

However, the sudden rise in concern for the physical fitness of the masses did not lead to criticism of intercollegiate athletics as a failure. On the contrary, the status of collegiate sport was enhanced. Universities and colleges provided that any male student could receive full credit for completing the physical education requirements for graduation by making any team representing the school in intercollegiate athletics. And since participation in one sport in intercollegiate athletics was equivalent to two semesters or three quarters of physical education at most institutions, intercollegiate sport received the added stimulus of being both an accredited college activity and a means of avoiding physical education courses (which apparently were not among the more popular curricular offerings). Thus, collegiate athletics flourished as never before. And soon the physical educator's winning record as a coach became more important than his skills as a teacher.[12]

JOURNALISM AND THE "SELLING" OF SPORT

In the years between World War I and World War II, organized amateur and professional sports intensified their grips on the American public. The increase in public attentiveness to organized athletics was

---

[10] Moore, p. 15.
[11] Hackensmith, p. 412.
[12] Ibid., p. 396.

aided by two new factors: the Great Depression and the emergence of the athlete as a national hero. The image of the athlete as hero was fostered and created by the newspapers, with their staffs of syndicated writers, as well as by public-relations specialists employed by educational institutions and professional sports organizations.

Between 1890 and 1918, America had certainly developed some nationally heralded sports heroes. By the first World War, Jim Thorpe, the Native American, had already become an international sports legend; the first Davis Cup team of 1900 had received national plaudits as heroes and the Davis Cup—donated by Dwight W. Davis, a Harvard student and a member of the first team—had already become a greatly sought-after trophy by both England and the United States; and Ty Cobb's name was almost sacred in the world of professional baseball.

But the celebration of these few outstanding heroes in the press and among the populace, impressive as it was, did not even approach the total impact of newspaper coverage, broadcast time, and other public fanfare expended on literally countless actual and prefabricated sports heroes during what one author calls "Sports' Golden Age"— roughly the years 1919–30.[13] During this period, strong impetus to the growth of American sport, both amateur and professional, was provided by three factors—affluence, the increased popularity and significance of the automobile in the life of the average American, and the newspaper industry.

After World War I, the United States experienced an economic boom having no parallel in American history since the onset of the Industrial Revolution. Still riding the wake of a war economy that had provided jobs and money for all who were willing to work, most of the "good things in life" had been brought within reach of the common man.

The war had also had other effects. It had provided a major stimulus for improvement in Henry Ford's mass production and assembly line processes—improvements which were rapidly adapted after the war for production of consumer goods. And there was a waiting populace both eager and able to buy the, by now, not-so-novel automobile. The car slowly became a necessity rather than a luxury. It enabled people to move greater distances in shorter periods of time than ever before. And much of this movement was expended traveling, sometimes 100 miles and more, to witness, firsthand, athletic events that had theretofore been practically inaccessible to all except local clientele. The auto industry also provided the means by which newspapers were distributed over larger areas and with an efficiency never before known.

American ingenuity and prosperity had also brought another medium

---

[13] John Durant and Otto Bettman, *Pictoral History of American Sports* (New York: A. S. Barnes and Co., 1952), pp. 150–98.

of mass communication into prominence—the radio. It was essentially the press, by way of both the newspaper industry and the radio, that stimulated and whetted the sports appetites of the countless thousands of Americans who, between the years 1919 and 1929, drove cumulative distances of thousands of miles to witness athletic events.

While many saw the role of the press as the natural and wholesome outcome of one of the greatest eras in American sports history, criticism of both the scale and the methods of sports reporting was rampant. Much of this criticism accused the press of being lackeys for the sports industry, both amateur and professional, and of prefabricating heroes of national stature out of men who sometimes were questionable in both character and ability. The press was accused of violating journalistic ethics by using newspapers and radio to promote the economic interests of those who made sports a business and to paint a picture of organized athletics which bore little resemblance to the actual subject.[14]

Colleges and high schools were also caught up in the sports mania, as is reflected in the volume of reporting space expended on such athletic events. Educational institutions formed and funded professional public relations agencies. Full-fledged magazines and newspapers with color supplements replaced mimeographed throw-away sheets at athletic events, as the commercialization of sports in educational institutions became so effective that the academic reputations of some leading colleges and universities were rendered secondary to their athletic standings.

COMMERCIALIZATION

The efforts made to "sell" collegiate sports were highly successful as reflected in the following facts:

At Yale University, a crowd of 20,000 had been recorded in 1890 as the largest number ever to attend a collegiate football game; by 1928, the number had grown to 80,000. The price of tickets to the 1890 games between Yale and Harvard was fifty cents per ticket. In 1891, the price was raised to one dollar and a frightful uproar ensued. However, following World War I, the price was raised to two dollars and a half; in 1921, to three dollars; and, in 1927, to five dollars per ticket, and, not only was there no outcry, but members of the public considered themselves lucky if they were able to obtain a ticket.[15]

It had been alleged that an emphasis on intercollegiate athletics

---

[14] For an in-depth analysis of sports and its problems during the postwar decade, 1919–28, see John R. Tunis, *$port$* (New Haven: Quinn and Boden Co., 1928).

[15] Ibid., pp. 118–25. (These increases far outpaced changes in the general level of prices.)

would benefit the entire educational community. But the benefits did not accrue in the manner that many had expected they would. For instance, there is some evidence that not even physical education departments received direct monetary benefits of any significance from the enlarged gate receipts from athletics. In 1927, the gate receipts from sports at Ohio State University were $275,723.73. Of this amount, nothing went to academic departments and only $13,000 went to intramural physical education activities for the larger student body. Of the original amount, $127,017.83 went toward the building of a six-million-dollar stadium complex for sports activities.

Stanford University took in $194,000 in 1926 as a result of intercollegiate sports activities. Of this amount, $7,500 went to intramural physical education activities. There is no record of any money derived from sports going to academic departments.

Fordham University, in 1924, took in over half a million dollars in football gate receipts. Of that sum, nearly $300,000 were spent on coaches' salaries, traveling expenses, publicity, and uniforms. Now it is quite possible that the income from sport *did* benefit academic parts of colleges and universities even though funds were not specifically earmarked for such purposes. Under such circumstances, it would be very difficult to document such benefits. This fact notwithstanding, the above cases were by no means atypical examples of the obvious distribution of payoffs resulting from the commercialization of collegiate sports.

Professional sports, too, had grown and benefited financially. The golden age of sports ushered in the first "bonus babies" in professional baseball, and raids on colleges were frequently made in an effort to capitalize on the talents of highly publicized amateurs. So intense and widespread were such activities that the National Collegiate Athletic Association felt compelled to explicitly define what an amateur athlete was.

Policing the so-called shamateur baseball participants became a frustrating and almost hopeless task for member institutions in the NCAA's eight regional districts. For many college athletes succumbed to the tempting financial offers of professional baseball teams to join the summer roster with an option to return to school in the fall to participate in college athletics as a "shamateur athlete."[16]

As a result of this development, America became the first country in history to spend in excess of four billion dollars in a single decade, 1919–29, for seats at sporting events. One would think that during periods of economic depression the sports mania sweeping America would have abated somewhat. But the enthusiasm did not decrease.

---

[16] Hackensmith, p. 425.

While gate receipts certainly dropped drastically, public interest in sports reached a new high. As one author states in reference to depressions: "During depressions with thousands out of work, sports help to refocus our attention on the Great American Values and ideals, and also help us to remember that life does not begin and end with the dollar."[17]

Likewise, the Great Depression of the 1930s, far from stemming the tide of sports enthusiasm, provided a situation which stimulated a heightening of sports interests. And during this time when bad news was plentiful and times were generally hard, the press was happy to contribute its part to sustaining public morale by reporting the sporting news.

World War II had effects on the development of sports in America which were similar to those of World War I, with the public construing the exploits of highly trained athletes as evidence of the virility of an American society embroiled in war.

But there were some significant substantive differences which emerged from World War II. The most outstanding of these was the introduction of minority-group athletes—particularly Afro-Americans—into major amateur and professional athletic organizations on a massive scale.

MINORITY-GROUP ATHLETES

Though Jim Thorpe and Jack Johnson were early involved in organized athletics, the so-called big-time sports had remained segregated and almost totally closed to minorities of color in both the collegiate and professional spheres. Even the seating arrangements at most athletic events were segregated. The aftermath of World War II was to change this situation significantly—particularly for the Afro-American athlete.

Little documentary evidence exists on the early participation of blacks in organized athletics. However, it is clear that it was through boxing that blacks first became engaged in American sport. Tom Malineaux, a Virginia slave, was this country's first recognized heavyweight champion, in 1800. Boxing was to continue for almost a century to be the only area of sport in which blacks could participate on an equal footing with whites.

By the time Jack Johnson beat Tommy Burns in 1908 for the heavyweight championship, boxing matches featuring black and white combatants had become commonplace both in this country and in

---

[17] John A. Krout, *Annals of American Sport* (New Haven, Conn.: Yale University Press, 1929), p. 295.

Europe. But all other sports had remained affairs for "whites only." And Emancipation aggravated the problem of segregation rather than aiding in its solution.

Prior to the enactment of the Emancipation Proclamation, most black people were excluded from organized sports. Free Afro-Americans, those few blacks who were legally defined as United States citizens, participated to some degree in full-fledged athletic events—particularly baseball and boxing—but the evidence indicates that such occurrences were rare. The full impact of the black man upon the development of sports awaited Emancipation and more particularly the widespread establishment of black athletic clubs and educational institutions.

With the end of the Civil War and the enforcement of the two Emancipation Acts, passed in 1862 and 1863, slavery was officially abolished in America. In March of 1867, a vengeful United States Congress passed the First Reconstruction Act, aimed at defeating the conservative reconstruction policies of President Johnson and enabling blacks to achieve greater freedom in their new roles as citizens.

However, by the 1880s, it became apparent to many blacks that Reconstruction had failed and that slavery had been abolished only to be replaced by a system of segregation and "Jim Crowism" which was in some ways harsher than "that dreaded institution," as slavery had come to be known among the more liberal segments of the American populace.

Some blacks migrated North when Reconstruction was seen to be on its last legs. They were spurred on by wistful stories, passed by word of mouth among the mostly illiterate freedmen, that portrayed the North as the promised land that had been sung and talked about for so many decades in the slave quarters after long days of work and drudgery.

. But most blacks, trapped in the South by simple impoverishment, turned to a cruel system of sharecropping rather than to northward migration in search of an opportunity for a better style of life. And here most stayed until World War I.

As was the case with whites, World War I created both new hopes and new problems for the Afro-American. For the average black, living in the North had always been preferable to life in the South—at least from his perspective as a sharecropper in the fields of still-intact southern plantations. The North did, in fact, offer him more economic opportunities—in public relief if not employment, more security from lynching and as a citizen, and generally greater freedom as a human being—this despite widespread and often intense racism and discrimination. Nevertheless, these perceived attributes of the North did not encourage more than a trickle of black migration prior to 1914.

In 1914 and 1918 both "push" and "pull" factors operated to generate what Rose, Frazier, Myrdal and others have termed the "Great

Migration."[18] The push factors had been generated by the capitulation after 1876 of the northern politicians to southern interests on matters pertaining to the economic and political survival of blacks in the South. The result was the demise of Reconstruction and the very evident fact that the promised "forty acres and a mule" were never to materialize. Economic privation, political disenfranchisement, and social oppression combined as "push" factors. The pull factors making themselves manifest during the early years of World War I were also tremendously influential.

A great number of blacks at the start of the Great Migration were attracted to the North by the opportunities that war and industrialization offered. They had found their chances in the South particularly bad, and they often heard of job openings in the North. Blacks already in the North not infrequently wrote letters to relatives in the South which testified that greater opportunities existed on the other side of the Mason-Dixon line. Such letters were passed around the community and handled with the care comparable to that with which a believer would protect a sacred parchment.

A desire to improve oneself economically was, of course, the chief motive for going North. Men often left their families in the South and went North, planning to send for them after work and living accommodations were found. With the country at war and many whites in uniform, jobs for blacks were more plentiful than at any other time in history. And though discrimination relegated most Afro-Americans to the less desirable occupations, there was work and there was a steady income.

From this point on, the story of blacks' lives in the new urban settings paralleled that of whites. Slums, social and cultural discontinuity, crime, disease, and sanitation problems prevailed. Added to this was the devastating impact of unexpectedly harsh racism and discrimination. It was these last two factors which most influenced the role of Afro-Americans in the development of sports, as they have the general character of black life styles in American society as a whole.

The great movement toward the development of recreational activities among the masses and in educational institutions between the Civil War and World War I never touched the black population of America. De facto segregation abounded in the North to such a point that it was a common saying by 1915 that, "In the South, blacks can get as close as they like but are not allowed to get too much; in the North

---

[18] For detailed analysis of the factors influencing the "Great Migration" see: Arnold Rose, *The Negro in America* (Boston: Beacon Press, 1944). Gunnar Myrdal, *An American Dilemma* (Boston: Beacon Press, 1956), by permission of Harper and Row. E. Franklin Frazier, *The Negro in the United States* (Chicago: University of Chicago Press, 1949).

they can get as much as they want, but they can't get too close." While this statement was most certainly an oversimplification of two very complex situations, it did manifest some degree of truth. This was particularly true in the realm of recreation.

Recreation is basically a very intimate social activity requiring a lack of stresses and strains. It cannot be forced upon a person. Whites, though many worked daily along side blacks in factories and industry, chose, by and large, to take their recreation to themselves. Getting away from their black coworkers was relegated to the same sphere as getting away from the job. Thus, Sundays provided both relief from the drudgery of often dull, monotonous labor and relief from the strains of the close, occupation-related social contact with blacks that had little precedent in American history.

However, blacks too sought relief from the strains and rigors of daily life and they too turned to recreation activities to achieve this. While they most certainly had nowhere near the resources, professional advise, or facilities made available to whites during the first two decades of the twentieth century, they nonetheless developed athletic clubs which, by the evidence available, rivaled those of the whites in talented participants and in the general quality of their activities. As was the case with the white clubs, returning, black, Civil War veterans had significant influence on the development of baseball, and later, football and basketball, into full-fledged sports activities.

Thus, the major impetus for the development of a separate sphere of black sport in the years preceding and during the World War I was generated by racism and discrimination. Blacks were excluded from white athletic clubs, so they established their own. Here too, since blacks shared the American cultural value of competitiveness, an emphasis upon competition soon displaced the recreational functions of the physical activities pursued and severely limited the number of people who actually had developed sufficient talent to participate. This separate sports development was to persist into and slightly beyond the World War II years.

By 1947, the reasons given by what had become a "white sports establishment" for the exclusion of blacks from major sporting events had developed into a whole ideology of beliefs and assumptions.[19]

Some whites believed that "racially pure" white teams would not compete against blacks or participate on an integrated team. And, although this assumption may have been true, there is no evidence that it was actually tried prior to 1947. Some coaches, owners, and athletic administrators claimed that their fans would not attend games played

---

[19] Edwin B. Henderson, *The Negro in Sports* (Washington, D.C.: Associated Publishers, Inc., 1949), pp. 15–37.

by integrated teams. Still others alleged that blacks were simply too spontaneous and impulsive in nature to participate within the structure of sports rules with the same degree of sophistication as whites. And others envisioned riots and fights if whites lost to black teams or vice versa.

Whatever the justifications expounded for black exclusion, the evidence indicates that they were based upon stereotypes and speculation. Nevertheless, discriminatory and exclusionist attitudes spurred blacks to establish and maintain their own clubs which were in their fullest bloom in the years 1914–47.

All-black baseball and basketball leagues proliferated, and, after World War II, served as springboards into "big-league" professional sports. Although it is difficult to document the histories of black athletic teams, the limited evidence suggests that they performed as well as white teams in most instances. After World War I, there are a few recorded instances where informal "sessions" were held between black and white basketball teams. The results of these events were predictably mixed. Blacks won some and lost some. In 1928, for example, the black Renaissance Five defeated the famed all-white Boston Celtics—the leading white basketball team of the time.

Such victories were not atypical, though such biracial events were, and they went unnoticed by the white sports reporting establishment of the day. To report such stories might have encouraged these events and, as one newspaper editor stated, "America is not ready for this."[20] Much the same was true of black-white baseball events.

This highly segregated pattern did not pertain to boxing, however, the sport most heavily participated in by blacks. Though some white champions such as John L. Sullivan had hidden behind the color line and refused to fight black contenders, nonchampionship and some championship boxing was common between the races. With Jack Johnson's achievement of champion status in 1908, the floodgates were opened to all challengers.

Though black professional and amateur athletic organizations managed to survive and even prosper in some cases, most of them were economic failures. They tended to be fly-by-night affairs with uncertain schedules and rosters.

The trend toward an emphasis upon intercollegiate athletics which started in the early 1900s was to engulf black educational institutions as it had white schools. This development brought stability to black sports, but enduring American racism and discrimination determined the directions of black intercollegiate sports as it had the roles of blacks in the development of sports in the larger society.

---

[20] Ibid., p. 39.

Jackie Robinson broke the color barrier in the lower echelons of American sport but almost a quarter of a century after this "breakthrough" racial quotas, exclusion, and other forms of discrimination persist. (UPI)

Black educational institutions grew primarily out of the ever increasing pressures toward racial segregation and the awesome need to educate millions of newly freed Afro-Americans in the decades after the Civil War. While, during slavery, it had been illegal in many states to educate blacks, after the war, black colleges sprang up all over the United States.

Such institutions as Hampton in Virginia, Howard in Washington, D.C., Tuskegee in Alabama, and Lincoln in Jefferson City, Missouri, became models for black education. Most of these subscribed to the Booker T. Washington dictum, "Separate as the fingers but like one as the hand" and were supported by philanthropic whites and state funds.

All too often the thrust of the curricula of these institutions was nonintellectual in character, offering instead practical skill courses. Although there was a great deal of criticism of this vocational orientation—the most notable of which was voiced by W. E. DuBois—this "practical" orientation prevailed and does to this day. The emphases were upon agriculture, mechanical skills, music, and physical education. Yet, despite these educational shortcomings—or perhaps because of them—black colleges provided an avenue of athletic prominence for aspiring young black males who literally had no other avenue of recognition open to them.

With the commencement of World War II, America mobilized and propagandized her people for the impending struggle against the then "honorary Aryan" and imperialistic Japanese and the armies of the self-proclaimed "master race" holding sway in Nazi Germany. Blacks were soon drafted, as were all other able-bodied men, excepting Japanese-Americans who were legally defined as potential enemies and consigned to concentration camps.

Having fought against the racist domination of Hitler, blacks returning from the war had little tolerance for antiblack sentiments in America. It was not long before the National Association for the Advancement of Colored People had prevailed, through litigation and other pressures, upon the United States government to end segregation in the military. President Harry S. Truman issued the order in 1948. This was only one manifestation of the rising tide of black impatience with racism, discrimination, and segregation.

One year before this action by Truman, in 1947, the sports world had been rocked to its foundations by Branch Rickey's announcement that he had signed an Afro-American from the University of California at Los Angeles to a professional baseball contract. While there was a great deal of discontent among some segments of the population over this occurrence, there was nowhere near the catastrophic reaction some had predicted and expected.

Upon the acceptance of blacks into professional baseball, football and basketball soon followed suit. And then, in 1954, the United States Supreme Court declared unconstitutional forced segregation of all public educational institutions. This act gave many previously hesitant all-white institutions the basis they needed to go into the South and the black communities of the North to recruit black athletes. For, by now, the trends established in the early 1900s toward the commercialization of intercollegiate athletes had reached maturity.

Athletics on the campus was big business, and only those schools in hard-core segregationist areas of the South and Southwest were willing to allow talented black athletes to escape their grasp and be absorbed into other educational institutions merely because of an accident of birth. Black educational institutions which had inadvertently developed a vested interest in segregation found themselves losing valuable athletic talent to such institutions as Iowa, Illinois, Indiana, Michigan, and other athletic powerhouses.

With the emerging widespread popularity of television in the early fifties and the economic prospects offered by the new medium to colleges and universities, there was even greater incentive to recruit for talent regardless of color. Television also gave the black athlete an incentive to attend the integrated school.

Black colleges were not then and are not today included in the regular schedule of televised collegiate athletic events. Thus, the black athlete found it to his advantage to attend a large, predominantly white school since he would receive greater public exposure through the newspapers, over the radio air waves, but, most important, on television. For many, this would mean more money and a better opportunity to sign a professional contract when his collegiate eligibility ended.

Other minorities, too, have benefited from the development of sports in America and the factors which have influenced it, but to a much lesser degree than have the numerically more powerful blacks.

Due to the territorial relationship between Puerto Rico and the United States, some Puerto Ricans have found their way into big-league baseball and, to a lesser degree, into other sports. Some Cuban immigrants have likewise propelled themselves into affluence through participation in professional sports—again primarily baseball. Both the Puerto Rican and the Cuban athletes have gained from the strides made by the Afro-American in the field of organized athletics in America.

The equipment and sporting facility industries which have grown up around organized athletics, the development of instantaneous means of mass visual communication, and more scientific approaches to sports —using skilled statistics experts, computers, and psychologists—have all contributed to propelling American sport into a prominence and significance rivaled only by long-established social institutions.

Yet, sport today is riddled with problems. Discrimination and quota systems persist even though sport in America is generally held to be one of the nation's most "integrated" activities. There are continuing reports of alleged inhumane treatment of athletes, both black and white, on college campuses and in professional sports throughout the country. And, though these accusations are typically denied by coaches, owners, and administrators, athlete strikes, rebellions, and boycotts have been widespread.

And finally, slowly but surely, the pressures and concerns of social and political issues that are causing upheavals in the greater society today have begun to create ripples also in the "sacred" realm of organized sports. A university football team decides not to participate in spring practice in order to protest America's military involvement in Southeast Asia; blacks demonstrate against racism in America before the eyes of television cameras and the entire world at the 1968 Olympic Games; and student governments cut off funds supporting athletics in their respective colleges in order to use those funds for minority scholarships and ethnic study programs. Because of these trends, some believe that sports are on the decline. But, be this as it may, sports today have arrived at a stage of high social stature and affluence—by way of such diverse historical events as wars, a depression, and Supreme Court orders, not to speak of the more massive and continuing contributions of industrialization and urbanization. Each year "little" leagues, junior high schools, high schools, colleges, and universities draw upon American communities for talent while professional sports enterprises draw upon colleges and universities—all under the aegis of a "sports creed," or ideology, which espouses, among other things, the development of socially acceptable character traits, a high value upon brotherhood, and a commitment to the American ideals of individualism, fair play, and honest competition.

3

Definitions and clarifications

IT IS GENERALLY desirable to be clear as to what we are talking about. We already have seen, especially in chapter 1, that scholars who have dealt with sport have used key terms in diverse ways. Even when the central concepts were originally defined in a reasonably consistent and precise manner, subsequent usage has brought about an ever-expanding inclusion of broader and more complex referents. While these elaborations of meanings may indicate the dynamic quality of the emergent field of sport sociology, a condition of continuing imprecision and change in crucial concepts obviously must be avoided.

This chapter aims to clarify the meanings of the concepts "sport" and "sports" and to differentiate these terms from others with which they are often confused. I will begin by drawing upon the works of certain authors who have attempted to delineate some key features distinguishing the activities of concern here. By contrasting their various characterizations of "play" with my own interpretations of the nature of this activity, I will demonstrate how the conceptual understandings employed here differ from those of the authors cited. In this way, the foundations of the treatment given subsequent concepts can be established while, simultaneously, the differences between my conceptual definitions and those of previous authors can be demonstrated. Once I have dealt with the concept "play," direct reference to the authors whose works are highlighted will be dropped as I embark upon the task of developing operational definitions of the remaining concepts.

PLAY

The root meaning of the word "play" is "to bestir oneself."[1] But, obviously, both the connotations and denotations of the concept have much deeper meanings than its linguistic origins would imply.

Huizinga designated as "play" all activities which are: "free activities standing quite consciously outside ordinary life as being not serious, . . . connected with no material interest, . . . confined to its own proper boundaries . . . and carried out according to fixed rules."[2]

This rather loose definition has several defects. Infants and animals play without any knowledge of rules, and activities such as whittling and drawing, even when they conform to rules, are not spoken of as play. Play may also be serious within its own boundaries, though not within the bounds of "seriousness" more properly pertaining to other activities in daily life such as work, maintaining good health, and so forth.

Caillois sees play in terms of a series of characteristics: it is free, separate, uncertain, unproductive, and governed by both make-believe and rules.[3] This delineation of play seems more useful than the statement of Huizinga. It also provides a basis upon which to assess the character of game, sport, contest and recreation. Although Caillois does not detail these dimensions of play in the manner which follows, it is felt that these extrapolations clarify what is meant *here* by play.

"Free" as used in the present work with regard to play signifies that the individual voluntarily engages in the activity and also that he may commence and terminate his engagement at will.

Thus, the first feature of play is that it is an activity sustained between two boundaries in time, t_1, that point at which the individual *voluntarily* commences the activity, and t_2, that point at which he *voluntarily* terminates the activity. This characterization of the free nature of play differs greatly from the trait "free" as understood by Huizinga and others.

For instance, Weiss holds that play need not be free and that it may be forcibly begun and terminated.[4] He uses as his evidence the notion that parents often force their children to "go outside and play," and that children may be made to terminate such activities by their parents. The central element confounding Weiss' proof by example is the question of boundaries. While parents may and do order their chil-

---

[1] Paul Weiss, *Sport: A Philosophical Inquiry* (Carbondale and Edwardsville: Southern Illinois University Press, 1969), p. 139.

[2] Huizinga, *Homo Ludens: A Study of the Play Element in Culture* (Boston, Beacon Press, 1938), p. 13.

[3] R. Caillois, *Man, Play and Games* (New York: Free Press, 1961), p. 3 ff.

[4] Weiss, p. 139.

dren to go outside and play, such activity never starts simply as a result of force. In fact, if force is the predominant stimulus for engaging in "play" it is not play at all. Typically when parents issue such an order, they are more interested in the child going outside than they are in his activities once he is out—so long as those activities are within the bounds of proper behavior. The child may mope, sit in the shade, read a comic book, wash the windows, or carry out any number of other acceptable tasks, any of which may fall well outside of the realm of play.

Once outside, however, the child *may* enter into play voluntarily. It is only at this point that play begins—not at the point where upon the parents order the child outside. Upon issuing such an order, the parents merely terminate or interrupt a child's present activities and, by sending him outside, bring about new conditions under which the child may potentially enter into play. Few parents actually go outside to make sure that the child is in fact playing or to actually coerce him into playing.

It is at the point where the child himself actually chooses to play as opposed to engaging in other types of behavior that play begins. If one is, in fact, forced to engage in what some may construe as play, he is in reality being subjected to a type of punishment—much the same as the punishment meted out to a participant in football who shows up late for practice and is ordered by the coach to run three laps around the practice field. Such involuntary engagement violates one of the principles of play to be discussed later—that play must be separate, or bounded off, from the concerns, influences, and seriousness of phenomena falling outside of the play activity itself. And clearly an order to play, regardless of its source, interjects into the play act elements of seriousness, concern, and stimulation originating neither in the act nor in the desires of the actor.

Similarly, Weiss' notion that play may be forceably terminated is seen as invalid. A child who is ordered to cease play seldom halts such activity in the way that an egg thrown against a brick wall would halt its flight through the air. Rather, the child will typically cease his play in a gradual manner under normal circumstances, just as a car will come to a gradual stop at a stop sign. Only under abnormal circumstances will a child stop play instantaneously, that is, when severe punishment or scolding is imminent or when danger emerges in the play situation.

At that point wherein de-escalation of play involvement begins, play activity ends. Again, the termination is due to violation of the principle of play that requires separation from concerns, influences, and seriousness emanating outside of both the actor's desires and outside of the play act itself. At the moment that the child is psychologically *concerned* about such outside phenomena as the intrusion of danger into the play act or an order to cease play, play ends (t_2) although the child may continue to engage in the activity for a brief time. But in Weiss' view, it is not at the point t_2 that the parents' order to cease play is heeded, but at the point where the actual activity stops. This is invalid. The child actually ceases play of his own volition when he begins the psychological process of weighing and considering the parents' order. Since he has the option to ignore it, and to worry later about suffering the consequences of doing so, he in effect volunteers to terminate play the moment he allows the order to disrupt his involvement in the activity. Thus, play must of necessity be free, that is, voluntarily begun, voluntarily continued, and voluntarily terminated.

Caillois's second characteristic of play, closely related to his first, is that of separateness. But his description of separateness is inadequate: by separateness he seems to mean no more than "limited in time and space." But all human activities, including the phenomenon of living itself, are limited in time and space. Temporal and spatial limitations alone are therefore insufficient to demarcate play as being significantly different from any other human activity.

Here, separateness is understood to mean that an act, in order to constitute play, must not only be limited in time and space but must also be exclusive of influences, concerns, and seriousness originating outside of the play act itself. Play must be bound off from the daily pragmatic concerns of the world. This does not mean that the activities of children seen by some psychologists and social psychologists as "role playing in preparation for life" do not constitute play. For it is role playing and preparation for life only in the eyes and minds of the observers of the behavior—not in the minds of the children.

Such functions as preparation for adult roles through participation in play activities typically are of no concern to the child. When the child engages in what social scientists see as assuming the roles of doctors, nurses, firemen, and so forth, and attend meticulously to what are taken to be essential parts of the role, not only are they not consciously preparing themselves for adult life (Why, otherwise, are not all adults firemen, nurses or doctors? And why did I never play sociologist to my recollection?), but they hold the activity outside of the realm of reality altogether as a separate domain needing no justification or productive direction.

Play is thus bracketed off from the realities with which the individual must contend in his daily life. Regardless of who is "playing," they must go through this bracketing process. As stated, even the play of the smallest child has little to do with his daily life concerns. He holds in abeyance the usual attitudes toward eating, talking, pushing, pulling, crawling, and walking. These are efforts usually initiated in order to fulfill some goal beyond themselves. Made a part of play, they are cut off from the implicit goals of satisfying the child's hunger, curiosity, or sense of security. When he plays, he moves in a sphere where he is in charge and where he may reinterpret what objects are and what they do. Like the adult, daily activities force the child to remain attentive to what will affect his welfare inside a larger world. But, in play, due to its separateness, he moves inside a world where he is in charge and can thus be more at ease to pursue his pleasure.

Caillois's third term, seriousness, is also of significant import as a characteristic of play and is related to the notion of separateness. In play, seriousness is bounded off from all else. In our daily lives, we move through a cluster of different but intimately related roles. For instance, the role of being a man may be interwined with the roles of husband, father, chief provider, and citizen. The degree of seriousness with which the person functions in one area of this role cluster has profound implications for his functioning in all others—as Mirra Komarovsky shows in *The Unemployed Man and His Family*.[5] Thus, because of the interrelatedness of his seriousness of involvement in each role in the cluster, a man who fails as a provider has also failed somewhat as a father, as a husband, as a productive citizen, and as a man to the extent that his masculine self-image and social status is diminished.

In play, to the contrary, seriousness is of consequence only with respect to what happens inside of the bounded realm of the play activity.

With regard to seriousness, play is as exclusive of concerns of religion, art, and science as it is from those of daily life. For, like daily life, these have as part of their meaning an aim to achieve some result with respect to reality. In short, they have goals beyond participation in the religious, artistic, or scientific processes. This makes them serious in much the same way as daily life is serious, though they often yield great satisfaction and are sometimes devoid of pragmatic significance.

To say that play is "uncertain" merely means that no preparation or planning is needed. Caillois's characterization of play as "unproductive" is understood here to mean nonutilitarian rather than what Weiss and Caillois both view in the more narrow sense as merely noneconomic. In order to be play, an activity must be devoid of utilitarian value, not only in product but also in process. Play necessarily is exclusive of all efforts aimed at producing valued ends or products and also of all efforts with the goal of conditioning or preparing one to produce or engage in the means of producing such valued ends or products. The bracketing off of play from the activities of daily life predisposes it to restriction within nonutilitarian bounds. Thus, none of the following actors could be considered as engaging in play: the office worker or executive who takes part in a badminton match in order to relax and take a break from the

---

[5] Mirra Komarovsky, *The Unemployed Man and His Family* (New York: Dryden Press, 1940).

rigors of work; the professional participant in football; the high school and college football participants who see themselves as preparing for a college athletic grant-in-aid or for a professional football career; persons who engage in such activities as card games with the goal of winning or gaining financially; or participants in checkers or chess. (This point of utilitarian versus nonutilitarian emphasis will be returned to later in discussions of other concepts.) Thus, a child's play act includes both the meticulous building of a sand castle and what would appear to be his wanton destruction of it.

The make-believe element in play is understood here to mean that the individual voluntarily puts himself in a role which is an integrated part of the play act but at the same time is a role with which the individual in reality does not identify. On the surface, there may seem to be some contradiction between the element of play termed "seriousness" and this element of make-believe or fantasy. But the contradiction is in fact spurious.

As stated, in order to engage in play, the individual must involve himself in activities separated from those in which he normally participates in daily life. This separateness demands that all but the most basic ascribed roles be eliminated from play. Thus, a child may play doctor, but a person who in real life is a doctor cannot. A doctor may buy a set of electric trains and "play" engineer, but a person who in real life is a train engineer may not. A tomboy may play the role of the football participant, but an actual football participant or a young man who aspires to participate in football for utilitarian reasons may not.

In those circumstances where the doctor "plays" doctor, the train engineer "plays" with the model trains, and where the football participant or aspirant "plays" football participant, the identification with the central role of the play act is too great for the act to be designated play even when such identification is not conscious.

For even in a supposed play situation, those individuals who in reality are engaged in these activities are soon beset by the same pressures that are upon them while pursuing those activities in their real life roles.

Both Caillois and Weiss are mistaken in their assertion regarding rules in play. Caillois states that rules must of necessity govern play activities. Weiss believes that rules may or may not be part of the play process. I feel that both are wrong. If rules were in fact a necessary element in play activity, the elements of voluntary commencement and termination of play, that of nonutilitarian engagement, and the element of separation from seriousness would all be negated. Rules imply goals, direction, and commencement, and terminal points for play activities that may be determined outside of the boundaries of the play act and beyond the control of the actor. When rules are interjected into a play act, it ceases to be play and begins to approximate a contest, a game, and even sport activity.

Play, of necessity, must be spontaneous and free. Even where there is danger to the life and limbs of the actor engaged in the play act, a situation where rules of behavior are clearly warranted, so long as the danger is ignored and concern over it is not interjected into the play act by the actor and rules of behavior are not brought to bear on the activity, then the actor may literally play himself to death.

These various characterizations of play may thus be summed up in the following statement: Play is a voluntary and distinct activity carried out within arbitrary boundaries in space and time, separate from daily roles, concerns, and influences and having no seriousness, purpose, meaning, or goals for the actor beyond those emerging within the boundaries and context of the play act itself.

RECREATION

Recreation is a concept closely related to play and more commonly used by physical educators than by social scientists. It means literally to re-create or to refresh oneself in body and/or mind. Therefore, by definition, recreation is different from play though the two terms are often used interchangeably. This confusion stems partially from the fact that play and recreation are quite similar. Recreation, first of all, involves a degree of voluntary engagement. No one can be forced to refresh himself. The individual may also terminate and commence, voluntarily, the recreational act. Recreational activity is also limited in space and time by the actor and requires no preparation or training. Recreation is also nonutilitarian in product. Role relevance is restricted to the recreational activity by the actor.

But with mention of these characteristics, the similarities between play and recreation ends. Because recreation is likely to commence with the perceived need for re-creating or refreshing the body and/or mind, entering into the recreational situation is not wholly a matter of individual choice, though as stated, the elements of voluntary commencement and termination of activity are matters of prerogative. Entrance into such situations is usually influenced by the degree of exhaustion or overwrought condition of the actor's mind and/or body as a result of his activities in daily life. But the recreational situation and the recreational act are not necessarily coextensive.

Separateness, too, is a characteristic of the recreational act. But, unlike play, where separateness is total, in recreation there is determined effort on the part of the actor to engage in activities *different* in some significant aspect from those which he engages in during his daily life. Typically, he consciously seeks to avoid the "busman's holiday."

Thus, by virtue of the fact that the recreational act is influenced by the character of the actor's daily activities, recreation is not completely separate from the actor's real-life role cluster. However, it is separate from the more pressing specific concerns of that role cluster.

Recreation typically involves little fantasy or make-believe. For the thrust of recreation is not to become that which one is not but, rather, to divorce oneself temporarily from the pressures and role responsibilities associated with the position he occupies in his day-to-day life.

The policeman who engages in surfing on his day off does not typically lose himself in a fantasy that he is the world's greatest surfer, either consciously or unconsciously. Instead, he attempts to absorb himself in the activity, thereby temporarily allowing his real-life role to recede into the background of his consciousness. And "forgetting" one's real-life role is quite different from taking on another.

The goal of recreation or refreshment also affects the element of seriousness within the recreational act. The actor's attitude of seriousness and its duration are influenced by the length of time it takes him to refresh himself and the rate of progress he makes toward that goal, as well as by stimulation emerging out of involvement in the recreational process itself. Here again, factors originating outside of the recreational act (those of degree of exhaustion, individual propensity to "bounce back," and the amount of attentiveness and time that the actor can afford to give recreation as opposed to his daily activities) constitute significant influences in limiting the actor's freedom of action.

Recreation may or may not be carried out within the structure of rules. Taking a walk constitutes recreation as much as engaging a basketball so long as either removes the actor from the mental and physical exertions of his daily life. If a recreational activity has rules, these may be formal or informal.

Recreation, then, is an activity which is for the most part voluntarily engaged in by the actor, different in character from those activities exerting mental and physical pressures upon him in his daily life, and having the effect of refreshing him in mind and/or body.

CONTEST OR MATCH

A contest, or match, and game are not sharply distinguishable today in all circumstances, but they differ in ways significant enough to demand separate treatment. Contest and match may be used interchangeably. One may refer with equal validity to a boxing contest or a boxing match, a wrestling contest or a wrestling match, a chess contest or a chess match, a tennis contest or a tennis match.

One may technically refer to these activities as games when the opposing participants are in fact representing larger collectivities, that is, boxing, tennis, wrestling, and chess are components of the Olympic Games. However, such reference overrides the most salient characteristic of contests or matches—they are in their pure forms *individual* in both effort and consequence. The participants are opposing individuals who are the sole beneficiaries of participation, goal achivement, or failure.

In modern urban civilizations with their characteristic impersonality, their emphasis upon achieved prestige and status in a situation where not all can have great prestige and high status, and their tendency to diminish the intensity of primary group identification, fewer and fewer true contests occur.

In the Olympic Games, originally a series of contests between individual actors, each participant now adds to or detracts from the prestige of the country from which he comes depending upon whether he wins, places, or loses in his particular event. The stated aim of the United States Olympic Committee in every Olympiad since World War I has been to "win the Olympic Games," usually meaning to beat the Russians or whoever else may be currently seen as America's chief protagonist in areas of international competition. The attention given the 1972 chess match between the American Bobby Fischer and the Russian Boris Spassky is a more recent example of the erosion of the match or contest as an activity form.

I feel that, in the not too distant future, true contests will be about as easy to find as dinosaurs—if such activities have not already fallen victim to forces emanating from the social, political, and ideological conditions endemic to the larger world.

The root meaning of contest is "to testify with" or more accurately, "to test against."[6]

Contests typically pivot around the demonstration of individual excellence in speed, endurance, accuracy, strength, coordination, and/or mental acuity. These may also be characteristics of the game, but in the contest it is the outcome for the individual that assumes most immediate priority. His role as "contestant" has no relevance beyond the boundaries of the contest itself.

In the true contest, engagement by the individual must be voluntary. Because of the element of self-discovery, the participant cannot be forced to become involved as a contestant. In the game, the group exerts pressure upon its representative participants to succeed and the responsibility for and the consequences of success or failure are shared to some degree. But, in the contest, the emphasis is put upon individual struggle, and, likewise, the consequences of the outcome are individual in effect.

---

[6] Weiss, p. 151.

Though there may be great variation in seriousness brought to the contest situation by different individuals (depending upon the significance of the activity to the maintenance of a subject's self-image and ego) it would appear fairly certain that an awareness of an informal group identification with one contestant or another would *heighten* the perceived seriousness of the contest for all involved.

In other respects, the contest is like the game and need not be further enlarged upon here. This holds with regard to such characteristics as preparation, the diminished existence of fantasy, and restrictiveness in space and time.

A contest then is an individually focused activity emphasing self-discovery through competitive struggle within the context of informal or formal rules and having no consequences beyond those affecting the individual and emerging within the contest activity.

GAME

The root meaning of "game" is "to leap joyously."[7] In modern times, however, the meaning is more correctly used with reference to play than to game. For though there is room for spontaneity in the game, the restrictive structure created by rules and the degree of seriousness manifest in the game typically preclude action such as that denoted in the root meaning of the word. Such spontaneity is kept well within the bounds of rules although these may be highly flexible.

The game always has goals. But, unlike recreation, the goals of games are not restricted to ends emerging out of the process of engaging in the activity. Rather, the game process is a means through which the actor or actors seek to achieve goals beyond the benefits of participation. Hence, unlike in play where a child will cease the activity once he is tired or bored, and unlike recreation where an actor will cease activity once he is tired, bored, or refreshed, a participant in the game will persist in the activity despite tiredness, boredom, or an interest in other activities.

This persistence of participation, often beyond the limits of interest and enjoyment is due to four basic factors: the existence of goals emanating from outside of the game act; a structure determined by formal or informal rules; a seriousness arising out of concerns and interests beyond the realm of the game act; and the fact that games are collective in character.

The essence of the game process is to test participants' abilities in a situation structured by either formal or informal rules. The goals may involve tests of physical ability and/or mental ingenuity. Further, this testing typically is undertaken in a situation of collective interaction and

---

[7] Ibid., p. 145.

representation, with the consequences of the game being shared by the memberships of the collectivities involved.

The chief characteristic of any game is rivalry or competition. If there are no opposing forces, there is no game. If the participants on the opposing sides are representative only of themselves and not collectivities, there is no game. Rather, they would be engaged in a "contest."

Because of the fact that the goal of winning carries along with it such products as prestige, influence, and status—all elements not emerging from within the game process itself (e.g., one does not receive a specific increment of influence or prestige for each point scored in a game) the game manifests a seriousness far beyond that exhibited in the play act or in recreation. This is due to several facts. First, not only does the prestige and status of the individual participant in the game hinge on its outcome, but that of his group also. Thus, increased pressures are placed upon the participants to succeed and they assume a much more serious attitude toward the task at hand.

Second, the fact that formal or informal rules always govern a game situation means that there is a finite time period within which to achieve a stipulated goal in a game; there are specifically acceptable ways of achieving that goal; and the decision as to whether the goal has been achieved or not is determined by impersonal and disinterested forces beyond the control of the participants. The participant in the game is therefore forced to utilize his physical, mental, time, and space resources in the most efficient manner, given the limitations imposed upon the game situation. This generates an intensity, attentiveness, and seriousness unknown in play and recreation.

For these reasons, despite the root meaning of game, one seldom sees a game participant "leaping joyously" until his goal has been successfully achieved. And for every person leaping with joy, there may be at least one who is baleful.

Again, due to the nature of the game—its goals, seriousness, and rules—the participants do not have the prerogatives of beginning or ending their participation in the activity as they might choose. Unlike play and recreation, where the actor may begin or end the act as he pleases, woe unto the game participant who exercises such individualism. The game participant who loses interest in the game, tires, or becomes bored and removes himself from the game situation is seen as a "quitter" by both participants and spectators—no matter how formal or informal the rules of the game might be. Even under conditions where the participant believes himself to be injured, his removal from the game is not a matter of his prerogative. Depending upon whether he removes himself or is removed by someone with authority to do so under the rules of the game, he may be a quitter and a heel or a hero who has sacrificed his own well-being in order to win for the group. This characterization typically holds whether the game is one involving physical prowess or the utilization of mental ingenuity in devising strategy. Thus, the commencement and termination of participation in the game is determined by rules, the nature of the game's goals, and the seriousness of the activity. The actor's responsibilities are not completed until the game is terminated by a win, loss, or draw on the part of one opponent or the other. And a premium is placed upon winning.

Unlike the cases of play and recreation, in the game an actor can be forced to participate. This forced participation may even lead to the successful achievement of the goal of the game. This result is possible because the key goals of the game are not of primary relevance to the individual or derived solely from the process of his carrying out the game activity. Rather, the chief goals are of relevance to the group and emerge from a context greater than that of the game itself.

Thus, the group may prevail upon the unwilling prospective participant to enter the game situation for the good of the collectivity. It may coerce him to do so with the implicit suggestions that he will be ostracized or will have failed the entire group if he does not; or the group may question the loyalty of the individual.

In those cases in which a particular collectivity goes outside of the group to recruit representatives to participate in the game on its behalf, the positive attributes and status of the group may be cited in efforts to induce the individual to participate on its behalf. But under any circumstances, voluntary participation is not a necessary element in the game.

Again because of structure determined by formal or informal rules, it is not the prerogative of the individual to set the limits of the game in space and time. Unlike the actors in recreation and play, the game participant is confined in space, as he is in time. Outside of defined spatial and temporal boundaries, his activities become irrelevant to the outcome of the game and may even constitute violations that might impede success in achieving the goals of the game.

Also, because of the seriousness of the game, there is little fantasy or make-believe on the part of the participants. In a situation where one must make the most efficient use of all resources available, there is little opportunity for fantasy. In fact, engaging in fantasy is detrimental to achieving a successful game outcome. So just as the individual must not lose himself in the game process to the extent that he loses sight of the primary goals of the game, likewise he must not engage in distracting fantasy during the course of the game.

One last characteristic of the game pertains to preparation. The game may or may not be preceded by preparation. However, the more valued the goals of the game by the group, the greater will be the preparation for it by the participants. This preparation may involve physical conditioning, the devising of strategies, and/or practice. At this point, the game begins to approximate a sport.

A game, then, is an activity manifest in physical and/or mental effort, governed by formal or informal rules, and having as participants opposing actors who are part of or who represent collectivities that want to achieve a specific goal that has value beyond the context of the game situation, that is, prestige, recognition, influence, and so forth. Clearly this definition of game has applicability in many diverse areas of human interaction.

SPORT

Sport derives its root meaning from "disport," meaning "to divert oneself." It carried the original implication of people diverting their attention from the rigors and pressures of daily life by participating in the mirth and whimsy of frolic—some physical activity. However, today, sport often is anything but a diversion to its participants. In fact, for many participants it is sport that produces the primary stresses and strains in their lives.

Sports differ radically from recreation, contests, and games, although they may contain elements prominent in each of these. Moreover, sports have virtually nothing in common with play.

It is only in sports that the participant can accurately be termed an "athlete." The following discussion will clarify these points.

One of the most salient features of sports is that they always involve physical exertion. This physical exertion is an imperative characteristic that cannot be overstressed. Without it there simply is no sport activity.

Another imperative feature of sports is that these activities are always formally structured and organized within the context of formal and explicit rules of behavior and procedure. These rules typically are historically based. Changes in rules are regarded as legitimate and binding only if made by officially mandated bodies carrying out their tasks in accordance with predetermined procedures.

Thus, the athlete involved in the sports or athletic activity (the two terms are synonymous) is functioning within well-established traditions that are preserved in formulations of what is required and permitted, as well as in formally documented and up-dated records and histories.

While few athletes have an intimate knowledge of the histories of their sporting events, they most assuredly are conscious of standards in their activities, of the levels and status of previous achievements in their events, of the teachings of their coaches, and, most of all, of the presence of disinterested and impersonal referees or judges who make the existence of formally prescribed rules of action and process always amply evident. Thus, the athlete differs radically from children at play who recite the same verses generation after generation, but have no sense of history or tradition, cumulative, causal, or explanatory.

Participants in sports are *always* representatives of groups or organizations. And, just as in the case of the participant in the game, the representation of or affiliation with a group brings about a heightening of the pressures on the individuals involved in the effort. The resulting intense seriousness of purpose is manifest in several ways.

First, all sports necessarily demand meticulous preparation on the parts of all having a direct input into the determination of the outcome of the sporting event. Thus, coaches carefully plot strategies, athletes prepare and condition themselves mentally and physically, and extensive practice sessions are carried out with the purpose of coordinating the various efforts. All such preparations are aimed toward one goal— winning.

Second, in sports all roles and positions are explicitly named, defined, and delegated; the relationships and responsibilities of each relative to another are clearly detailed.

And, finally, the seriousness of purpose in sport as a social phenomenon is manifest in the fact that formal organizational structures and relationships are necessary. This formal organization typically rivals that of other large-scale bureaucratically structured enterprises in terms of role specialization, the complexity of its internal functions, and the hierarchically arranged authority relations among positions.

In sports, the athlete may seek self-discovery as does the contestant, but this search is secondary to the central effort of using whatever personal resources that he might have, for example, physical power, as efficiently as possible to defeat the opposition within the boundaries of the rules governing participation.

Sports are utilitarian in product but not necessarily in process. Sports always involve efforts to attain valued factors beyond those emanating from mere participation. Thus, the athlete, like the participant in the game, may engage in the sport activity even though he may not enjoy it and may even persist in this involvement beyond the limits of his interest, stamina, and personal welfare.

Like the participant in the game or contest also, the athlete in sports has no control over the temporal and spacial dimensions of his activity. Both of these boundaries are set by rules and enforced by judges and referees. The athlete may neither enter nor leave the activity as he desires. For to do so would constitute a breach of his role responsibilities to the collectivity which he represents or is a part of. And, unlike the participant in the game who may face ridicule or ostracism for "quitting" before the rules stipulate that he may, the athlete not only faces the possibility of ridicule or ostracism for such behavior, but, due to the formality of his role and position to which he is usually bound by contract in relation to others in the organization, he may also be fined, dismissed, or otherwise legally and officially punished.

Sports, being the formal, rational, goal-directed endeavors that they are, provide little opportunity for fantasy or make-believe on the part of the various persons whose actions contribute directly to determining the outcome of sports events. These activities, to the greatest extent possible, constitute calculated, rationally planned efforts.

Because sports activities are utilitarian in product, they are much less sharply separated from daily concerns than play, recreation, games, or contests. In fact, sports, for athletes, coaches, and the owners and administrators of sports organizations, constitute the central realm of endeavor and involvement in the daily rigors and pressures of life. And in a real sense, sports are intimately intertwined with the daily cares of even the fan or spectator. Indeed, this fact constitutes part of the central thesis of this book.

Sports have typically evolved from games. Games become sports after rules are formalized, a history and tradition is generally recognized as having been established and accurately recorded and documented. New games may be created overnight, as may contests. But sports are not suddenly created, but rather are the products of a nondeliberate, nondirected evolutionary process.

The element of "role relevance" also demarcates sports from the activities previously discussed. Because of the utilitarian features of sports, the fact that the athlete is an integrated component of a formally coordinated activity affecting the outcomes of large organizations and collectivities, and because of the notion that he is superbly conditioned and trained, some interesting anomalies arise. For instance, the black athlete is accepted in some circles of American society in which black people in general find difficulty in being accepted. His role status as athlete surpasses his role status as a black person in terms of social acceptance.

Weiss explains the role relevance of "athlete," perhaps with some poetic license, in this way: "[In this society] an athlete . . . is treated as a sacred being who embodies something of the divine in him. He is credited with the dignity of embodying a supreme value."[8]

Sport, then, is defined here as involving activities having formally recorded histories and traditions, stressing physical exertion through competition within limits set in explicit and formal rules governing role

---

[8] Ibid., p. 153.

and position relationships, and carried out by actors who represent or who are part of formally organized associations having the goal of achieving valued tangibles or intangibles through defeating opposing groups.

The following tables present comparisons of the activities denoted by the concepts discussed above.

From Table 3-1, it should be evident that, as one moves from play to sports, the following occurs:

TABLE 3–1

Profiles of activities denoted by central concepts

		Activities denoted by:				
	Determining attributes	*Play*	*Recreation*	*Contest or match*	*Game*	*Sport or athletics*
1.	Activity exclusive of concerns and influences emanating from outside of contest of act	X				
2.	Existence of fantasy or make-believe	X				
3.	Actor(s) commences activity at will	X	X			
4.	Actor(s) limits act in space and time	X	X			
5.	Actor(s) terminates activity at will	X	X			
6.	Activity not necessarily utilitarian in product (may be devoid of economic, material, prestige, power, or status-achievement goals)	X	X			
7.	Competition not a necessary component	X	X			
8.	Activity characterized by a necessary degree of spontaneity (not restricted by formal and informal rules of procedure)	X	X			
9.	Relevance of role restricted to boundaries of activity	X	X	X		
10.	Individualistically focused and oriented	X	X	X		
11.	Actor(s) involvement in activity necessarily voluntary	X	X	X		
12.	No imperative formal hierarchical arrangement of roles and positions	X	X	X	X	
13.	Physical exertion not a necessary component	X	X	X	X	
14.	Preparation for participation in activity not a necessary component	X	X	X	X	
15.	No formal stabilized history or tradition necessary	X	X	X	X	
16.	Activity inclusive of concerns and influences emanating from outside of context of activity		X	X	X	X
17.	Nonexistence of fantasy or make-believe		X	X	X	X
18.	Actor(s) may not commence activity at will			X	X	X
19.	Actor(s) may not terminate activity at will			X	X	X
20.	Actor(s) does not have prerogative to limit activity in space and time			X	X	X
21.	Activity utilitarian in product (emphasis on attaining economic goals, prestige, power, status, self-esteem, etc.)				X	X
22.	Competition necessary component				X	X

	Determining attributes	*Play*	*Recrea-tion*	*Contest or match*	*Game*	*Sport or athletics*
				Activities denoted by:		
23.	Activity necessarily characterized by formal or informal rules, regulations, restrictions or limitations which must be adhered to			X	X	X
24.	Activity not necessarily voluntary; may be forced				X	X
25.	Relevance of role not restricted to activity				X	X
26.	Activity necessarily collective in character				X	X
27.	Preparation for participation in activity necessary					X
28.	Formal history; recognized records and traditions					X
29.	Physical exertion a necessary component					X
30.	Imperative formal hierarchical arrangement of roles and positions					X

1. Activity becomes less subject to individual prerogative, with spontaneity severely diminished.

2. Formal rules and structural role and position relationships and responsibilities within the activity assume predominance.

3. Separation from the rigors and pressures of daily life becomes less prevalent.

4. Individual liability and responsibility for the quality and character of his behavior during the course of the activity is heightened.

5. The relevance of the outcome of the activity and the individual's role in it extends to groups and collectivities that do not participate directly in the act.

6. Goals become diverse, complex, and more related to values emanating from outside of the context of the activity.

7. The activity consumes a greater proportion of the individual's time and attention due to the need for preparation and the degree of seriousness involved in the act.

8. The emphasis upon physical and mental extension beyond the limits of refreshment or interest in the act assumes increasing dominance.

Table 3-2 illustrates the fact that the items characterizing the five activities form a perfect Guttman-scale pattern having no errors and 100 percent reproducibility as we move from play to sport. Note that play and recreation are very similar, that contest/match is a genuinely intermediate case and that game and sport are paired similarly. Note also that there is *no* overlap at all between play and sport. As defined here and employed throughout the remainder of this work, these are fully independent concepts.

TABLE 3-2

Comparison of profiles portrayed in Table 3-1

Type of activity	Defining characteristics																													
	1	2	3	4	5	6	7	8	9	10	11	12	13	14	15	16	17	18	19	20	21	22	23	24	25	26	27	28	29	30
Play	x	x	x	x	x	x	x	x	x	x	x	x	x	x	x	x														
Recreation			x	x	x	x	x	x	x	x	x	x	x	x	x	x														
Contest or match								x	x	x	x	x	x	x	x	x	x	x	x	x	x	x								
Game										x	x	x	x	x	x	x	x	x	x	x	x	x	x	x	x					
Sport												x	x	x	x	x	x	x	x	x	x	x	x	x	x	x	x	x	x	x

So, far from being play, recreation, "fun and games," or mere diversion, sports assume the character of occupational endeavors for participants, and of businesses for coaches, administrators, and owners. The "businesslike" quality of the role relationships among these positions and the rigidly defined role responsibilities and rewards attached to each become crucial factors in determining the overall functioning of sports in American society. This is true in both amateur and professional sports where the only real differences between the two typically pertain to the intensity and roughness of the activity and the fact that professional participants may legitimately receive economic or material remuneration for their services to the groups or organizations which they represent and amateurs may not.

As used in this work, then, the concept "sports" refers to athletic activity and is synonymous with athletics. The singular form, "sport," refers to the complex of values, positions, roles, and other accoutrements designated here the "institution of sport."

part two

The American sports creed

THE REMAINING CHAPTERS of this book examine the institutional complexities of sport. Emphasis is placed upon the institutionalized role relationships among those involved in sport, the character of its focal activities, the content and functions of what is called here "the American sports creed." "Creed" and "ideology" are used interchangeably. Of course, neither word is used in a derogatory sense. Rather, the terms are "neutral and describe any system of beliefs, publically expressed with the manifest purpose of influencing the sentiments and actions of others."[1]

One goal of the remainder of this book is to illuminate the institutional character of and the role relationships within the realm of organized sports in contemporary American society. A second objective is to answer two questions concerning the sports creed: Why does the sports creed espouse what it does? What are the relationships among the sports creed, the character of human relationships within the institution of sport, and the cultural heritage of American society as a whole?

The primary aim here is neither to debunk nor to evaluate the "right" or "wrong." While any judicious analysis of social phenomena carries with it some nuance of approval or criticism, here criticism is meant as a service to analysis and not as an end unto itself. Though tempted at points, I have made a strenuous effort to abstain from polemical statements and purely idiosyncratic interpretations of data. It is

---

[1]Frances X. Sutton, S. E. Harris, C. Kaysen, and J. Tobin, *The American Business Creed* (Cambridge, Mass.: Harvard University Press, 1956), p. 2. This book provides a basic theoretical foundation for the present analysis.

within this context that the cited omissions, exaggerations, contradictions, and ambiguities of the sports creed should be understood.

The present discussion uses the theoretical framework of Sutton et al., *The American Business Creed.* This book presents a clear, coherent theory applicable to the present work, and it provides a format within which a body of chaotic and often contradictory information pertaining to sports can be productively organized.

Broadly speaking, achievement of useful answers to the questions stated above depends upon an analysis of the strains and conflicts inherent in the various role and status relationships within the institution of sport and between those persons who are involved primarily within the sports realm and those who are not. These conflicts and strains are viewed as emerging from several sources: (1) conflicts between the demands of particular positions in sport and the broader values of society; (2) gaps between the demands of particular positions in sport and the capabilities of the human beings who hold them to fulfill these demands; (3) inherently conflicting demands built into the social definitions of certain positions in the sport sphere.[2] This tripartite statement constitutes the general proposition that is applied in the analysis of sports in American society. The chief endeavors here are to demonstrate (1) that a great deal of the present turmoil as well as a good many of the traditional impediments to harmonious functioning in the sport realm are due to strains inherent in particular sport roles and in the sport institution as a whole and (2) that the major themes of the sports creed or ideology constitute verbal and symbolic resolutions to these conflicts. These then are the specific propositions at issue. Examination of the particular means of disseminating the sports creed, as well as an analysis of the economics of the sport institution, will also be undertaken.

Adopting Sutton's phraseology, my central thesis is that persons involved with sport, particularly coaches and athletes, adhere to their particular kind of ideology because of "emotional conflicts, the anxieties and the doubts engendered by the actions which their *roles* compel them to take, and by the conflicting demands of other social roles which they must fulfill in their various communities and in the society at large. Within the resources of the cultural tradition of America and within the limits of what is publically acceptable, the content of the [sports ideology] is shaped to resolve these conflicts, alleviate these anxieties, and overcome the doubts. For the person directly engaged [in sports endeavors—especially athletes and coaches], the function of the ideology is to help maintain one's psychological ability to meet the demands of his [role]."[3]

---

[2] Ibid., p. 1.
[3] Ibid., p. 11.

While it is conceded that not all coaches or athletes, for instance, will react identically to similar strains, nevertheless the majority of individuals socialized in American society are bound to find some of the demands inherent in certain sport roles to be disquieting. Moreover, one can infer that individuals engaged in sports endeavors will experience certain common patterns of strains as a result of institutional features and certain characteristics of American society. A major proportion of the present work is concerned with the disclosure of these "patterned" strains, their sources and consequences.

The data used and analyzed in Part II were gathered from four sources: (1) a content analysis performed on a sample of one-third of the issues of *Athletic Journal;* (2) recent newspaper articles, magazine editorials and feature articles, speeches, letters, and various legal documents in the files of the Institute for the Study of Sport and Society; (3) data collected by Eldon E. Snyder of Bowling Green University pertaining to athletic dressing-room slogans; (4) contemporary biographies, newspaper articles, and other literature pertinent to sport which I have collected over the past six years.

Information relevant to the substantive content of the sports creed in America emanated from many diverse sources. It is to be found in the sports columns of newspapers, in advertisements of all kinds, in the speeches of political leaders, within the fabric of theatrical plays, in poems, and so forth. The tremendously varied potential sources of such information obviously makes the possibility of achieving a statistical sample of *all* such data remote. However, some systematic sample of data clearly is desirable as a foundation upon which later analysis of information from more varied sources can be based. Attention was therefore focused upon one of the journals subscribed to by a significant segment of persons affiliated officially with sports in America, as either coaches or administrators.

This decision was based upon several factors. It is to the major sports journals that most coaches and administrators submit their ideas and articles reflective of serious professional concerns pertinent to athletics. Valid assessment of opinions, beliefs, and principles can thus be aided by focusing upon a journal recognized as creditable among coaches and administrators.

Second, by concentrating upon a professionally accredited journal as the source of primary material, the problems of sampling and access to relevant materials are greatly reduced. A journal which is published on a regular schedule and then over the years is bound into volumes can be readily sampled in a systematic fashion.

Third, it would be unnecessary as well as inordinately costly to inspect *all* statements made over the years in literally thousands of publications. While content analysis of the articles appearing in even a single journal is a tremendous task, such an undertaking is at least feasible and much time is saved by the aid of the journal's standard table of contents, structure, and summary statements at the end of each article.

The journal chosen for this content analysis was the *Athletic Journal,* America's first professional journal for coaches. It has a publication history going back to 1919; its emphasis and subject composition have been consistent and unbroken; and it has maintained and even expanded its appeal to professional athletic practitioners and administrators.

In a search of the libraries located at San Jose State College, the University of California at Berkeley, and at Stanford University, I found that the earliest available edition of *Athletic Journal* was that of September 1930. It was possible to secure for analysis all volumes commencing with volume 11, September 1930–June 1931, to volume 49, September 1968–June 1969. During the period from the first issue of volume 11 to the last issue in volume 49, *Athletic Journal* published 390 separate issues. It seemed impractical and unnecessary to analyze all 390 issues, averaging slightly over sixty-eight pages each. It was thus decided that a sample would be taken.

The major sample population was comprised of journal issues rather than articles, since not every article contained relevant materials. Some articles dealt with new equipment, new strategies in team sports, or some other subject matter not directly relevant to the sports creed. But each issue did contain some references to opinions or beliefs about what is termed here the sports creed.

It therefore seemed adequate to include every third issue from each annual volume, making the sample population one-third the size of the total number of issues published. Thus, *130* issues out of a total of 390 were analyzed.

In order to determine the issue with which the sampling would start, a table of random numbers was used. As a result, each issue had an equal probability of being included in the sample. By chance, the number thirty-two was chosen. Starting with the thirty-second issue published after September 1930 volume 14 number 2) every third issue became part of the sample. This procedure was continued until each of the thirty-nine available volumes had been sampled and at least three issues from each had been sampled.

The end product of a content analysis of articles appearing in the 130 publications making up the sample was that verbal expressions constituting a sports creed were coded and categorized into a relatively small number of classifications. The *recording unit* for the analysis was the sentence. The *context unit*—analyzed in order to assess the overall treatment of the recording unit by the writer whose statements were being studied—was the paragraph.

This initial content analysis resulted in twenty-one sentence classifications, one of which was labeled "miscellaneous." In order to check the accuracy of the coding process for the twenty substantive classifications, a sample of 200 sentences was drawn from the recording unit population and submitted to three graduate students who were writing their master's and doctor's theses on sports—two from San Jose State College and one at the University of California at Berkeley.

Since the sentences had been coded prior to giving them to the students, a comparison of the students' work with the original coding results provided an index as to the reliability and consistency of the content analysis.

Although manifestations of the sports creed were found throughout all sampled issues of *Athletic Journal,* these were rather heavily concentrated in staff editorials and commentary-type articles by coaches and athletic administrators. In the middle 1950s, however, the journal altered its format by cutting the length and reducing the regularity with which it presented such features. Meanwhile, it gave more space to advertisements for athletic equipment and to articles dealing primarily with details of the technical aspects and coaching techniques current in the various sports (football formations, defensive strategies in basketball, high-jumping styles, etc.).

Many articles and even advertisements containing aspects of the sports creed continued to appear after the cessation of regular editorials and articles focusing primarily upon commentary about the sports scene. But, given the significant occurrences in sport since the middle 1950s, resort to auxiliary and more current sources of additional data was felt to be desirable. These additional sources were also useful from another standpoint: they would provide some indication of the substantive continuity of the sports creed and point up aspects of the creed which were evoked primarily by social atmospheres created by unique past societal events such as the Great Depression of the late 1920s and early 1930s and by World War II.

The first source of additional data was the Institute for the Study of Sport and Society directed by Jack Scott. As part of its activities, this organization maintains a continuing file on socially relevant occurrences in organized athletics. Part of the input into this file is collected by regular volunteer staff members at the institute, but the overwhelming majority of it is gathered by a professional magazine and newspaper clipping service. In all, over eleven hundred articles from these files were read and appropriate aspects of their contents coded for the present study. Sample articles were also photocopied so that portions could be used as illustrative materials throughout this work.

The institute also maintains a file on all available official and legal documents and rulings having an overall effect on some level of sports activity. Most of these records give information about decisions of the various courts and, to a greater degree, rulings by the governing bodies of sports (such as the National Collegiate Athletic Association and the National Football League). To a limited extent, these materials were found to be useful as reference sources.

A second source of additional and less "dated" materials was the body of data collected by Eldon E. Snyder of Bowling Green University on the use of dressing-room slogans as a means of socialization. In the spring of 1969, Mr. Snyder, with the cooperation of the Ohio Association for Health, Physical Education and Recreation, drew a systematic sample of 270 high schools (or one-third of the schools affiliated with this organization). A questionnaire was sent to the basketball coach and two basketball team members from each of the 270 schools. One open-ended item on the questionnaire asked for a listing of slogans put up in the dressing room facilities provided for each team involved in the study. Of those contacted, 65 percent of the coaches responded as did 50 percent of the athletes. These responses showed that 71 percent of the coaches and 61 percent of the athletes indicated that the slogans or statements listed were put on dressing room walls and bulletin boards by coaches.[4] Clearly, the slogans gathered through this study represent a valuable source of data for the purposes here.

The final source of up-to-date information was my own file on magazine articles, newspaper clippings, and other literature pertinent to the task here. From these materials, some 557 articles were read and analyzed. Of these, over half (293) were discarded since they were duplicates of articles found in the files of the Institute for the Study of Sport and Society.

Despite the relatively wide range of sources tapped, the data analyzed here cannot be said to represent a statistical sample of the information available. I am satisfied, however, that the creedal statements derived and presented are representative of the core of publically expressed beliefs held by those directly involved in organized sports at all levels in American society.

After inspecting data from sources other than *Athletic Journal*, I made two major adjustments so that this study would reflect the overall and continuing character of the dominant sports creed in America more accurately. A number of preliminary categories developed from data taken during the examination of *Athletic Journal* were eliminated because, in my opinion, they were not significantly evident as patterned beliefs consistent throughout all the data analyzed. The substantive content of a category of statements labeled "miscellaneous" was also

---

[4] Eldon E. Snyder, "Athletic Dressing Room Slogans as Folklore: A Means of Socialization," paper presented at a meeting of the American Sociological Association, August 30, 1970.

dropped once it became clear after analysis of auxiliary materials that these represented, for the most part, "unique" idiosyncratic sentiments.

The number of categories derived from the analysis of all the above-mentioned sources was finally reduced from the twenty-one developed through the foundation analysis of *Athletic Journal* to twelve. These twelve specific categories are viewed here as being encompassed by seven central themes in the sports creed:

I. Character: encompasses (1) general statements pertaining to character development and relating sports to such traits as clean living, proper grooming, "red-bloodedness," and so forth; and statements specifically relating sport to the development of (2) loyalty and (3) altruism.

II. Discipline: relates sport to the development of (4) social and/ or self-control.

III. Competition: composed of statements and slogans relating sport specifically to (5) the development of fortitude and more generally to (6) preparation for life and (7) providing opportunities for advancement for the individual.

IV. Physical fitness: (8) statements and slogans relating sport to the achievement of physical health.

V. Mental fitness: encompasses statements relating sports to the development of (9) mental alertness and to (10) educational achievement.

VI. Religiosity: (11) expression relating sports achievement to traditional American Christianity.

VII. Nationalism: (12) statements relating sports involvement to the development of patriotism.

Each of these general themes and the more specific claims concerning each will be discussed in detail later.

For the most part, the chapters of part 2 describe the milieu within which the sport creed assumes significance in the symbolic resolution of strains inherent in particular sports roles and in the functioning of the sport institution as a whole. Chapter 4 briefly establishes the character of ideology and the validity of conceptualizing as ideology publically expressed beliefs about sports. Since the theoretical format employed here is adopted from *The American Business Creed*, the reader is referred to the original work (chap. 1, pp. 1–15, 303–10) for more detailed discussion of the character of ideology and for additional references on the subject. Chapter 5 discusses sport as a social institution and outlines the claims made on its behalf within the dominant sports creed. Chapter 6 focuses upon coaches, the executives of the individual sports unit. Chapter 7 deals with athletes. Chapter 8 is concerned with the fan and the nature of his role in the institution of sport. In chapter 9, the subject is the economics of sports in America. Chapter 10 examines the claims of the dominant sports creed presented in chapter 5.

4

Public beliefs as ideology

The American sports creed:

Athletics develop dedication and a desire to excel in competition, a realization that success requires hard work and that life must be lived according to rules. An athlete learns a sense of loyalty and a respect for discipline, both of which are lacking in this country today . . .[1]

Jess Hill
Athletic Director
University of Southern California

The humanitarian counter-creed:

. . . athletics for athletes . . . would be run in a democratic manner and all those involved would have a say . . . Unlike today's static, authoritarian, tradition-bound athletic programs, it would allow radical change in order to serve properly each new group of athletes . . . The most dire consequences would be . . . [some] rather unorganized athletic contests. The athletes themselves would suffer the consequences of any irresponsibility, and what better way is there for youth to discover the importance of mature, responsible behavior . . .[2]

Jack Scott
Director of the Institute for the
Study of Sport and Society

---

[1] In Tim Saasta, "Athletics: A Question of Values," *Daily Trojan*, September 27, 1971, p. 4.

[2] Jack Scott, *The Athletic Revolution* (New York: Free Press, 1970), p. 213.

The equalitarian counter-creed:

. . . The roots of the revolt of the Black athlete spring from the same seed that produced the sit-ins, the freedom rides, and the rebellions in Watts, Detroit, and Newark. . . . The Black athlete is for the first time reacting in a human, masculine fashion to the disparities between his heady artificial world of newspaper clippings, photographers, and screaming spectators and the real world of degradation, humiliation and horror that confronts the overwhelming majority of Afro-Americans. A more immediate call to arms . . . has been the Black athlete's realization that all his . . . clippings, records and photographs . . . will not qualify him for the quarterback position, a head coaching job, or a manager's position with a big-time sports organization . . .[3]

> Harry Edwards
> *Organizer of the Olympic*
> *Committee for Human Rights and the*
> *1968 Olympic boycott movement.*

THE STATEMENTS QUOTED above represent three clusters of attitudes, opinions, and values manifest in the institution of American sport. They undoubtedly have a familiar ring to many Americans. Such publicly expressed views constitute the substance of competing sport-related ideologies in America.

Clearly, then, what has been referred to here as *the* American sports creed is by no means the sole body of beliefs and value orientations focusing upon sports in the United States. Far from being monolithic, attitudes and opinions about sports are highly diverse and not infrequently antithetical in character. Unquestionably, however, there is one ideological system of values, attitudes, and perspective which does at present predominate.

The purposes of this chapter are to clarify the unique features of "ideology" and to explain why the dominant sports creed and competing sport-related belief systems are classified as such.

CHARACTERISTICS OF IDEOLOGY

It is commonplace in America today for ideologies of all types to come under attack on the grounds that the claims which they make lack empirical validity. Yet, an examination of ideologies as social phenomena reveals that rigorous external validity and even internal consistency are far from common traits. For, unlike science, the objective of ideology is not to broaden understanding through the development of logical, valid, and systematic "proofs" of relationships existing in the "real world." Rather, the objective of ideology is to influence social action and atti-

---

[3] Harry Edwards, *The Revolt of the Black Athlete* (New York: Free Press, 1969), pp. xv–xvi.

tudes regarding the particular subject with which it deals.[4] This distinction is fundamental to the remainder of this work.

Generally speaking, the more salient features of ideology are *selectivity, simplicity, symbolism,* and *public acceptability.*

Selectivity. All ideologies are highly selective as to the subjects they address. For instance, if one were interested in the problems of racism and authoritarianism in sports, the pronouncements and writings of athletic directors, coaches, and sports public-relations personnel would not be particularly promising sources of information. These are subjects which people holding such positions are likely to omit from the image of sports which they put forth for public appraisal. Ideology is likewise selective in citing empirical evidence. Therefore, while many critics of policies and practices prevalent in collegiate athletics have cited the large number of athletes recruited to certain colleges who expend their athletic eligibility but graduate belatedly or not at all, coaches and athletic directors expound upon the educational opportunities provided by sports to individuals who might otherwise never attend college. Ideology is selective in its use of logical argument. For example, the dominant sports creed is adamant in its view that varsity sports participation provides an essential and indispensable component of a student's total educational experience; and it points out that traditional American educational philosophy has long emphasized the school's responsibilities for both the intellectual and physical health development of its charges. Yet, the creed makes no attempt whatever to deal with the facts that most students never participate in varsity sports programs (due to the structure and functioning of sports in American society) and, further, that women students are excluded from practically all such programs as participants or coaches.

The selective character of ideology is determined primarily by its *evaluative* character, in the service of its objectives of influencing social conduct. In seeking to influence actions and attitudes, the ideologist overlooks complications of logic and consistency which would dilute his argument. Such omissions may be deliberate, but probably quite often, they simply never occur to him.

Simplicity. Ideology is simple and clear-cut with sharp lines, no grey areas, and no fuzziness. Therefore, in the dominant sports creed one finds slogans such as "The difference between winning and losing is hustle," and "A man shows what he *is* by what he *does*."[5]

---

[4] F. X. Sutton, S. E. Harris, C. Kaysen, and J. Tobin, *The American Business Creed* (Cambridge, Mass.: Harvard University Press, 1956), p. 3.

[5] Eldon E. Snyder, "Athletic Dressing Room Slogans as Folklore: A Means of Socialization," paper presented at a meeting of the American Sociological Association, August 30, 1970, p. 11.

In both these examples, mitigating circumstances and a multitude of possible intervening factors are ignored.

Symbolism. Extensive use of *expressive* symbols is another characteristic of ideology. According to Sutton et al.: "An expressive symbol is a word or set of words which excites in the reader [or listener] feelings of like or dislike or other emotional reactions."[6]

Thus, in the dominant sports creed, concepts such as "team man" and "competitive" are often juxtaposed with such terms as "freethinker" and "quitter." Each of these words is a symbol which not only conveys some meaning but also is aimed at mobilizing the emotional approval or disapproval of the audience. Each provokes likes or dislikes and related moral judgments.

Public acceptability. According to Sutton et al., the orientation of ideology subjects it is substantial control by its audience. In the case of sports, although there is tremendous emphasis put upon teamwork and intraorganizational cooperation—and, though from the professional levels down through "little league" sports, public taxes, mandatory fees, and/ or philanthropic donations provide substantial sources of fiscal support —the dominant sports creed cannot and does not advocate a socialistic or communistic economic or social philosophy for either the sports institution or society at large. For to the vast majority of Americans, including many if not most of those directly involved in sports, such philosophical and political orientations elicit negative sentiments of dislike and disapproval—even though only a relatively small proportion of the American public could define socialism or communism in any very precise manner.

The qualities of selectivity, oversimplification, symbolism, and public acceptability have helped us to assess the ideological character of the dominant American sports creed. The same qualities are equally applicable to diagnosis of the nature of the two major competing creeds. For it appears that the humanitarian and the equalitarian creeds also are selective, overly simplistic, make extensive use of expressive symbolism, and are tailored in substantive content to be acceptable to particular segments of the public.

The validity of these points will be illustrated in later chapters. The main thing to remember here is that the dominant American sports creed, the humanitarian creed, and the equalitarian sports creed differ not so much in the character and "truth" of their respective pronouncements as in the value orientations they emphasize.

Ideology as used here refers explicitly to "publicly expressed statements." For some, this perhaps raises the question of whether or not publicly expressed statements can be taken as the "real" creed or ideol-

---

[6] Sutton et al., p. 5.

ogy adhered to by those who are in some way involved with sports. Do such statements in fact constitute mere "smoke screens" obscuring from public view the values and beliefs actually held by such persons? Let us focus momentarily upon coaches' expressions of the dominant American sports creed and then briefly recapitulate Sutton's explanation of the validity of regarding public expressions as reliable manifestations of personal beliefs.

It has been frequently alleged, particularly by dissident athletes and other critics of established sport, that coaches express claimed virtues of sports, despite evidence to the contrary, simply because coaches as a group are incorrigible liars. While coaches, like most everyone else in the society, undoubtedly opt to prefabricate or bend the truth in the name of expediency from time to time, it has yet to be demonstrated that as a group they singularly possess any extraordinary inclination to do so. Further, since the American public apparently believes the claims expressed, the inference to be made from the allegation that coaches say what they do because they are incorrigible liars is that, correspondingly, the American public is made up of gullible fools—if not outright liars also. Such logical pursuit of the "liar" explanation leads down a road which must ultimately end with the conclusion that coaches and the general public are engaged in some massive, conscious conspiracy against athletes. Clearly this conclusion is untenable and must be discounted.

Another prevalent notion among dissidents is that self-interest underlies expressed claims for the virtues of sport. Here the notion is that coaches in particular actively promote the sports creed because it is "in their interest" to do so. There are several problems with this explanation. First of all it does not explain the *athlete's* belief in the creed as manifest in the countless biographies and autobiographies presenting "what sports have done for me" testimonials. Neither does it explain the fans' belief in the creed. For, in its essence, narrowly defined "self-interest" as an explanation is merely a more sophisticated version of the "coaches are incorrigible liars" explanation, and it suffers from the same shortcomings. Assuming for the moment that coaches make the claims constituting the sports creed out of a narrowly defined self-interest (i.e., they lie), if the American public's apparent belief in the expressed claims is to be accounted for within the context of the self-interest explanation, it must be assumed also that the public is a conscious coconspirator in the deceit or that it is extremely gullible—the current "Lumpen Neanderthal" so to speak.

There is also another difficulty associated with the self-interest explanation. This difficulty revolves around the scope and meaning of the term "self-interest." If the term is clearly and precisely defined, the explanation becomes patently inadequate. If the term is stretched to cover every contingency, the explanation loses all meaning. If the former alternative is applied to the question "Why do coaches oppose 'hippie-style' dress and grooming standards among their athletes?" it should be clear that self-interest does not provide an adequate explanation of this patterned coaching behavior because it really is not in coaches' interests to dismiss athletes from their squads. Neither is there any evidence that coaches consider it in their own best interests to inject ill-feelings into their relationships with athletes. And so, under a "normally defined self-interest" explanation, there is no adequate basis for the simplicity, certainty, and prevalence of coaching opposition. If we stick with the explanation, we can only dismiss such opposition as evidence of patterned error or ignorance. But this of course is not an explanation but an example of how problems are defined out of existence. It is therefore unsatisfactory.

With regard to a broadening of the concept of self-interest, Sutton states: "A broadening of the concept of interest to take into account non-rational action is of course possible. The problem is to do it in some reasonably clear and systematic way."[7] It should be taken as axiomatic that what coaches say is somehow related to their motivations, and hence that, in a very diffuse sense, they are speaking in their own interests. To use the term "interest" in such a broad way, however, is to deprive it of any explanatory value. It becomes so broad as to be, practically speaking, tautological: to wit, coaches say what they say, because they are motivated to say it.

Now, logical alternatives to accepting publicly expressed statements as manifestations of actual beliefs are (1) to infer beliefs from observed actions, (2) to accept privately expressed statements as indicative of actual beliefs. Regarding the question of how beliefs might be inferred from observed actions, Sutton states that

> This seems to involve a hazardous kind of speculation and raises the very difficult question of the relation between beliefs and actions. Actions are not simply consequences of beliefs; and where the interest is in expressed beliefs, it seems desirable not to complicate matters by trying from the very first to treat actions as evidence of beliefs.[8]

In short, inputs into the determination of observable actions may derive from a multitude of diverse sources other than the actor's personal beliefs. It should be remembered that a basic premise of the present work is that not only are patterned *actions* of persons involved in sports attributable to their particular positions and role responsibilities, but that the *motivations* behind their expressed beliefs also have their origins for the most part in those same positions and responsibilities. It is rare, then, that one can justifiably infer a unilinear nexus between

---

[7] Sutton et al., p. 5.
[8] Ibid., p. 13.

action and belief in sport or, indeed, any other sphere of social interaction.

With regard to private as opposed to public expressions of belief:

. . . the beliefs which a person expresses in any social situation are to some extent determined by the expectations of others in that situation. The common feeling that we "really" express ourselves in those intimate, familiar contexts we call "private" rests not on the fact of *no* constraints on what we say in these contexts, but on a difference in degree of constraints.[9]

Obviously, one may quite comfortably express views in private or anonymously which are not admissable as more public expressions. However, as Sutton states "The extent and significance of divergences of this kind can easily be exaggerated. There is a strong tendency for the social constraints which make some statements inadmissable in public to be internalized by individuals. That is, the controlling norms become part of the individual's own structure of attitudes and beliefs; and inhibitions become personal and automatic rather than controlled by the social situation. Insofar as this happens [it is assumed here] that a man believes what he says in public and that this will not differ significantly from at least some of the things he says in private."

Furthermore, where conflicting or inconsistent value orientations prevail within a given society, one may publicly *or* privately express statements indicative of conflicting beliefs without impugning the validity of either. For instance if, as Robin Williams states, American society is simultaneously supportive of values which emphasize a commitment to "principles of equality, of humanitarianism, and of political freedoms," and also of strong counter-traditions centered around "ascription of value and privilege to individuals on the basis of race," then statements indicative of adherence to one value set need not necessarily negate the possibility (or more accurately the probability) that the alternative value set is likewise adhered to—especially by dominant group members.[10] Coupling the above discussion of the relative validity of private versus public expressions of beliefs with the notion of conflicting or inconsistent value demands, it follows that one cannot infer conclusively from the statement below that the decision makers controlling the racial composition of the team in question do not adhere to valid humanitarian and egalitarian beliefs: ". . . A scout [from a major league team] made the comment during an interview that his team was looking for a good white outfielder because they had enough colored players."[11]

In fact, there is not sufficient information in Chornofsky's report

---

[9] Ibid., p. 14 ff.

[10] Robin M. Williams, Jr., *American Society: A Sociological Interpretation* (New York: Alfred A. Knopf, 1966), p. 466.

[11] Harold Charnofsky, "Baseball Player Self-Conception versus the Popular Image," in *International Review of Sports Sociology* 3 (1968): 44.

to assume that the decision makers involved even harbor racist values since their preference for a white outfielder could be prompted by factors other than their own personal desire (e.g., concern for continued fan support, team harmony, etc.). While this situation definitely implies some question of ethical priorities, it does not necessarily indicate an adherence to racist values.

Overall then, it should be expected that divergences would be small between expressions of public and private beliefs within the boundaries of "normal" constraints for these situations—(i.e., extraneous force, coercion, or other pressures are not brought to bear). In terms of empiri-. cal support for this assertion, Sutton found discrepancies between public and private expressions of belief within the context of the American business creed to be insignificant.[12]

So, owing to their ideological character, the patterned sports-related beliefs focused upon in this work frequently assert with dogmatic certainty that which the social scientist finds to be either contradicted by empirical evidence, or too inconclusive to justify decisions either pro or con, or simply shrouded in ignorance and doubt. Although a comparative process will be utilized throughout the remaining chapters of Part II, a few initial examples of the contrasts of assertions which are typical of the dominant sports creed with the presently available scientific knowledge will perhaps provide further context for our characterizations.

The dominant American sports creed:

A program in sports may be justified on the grounds that . . . it will develop worthwhile character qualities such as reliance, perserverance, determination and a willingness to abide by rules . . .[13]

Contrast the thrust of this early assertion, which remains today a major component of the sports creed, with the more recent findings of Ogilvie and Tutko. Based upon the analysis of data gathered by administering their "Athletic Motivation Inventory" to 15,000 athletes, the authors concluded:

It seems that the personality of the ideal athlete is not the result of any moulding process, but comes out of the ruthless selection process that occurs at all levels of sports. These athletes are well organized and self-disciplined in the first place and always were . . . Young athletes today are going into sports for their own personal enjoyment and they no longer accept the authoritarian structure of sports or the emphasis on winning. . . . Indeed there is evidence that the athletic competition limits character development in some areas . . .[14]

---

[12] Sutton et al., p. 15.

[13] Gordon R. Fisher, "School Athletics Become Increasingly Valuable," *Athletic Journal* 13, n. 8 (April 1934): 16.

[14] Bruce C. Ogilvie and Thomas A. Tutko, "Sports Don't Build Character" *San Francisco Chronicle*, September 23, 1971, pp. 63–64.

With regard to a subject closely related to the question of general character development, delinquency among male youths, the sports creed states emphatically "Stay out for sports, stay out of courts."[15] However, in the concluding remarks of a study focusing on "Some Social Sources and Consequences of Interscholastic Athletics," Walter E. Schafer expresses less certainty about the relationship between sports participation and delinquency.

> We have seen that, as predicted, athletes are less often delinquent than non-athletes . . . Of course it is . . . possible that athletics attracts conforming types of boys in the first place. Stated differently, the negative relationship between athletic participation and delinquency may not be the result of the deterring influence of athletics at all, but rather to the selection of conformers into the athletic system. This must be taken as a serious alternative explanation since deviant boys may have been formally and informally screened out of sports by coaches during junior high school and even before.[16]

Data gathered by Ogilvie and Tutko tend to support Schafer's cautious approach to the interpretation of his findings:

> Most programs in competitive sports are really directed towards the young people who have the least need for athletics in terms of enhancing their characters. The young people who have the highest need for personality growth experiences have a higher probability of being eliminated. The youngster who has the most to gain from the development of motor skills and ego gratification tends to have the least probability of being encouraged by the educational system.
> The data from our present study shows that the youngsters who remain in competitive sports have developed *prior to their participation* a higher emotional stability, a higher degree of self-control and social responsibility, and they are significantly more resistant to the effects of failure . . . We've found then that distinctive formal and informal selective factors operate to limit opportunity for the deviate, the emotionally unstable, and the undisciplined to secure rewards from sports.[17]

The differing objectives seem clearly implied by the above contrasting treatments of exemplary subject matter by the social scientists as opposed to the adherents to sports-related beliefs. The differences amply justify the classification of such patterned beliefs as component elements of a sports creed or ideology.

One final caution. It is not to be assumed that discrepancies be-

[15] Snyder, p. 12.

[16] Walter E. Schafer, "Some Social Sources and Consequences of Interscholastic Athletics," in *Sociology of Sport,* ed. Gerald S. Kenyon (Athletic Institute, 1969), p. 43.

[17] Bruce C. Ogilvie and Thomas Tutko, "The Mental Ramblings of Psychologists Researching in the Area of Sports Motivation" (Department of Psychology, San Jose State College, 1967).

tween creedal statements and scientific research findings constitute the sole or even the primary basis for determining the ideological character of any particular assertion. Therefore, the main line of demarcation is centered not upon the question of whether or not publicly expressed statements are "right" or "wrong," but whether or not they are founded upon logical, objective inquiry or upon faith.

For this reason, despite the fact that recent scientific findings provide some, although inconclusive, support for the dominant sports creed's positive statements regarding the role of sports in the social control of the young, such statements are still ideological in nature because the available evidence is much too weak and scanty to justify the degree of certainty expressed.

Let us proceed to an outline of the concepts and approach to be employed here.

STRAINS AND IDEOLOGY: A THEORETICAL STATEMENT

Sutton et al. present their theory within the framework of a series of eight propositions. The logic and development of these propositions are presented exactly as stated by Sutton because of their theoretical "fit" relative to the subject matter to be discussed here and the importance of presenting a precise statement of the original theoretical arguments and foundations.[18] Where appropriate, necessary insertions have been made in brackets.

(1) By far the greatest part of human action is performed unreflectively. We do not stop to think how we should walk, wash our hands, or greet our friends. In contrast to older, more rationalistic theories of human action, modern thought tends to stress the unreflective, automatic course of most human action . . . ordinary human action appears inevitably to proceed with the "carelessness and inattention" which Hume advocated as the only remedy for man's estate.

The most dramatic evidence that inattention is essential to normal human action appears in psychopathology. It is precisely a self-conscious attention to matters ordinarily ignored that characterizes many of the bizarre phenomena known as obsessions and compulsions. For example, Janet has reported the case of a young girl who was always aware of the number of fingers with which she touched an object, and bound herself to certain rules which made touching a very complicated venture. . . .

If the psychoneurotic reminds us that we execute most daily actions without reflection, more normal but exceptional persons remind us of our inattention to problems of the society in which we live. Men like André Gide

---

[18] The eight propositions, references to other authors' writings, and the arguments presented in support of each proposition are to be found in Sutton et al., pp. 305–309.

who question the propriety of accepting advantages of birth trouble themselves about a problem which could trouble many people but rarely does. Our society is one with very marked egalitarian values and much ideology in support thereof. Still it does not demand any radical denials of the ties of kinship, even though these ties inevitably lead to differential advantages which are difficult to justify.

(2) The roots of this normal unreflectiveness lie in the very nature of societies and the way in which they mold the personalities of their members. No society simply presents its members with a random set of choices of possible behavior; it indicates the approved ways, and rewards or punishes as these are adopted or rejected. The molding of human behavior is so definite, even in societies like our own, that many alternative ways of doing things remain unconceived or stoutly rejected as "unnatural."

(3) Fortunately or unfortunately, societies and personalities are never completely free from difficulties and disturbances. Any society must cope with a variety of functional problems. It must provide means for dealing with the natural environment, for allocating goods and services among its members, for maintaining order, etc. Complete success in handling these problems is never attained. . . . Individuals living in societies experience these imperfections as *strains;* they must at times face situations where the expectations they have learned to view as legitimate are thwarted, or where they must wrestle with conflicting demands. In addition . . . human personalities are apt to carry a heavy freight of unresolved problems arising in earlier experiences.

(4) Strains then are "normal" in any society. Situations regularly arise in which the individual must work out solutions in the face of difficult or conflicting demands. It is at these points that he must think explicitly about the courses of action he may take, and hence look for guiding principles which can help his decisions. If the fundamental pattern of human action is unreflective conformity with the cultural tradition, there is nevertheless a general need for bodies of explicit ideas which may be used when strain arises."

"While we tend to exaggerate the importance of conscious thought in action (simply because it is there that our attention focuses), we must not go to the opposite extreme. No society could function effectively without some means of guiding conscious decisions, and in a society like ours they assume exceptional importance. . . . In some cases, explicit ideas have a clear empirical reference and help directly in the solution of well-defined empirical problems; in other cases they have no such reference but they still play an important part in the functioning of societies. . . .

(5) The strains to which the members of a particular society are subject do not simply vary at random; they are patterned. Human behavior in social systems is patterned in a body of institutions and role, and strains are patterned accordingly. . . . The "career-marriage" problem represents a patterned strain in the role of the adult female. Any role in a social system is likely to involve patterned strains of greater or lesser severity.

(6) The reactions to a given strain are not entirely random. There is some patterned linkage between strains and reactions. . . .

(7) Ideology is a patterned reaction to the patterned strains of a social role. . . . Where a role involves patterns of conflicting demands, the oc-

cupants of that role may respond by elaborating a system of ideas and symbols, which in part may serve as a guide to action, but chiefly as broader and more direct functions as a response to strain.[19]

The fundamental relation [to be considered] then, is one between strains and ideology. But the links between them are by no means simple: a one-to-one correspondence between particular strains and specific ideological content is not to be expected. . . . the ideology is a symbolic outlet for the emotional energy which the strain creates. . . . While the relations between strains and the content of ideology are not simple, neither are they merely chaotic. The objects on which reactions ultimately settle may be only symbolically related to their origins, but presumably not just anything is appropriate as a symbol. A hostility to [hippies] is engendered by certain strains in our society, and the choice of [hippie] as a symbol is not just a random choice. . . .

(8) The [coaching] role is filled by many individuals of varying personalities. Individual [coaches] will vary widely in their quantitative reactions to the strain-producing situations in their role. What might overwhelm some, will appear as exciting stimuli to others. But the patterned strains of the role, arising from basic conflicts in it which all [coaches] feel to some degree, can be expected to show strong qualitative uniformities; and correspondingly the ideological reactions can be expected to be qualitatively similar.

In addition to the patterning of behavior imposed by particular role definitions in a society there is the further patterning of personalities due to a common cultural tradition. American [coaches] come to their roles with personality structures susceptible to certain general types of strains and prepared for coping with role demands in particular ways. . . .

Role-patterned strains are not, of course, the only problems in the personalities of individual [coaches]. Many other problems may lie deeper, below the level of conscious worries and conflicts. In this respect as in others, the personalities of individual [coaches] may be presumed to vary widely. . . . Strains arising in one role-context may be heightened in their seriousness by strains generated in other role-contexts, past or contemporary. . . . The strain-producing features of the [coaching] role may act both (1) as primary sources of strain, and (2) as secondary symbolic foci for strains generated in other contexts. For purposes [here], it does not greatly matter what the relative importance of (1) and (2) may be.

---

[19] Here Sutton et al. reiterate a caution which is significant to the present work as well. They state "We focus on the significance of ideas in the emotional adjustment of personalities because we wish to understand why certain ideas are expressed, repeatedly and vehemently. The fact that holding a particular belief may serve to ease emotional strains for the person who holds it, in itself carries no implications for the validity or invalidity of the belief. The popular reaction to [focusing] on the psychological function of belief—that it implies casting doubt on its validity—nonetheless contains some truth. Where a particular belief is so clearly dictated by objective circumstances that any other would be spectacularly wrong, there is little interest in psychological analyses. But this is a far cry from regarding all motivational analysis as radical debunking of discussion of complex social issues. The views of individuals on the income tax may be profitably analyzed in terms of strains in their personalities without the implication that all discussion of the level of the income tax is sound and fury which might better be dispensed with."

Applied to the dominant American sports creed, then, Sutton's theory links the specific emphasis of the creed to patterned strains in sports-related roles. Here the application has been directed at the role of head coach but, as will be demonstrated, the theory has significance for the roles of fan, athlete, and assistant coach as well as to those of dissidents adhering to the competing humanitarian and equalitarian sports creeds.

Our next task is to demarcate the scope of sport as an important social institution and to delineate its claimed achievements as expressed in the dominant American sports creed.

Sport as a social institution

THROUGHOUT THE DISCUSSION thus far references have been made to the "institution of sport" in American society. But "sport" consists of many complex and varied activities, values, positions, and role relationships. Is it justifiable to talk of sports as an institution?

We will use the definition of an "institution," offered by Williams, as

a set of institutional norms that cohere around a relatively distinct and socially important complex of values. The central core of an institution is a set of obligatory norms. In the fully developed case, institutional norms are: (1) widely known, accepted, and applied; (2) widely enforced by strong sanctions continuously applied; (3) based upon revered sources of authority; (4) internalized in individual personalities, (5) inculcated and strongly reinforced early in life; and (6) objects of consistent and prevalent conformity.[1]

It follows from the substance of these definitions that institutions "define problems and approved solutions" and thereby "channelize" human experiences along certain lines while ignoring or prohibiting other possibilities.[2]

Now in a complex society such as the United States, publicly ex-

---

[1] Robin M. Williams, Jr., *American Society* (New York: Alfred Knopf, 1970), p. 37. Williams' basic approach to the analysis of institutions is to classify norms according to the major "needs" or value centers they are most closely associated with, e.g., economic, political, religious, educational, etc.

[2] Ibid., p. 38.

pressed and supported institutional values frequently fall far short of accounting for actual behavior. Therefore an analysis of these values de facto renders a highly selective and incomplete picture of society. However, discrepancies between ideal norms or values and actual patterns of behavior do not negate the fact that institutional structures do emerge and are perpetuated which regulate much human behavior in specific areas of social interaction.

Before applying these conceptions to sports, we need to ask *who* it is that is affected by the values centered upon sports activities. According to Kenyon "The cognitive world of most people includes sports. The amount of sport information made available to persons in most countries makes it almost impossible to avoid learning something about it."[3]

But obviously Williams' concept of the "channelizing" effect of institutions implies more than mere cognizance of sports endeavors, since many informational inputs may in fact be matters of indifference—affectively neutral in impact. Thus, some element of "involvement" must be taken into account, that is, the relative centrality of sport-related values to the outcomes of the various persons who are aware of sports activities. The notion of "relative centrality" refers to the significance of sports activities in relation to one's interests, life concerns, and outcomes. As relative centrality decreases, overt behavioral responses to the value demands and consequences of sports likewise decrease—ultimately, of course, diminishing to zero in the case of an individual totally unaware of sport.

Clearly, a description of each specific individual's involvement in sports would be both impossible and unnecessary. A more useful approach is to specify involvement by social role and position. Such specification can be aided by an adaptation of Kenyon's classification of types of involvement. He subdivides involvement as "overt behavior" into "primary involvement," referring to actual participation, and "secondary involvement," referring to all other forms of participation including participation by way of consumption (coaches, team leaders, fans, etc.) and via production (manufacturers, retailers, promoters). For our purposes, however, Kenyon's delineations require further specification. Using his concepts of primary and secondary involvement as foundations, Table 5–1 presents a more refined analysis.

Within the context of Table 5–1, a sizable portion—if not a majority —of American society's members would be found under one heading or another indicative of substantial involvement in sport.

---

[3] Gerald S. Kenyon, "Sport Involvement: A Conceptual Goal and Some Consequences Thereof," in *Sociology of Sport,* ed. Gerald S. Kenyon (Athletic Institute, 1969), pp. 79–80.

TABLE 5-1

Centrality of sports-related values by role, position, and degree of involvement

Primary involvement				Secondary involvement			
Direct	Indirect			Producer			Uninvolved
				Direct		Indirect	
Participant (A)	Instrumental leader (B)	Regulator or administrator (C)	Expressive leader (D)	Fiscal (A)	Entrepreneural (B)	Consumer (C)	Uninvolved
1. Superstar 2. Captain 3. First string 4. Substitute 5. Athlete incapacitated by sports injury	1. Coach or manager 2. Doctor 3. Trainer 4. Water boy	1. Sports governing bodies 2. Rules committees 3. Athletic director 4. Referee, umpire, field judge, etc.	1. Public relations personnel 2. Cheerleader 3. Band 4. Former outstanding team members, alumni	A. *Professional sports* 1. Owner 2. Promoter B. *Amateur sports* 1. Educational institutions 2. Alumni 3. Philanthropic "sportsmen"	1. Sports equipment wholesalers 2. Retailers 3. Salesmen 4. Concessionaires	1. Relatives and close friends of primary level actors 2. Fans ("fanatics") 3. Occasional spectators	1. The cognizant but nonaffected (some newly arrived foreigners who are unfamiliar with American sports; Americans who simply pay little or no attention to sports, etc.) 2. The noncognizant (The new born, the mentally incapacitated, the extremely alienated or isolated, etc.)

THE FUNCTION OF SPORT

Apart from the question of who is affected, what "needs" or functions are served by sport? If sport in fact constitutes an institution, what are the consequences or functions of its "channeling"? And, toward what values or goals does its channelizing of activity lead?

The answers to these questions depend both upon the content of the sports creed and upon the relationship between this content and other parts of America's cultural heritage. In a direct sense, sports activities produce no material commodities analogous, say, to the automobile production of General Motors. It may be said that sports activities produce entertainment for the spectator and income for coaches and for athletes at the professional level. But motion pictures also provide entertainment as do phonograph records, live theater, and art shows. However, only rarely does one of these other components of the "entertainment industry" surpass sport in terms of the sustained "fanatical" devotion and loyalty that it commands from many of society's members. Thus, Beisser points to a striking characteristic of sport fans:

> One may explain the willingness of fans to pay for their sports events— and they pay handsomely—on the basis of entertainment. But does entertainment alone account for spectators who willingly endure inclement weather and personal sacrifice for the sake of a sport, for example, the loyal New York Mets fan who steadfastly supported their team in baseball's most miserable showing? Or the rioting that accompanies Stanley Cup competition in ice hockey? Clearly, one must look deeper than casual amusement to understand the fan's loyalty, commitment, and willingness to sacrifice . . .[4]

And though some coaches and outstanding athletes often receive very large salaries, in any realm other than sport all but a few of the very highest salaries would be regarded generally as inadequate—given that occupational security is virtually nonexistent and that high risk of serious injury are involved. Yet the fans continue to fill athletic facilities, sometimes paying fantastic prices, to see highly regarded teams or individuals confront each other. And there is no shortage of willing participants. In fact, over a million and a half amateur athletes each year—from the little leagues up through collegiate and semiprofessional sports—literally risk life and limb for nominal or no financial renumeration whatever. There must be something more involved here than mere "entertainment"—or even the creation of additional occupational positions or of opportunities for educational advancement.

In searching for this "something more"—this additional qualitative characteristic of sports, let us recall an earlier reference to a statement by Loy and Kenyon:

---

[4] Arnold Beisser, *The Madness in Sports* (New York: Appleton, Century, Crofts Publishing Co., 1966), pp. 6–7.

. . . sociologists [in the Soviet Union] working within a Marxist context . . . assume certain end products [of sport] to be implicitly established, namely, the shaping of various social institutions to facilitate the ultimate achievement of a communist society.[5]

Similarly, the observations below from the *Peking Review* indicate that the Russians are not alone in their belief in the socially and politically supportive potentialities of sports:

Holding high the great red banner of Mao Tsetung thought, Ni Chih-chin has trained painstakingly for many years with unmatched perseverance, displaying the revolutionary spirit . . . His training plan was drawn under the guidance of Mao Tsetung Thought . . . then the moment for tempering the revolutionary will . . . up and over the 2.22 meter mark—a new national record. . . . The evening of the day he broke [the record], he again opened his book of the *Selected Works of Mao Tsetung* and read aloud: "To win country-wide victory is only the first step in a long march of ten thousand miles . . ."[6]

In America, of course, the meaning of sports is interpreted within the context of a particular social and political heritage. Hence, the late General Douglas MacArthur echoes a familiar sentiment when he says of sport

It is a vital character builder. It molds the youth of our country for their roles as custodians of the republic. It teaches them to be strong enough to know they are weak, and brave enough to face themselves when they are afraid. It teaches them to be proud and unbending in honest defeat, but humble and gentle in victory . . . It gives them a predominance of courage over timidity, of appetite for adventure over love of ease. Fathers and mothers who would make their sons into men should have them participate in [sports].[7]

Given the explicit and implied potentials of sports as viewed from each of the three sociopolitical perspectives above—Russian-style Marxist-Leninism, Maoism, and, for want of a more precise concept, Americanism—it may be assumed (1) that most sports activities have few, if any, intrinsic and invariant socially or politically significant qualities (2) and that those qualities which such activities do possess are sufficiently "liquid" to fit comfortably within many diverse and even conflicting value and cultural traditions.

Now, while the range of possible human physical activity may be quite broad, there are nonetheless boundaries or limits in this regard

[5] John W. Loy and Gerald S. Kenyon, *Sport, Culture and Society* (New York, Macmillan Co., 1969), pp. 9–10.

[6] "Ni Chih-chin—The Man Who Set the World Record in Men's High Jump," *The Peking Review*, no. 7 (February 12, 1971), pp. 18–19.

[7] Cited in "Education in America" (prepared by the staff), *Saturday Review*, October 16, 1971, p. 38.

which are determined by mankind's anatomical and physiological structure as a species and by the limiting influences of his environment, for
instance, gravity. Thus, any particular movement is relatively quick or
slow, any individual is relatively strong or weak, and so forth. All physical endeavors involve, in a substantive sense, merely the coordination
and/or use of body movement, strength, speed, and endurance toward
the end of accomplishing a particular goal; these actual substantive features are in and of themselves neutral. They simply fall within or outside
of the physical capabilities of each individual. In sports, a premium is
put upon pressing toward the upper limits of man's physical capability.
For this reason, sports activities usually exact a price from the athlete
in terms of physical exertion far beyond the "intrinsic worth" of the immediate goal accomplished (e.g., jumping over a bar seven feet high is
itself of no direct concrete value—and may, in fact, result in some form
of injury). Accomplishment in sports then is de facto exceptional in
terms of both its quality and its goals relative to the "normal" physical
efforts required of people in most societies in meeting their day-to-day
role responsibilities. *It is this, the relatively extraordinary quality of the
physical requirements involved in sports activities that is the first key to
the functions of sport as an institution.*

All societies must solve the basic problem of regulating human behavior and directing efforts. In every society, "cultural blueprints" are
developed that express axiomatic and unconditional ideal norms which
are typically very plastic and nonspecific in terms of detailed application. Especially in highly heterogeneous societies, where dependence has
shifted increasingly from primary to secondary forms of social control,
the pressure to regulate and coordinate the values and perspectives
operant in human interaction and day-to-day problem solving is imperative. Such cultural blueprints typically involve some definition of the
"good" citizen and thus set boundaries upon acceptable behavior and
goals.

By infusing exceptional, but "intrinsically" neutral, physical activity
with socially significant values, societies reinforce prevalent sentiments
regarding acceptable perspectives and behavior. They thus establish
avenues of communicating to the populace those values focusing upon
solutions to critical problems, most notably those involving needs for
societal integration and goal attainment.

It will be recalled from chapter 3 that sports activities are, in a
direct sense, nonutilitarian in product but utilitarian in process. Hence,
social concern is, officially or ideally, focused on the *quality of performance* by those involved in sports as primary participants. This focus upon
the presentation of a "high-quality performance," the "exceptional" character of the physical demands involved in the achievement of any consequent success in sports, and the existence of a system of shared value

orientations common to both the institution of sport and the larger society combine to attract widespread public attention and interest.

Sport thus is strongly marked by nonutilitarian loyalties and commitments, by much ritualized or ceremonial behavior, by expressive symbolism, and by ideological creeds justified in terms of "ultimate" values or ultimate conceptions of the good life.

In sum, sport is essentially a secular, quasi-religious institution. It does not however, constitute an alternative to or substitute for formal sacred religious involvement.

Nor does it typically espouse values which are in conflict with the general prescriptions of such religious bodies. Rather, since the socially significant secular values infused into sports activities typically have their roots in large part in the religious and moral heritages of the societies in which these activities are pursued, values disseminated through the institution of sport are (1) more supplemental and complementary than contradictory to established religious doctrines, and (2) they apply more directly to day-to-day secular concerns of a society's members.

If this characterization is correct, one would expect that any attack upon the institution of sport in a particular society would be widely interpreted (intuitively, if not explicitly) as an attack upon the fundamental way of life of that society as manifest in the value orientations it emphasizes through sport. Hence, an attack upon sport constitutes an attack upon the society itself. As we shall see later, this interpretation is affirmed by persons both supportive and critical of the functioning of sport in America. At this point, however, suffice it to say that there exists more than a minimal degree of plausibility in an assertion I have often made: "If there is a universal popular religion in America it is to be found within the institution of sport."

To reiterate then, sport is a social institution which has primary functions in disseminating and reinforcing the values regulating behavior and goal attainment and determining acceptable solutions to problems in the secular sphere of life. The channeling functions carried out in a general fashion through the religious institution (or through the dissemination of political ideology in atheistic societies) are thus extended and supported. This channeling affects not only perspectives on sport, but, it is commonly assumed, affects and aids in regulating perceptions of life in general. And herein lies the primary significance of sport as an institution.

Other observers have agreed with this general characterization of sport. For instance, Boyle states:

Sport permeates any number of levels of contemporary society and it touches upon and deeply influences such disparate elements as status, race relations, business life, automotive design, clothing styles, the concept of the hero, language, and ethical values. For better or for worse, it gives form and substance to much in American life . . .[8]

Within the context of the discussion of sport as an institution, we find some evidence supportive of the frequent claim that sports is "political" in nature, though this label typically is denied by persons responsible for the control and regulation of sports activities. If, in fact, our own diagnosis of the functions of sport is correct, then the institution of sport and the political institution in America do share to some degree a common focus. While, unlike the political institution, sport is not directly involved in political implementation, it does share with the polity the function of disseminating and reinforcing values that are influential in defining societal means and in determining acceptable solutions to problems, that is, goals to be attained. The fact, however, that sport as an institution is involved only with value dissemination rather than implementation means that its pronouncements need not stray from ideal values. For it is only within those institutions concerned with the actualization of political values in the general society that responsible persons of necessity must show flexibility in terms of their guiding ideology. While this characteristic of the institution of sport renders it ideal as a vehicle for value dissemination, it also renders the institution susceptible to criticisms that it operates consistently in ideological concert with the political right. To the degree that the political leanings of significant persons holding positions of control in sport can be assumed to be indicative of the political demeanor of the institution as a whole, there is some empirical basis for the assertion that sport is both political in character and basically conservative. For instance, Walter Byers, director of the National Collegiate Athletic Association, in the April, 1970 *NCAA News Letter* wrote an editorial endorsing the political stance of Vice-President Spiro Agnew and denouncing those who criticized Agnew's conservative political position. There is also some evidence that the more conservative political figures tend to more strongly indorse the claimed benefits of sports activities. Max Rafferty, former California State Superintendent of Public Instruction and generally considered to be on the political far right, has stated

Critics of collegiate football are kooks, crumbums, and commies . . . hairy, loud-mouthed, beatniks. Football is war—without killing. Athletes possess the clear, bright, fighting spirit which is America itself.[9]

---

[8] Robert H. Boyle, *Sport: Mirror of American Life* (Boston: Little Brown, 1963), pp. 3–4. See also Loy and Kenyon, pp. 67–70.

[9] N. Von Hoffman, "College Sports," *Washington Post*, November 25, 1970, p. B1.

Similarly, in Robert Lipsyte's by-lined column, "Sports of the Times," in the *New York Times* of June 7, 1971, Vice-President Spiro Agnew stated:

I believe that sport, all sport, is one of the few bits of glue that holds our society together, one of the few activities where young people can proceed along traditional lines . . . where he can learn how to win . . . and how to lose . . .

A correlation between conservatism and fan enthusiasm for sport is suggested by the findings of a Gallup Poll (reported by William A. Seevert in the *Chronicle of Higher Education,* January 25, 1971, p. 1) indicates that the more politically conservative a region of the nation is, overall, the greater the perceived interest in sport. Of the college students polled in the relatively cosmopolitan western and eastern parts of the United States, 57 percent in the East felt interest in sport to be declining as did 44 percent in the Far West. By contrast, only 39 percent of students in the Midwest, and, in the traditionally more conservative South, only 35 percent felt sports interest to be on the wane.

This fragmentary evidence gives some plausibility to the idea that sport as an institution is conservative in its political affinities. The contention here is that both the apparently intrinsic political character of sport in America and the conservativeness of its appeal are mainly due to its characteristics as an institution—although the political conservatism of people holding certain key sports-related positions certainly might contribute to and highlight the overall political demeanor of the institution. An additional speculative hypothesis is, of course, that, due to the conservative political character of sport as determined by its functions in society, there is a tendency for those drawn into sports and filling instrumental and regulatory positions to adhere to conservative political philosophies. Though this supposition is certainly plausible, conclusive evidence in support of this idea is not now available. We shall explore the question of "conservatism" in sport again later in connection with an analysis of the coach's role.

THE CLAIMED ACHIEVEMENTS OF SPORT

Implicit to the above discussion of sport as an institution is the expectation that in America, claims made on its behalf will generally reflect American social values that define what is "good," "wholesome," or otherwise worthwhile. Claims made by the dominant American sports creed appear to substantiate the ideas upon which this expectation is based. But before beginning our presentation, three significant facts should be pointed out. First of all, it should be reiterated that, at the societal level, the prevalent claims made on behalf of sport are fundamentally conservative. This is true of sport in all but the most unstable of societies—Russia, the Peoples Republic of China, and America included.[10] Within a particular society, it is only when social instability becomes rampant that competing sports-related creeds or ideologies emerge within the established sport institution. In the stable society, however, sport is invariably portrayed, through a sports creed, as supporting established or traditional beliefs and practices and as discouraging any adherence to "new" or foreign ideas and ideologies. Sport is seen also as discouraging adoption of "radical" means, even if these means are outwardly more in conformity with value *ideals* than those implied by a particular sports creed. And sport in American society is no exception. This fact has become a pivotal issue in the ideological struggle between critics and supporters of the established sports institution.

Second, virtually none of the presently claimed benefits of sports make mention of any direct positive effects upon females. This fact requires some explanation since females are not only capable of but actually do participate in a wide variety of sports activities. Also females are typically involved in male-dominated sports at both the primary level as expressive leaders and at the secondary level as spectators, relatives, and as friends of primary-level persons. While available evidence will not conclusively show that sport as an institution is antifemale in ideology, there definitely is much resistance to attempts by women to fill positions and roles traditionally occupied by males—for example, major league umpire, jockey, football referee. Whether the absence of any reference to females in creedal claims on behalf of sport constitutes an act of conscious omission or unconscious commission is not conclusively clear. If the following analysis of sport is accurate, however, it would appear that it is more the product of the latter than the former. And, finally, the claims made on behalf of sport are primarily nonmaterial in substance. This is viewed as resulting mostly from the fact that, in a direct sense, it is nonutilitarian in product as was mentioned earlier.

Praise for the claimed positive contributions of sport to American society permeates the entire fabric of the sports creed. The emphasis is upon the nonmaterial, intangible benefits to be derived from involvement in sport. These claimed benefits are encompassed within two overall themes, one stressing sport's service to society while the second emphasizes the services provided by sport to the individual.

According to the dominant creed, the chief overall achievement of sport has been its contribution to the maintenance and perpetuation of America's "esprit de corps." Since the creed also portrays "the Ameri-

---

[10] For detailed discussions of sport, nationalism, and ideology in Russia and the Peoples Republic of China, see Henry W. Morton, *Soviet Sport* (New York: Collier, 1963) and Jonathan Kolatch *Sport, Politics and Ideology in China* (New York: Jonathan David Publishers, 1972).

can spirit" as having a more or less rigid cause-effect relationships with this nation's material wealth as well as with the maintenance of its political and military integrity, the crucial value of sport to the very survival of "the American way of life" is clearly suggested and, in many cases, explicitly stated.

Athletics offer the greatest opportunity for character development of any activity . . . The fundamentals of character are gained through participation in sports under right leadership, and a person who lacks these fundamentals may be sensitive, refined, and cultured but will lack the vital character qualities most needed and esteemed by this society.[11]

Those of you who are promoting sports in America are making the heroes of America. You are developing the heroic youth . . . In order to develop character you must create the situation for securing the traits desired. Sports is rich in such situations . . . They provide the training ground for creating the virile qualities necessary to our way of life.[12]

And, as Sandy Padwe observes, contemporary views on American sport are quite similar to those of the 1920s and 1930s: "It is commonly held that the competitive ethic taught in sports must be learned and ingrained in youth for the future success of [American] business and military efforts."[13]

The strength of the traditional belief that the role of the sports institution in America is and should properly be that of supporting traditional American values is further indicated by the comments of Sandy Padwe.

Sports and Politics Must Be Separate—At Least *Some* Politics That Is

The righteous have repeatedly warned us over the last several years that sports and politics must remain separate.

Naturally, they are very strict about this. Only their viewpoint may be aired.

Take the people out in Pasadena, Calif., who run the Rose Bowl. The University of Michigan band, with backing

---

[11] M. M. Hussey, "Character Education in Athletics," *The American Educational Review* 33 (November 1938): 578–80.

[12] George J. Fisher, "Athletics and the Youth of the Nation," *Proceedings: The National Collegiate Athletic Association,* 1927.

[13] Sandy Padwe, "Midget League Sports Rapped," *Philadelphia Inquirer,* February 14, 1971.

from the student body, asked that it be allowed to present a four minute "peace segment" as part of its performance between halves of the Michigan-Stanford game New Year's Day.

The band wanted to release 100 black balloons and play taps. The Rose Bowl people refused, saying the contract with the schools in the game prohibits such political activity.

And so it was more of the same from Pasadena this year: the girls, the floats, the military marches, the usual red-white-and-blue pageantry of football.

There are very few things in this country that can match the patriotic orgies of the bowl games and football's halftime performances in general.

Usually, the Orange Bowl is best. Anita Bryant does "The Battle Hymn of the Republic," a neon American flag glitters over one end zone, fireworks explode into the warm Miami night. . .

In Memphis, a Liberty Bowl official described that game's halftime show: "We're able to depict a patriotic scene that evokes the greatest emotional outburst. The finale is traditional. Every spectator receives an American flag and we wind up with 50,000 people waving the flag."

That information comes via the American Broadcasting Co., which televises the game.

It was ABC, you will remember, which refused a half-time program last year in which the University of Buffalo band presented a program with three themes: anti-war, anti-racism and anti-pollution.

The network based its refusal on the fact that the haftime show was a "political demonstration."

But later that year, ABC televised the halftime ceremonies from the Army-Navy game honoring some Green Berets, who, a week before had staged a raid on a suspected prisoner of war camp in North Vietnam.

It is not unusual at bowl games to see formations of military jet planes flying over the different stadia with three planes instead of the usual four. The open spot in the formation symbolizes American prisoners of war and those who have died in action. . . .

Following last year's Super Bowl, the National Broadcasting Co. and the Columbia Broadcasting System maintained that the televising of the jet formations was non-political because it was "hard not to sympathize with the prisoners."

And it is hard not to. But the prisoner issue in the Vietnam war is a politically sensitive area. The government's use of the fighter formation was political exploitation at its best—or worst—depending on your politics.

Sometimes, the super-patriotism is a little too much. The National Football League has an employee who once received the assignment of checking on league teams to make sure the players were in the proper National Anthem formation: parade-rest, helmets under arms, lines straight.

One time, Minnesota defeated the St. Louis Cardinals, prompting a St. Louis columnist to write (nor humorously, either) that he knew the Vikings would win because "they showed greater discipline during the playing of the National Anthem" . . .[14]

There are also other examples which suggest a belief that sport is and should be supportive of the "American way of life." The most obvious of these, of course, are the attempts of various political figures to associate themselves with athletics, and of athletes, sports organizations, and sports governing bodies to associate themselves with various occurrences which are more generally significant to the outcomes of the greater society. For example, President Richard M. Nixon, frequently referred to as "the nation's number one sports fan," made sports headlines on at least three different occasions in the summer of 1971: when he launched

---

[14] Sandy Padwe "Sports and Politics Must Be Separate—At Least Some Politics That Is," *Philadelphia Inquirer*, December 14, 1971, p. 35.

a national fund raising drive to build a memorial to the late professional football coach Vince Lombardi on June 9, 1971; when he presented the keynote address at the professional football "Hall of Fame" inductions at Canton, Ohio, on July 30, 1971; and when he greeted the Oakland A's baseball team and had an extended conversation with pitching ace Vida Blue in Washington, D.C., on August 17, 1971.[15] Also, when Defense Secretary Melvin Laird was assigned to throw out the first baseball to the former Washington Senators at their home opener for the 1971 baseball season, he elected to have a wounded Vietnam veteran do so instead and then proceeded to give a short speech on the similarity between American efforts in Vietnam and baseball.

These efforts at association are by no means unidirectional. Such patriotic gestures as those carried out by the NCAA and the various professional athletic leagues in sponsoring trips to Vietnam by noteworthy collegiate and professional sports figures are commonplace.[16]

Even the lexicon and imagery of sport have become intermingled with that formerly associated with other spheres of societal endeavor, and vice versa. One finds frequent reference to the "Nixon game plans" regarding the President's political and economic strategies, on the one hand, while people involved in sport speak of "throwing the bomb" in football and "blitzing" one's opponent in basketball on the other.

On a second level, there is a creedal theme which emphasizes service to the individual. Here, it is alleged that sport provides a *service to the individual* by preparing him to meet the challenges of competition during later life in the greater society. For the athlete in particular, this preparation includes the development of mental and physical fitness, good character, discipline, competitiveness and courage, and opportunities to experience challenges leading to personal achievement and social recognition. Of course, ultimately it is the nation as a whole which is viewed as inevitably benefiting from sport regardless of the benefits accrued by specific individuals.

Though the cumulative impact of the claimed benefits of sports on society and individuals cannot be measured or quantified, a comparative perspective is clearly implied. That is, the creed suggests that without sport, American youth would have less character, be less physically and mentally fit, less courageous, less disciplined, have less opportunity for achievement and thus America would on the whole experience a decline in its quality of life. Just because the cumulative impact of these claimed benefits cannot be measured, is not a basis for assuming that the claims

---

[15] See the *San Francisco Chronicle* "Lombardi Memorial Planned," June 10, 1971, p. 47; "Nixon at Hall of Fame Induction," July 31, 1971, p. 41; "Nixon Greets A's," August 18, 1971, p. 51.

[16] See "Gridders Visit Vietnam," *Los Angeles Times,* May 30, 1971, Section D, p. 5.

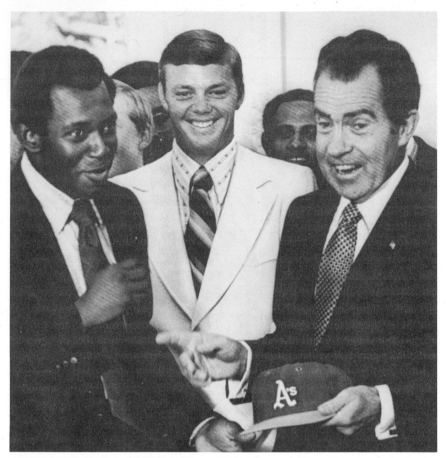

After being invited to the White House, Vida Blue and Dave Duncan chat with President Richard M. Nixon, the self-designated "number one" fan of the nation. (San Jose Mercury-News)

are false. They should more accurately be understood as simply being one-sided and highly selective. No broad and unbiased appraisal would attribute the quality of American life so resolutely to the operation of a single institution. Further, with regard to the claimed opportunities offered by sport to the individual, even more obvious selectivity is at work. The creed abounds with testimonials and stories detailing how sports opened up opportunities to a better life, but there is no mention of the more tragic side of sports involvement or the fact that for every winner there is at least one loser; for every athlete who makes the team there is one less position available for someone who desires to participate. There is no attempt to remind the public of recorded cases of athletes who committed suicide after experiencing disappointing athletic careers.

For instance, in 1971, Bruce Gardner, an aspirant major-league baseball pitcher and former University of Southern California All-American, committed suicide on the USC baseball diamond after failing several times to make the major leagues. A friend characterized the chief cause of his suicide in this fashion: "The thing was," Biales said, "that he always thought he could make it in the majors. He was always bringing that up. That's the one thing he wanted."[17]

And it is not just those who aspire to "big-time" sports careers who are negatively affected by failures in athletics. On October 29, 1971, a high-school quarterback committed suicide. According to news reports,

> . . . The dead youth was found Thursday afternoon, dead of an apparently self-inflicted gun shot wound . . . The prevalent belief is that he was despondent over his team's 0–7 season record. Authorities would only say that the suicide involved personal problems. . . .[18]

And then, of course, there is the case of the "normal" athletic failure, epitomized by the son of Willy Loman in Arthur Miller's classic play, *Death of a Salesman*. Miller, a former athlete himself, poignantly describes the more pernicious influences of athletics. Willy Loman, the central character protagonist, reminisces at the end of act 1 about his son who was a high-school athletic star who never quite made it, a "has been" who never really was:

> Like a young god. Hercules—something like that. And the sun, the sun all around him. Remember how he waved to me? Right up from the field, with the representatives of three colleges standing by. And the buyers I brought, and the cheers when he came out—Loman, Loman, Loman! God Almighty, he'll be great yet. A star like that, magnificent, can never really fade away![19]

But Willy's son, as have thousands of other athletic heroes, did fade away. As Jack Scott points out, for every youth lifted out of a coal-mining town or taken from the ghetto by an athletic scholarship, there are hundreds of other lower-class youths who have wasted their lives futilely preparing to be a sports star.

While the first two cases present rather extreme and unusual responses to athletic failure, they do nonetheless point up the selectivity involved in the sports creed's claim—also illustrated by the creed's silence concerning the stereotypical "athletic bum" who shows up season after season, always failing to make the grade. Examination of this side of sport would undoubtedly yield more tempered conclusions about the

---

[17] "He Wanted To Be A Star," *San Francisco Chronicle*, June 8, 1971, p. 46.

[18] "High School Team Decides To Play Despite Suicide," *Fremont News-Register*, October 30, 1971, p. 37.

[19] Arthur Miller, *Death of a Salesman* (New York: Viking Press, 1958), p. 68.

impact of the institution upon the quality of American life and its benefi-cence toward the individual.

MALES, FEMALES, AND THE CLAIMED ACHIEVEMENTS OF SPORT

The perceived relation between sport and the quality of life in American society is central to an understanding of the predominantly male-oriented tenor of both the sports creed and of sports activities in America. Sports are seen as primary vehicles for enculturating the youth who will "be the future custodians of the republic," in the words of the late General MacArthur. In America, roles involving the establishment and maintenance of security, leadership, control, and other instrumental functions are typically reserved for males. Therefore, given the claimed relation between sport and the greater society, it is to be expected that the focus will be upon males, with females being more or less ignored and excluded from the claimed benefits of sports.

Even some women involved in "female sport" and holding adminis-trative positions in regulatory bodies adhere to a belief that sports ac-tivities not specifically designated for women are in fact harmful to them, even though there is no conclusive proof that this is the case. For in-stance Nell Jackson, head of the National Amateur Athletic Union's Com-mittee on Women's Track and Field, in the January 1971 issue of *Runner's World* stated that women's participation in long-distance races tradi-tionally run by men "hurts the women, and hurts the women's program in general." She further derides the very idea by stating that marathoning involves "only a few older women out for a lark."

In a rebuttal to Jackson in a subsequent issue of *Runner's World*, Pat Tornawsky, a female marathon runner herself, presents evidence that the former's assertions are incorrect. She further characterizes Dr. Jack-son's attitude as "the last gasp of Victorian over-caution."[20]

But it is not only "Victorian" *attitudes* among people controlling sport in America that contribute to the predominantly male-oriented character of creedal beliefs prevasive throughout the sport institution. Some sports governing bodies have official rules prohibiting men and women from competing together, as do some states. Thus the AAU's rule forbidding males and females to participate together and the New York State Board of Education's rule prohibiting coeducational athletics[21]

---

[20] Pat Tornawsky, "Women vs. the Myth," *Runner's World* (March 1971), pp. 16–17.

[21] Ibid., p. 16 (According to a *New York Times* report of February 4, 1971, Chancellor H. B. Scribner recommended that coeducational athletics be allowed in New York state secondary schools in noncontact sports. The legal issue had been raised when a coed named Phyllis Grabner attempted to join her male high-school tennis team. Her coach said she had the skill to qualify, and a civil liberties com-plaint was subsequently filed with the City Commission on Human Rights.)

operate not only to curtail such activities but also to assure that females will not engage in sports activities specifically intended for males, especially in the case of high-budget team sports. This kind of regulation adds overt reinforcement to the covert omission of reference to women in the sports creed.

Such attitudes and rules as the above have their roots deep in the history of Western culture in general and Western sport in particular. The specifics of this cultural heritage as it affects female involvement in sport will be delineated in chapter 7. For now, it is sufficient to point out that, in America, the tradition of male-domination in sport is a manifest in a concern that women adhere to the female role as it is in a concern for women's physical well-being. For instance, in 1909, Mrs. Frank Roessing and Elizabeth Burchenal speaking to the Playground Association of America stated that

. . . Sports for girls should be encouraged [but] the fighting element should be eliminated and . . . proper safeguards should be made against injury . . . A difference needs to be made between boys and girls athletics: Let the former be for fighting and the latter be for fun . . .[22]

In 1928, Frederick R. Rodgers echoed the above sentiments:

. . . Competitive sports tend to develop behavior patterns which are contrary to feminine nature. Natural feminine health and attractiveness . . . are certainly impaired if not destroyed by the belligerent attitudes and competitive spirit the development of which intense athletic activity inevitably fosters. One has only to postulate a female Roosevelt to reduce to absurdity the claims of those who foster the masculinization of girls. Neither men nor any normal woman would embrace or willingly tolerate any tendency toward such an eventuality, yet competitive athletics will bring it about more surely than any other human behavior . . . Games and recreation of all types for girls, by all means, which develop charm and social health, but athletic competition in basketball, track and field sports and baseball. NO![23]

That these attitudes are still quite prevalent today is indicated by the many cases of females being denied access to positions in sport which have traditionally been held by males. And it is not just the athlete positions that are sexually restrictive but such positions as coach, umpire, referee, athletic director, manager, and league commissioner as well. For this reason, sport is perhaps the most sexually segregated of America's civilian social institutions.

Another factor which deserves mention in any analysis of female roles in organized sport in America is the possibility of male anxieties

---

[22] Mrs. Frank Roessing and Elizabeth Burchenal, "Athletics for Girls," taken from the proceedings of the 1909 Congress of the American Playground Association.

[23] Frederick R. Rodgers, "Olympics for Girls," *School and Society,* 30 (August 10, 1929): 193–94.

over female athletic potentials. There is not sufficient evidence to support even the speculation that women pose any real "threat" at present to men in competitive performance in most popular sports (e.g., football, basketball, baseball, track and field, boxing). Thus, despite some privately held suspicions among a few once-prominent female track and field athletes that so-called sex tests were primarily aimed at maintaining the relative distances between men's and women's performances, it seems more likely that these tests were adopted to control "unnatural" competitive advantages *within* women's sports events—especially at the international level. After a woman reaches a performance level which so far outdistances her competitors that she becomes singularly conspicuous, her "womanliness" apparently becomes suspect. It is significant in this regard that there have been virtually no demands for sex tests for men, no matter how low or high the quality of their performances have ranged. On the other hand, it has been in Western countries—particularly in the United States and England—that sports officials have most strongly advocated such tests for women.

Certainly there are potential dangers of injury to females engaging in contact sports with males. But the pervasiveness of anticoeducational attitudes extends to noncontact sports and there is widespread opposi-

---

Biennal Sex Tests for Girl Athletes?

London—Marea Hartman, secretary of the British Women's Amateur Athletic Association, started a move yesterday to make international women athletes undergo the sex test every two years.

She will propose the rule change at a meeting of the International Women's Athletic Commission during the European Track and Field Championships at Helsinki next month.

At present one sex test is enough. Once a girl has proved to doctors that she's female she doesn't have to take the test again for the rest of her track and field career.

"I want to be assured that certain people who have undergone a sex test would pass another one," she said.[24]

---

[24] "Biennial Sex Tests for Girl Athletes" *San Francisco Chronicle*, July 13, 1971, p. 43.

tion against females participating in any sports seen as "more appropriate" for males. Such attitudes are connected with beliefs about the claimed benefits of the institution of sport for the individual and the nation. Expressions of the sports creed typically suggest that the benefits accrued from sport most directly affect the athlete, though everybody involved is believed to be affected in some positive way. Let us now turn our attention to the major tenets of the dominant American sports creed.

THE DOMINANT AMERICAN SPORTS CREED

I. Character development

Back of the trained mind and trained body, there must be that something we call character. A man possessed of the right character will use his mind to benefit society. . . . Sports are [of value] as a means of developing desirable social character traits.[25]

The most frequently stated benefit of sport for the individual is its role in the development of "character." However, in no instance did the present study find any effort by persons expressing a belief in the intrinsic character-building capabilities of sport to explicitly define the concept. Rather, the quality, "character," was typically assumed to be understood as desirable and wholesome, or it was defined implicitly by association with such adjectives as "clean-cut," "red-blooded," "upstanding," "desirable," and so forth. Thus, the undefined use of "character" in the sports creed relies on the more or less intuitive understandings of the concept within the context of traditional American culture.

During the 1960s, the traditional emphasis upon the development of character through sports participation was both dramatized and heightened through the highly publicized controversy concerning proper hair length for athletes. Why should a matter so simple as hair length become the focal point of such pervasive and heated debate? Let us look for a moment at the issue of hair.

Jack Scott, director of the Institute for the Study of Sport and Society, has held that the anti-long-hair sentiments held by many coaches are due primarily to fears of homosexuality stemming from their own "latent homosexual" tendencies. In Scott's words,

No one loathes the homosexuals quite as much as the latent homosexual, and long hair on a male, since it has in recent times been associated with femininity, will arouse the anger of the latent homosexual like almost nothing else can. Not only does it upset the coaches' sex cues, but if a coach allowed his athletes to have long hair people might suspect [the coach] of being queer— at least that is the way that a latent homosexual coach would see the matter. A male who has a secure masculine self-image will not have homosexual

---

[25] "Editorial," *Athletic Journal* 13 (April 1933): 22.

phobias, whereas a male who does not feel confident will spend his time projecting a super-masculine image.[26]

Now, it is not unreasonable to suppose that some individuals engaged in sports at all levels and in all roles might be considered homosexual or to have homosexual tendencies. Nevertheless, there are some rather obvious flaws in Scott's argument. First, long hair has been associated with femininity in America for many decades and so Scott's argument does not account for the emergence of the hair controversy in sport *now*. Second, unless one is prepared to assume that the coaching profession is singularly or even predominately populated by persons having homosexual tendencies, the "latent homosexuality" theory would not hold. As the following statement indicates, Scott apparently has been prepared to go beyond assumption and state this explicitly:

> What I am proposing is that coaches as a group have problems with latent homosexuality. How does a latent homosexual prevent himself from manifesting this latent potential into overt acts? Even more importantly, how does he insure that no one will suspect him of being queer, fag, or fay? . . . He projects a super-masculine image . . . and dresses in a manner and walks in a way, that might be becoming of a high school football star . . . He will do almost anything so as not to be suspect.[27]

I do not share Scott's views. For not only are there no in-depth studies available on the sexual dispositions of coaches as a group, but the confusing and contradictory state of findings reported in the scientific literature on homosexuality itself prohibits conclusive statements even as to the criteria for determining the "condition," if a "condition" is in fact what it is.[28]

A second notion as to the genesis of the "hair controversy" in sport essentially holds that the anti-long-hair sentiments expressed by many coaches and others involved in sport stems from their adherence to military codes of personal grooming. In this regard, Scott points out

> Soldiers and athletes have the same grooming requirements:
> 1. clean shave
> 2. close haircut
> 3. shined shoes
> 4. regulation dress (gray slacks, blazer)[29]

Specifically, the idea is that short haircuts and clean-shaven faces among men came into being as grooming practices during World War I. Up

---

[26] Jack Scott, *Athletics for Athletes* (Berkeley, Calif.: Other Ways Books, 1969), pp. 28–29.

[27] Ibid., p. 29.

[28] Mary McIntosh, "The Homosexual Role," in *Family in Transition*, ed. Skolnick and Skolnick (Boston: Little, Brown, and Co., 1971), pp. 231–41.

[29] Scott, p. 7.

until that time, many military men wore beards and mustaches (General Grant, for instance) and even shoulder-length hair (General George Custer). But during World War I, with its stalemates and trench warfare, long hair and beards became health hazards, providing havens for lice and other vermin. Close haircuts and frequent shaving became established practices and were enforced whenever possible. These military grooming policies were carried over into World War II and the Korean War. Thus the American heroes emerging from these three wars were always clean-cut and close-shaven. The assumption is that coaches, motivated by self-interest and patriotic attitudes, decided that if close haircuts and clean shaves constituted minimum standards of grooming for America's most valiant sons, then the adoption of such standards for athletes could not help but bolster the image of sports as wholesome, clean, all-American activities.

There are several problems with this argument. Hair styles like other aspects of men's grooming are cyclical. That is, they fluctuate between extremes ranging from almost bald haircuts to the opposite extreme of long hair. For instance, just prior to the Civil War, hair was worn short and beards were not usually worn inside or outside of the military.

Furthermore, the argument implies two dubious assumptions: that the military is the most important if not the sole determiner of hair styles from the perspective of the coaching profession, and, in turn, that the codes of grooming in the military are primarily determined by the limitations of proper health and sanitary conditions. There is little evidence to support either of these assumptions.

While it is possible that some persons in sport may in fact be against long hair due to their own latent homosexuality or their affinity for military-style haircuts, the contention here is that the anti-long-hair sentiments expressed by most of these persons reflect their beliefs that sports do and should build character. In American society during the 1960s, long hair came to be associated with political philosophies and life styles which differed from those traditionally deemed appropriate and desirable by the majority of this society's members. In their roles as coaches, many individuals have thus reacted in an almost visceral fashion to the *assumed challenge to established values* represented by such hairdos and other subcultural or counter-cultural accoutrements of grooming. In past times, few if any of the dozens of hair-related incidents would have been considered newsworthy or of sufficient gravity to disrupt an athletic organization. From the late 1960s to the end of 1970 and beyond, however, many coaches viewed long hair and beards as indicative of political and social philosophies which were inconsistent with the "American way of life." Ara Parseghian, head football coach at Notre Dame University stated, for instance, in 1969 that

The fad started with the hippies. I saw them in Haight-Ashbury. Wearing a beard or a moustache or long hair doesn't necessarily make anyone look like the scum I saw there but it gives an empathy for a movement that certainly is the direct opposite of what we strive for in football. Sports is goal-oriented. The hippie movement is geared to shiftlessness . . .[30]

The general consensus during the late 1960s that the "natural" hairdos worn by blacks were the insignia of political militants with regard to racial issues led to numerous confrontations between white coaches and black athletes. When the Black Student Union at Oregon State University, for instance, demanded that black athletes be allowed to wear mustaches, beards, and "Afro" hairdos as an expression of their cultural heritage, letters poured in to the coach who was the focus of the greatest pressure—head football coach Dee Andros. One letter signed "The Class of '32" stated emphatically ". . . Don't give in to the militants . . . students have to abide by rules or the country will go down . . ." As a result, Andros stated "The day might come when I will allow neat mustaches, . . . but I will not do it to appease some pressure group."[31]

Some coaches side-stepped the issue of the values implied by unconventional hair-grooming methods and simply claimed scientific grounds for their preference that their athletes have clean shaven faces and short haircuts. Lee Corso of Louisville University stated, in football "research shows that long heavy hair prevents the helmet from fitting properly, absorbing shock, et cetera. If these guys want to get headaches, let 'em go ahead, have lots of hair, have lots of headaches."[32]

In a search of the literature on sports medicine, I found no evidence to support Corso's statement. Also it would seem that a larger helmet would solve any problems resulting from too much hair. As Bob Devaney, the University of Nebraska head football coach, said, "Hair and a Fu Manchu beard [as worn by] Joe Namath of the New York Jets don't seem to hurt. Joe seems to pass alright."[33]

Still other coaches took a more sophisticated approach to the hair issue. Nonetheless, a distinction between legitimately established cultural tradition and subcultural or counter-cultural fad was still implied. John Wooden, basketball coach at UCLA has stated: "If a boy comes to me and wants to wear long hair or a beard, I ask him to prove to me that it is part of his ethnic culture. If he can do it, he can wear it."[34]

---

[30] Ara Parseghian, cited by John Underwood, "The Desperate Coach: Cut That Thing Off," *Sports Illustrated,* September 1, 1969, p. 22.

[31] Cited in Underwood, p. 23.

[32] Cited in Underwood, p. 22.

[33] Boby Devany in Harry Edwards, *The Revolt of the Black Athlete* (New York: Free Press, 1969), p. 124.

[34] George Solomon, "High School Coach Finds Winning Isn't Everything," *Sports Focus,* May 5, 1971, p. 1.

The hair controversy has not been restricted to amateur sports. In May of 1971, the new coach, of the Cleveland Browns, Nich Skorich, took a look at the crop of newcomers in rookie camp and their crop of long locks. Before the day was over, Skorich had handed down a ruling on hair. "No hair will stick out from below the helmet," he said. "Sideburns will be no longer than the bottom of the ear and moustaches must not come below or beyond the bottom lip."[35]

Now clearly, there is nothing intrinsically debilitating about long hair in terms of its impact upon one's character. The following case points up the issue.

Significantly, it is now common to see long hair and even beards on

---

Barred from Meet, "Longhair" Saves Life

Indianapolis. Ind.—Steven Michaluk, 25, Air Force veteran and student at Indiana-Purdue University here, was driving Tuesday to a gymnastics meet from which he had been barred as a participant because he wears his hair long.

As he drove into the highway bridge over the White River, a truck and another car collided. The truck, driven by Raymond Young, 75, Plainfield, Ind., went through the guard rail into the river where it began slowly to sink.

Michaluk jumped from his car, stumbled down a concrete embankment and swam to the truck, motioning the elderly driver to roll the window down.

Young, although injured and in shock, managed to do so. Michaluk grabbed him by the collar and pants, pulled him out, and swam to shore. Young was hospitalized.

Michaluk, who is a trained gymnast and a lifeguard, said he had been told Monday he could not participate in a high school gymnastics demonstration because of his hair length. But he had planned to watch.

He got to the show too late.[36]

---

[35] See "Names and Places," *San Francisco Examiner,* May 11, 1971, p. 46.

[36] "Barred From Meet, 'Longhair' Saves Life," *Berkeley Daily Gazette,* May 12, 1971, p. 1.

both amateur and professional athletes. The military forces, too, during 1971, altered their hair grooming codes. But the acceptance or tolerance of beards, long hair, and moustaches has also changed. Military officials have made it clear that the liberalization of grooming requirements in the Army, Navy, and Air Force is an attempt to make military life more attractive to the young man who is influenced by today's popular civilian hair styles. Their fear was that such persons were being discouraged from joining the armed forces or re-enlisting partly because of out-dated grooming requirements.

The longer hair styles and even beards seen in the athletic realm today likewise are a result of increased tolerance for these in the society as a whole. If the "counter-culture movement" among young whites and the "black liberation struggle" mounted by young blacks have accomplished little else, it does appear that they have succeeded in exposing the American public to long hair and beards with such regularity that these are no longer considered by many to be out of the ordinary. Hence, in most quarters, including sport and the military, modestly long hair and beards are no longer perceived de facto as being indicative of empathy with or possession of "bad" character traits.

Such acceptance has not been extended, however, to other aspects of the counter-culture life style, which has found some adherents inside of the sports sphere. For instance, at Springfield College of Springfield, Massachusetts, a freshman charged that he was dismissed from the school's cross-country team because he refused to take off his headband during a meet. The coach, Vernon Cox, reportedly allowed freshman Thomas Clear to wear the headband during practice but not during meets. Clear claimed that the headband kept sweat out of his eyes during races.

Clear, who described himself as a political radical, had joined the "athletic wing of the New Left Movement" called the "Woodstock National Athletic Association." Headbands, beads, and other personal ornaments are considered by many to be the insignia of radical political leanings.

Coach Cox, when asked about the headband case, stated simply that "Clear's actions were not conducive to the unity of the team."[37]

Though the long-hair issue is the latest and most widespread "character-related" controversy to come to light in sport, it is by no means unique. In fact, there have been numerous cases in sports of athletes being disciplined, suspended, and even banned from sport completely for nothing more than an alleged lack of conforming behavior. Noteworthy contemporary cases include Muhammed Ali, stripped

---

[37] See *San Francisco Chronicle,* October 17, 1971, p. 54, "Head band Hassle Halts Springfield College Runner."

of his heavyweight boxing title for refusing to comply with the selective service laws, Tommy Smith and John Carlos being ordered out of Mexico City, and Wayne Collett and Vince Mathews being banned from the Olympics after they carried out demonstrations in protest of racism in American sport and in American society. Sometimes an athlete's own behavior may not be at issue at all. Thus, Ben Davis, a defensive safety man for the Cleveland Browns professional football team was suddenly removed from the squad's active roster when his sister, Angela Davis, was placed on the FBI's "ten most wanted" list. After her capture, he was just as suddenly "picked up and reactivated." But perhaps the classic case of retaliation against an athlete for a perceived lack of conforming character is that of Paul Leroy Robeson. Robeson, despite his athletic and scholarship credentials, is the only two-time Walter Camp All-American who *is not* in the College Football Hall of Fame, though the Hall of Fame is located at Rutgers—Robeson's alma mater. Furthermore, Robeson was the first all-American in Rutger's history.

In *College Football,* published by Murray and Company in 1950 and billed as "the most complete record of collegiate football ever compiled," the 1918 Walter Camp All-American team lists only ten athletes. Robeson's name has been deliberately omitted, making this squad the only ten-man team in All-American history. Because of his "radical" outspokenness on behalf of black Americans and his alledged communist leanings—both considered to be indicative of fundamental character flaws by many segments of the American public—Robeson was reduced from the "football genius" Walter Camp came to admire to one of the most obscure figures in American sport. In short, football history has been rewritten to all but totally exclude Robeson and thus relegate him to the status of an "Orwellian nonperson."[38]

Like the characterization "clean-cut," other adjectives are also associated with the undefined concept of character in the literature. The most frequent of these are the words "upstanding," "personable," "good," "wholesome," "red-blooded," and in numerous cases it is simply claimed that "American character" is developed through participation in sport.

However, frequent mention is also made in the sports creed of some specific attributes believed to be developed through sport as components of character. For the purposes of this work, these factors are treated separately from the general concept of character, though they are understood as being encompassed by it. They are two: loyalty and altruism.

Both loyalty and altruism are typically expressed as products of a

---

[38] For some contemporary views on Robeson's situation see, Stan Isaacs, "Football's Shrine Needs Paul Robeson," *Newsday,* July 30, 1971, p. 92. See also Harry Edwards, "Paul Robeson: The Embodiment of The Athlete's True Heritage," *Freedomways Magazine* 2 no. 1, (first quarter, 1971).

Julius Sang stands at attention as U.S. gold medalist Vince Matthews (center) and silver medalist Wayne Collett stand casually with hands on hips. Collett later explained that his and Matthews' demeanor on the victory stand during the playing of the U.S. national anthem was meant to "reflect the casual attitude of white America toward black Americans." For their action, both Matthews and Collett were banned from Olympic competition for life by the IOC. (San Jose Mercury-News)

Tommie Smith leaves Mexico City after he and John Carlos were ousted from Olympic Village for "Black Power salute" on victory stand. (San Jose Mercury-News)

"team spirit" which is either emphasized as a desired attitude (in such sports as track and field for instance) or is actually required as a result of the structure and goals of sports such as basketball, football, and baseball. Many of the slogans common throughout the sports creed express sentiments reflecting a value upon loyalty and altruism.

Slogans and statements coded as expressions indicating a value on altruism were those which emphasized cooperation, concern about others, the desirability of an unselfish attitude, or which specifically mentioned "brotherhood" or altruism as end products of sports involvement. The following are typical of the most common expressions:

There is no "U" in team
There is no "I" in team
Who passed you the ball when you scored
Teamwork means success together—win together
The best players help others to be best players
Ask not what your team can do for you but what you can do for your team
We don't care who scores as long as someone does—self-sacrifice[39]

. . . The time will come when [the athlete] will have to hustle for his own food. What has all of this got to do with sport? Only this, there are some five million athletes in schools and colleges around this country who are being put through [their paces] by some 15,000 coaches. If these coaches do their jobs . . . they are helping to develop a race of men who will share the results of their toils and energy with those [who are] less fortunate . . .[40]

Slogans and other expressions of the high value placed upon loyalty are also to be found throughout the sports creed.

---

[39] Eldon E. Snyder, "Athletic Dressing Room Slogans as Folklore: A Means of Socialization," paper presented at a meeting of the American Sociological Association, August 30, 1970, pp. 11–13.

[40] "Editorial" (n. 25 above), p. 20.

An ounce of loyalty is worth a pound of cleverness.[41]

Athletics offer the best training in subordinating oneself to the welfare of the group to which he belongs; in controlling one's own appetites and desires for the sake of loyalty to something greater than oneself.[42]

The moral value of athletics are abundant. . . . [it] cultivates teamwork, especially the honorable ethic of loyalty and all that this implies [with regard to] courtesy and generosity in victory and defeat.[43]

The value placed upon altruism remains quite strong in sports:

When I recruit a kid I never promise him where he'll play or if he'll play. All I say is that I want him to be happy to be a member of the [team]. I don't want prima donnas. I probably have more fullbacks and halfbacks [prestige positions] playing guard and tackle than anybody.[44]

The principle of loyalty to one's teammates is recognized not only by those involved in sport but by many outside of sport as well. As a result, awkward situations sometimes arise, particularly within educa-

---

Double Standards Charge Leveled at U of A Officials

University of Arizona students have long suspected that the U of A administration has one standard for longhair militants and another for "straight" students.

Now they know it.

The university decided not to file felony charges against two prominent football players who admitted they were guilty of what would clearly be felonies off-campus. . . .

The two football players, while refusing to name names, admit that more than 25 members of the team participated in the thefts. . . .

Those that did know they are guilty. But what about the innocent players? Their names are blackened too by the university's silence.[45]

---

[41] Snyder, p. 13.

[42] J. P. Gavit, *College* (New York: Harcourt, Brace, 1925), p. 150.

[43] Henry Neuman, "Moral Values in Secondary Education" United States Bureau of Education Bulletin, 1917, p. 35.

[44] Dee Andros, cited in Underwood (n. 30 above), p. 23.

[45] R. L. Thomas, "Double Standards Charge Leveled Against U of A Officials," *The Arizona Republic,* April 3, 1971, p. 29.

tional institutions, when the principle of team loyalty conflicts with other ethical values, such as that of civic responsibility.

The differential treatment of "longhairs" as opposed to "shorthairs" by the administration notwithstanding, it is at least plausible that adherence to the principle of team loyalty is at work on the part of the two admittedly guilty athletes and also on the part of those team members who are innocent.

The principle of loyalty even covers behavior expectations with regard to coaches. In 1957, *Athletic Journal* published a "Code of Ethics" drawn up by a midwestern coaches' association. It was suggested that it be incorporated into the charters of all such groups and that each individual coach adopt it as his own personal "rules of behavior." The very first rule of this code is "a coach is loyal to his superiors and supports the policies of his administrators." The last tenet is "a coach is loyal to his profession and the Coaches Association."[46]

The code that says that coaches and athletes alike are expected to be loyal to their respective sports organizations is further pointed up by the two following cases.[47]

Controversial Coach Fired

A leader in forming the controversial League of Athletes, John Parker was fired last Nov. 4 as assistant track coach after he wrote an article for the Florida State College newspaper criticizing the athletic department. Now he has filed a suit for $11,650 against Ray Graves, the athletic director, charging that he had been denied right of free speech and free press under the Civil Rights Act, and that the firing was "arbitrary, capricious, unreasonable, discriminatory and not reasonably related to any substantive evil."

It is at least plausible that, because athletic involvement is believed to be conducive to instilling a high evaluation of loyalty, the refusal of the two athletes (in the University of Arizona case cited above) to name those team members also taking part in the thefts was tolerated by the coaching staff and administration, even though it meant the violation of another ethic. Likewise, the innocent athletes did not identify them-

---

[46] "Editorial" (n. 25 above), p. 24.
[47] In *San Francisco Chronicle*, September 29, 1971, p. 54.

Black QB Criticizes Coach, Barred

Atlanta—Eddie McAshan, Georgia Tech's candid quarterback, faced possible disciplinary action yesterday for hurling public criticism at his team's offensive planning.

"I was very surprised he would say things like that. . . . What the team needs most right now is loyalty," said his coach Bud Carson.

McAshan later admitted he made the remarks, but indicated the "story did not turn out as I expected it." He emphasized he did not mean to attack the coaching staff or the team.

"I have never known Eddie to be disloyal to his football team," Carson said.

---

selves. On the other hand, coach John Parker's criticisms of the athletic department and Eddie McAshan's criticism of his team's strategy did not endear them to their respective superiors. In sports, behavior which contradicts the belief that sports involvement does or should instill loyalty is seldom left unrebuffed.

II. Discipline

In the sports creed, expressions and slogans relating sport to "discipline" are second only to those relating it to "character development." Discipline is believed by many in sport to be *the* key factor in the operation of the athletic organization.

When a man signs a contract to play a sport . . . he obligates himself to comply with the rules that govern that sport as set down by his coach. This is understood by everyone who has been [involved] in athletics at any level . . . Is it too much to ask that a person sacrifice certain individual privileges for the honor of representing his school or state through athletics. Without discipline there could be no sports.[48]

Today, one frequently hears complaints that the discipline emphasized in sport has been exaggerated to the point of demanding "lockstep" regimentation. There is, indeed, some evidence of rather far-reaching requirements. Consider for instance the following memorandum

---

[48] John Didion (All-American linebacker at Oregon State University), cited by Underwood, "The Desperate Coach: Concessions and Lies," *Sports Illustrated,* September 8, 1969, p. 29.

sent out to the faculty and staff of a large southeastern university. Here, it seems that discipline has been extended beyond the boundaries of sports to relationships between persons in sports and those in nonsports roles.

MEMO TO: All Faculty and Staff
FROM: Paul Dietzel, Director of Athletics and Head Football Coach
SUBJECT: Faculty Football Breakfasts
DATE: September 3, 1971
The Department of Athletics would like for you to be our guest at breakfast on Thursday morning, September 9, 1971, two days prior to our football season opener with Georgia Tech. The football staff will brief you on the 1971 Gamecocks and give you a scouting report on our opponent. . .
At each breakfast we will follow this schedule:
7:00 A.M.—Coach Bill Shalosky blows whistle and Coach Dietzel asks blessing.
7:05 A.M.—Breakfast
7:20 A.M.—Coach Dietzel introduces offensive coach to discuss Carolina offense.
7:25 A.M.—Coach Dietzel introduces defensive coach to discuss Carolina defense.
7:30 A.M.—Coach Dietzel introduces scout to discuss opponent.
7:40 A.M.—Coach Dietzel comments, questions and answers.
7:55 A.M.—Coach Shalosky blows whistle; breakfast adjourns.
We hope to see you Thursday and at subsequent faculty and staff breakfasts.

Complaints and criticism notwithstanding, a high value upon the significance of discipline to the proper functioning of the institution of sports is held throughout all levels of sport. The perceived importance of self-discipline is reflected in sports slogans:

The boy who isn't criticized should worry.
Strong men criticize themselves.
He who flys with the owls at night cannot keep up with the eagles during the day.
Anger is a sign of weakness.
The way you live is the way you play.
Live by the code or get out.
Discipline.

Similarly, at the level of social control, one finds the following in the sports creed: "Stay out for sports, stay out of courts," "A true athlete is one year round."[49]
The emphasis upon discipline helps to support the assumption that sports participation enculturates athletes with a high regard for self-

---

[49] Eldon E. Snyder, pp. 10–13.

discipline and with a healthy respect for the necessity of social control. Thus, any advocacy of relaxation in discipline as an integral part of sport is seen as endangering the whole of American society. In response to a lecture given by Dave Meggysey—a former professional footballer who gave up the sport partly because of what he calls "the dehumanizing discipline" enforced by coaches and the "regimented" character of the game itself—a high-school principal made the following statement:

> Mr. Meggysey's ideas about running a team is a wonderful example of the revolutionaries' attempt to break down the basic foundations upon which this society is founded. If you are competing in sport, you have structure, line of authority, and someone making critical decisions. . . . Hard work, compromise, and sacrifice . . . are fundamental to this society and . . . in athletics but not to the "namby-pamby" type of life Mr. Meggysey sees for us all. . . . I personally feel that a man like Vince Lombardi or our present coach of the "49'ers," Dick Nolan, would have been insulted by the generalizations he made . . .[50]

According to Willard Waller, many in the educational institutions of America maintain a firm belief in the discipline-building capabilities of sports and, on the basis of this belief, have made athletics an integral part of the social control techniques applied in schools. Waller observes: "Part of the technique, indeed, of schools and teachers who handle difficult cases consists in getting those persons interested in some form of athletics . . ." Further, Waller asserts, the school authorities believe that: "This constitutes a wholesome interest, opens the way to normal growth of personality and inhibits abnormal interests and undesirable channels of growth."[51]

As if to exemplify the point, Ralph Schneider, president of the Philadelphia Men's Coaches Association states: "We know that we help keep boys out of gangs. We have proved we are effective in fighting vandalism, violence and drug use. The best lesson to be learned from sports is self-discipline in the social arena."[52]

In a time of turmoil and challenge for the institution of sport in America, F. Melvin Cratsley, basketball coach at Little Point Park College in Pittsburg, concurs in believing in the control functions of sport and in regarding any relaxation in discipline as ultimately a threat to the whole of American society.

> Athletics are our last stronghold of discipline. . . . It may be that they are in a life and death struggle all of their own. I read somewhere, I clipped

---

[50] William Hale, "A Memorandum" May 7, 1971 (From the files of the Institute for the Study of Sport and Society.)

[51] Willard Waller, *The Sociology of Teaching*, John Wiley and Sons, Inc., 1965, p. 114.

[52] Ralph Schnieder, "We Expect Them to Storm the Gates" in *Sports Illustrated*, September 6, 1971, p. 22.

it out, where the aim of the "New Left" is to replace the athlete with the hippie as the idol of the kids. I don't know if it can be done, but it seems society is intent on destroying Horatio Alger, Jr. The undisciplined Oddball is getting control. The good guy is outnumbered. America seems interested only in glorifying the loser. If you can't tell [athletes] what to do, if they don't kindle to discipline, they don't need a coach.[53]

Similarly, Bob Nichols, basketball coach at Toledo University states: "We can not condone outright refusal to obey orders."[54]

Thus, the belief that sports activities do and should instill discipline has contributed to an intolerance of any perceived laxity in discipline among those engaged in sport, particularly athletes.

III. Competition

The general theme of competition within the context of the sports creed encompasses three more specific points of emphasis. First, sports participation is believed to be conducive to the development of fortitude (understood here as a combination of courage, perseverance, and aggressiveness); second, sport is a means of "preparing the athlete for life," to meet the challenges of day-to-day problem solving successfully; and third, participation is believed to be a primary avenue by which individuals can be developed who will fulfill the needs of a democratic society both in terms of leadership and as visible examples that the system continues to be viable.

Many slogans in sport reflect the value placed on fortitude:

A quitter never wins, a winner never quits.
When the going gets tough, the tough get going.
Hustle: you can't survive without it.
It's not the size of the dog in the fight, but the size of the fight in the dog.
Winning is the second step, wanting to win is the first.
To explain triumph, start with the first syllable.
Hustle, guts, and desire make a winning team.
Desire.
Hustle.
Guts.
It's easy to be ordinary, but it takes guts to excel.
It takes courage to excel and we must.
If you come to the end of your rope, tie a knot and hang on.
The heart carries the feet.
Guts, desire, attitude.
What good is skill without guts and desire?

---

[53] F. Melvin Cratsley, cited by Underwood, "The Desperate Coach" *Sports Illustrated,* September 25, 1969, p. 71.

[54] Bob Nichols, basketball coach at Toledo University, Ibid., p. 70.

The emphasis upon fortitude as a necessary element for success in sport is a primary foundation for the belief that participation is conducive to the development of this personal trait. It is believed that,

. . . In competitive sport, it is necessary for a boy to mobilize at a given time and in a given place all . . . the courage that he possesses . . . in the face of strenuous opposition, . . . Athletics afford a laboratory for development in this regard . . .[55]

and that "athletics are a basic means of cultivating physical courage."[56]

Clearly, the relevance of fortitude is not seen as being merely an end unto itself or restricted to the realm of sport. An athlete's conduct under the pressures of competition is believed to be an accurate indicator of how he will approach the challenges of life, as reflected in the slogan "The way you play is the way you'll live."[57] But the faith that sport has the capability of *determining* to a significant degree how an individual will live also is reflected in sports slogans—for instance, "Send us a boy, we'll return him a man."[58]

Ultimately, however, the greatest benefactor of the fortitude and "training to meet the challenges of life" instilled in the athlete is believed to be "the American system." This benefit is particularly emphasized in the case of the creation of visible examples showing that "the system still works."

In 1927, Helen McAfee observed:

Nowhere has the tendency to democratize been greater than in sports . . . As the equalitarian economic process has gone on . . . more and more labor [class] persons have had the money and the leisure to become involved in sport.[59]

This "democratization" is viewed in the sports literature as a key factor in the establishment of sport as a laboratory in which all young men regardless of social class, can learn the advantages and rewards of a competitive system.

In a 1956 editorial, the publishers of *Athletic Journal* offered the following defense of athletic competition:

. . . Athletics provide the most primitive and clear-cut kind of competition. The desire to excel is not evil . . . America would be a sorry state if the

---

[55] Charles W. Kennedy, "Effect of Athletic Competition on Character Building" *The American Physical Education Review* 30 (October 1926).

[56] R. T. McKenzie, "The Functions and Limitations of Sport in Education," *Proceedings: National Conference on Education*, 1926, p. 15.

[57] Snyder, p. 14.

[58] Snyder, p. 14.

[59] Helen McAfee, "The Menace of Leisure," *Harper's Monthly*, May, 1927, p. 69.

next generation grows up with the idea that to compete [or] try to be better than anyone else is bad.[60]

Similarly, educator William Hale, in 1971, stated:

I do not accept the arguments about [sports] competition being responsible for one losing his virility, individual rights, and so forth. If we had a country of individuals who didn't value competitiveness, we would have chaos, anarchy, and zero productivity.[61]

Spiro Agnew echoes Hale's sentiments:

Coaches who let athletes tell them how to coach are not going to contribute much to the athlete's preparation for those hard times later on when he has to face the outside competition. . . .[62]

And finally, the editors of *Athletic Journal,* in a comparative appraisal of the role of sport in communist countries and in the United States, assert unequivocally that

. . . In true communist dogma there can be no first place nor can there be any competition. The ideal communism of Marx and Lenin would hold the speed of the fastest to that of the slowest . . . The free enterprise system is based on competition and for that reason our system of athletics has augmented our idea of political and economic life . . . prepares our youth for their roles in [these] . . . [Participation in] competitive sports must be taken as a rather general acknowledgement by the soviets that they have dropped any pretext at being a true communist state.[63]

The competitiveness of sport is thus seen as a means of imbuing youth with the "spirit" and fortitude necessary to face the challenges of adult life and to make a social system work that is philosophically founded upon the notion of free and open competition.

IV. Physical fitness

The theme of physical fitness in the sports creed expresses the belief that participation in sports helps to develop a physically healthy body, as well as an appreciation for physical fitness which carries over into the athlete's postparticipation years. Both the intensive physical conditioning that has become fundamental to virtually all athletic training programs and the healthy, robust appearance of many athletes encourage this belief. Thus, in 1922, Professor Maurice Caullery stated ". . . The practice and conditioning of sport helps to give American

---

[60] "Editorial," *Athletic Journal* 37 (September 1956): p. 17.
[61] Hale, p. 2.
[62] In R. Lipsyte, "Sports of the Times," *New York Times,* June 7, 1971.
[63] "Editorial" (n. 60 above), p. 16.

youth an elegance of body and a physical vigor which one cannot but envy . . ."[64]

Some statements go beyond the belief that sports participation simply develops a healthy, enviable body.

. . . The main purpose of any athletic activity . . . is the development of the general health of the persons concerned for the purposes of securing for society their effective work in later life . . .[65]

Sports slogans too reflect a high evaluation of physical fitness:

> *It's easier to stay in shape than to get in shape.*
> *How well-conditioned is the man next to you?*
> *Good training makes a good athlete.*
> *Fatigue makes cowards of us all.*[66]

Overall, then, physical fitness is believed to be a product of sports participation which benefits not only the individual athlete but also the society.

V. Mental fitness

The sports creed is replete with expressions attesting to the contributions of sports participation to the development of mental alertness and to educational achievement. "Mental alertness" seems to be understood as a continuous rationally optimistic awareness of one's potential and alternatives in any goal-directed activity. Sports slogans place great emphasis upon mental alertness:

> *It takes a cool head to win a hot game.*
> *It's all in a state of mind.*
> *You're as good as you want to be.*
> *The true champion is one who can conquer the fear of making mistakes.*
> *You always become tired mentally before physically.*
> *Alertness + hard work = a winner.*
> *Mental toughness.*[67]

It is believed that sport's contribution to mental alertness arises from the need for the athlete to coordinate mental concentration and motor skills during his participation in complex athletic activities.

. . . In the . . . complex forms of sports not only is the raw material for thought-motor images, memory of various situations, rules, and the like fur-

---

[64] Maurice Caullery, "Sports and Athletics," *Universities and Scientific Life in the United States* (Cambridge, Mass.: Harvard University Press, 1922), p. 75.

[65] C. F. Taeusch, "Athletics and Ethics," *School and Society*, December 10, 1927, p. 728.

[66] Snyder, p. 6.

[67] Snyder, p. 7.

*Sport "prepares young
men for their roles as
the future custodians of
the Republic." General
Douglas MacArthur rose
from schoolboy athlete
to national hero. (UPI)*

nished, but attitudes, associations, and habits significant for mental efficiency
. . . are developed.[68]

In defense, specifically of football, a sport which had come under
attack from some educators as being detrimental to the educational
process, Percy D. Haughton stated at the 1914 National Collegiate
Athletic Association Convention that

. . . Football requires more brains than brawn. A boy when he goes to his
football practice is getting just as good mental training as he does in the school

---

[68] William H. Burnham, "The Newer Aims of Physical Education and Its
Psycho-Physiological Significance," *American Educational Review* 27 (January
1922): 3.

room, if not better. I hope that as times goes on football as a source of mental training will be recognized.[69]

The belief that sports participation contributes to individual educational achievement has long been a basic argument for the continuation and even the expansion of athletic programs in educational institutions. In the sports creed, these believed contributions are of two main types. First, it is held that sports participation itself is of *direct* educational benefit.

. . . Our school sports are perhaps the most genuinely educative features that our schools possess. . . . They are honest, competitive, and thoroughly objective. The sports program involves throughout the selection and pitting of merit against merit in open, interesting struggle.[70]

Second, sports are believed to contribute *indirectly* to educational achievement by providing both incentives for students to stay in school and opportunities for more students to continue their educations beyond the high school level. Related to these indirect contributions is the belief that student athletes do better academically than nonathlete students of comparable intelligence.

The evidence pro and con on the relationship between educational achievement and sports involvement will be reviewed in some detail later in this work.

VI. Religiosity

Though it does not contain a consistent and unified body of exhorted religious principles, the place of sacred religion in the sports creed is quite conspicuous. A belief in religious precepts approximating those traditionally advocated in American society is both encouraged in athletes and informally perpetuated by athletic organizations and officials. Many, if not most (no accurate count is available), amateur and professional athletic organizations engage in some form of informally authorized religious exercises, usually just prior to competing. Several sports slogans suggest the typically generalized quality of the emphasis upon religion in the sports creed: "I can do all things through Him who strengtheneth me"; "Position of athlete and Christian: knees bent, eyes up."[71]

However, not all efforts to relate sport to formal religion are as general as the encouragement of a belief in a "divine being" or the

---

[69] Percy D. Haughton, "Mental Training and Football," in *Proceedings: National Collegiate Athletic Association*, 1914, p. 65.

[70] William S. Leamed, "The Quality of the Educational Process in the United States" in the Carnegie Foundation for the Advancement of Teaching, Bulletin no. 20, p. 133.

[71] Snyder, pp. 6, 14.

practice of prayer. For instance, at San Jose State College, head football coach Dewey King has sent out pamphlets containing fundamentalist Christian religious teachings as part of his regular preseason correspondence to his athletes. Nor is it only the coaches who inject sacred religion into sport. Athletic governing bodies and athletes are involved as well. *Newsweek* reported (January 11, 1971), upon the occasion of the Reverend Billy Graham being installed as grand marshal of the Rose Bowl parade, that

Religious fervor has become so much a part of the U.S. sporting scene that the most surprising thing about Graham's appearance . . . was that he wasn't invited before now.[72]

As an enthusiastic exponent of the virtues of athletic competition and the sanctity of the "Christian" athlete and coach, Graham has made sport a basic metaphor in his ministry.

The Bible says leisure and lying around are morally dangerous . . . Sports keep us busy; athletes, you notice, don't take drugs . . . There are probably more really committed Christians in sports, both collegiate and professional, than in any other occupation in America. The Bible reveals that St. Paul was an avid sports fan because he used so many illustrations from the Olympics in his letters . . .[73]

Many athletes, coaches, and sports organizations apparently agree with Graham's appraisal of the relationship between sport and traditional Christianity. The Fellowship of Christian Athletes (FCA), organized in 1956 to make evangelists of prominent athletes, now boasts more than 100,000 members including athletes and coaches from the high-school, collegiate, and professional sports ranks. Athletes in Action, a division of Graham's Crusade for Christ, provides a smaller but more zealous and aggressive platform for "winning souls" through sports.

The NCAA supports a religious emphasis in sports. For instance, it allows the Crusade for Christ to put on half-time shows at authorized NCAA basketball games whereupon former college basketball participants tell campus crowds how they "found Jesus."

Professional sports bodies are also supportive. The NFL, in 1971, sanctioned what was billed as a special "Weekend of Champions" at the Super Bowl in Miami, Florida. The affair involved athletes representing practically every major sport in America—football, baseball, basketball, track and field, weight lifting, and so forth. The concluding rally before some 25,000 persons focused upon the featured attraction for the "Weekend of Champions": evangelist Mike Crain, who practices "karate for Christ" by splitting ten inches of concrete with his bare hand to "demon-

---

[72] "Are Sports Good For the Soul?" *Newsweek*, January 11, 1971, p. 51.
[73] Ibid., pp. 51–52.

Using one of his frequent sport metaphors, evangelist Billy Graham warns young people of the evils involved in using drugs and dropping out of the "game of life." (UPI)

strate God's power." Says Crain "There is Communist power, Black power, White power, and Red power. But the greatest power is God's power."[74]

Other athletes also find sports participation and the Christian ministry to be compatible pursuits. Calvin Hill, a running back for the Dallas Cowboys professional football team, is an ordained minister.

Coaches and owners often welcome the religiosity with which sport of late has become draped. Louisiana State University's coach, Charles McClendon, credits a Graham campus crusade in the fall of 1970 with helping his football team win a victory over Auburn University. Dallas Cowboys head football coach, Tom Landry, presided over a Billy Graham Crusade for Christ held on the Cowboys' home field, the Cotton Bowl, in 1971.

While the sports creed does not make the blanket assertion that being an athlete will make one a Christian, it rather clearly holds that being a Christian will make one a better athlete. The view is rendered highly concrete by Dave Hannah, director of Athletes in Action: "Joe Namath is a good quarterback. But if he were a Christian, he'd be a better one."[75]

---

[74] Ibid., p. 51.
[75] Ibid., p. 52.

The religious theme in the sports creed is clearly Protestant in emphasis, though hardly systematically orthodox. The place of religion in sports is ill-defined but the emphasis is conspicuous enough to show that the creed recognizes and appreciates traditional Protestant religious values. It is, however, not from Protestant ethics that the sports creed derives its coherence. Rather, as will be illustrated later, the predominant values expressed emerge from strains inherent in the role relationships and functioning of the institution of sport itself.

VII. Nationalism

Like the religious theme, nationalism has a relatively vague and diffuse place in the sports creed. Nonetheless, the pervasive informal emphasis upon patriotic symbols and values makes it apparent that nationalism has a significant place in sport. Some expressions in the creed depict sports involvement as in and of itself conducive to the development of a patriotic attitude. With the naïve directness of its times, this 1904 statement makes the matter plain:

. . . The team [effort] represents the earliest form of organization of society and is one of nature's own methods of leading the youth into patriotism . . . What does it matter if a leg is broken now and then? It is worth a thousand broken legs if you can teach your boy to be a hero and a patriot . . .[76]

Some spokesmen of the creed, however, simply see patriotism as a necessary element in sports involvement. An incident at Adelbert College points up this perspective. Basketball coach Ron (Buzz) Ellis suspended an athlete from his team for failure to stand up during the playing of the "Star Spangled Banner." In Ellis's words "There are no rules in sports about standing up for the National Anthem, but there are no rules about dropping a player who doesn't do it either."[77]

In one sense, the main thrust of the sports creed is "nationalistic," supporting as it does many of the general values and certain traditional political and economic philosophies of American society. In addition, there is the symbolism of flag ceremonies and the honor guards made up of military personnel that have become part of the opening show at important athletic events. Some other patriotic gestures made by sports organizations have already been discussed (e.g., the sending of noted athletes to Vietnam to talk with the troops).

We have now sketched the basic themes of the sports creed. They represent beliefs publically expressed continually over the decades by persons involved in sports at all levels. Paradoxically, however, the chief and all-pervasive concern of persons actually participating in sports is discernible as a major theme in the sports creed only by implication.

[76] Henry S. Curtis, "A Football Education," *The American Physical Education Review* 9 (December 1904): 264.

[77] Ron Ellis, cited by Underwood, September 25, 1969, p. 70.

This is the concern with winning. Throughout the sports creed, the implication is that the reward of adhering to the values expressed will be a winning record. But the value of *winning* as an end in itself is not emphasized. It is simply implied that the more disciplined athlete *will* win, that the more religious athlete *will* perform better and will thus win, that the more mentally and physically fit athlete *will* win, and so forth.

The low profile of winning per se as projected through the sports creed is supported by most coaches. Only those with established reputations for fielding winning teams openly express a belief in Vince Lombardi's edict "Winning isn't everything, it is the only thing." Most allow themselves more latitude in terms of their own personal boundaries for achievement. The sports creed has hardly gone so far as to place a positive value on losing. Rather, it makes the fine distinction between losing honorably (i.e., having performed well and behaved in a sportsman-like fashion within the context of the rules in the face of impending defeat) and losing disreputably (i.e., having performed below assumed potential or having exhibited poor sportsmanship or "foul play" in losing). Thus, the all-important significance of winning is known, but likewise, there is the consoling "reward" of the "honorable defeat." Indeed, the "sweetness" of winning is derived as much as from anything else, from the knowledge of having defeated a courageous opponent who performed honorably. Without such a twilight zone—honorable defeat—between total victory and total defeat, the only alternative would be sports involvement solely for the value of having the experience. In essence, all sports endeavors would end in a tie—no winners and no losers. Such a no-win, intrinsic-reward form of "sport" could not at present become established without some widespread and fundamental alterations of the institution of sport and of American societal values as a whole. In this regard, Walter Camp stated as early as 1922

Its fine, isn't it, to tell the boys . . . they should play for the sport, never mind who wins? That isn't the way to bring boys up. One side or the other has got to lose. And boys who make the right kind of men are boys who go in and play as hard as they can to win, play fair, but play hard, take a whipping without a whimper and come back for more. Win if you can, lose if you must. And that is the sort of men we want to develop through sports . . .[78]

In American sport, then, the institutionalized and preferred outcome (that which characterizes the "great" event) is the hard-won victory by one team coupled with the honorable defeat of its opponent. A tie wherein neither opponent wins or loses is acceptable but is not institutionalized as a *goal* in sport. A tie, as one coach said, is "like

---

[78] Walter Camp, *Proceedings: National Collegiate Athletic Association,* 1922 Convention, p. 97.

kissing one's own sister." And the disreputable defeat is eschewed by all.

One final word about the infrequent case of the "disreputable victory." Such an occurence may entail some individual act such as the surreptitious and deliberate injury of an opposing star athlete by an overzealous participant. There is also the case of piling up unreasonable margins of victory over an opponent which is obviously overmatched. In this regard, one usually finds great criticism of the 65 to 6 football score or the 115 to 36 basketball score. Then there are the more "unusual" cases of disreputable victory:

Players Allow Giveaway Touchdown

The Florida Gators literally prostrated themselves Saturday night so senior quarterback John Reaves could break a major college passing record.

The action made University of Miami Coach Fran Curci hopping mad.

"It was the worst thing I have ever seen in football," said Curci after his Hurricane team lost to Florida 45–16 in the Orange Bowl.

"I used to admire (Florida) Coach Doug Dickey as a coach—his record speaks for itself—but tonight I lost all respect for him as a coach and as a man. What he did shows absolutely no class."

What aroused Curci's ire was a mass fall-down by the entire Gator defensive team with 1:10 left in the game to let Miami's John Hornibrook score from eight yards out. The action allowed Reaves to get his hands on the football and have a last-minute shot at breaking Jim Plunkett's passing record.

Florida took possession on the ensuing kickoff and Reaves fired a 15-yard pass to receiver Carlos Alvarez.[79]

In conclusion, consider the following editorial from *Athletic Journal* which manages, in a remarkably few words, to enunciate almost all of the major themes of the sports creed discussed here. Though its focus

---

[79] "Players Allow 'Give-Away' Touchdown," *Fremont News-Register,* November 29, 1971, p. 14.

was upon events of January 5, 1957, the values expressed are as prevalent today as they were then.

Ray Null, a former high school and college coach and more recently
athletic director at Detroit University, is currently on the sports staff of radio
station WHFB in Benton Harbor, Michigan. He concluded his sportscast of
January 5, with a stirring plea for athletics. Joe Rogers, the director of athletics at Benton Harbor High School, thought so much of Null's remarks that
he sent us a transcript. We quite agree that this is the type of affirmative
thinking which is needed in regard to athletics. Mr. Null's remarks follow:

"Many of us today listen to the grave address to Congress delivered by
Dwight Eisenhower, the president of the United States, in which he asked its
permission to use American troops to curb any armed aggression in the Middle East.

"Made us stop and think, didn't it?

"Many people often question the value of athletics—many people question professional athletics—the purity code—injuries—and the overall contribution of athletics to the American way of life.

"Let me assure you that no part of our educational curriculum contributes more to the seven cardinal principles of education than physical education.

"A young man's ability to think and act under pressure—his contribution
to a cooperative team effort—cannot be found in a textbook or in the classroom. The ability to adjust to adverse conditions—to react to a victory or a
loss—the value of conditioning and physical fitness—the importance of self-
sacrifice to obtain definite objectives and goals—leadership and the ability to
react with sound leadership and decision under stress—all this is physical education and competitive athletics' contribution to the development and education of our young Americans.

"Granted that all branches of learning and education contribute to our
national safety—for example: our chemists—our engineers—our doctors—our
dentists—our men of industry—all are important members of the American
team. But where can our young men better learn the value of team contribution than in athletics?

"Yes, sports fans, as our great president addressed the nation over this
radio station and many other networks this January afternoon, I thought that
in these trying days—when the blue chips are spread all over this great big
world of ours—many, many of the leaders of the various branches of our
fighting forces are American young men who on the gridiron, the hardwood
court, the diamond, and the cinder path learned the true value of leadership,
the value of organization, and the ability to think and act quickly under stress.

"It's a warm and nice feeling to know that the best in the world is a
red-blooded young American who appreciates the value of athletics as an expression of the American way of life. If my youngster has to serve his country
some day—that's his duty—that's fine—but I know one dad who hopes that
his colonel or battalion leader called signals with calmness and integrity when
thousands of sports fans' screaming voices stimulated rather than unnerved
him. Let us, as good citizens, never lose track of the value of sports. It is in-

deed very true that today we cannot all participate in sports—but certainly we can all try to be one."[80]

To give some idea of the stability of the sports creed over the decades, compare the following statements made by a University president in 1892:

. . . Sports have infused into boys and young men a greater respect for bodily excellence and a desire to attain it; they have supplied a new and effective motive for resisting all sins which weaken and corrupt the body and the nation; they have quickened admiration for such manly qualities as courage, fortitude, and presence of mind in emergencies and under difficulties; they have cultivated in a few the habit of command, and in many the habit of quick obedience and intelligent subordination; and finally they have set before young men prizes and distinctions which are uncontaminated by any commercial value, and which no one can win who does not possess much perseverance and self-control in addition to rare bodily endowments . . .[81]

Up until now, the various themes of the dominant sports creed have been dealt with in a "laundry-list" fashion. However, its component aspects are not as random as this treatment might suggest.

In essence, the creed can be analytically delineated according to whether a particular theme is "instrumental" or "managerial" in its function within the sport realm. Instrumental components relate to characteristics that are primarily useful as adaptive resources and neons for goal attainment. Managerial components have to do with system maintenance. These two "creedal strands" represent partial resolutions of fundamental inconsistencies in ethical norms. Table 5–2 depicts this analytical delineation.

TABLE 5–2

Instrumental and managerial foci of the American sports creed

Instrumental (goal attainment)	*managerial (pattern maintenance)*
II. Discipline: social control and/or self-control	I. Character: character development; loyalty; altruism
III. Competition: fortitude; preparation for life; opportunity for advancement	VI. Religiosity
IV. Physical fitness	VII. Nationalism
V. Mental fitness: mental alertness; educational achievement	

---

[80] "Editorial" *Athletic Journal* 37 (March 1957), p. 18.

[81] R. Eliot, "Values in American Athletics," *American College Athletics,* the Carnegie Foundation for the Advancement of Teaching, Bulletin no. 23, 1929, p. 294.

Without further elaborating upon these two creedal strands at this point, suffice it to say that these beliefs constitute *what* is said and believed for the most part about sport in America. The remaining chapters of Part II concentrate upon *who* makes and believes these statements, why, and the degree to which there is evidence that these professed attributes of sports conform to contemporary knowledge.

6

The coach

Every coach knows that he may be sacrificed at the end of a losing season, even though his team lost through no fault of his own. Here again is apparent the disposition on the part of certain people to want to punish someone for what they think of as their disasters and misfortunes.[1]

. . . There are too many coaches and there is too much coaching. More should be left to the initiative of the players.[2]

The coach is the last stronghold of the archaic family structure.[3]

Coaches are right up there with ministers in the concern that they have for others. Coaches try to do what a lot of papas haven't done or won't do. You won't see anybody try harder than coaches.[4]

The coach is the last chance for the preservation of dignity on campus.[5]

. . . Coaches are aggressive people, self-assertive. We know that they are highly organized and ordered. . . . That they listen to others . . . but pay little attention to what others say . . . They have fierce psychological endurance . . . But they are also inflexible in their profession as coaches.

[1] John Griffith, "Goats," *Athletic Journal* 13 (October 1932): 20.

[2] Charles A. Richmond, "Personality of Coaches," *Association of American Colleges Bulletin* 12 (May 1926): pp. 245–46.

[3] From Arnold Beisser, *The Madness in Sports*, in John Underwood, "The Desperate Coach," *Sports Illustrated*, August 25, 1969, p. 66.

[4] John Underwood, "The Desperate Coach," *Sports Illustrated*, September 8, 1969, p. 37.

[5] Ibid., p. 66.

They dislike change and experimentation; and they are extremely conservative politically, socially, and attitudinally.[6]

IN 1929, Howard Savage defined a "coach" as "a man or woman whose work it is to instruct participant members of . . . [an athletic organization] or candidates for such membership in the techniques and methods of one or more branches of athletics . . ."[7]

However, a relatively cursory reading of Savage's own discussion of the coaching role will reveal that his definition was simplistic and incomplete even at the time it was published. Certainly it is inadequate to encompass the role responsibilities commonly associated with the position of coach today.

From the first emergence of organized sport as a major spectator interest, the role of coach has been very complex. Its boundaries of responsibility have been more ad hoc than explicitly stipulated and defined. The coach has been viewed as the "executive" or the "patriarch" of the individual athletic unit, whether this be a team or an individual athlete such as a boxer or jockey.[8] And, as Sutton found to be the case with business executives,[9] the coach's essential responsibility is to "make decisions." For the coach, these decisions range all the way from choosing assistants (in the case of the head coach) to recruiting athletes, arranging sports schedules, deciding which athletes will be first string, what strategy will be employed, what is acceptable athlete behavior, grooming, and politics inside and outside of the sports realm, what and when an athlete will eat, when he will sleep, down to, in some cases, who an athlete can appropriately date. While this list of traditional decision-making responsibilities by no means exhausts the duties seen as normal for most coaches, it does illustrate the diversity of such responsibilities. And this diversity is common to coaching roles at all levels of sport.

Key to any analysis of the coaching role is a clear delineation of the occupational milieu in which the coach must operate. Because of the complexities affecting the coaching role in collegiate sports, the college coach will be the focus of attention here. Though space will not allow a thorough analysis of coaching roles below the collegiate level

[6] Bruce C. Ogilvie and Thomas A. Tutko, "Self-Perception as Compared with Measured personality of Male Physical Educators," paper presented at Second International Congress of Sports Psychologists, October 29, 1968, Washington, D.C.

[7] Howard Savage, "The Coach in College Athletics" in *American College Athletics,* the Carnegie Foundation for the Advancement of Teaching, Bulletin no. 23, 1929.

[8] *Coach* and *Manager* are viewed here as identical roles carrying different names. For example, the role responsibilities of the amateur baseball coach and the professional baseball manager essentially are the same.

[9] Frances X. Sutton et al., *The American Business Creed* (Cambridge, Mass.: Harvard University Press, 1956), p. 90.

(high school, junior high school, little league) or above it (postcollegiate amateur, semiprofessional, or professional coaching), it can be assumed that most of the discussion of pressures and responsibilities deriving specifically from the character of sport itself are more or less applicable to all coaching roles.

THE OCCUPATIONAL MILIEU OF THE COACH

In colleges and universities, the methods of hiring coaches vary among athletic conferences and schools. One prominent factor is whether the employing institution is publicly or privately supported. At public institutions (whether junior colleges, colleges, or universities), a coach typically must also teach. Under such circumstances, the coach often has "faculty status," implying that he is appointed by the same authority as other members of the faculty, that his rank in the academic community is comparable to that of heads of academic departments, professors, instructors, or lecturers, that his reappointment, promotion, or release is to be approached on the same basis, that a sabbatical leave of absence is accorded him just as it is to his colleagues in other departments, and that his post carries with it the right to vote in academic deliberative bodies. In short, the term "faculty status" should mean no formal distinctions between the coaches' status and the status of any other academic colleague. Coaches hired in public institutions are supposedly teachers as much as they are coaches. In order to insure that these separate responsibilities remain congruous, many such institutions group their athletic and physical education divisions into one department —a Department of Physical Education and Intercollegiate Athletics.

For the most part, the nominal balance between teacher-coach roles is not maintained in reality. Like the coach in professional sport or in many of the private schools, the teacher-coach usually perceives his main duty—if not his only real responsibility—as that of producing successful sports performances. Evidence tends to indicate that this deemphasis of teaching duties is not simply a matter of the coaches' personal preferences. In a survey covering the years 1960–69, I found that every coach who was dismissed or who resigned "under pressure" from California state colleges and universities met his fate in the wake of difficulties directly associated with their coaching responsibilities, for example, a won-lost record adjudged to be inadequate, problems with rebellions among athletes. Not one came under fire because of inadequate performance in the classroom.

At private schools, a coach may or may not have teaching responsibilities. Also, he may or may not have academic credentials equivalent to those required of faculty members belonging to other departments in these institutions. It was found, however, that most head coaches in private schools in California, for instance, possess at least a bachelor's degree and many possess the master's. Few have the educational doctorate or the doctor of philosophy degree.

In many cases the private institution separates physical education and intercollegiate athletics and establishes two distinct departments. The exact academic relevance of departments of intercollegiate athletics is unclear. Courses are listed in the curriculum catalogue under the department heading, and, in general, the course offerings conform to formats found under the headings of academic departments. But courses offered are typically low-credit subjects with an affixed notation such as "This course satisfies the general education requirements for physical education credits," alerting the prospective enrollee that he is exempt from physical-education requirements if he makes the grade in intercollegiate athletics. And, finally, courses offered in the departments of intercollegiate athletics are typically segregated by sex—men only. Intramural activities sponsored by these departments, however, may involve women.

The faculty or, more appropriately, the staffs of departments of intercollegiate athletics are usually perceived as having the lowest academic rating of any departmental membership on campus. Their academic credentials are typically in physical education and characterized primarily by an emphasis upon "methods" courses (Techniques of Teaching Basketball, etc.), and the question as to whether they are actually engaged in "teaching" in the traditional sense has always been a debatable issue in the minds of academic faculty.

The coach at the private school is usually selected for his job by the director of the athletic department in consultation with alumni groups, booster clubs, and other financial backers of the athletic program along with coaches already on the staff. Usually the academic faculty and the institution's administrator merely rubber-stamp the selection. In this case, however, there is no question as to the coach's chief responsibilities.

In professional sports, coaches are typically selected by owners or boards of directors for the commercial enterprise, in consultation with general managers or other knowledgeable persons. Here the coach's single duty is to win. If he does this, little or nothing else matters.

So, though coaches are hired under differing auspices at the various levels of athletic endeavor, it is clear that the main responsibility of any coach is to produce victories. In this sense, winning covers up for a multitude of other possible inadequacies. And if the coach is not winning or not conspicuously moving toward that goal, none of his other attributes are likely to be of any relevance. To this extent, coaches comprise a remarkably homogeneous group due to the pressures common to them all, regardless of the level of their sports involvement.

THE COACHING ROLE

As was stated, the feature most central to the coaching role is not any particular set of duties, but rather the general decision-making responsibilities charged to the coach. But the coaching role is also distinguished by the manner in which decisions are made. The emphasis is on "hard-boiled" rationality and practicality. Most often this approach to decision making comes out when coaches discuss perceived deficiencies in the approaches of others regarding problem solving— particularly those of academic faculties and administrators.

I think college administrators started [the athletic rebellion] by not making decisions, by backing down. Now they're scared to make *any* decisions— hard or soft. It probably originated with the Black problem. But today it's not race. It's kids of all types. They have the power.[10]

[The] faculty's questions showed that they knew nothing about what we were trying to do, why we said things the way we did. The faculty should not judge coaches . . . They don't understand the relationship at all. They give a boy an F and they're through with him. A coach can't do that. We live with our mistakes and decisions. We have a 24-hour responsibility. Faculties can't understand that . . .[11]

Too many administrators are weak in the face of pressure . . . a coach needs an iron clad contract to protect him against his superiors , , , so that a president or who ever is in charge can't lose his guts when the going gets tough . . .[12]

Where do you think undisciplined kids get their support? From the faculty . . . They've always been there, waiting for their chance . . . theorists who want to be political powers. The professor empathizes with the student to establish himself as a good guy . . .[13]

Coaches' criticisms of faculty and administration for hesitancy in decision making and presumed dependence upon theories and idealism rather than rational appraisals of realities are both curious and ironic. For it is precisely the high degree of uncertainty and the dependence upon educated and even "blind" hunches which distinguishes the decision making of coaches in their day-to-day role functions from the decision making of professors and administrators. This high degree of uncertainty coupled with the coach's situation of total accountability for athletic outcomes largely explain why coaches have enjoyed almost absolute decision-making authority.

Since 1967, however, coaches' decisions have been increasingly challenged and some coaches admit quite frankly that the day may not be long off when the "hard-boiled" approach will be a luxury which no

---

[10] Mel Cratsley cited in John Underwood, September 25, p. 70.
[11] Ray Willsey, Ibid., p. 68.
[12] Paul Bryant, Ibid., p. 68.
[13] Anonymous coach, Ibid., p. 70.

coach interested in keeping his job will be able to afford. Holding coaches responsible not just for the "won-lost-tie" outcomes of their decisions, but also for the ethical and professional character and implications of decision-making processes and the decisions themselves, has highlighted the uncertainty intrinsic to the coaching role. Some coaches interpret the challenges to their absolute decision-making authority as a threat to the survival of sport in its present form. For such coaches view all their decisions as relevant to one end—winning.

. . . Sports are in a life and death struggle all of their own . . .
. . . a way out . . . is to give a coach tenure and tell him it doesn't matter if he wins or loses and not to worry about whether his athletes flunk out or not. Either-or. Change the system or let a coach run his shop the way he sees fit. But don't tear him down the middle . . .[14]

The alternatives for handling the uncertainties from the coaches' perspective then are to either alter the character of sport in America or to "let the coach run his shop" autonomously. Coaches, through various athletic governing bodies, have made attempts to insure their autonomy, with or without the good wishes of faculties and administrators.

For instance, in 1969, a new rule was enacted into the NCAA constitution. It appears under "Institutional Aid," article 3, section 1, and states, in effect, that an athlete can get himself and his school into trouble by serious misconduct—conduct serious enough to warrant the coach taking disciplinary action and which involves "manifest disobedience." This includes violations of institutional regulations or "established athletic department rules and policies." Many coaches interpret this rule as shoring up a sagging authority structure. "This new rule will force administrators to support a coach. . . The rule tells us that we don't have to put up with troublemakers anymore . . ."[15]

Others, however, with a broader perspective on contemporary trends in athletics, see a third alternative. Thus, Ogilvie and Tutko state:

. . . We find most coaches uncertain and anxious about the changes taking place in sport . . . They know that they are not fully prepared for their task . . . Many coaches won't be able to stand the strain. Eventually the world of sport is going to take the emphasis off of winning at any cost . . . Inevitably these changes are going to force the least flexible coaches out of the business—perhaps as many as a third of them . . .[16]

---

[14] Dee Andros cited in John Underwood, September 8, p. 30.

[15] Ray Graves, Ibid., p. 31.

[16] Bruce C. Ogilvie and Thomas A. Tutko, "If You Want to Build Character Try Something Else," *Psychology Today* (October 1971), p. 63.

"Winning isn't everything. It's the only thing." Vince Lombardi at the height of his career after his Green Bay Packers beat Oakland Raiders in 1968 Super Bowl. (*San Jose* Mercury-News)

And as *Sports Illustrated* reports, a significant number of coaches who have come under fire have already been "forced out" of the profession.[17]

It is not entirely clear what factors determine the "inflexibility" which is apparently characteristic of many in the coaching profession. Analysis of the coaching role, however, does seem to offer some clues as to both the origins of this inflexibility and its perpetuation.

In American society, it is commonly accepted that the success or failure of an athletic unit depends almost entirely upon the competence or incompetence of its coach. This belief survives even though many of the occurrences which go into the determination of athletic success or

---

[17] See Underwood, September 8, p. 32.

failure are clearly beyond the coach's control. Some circumstances and pivotal incidents—outstanding performances by little-known opposing athletes, poor officiating, injury to key athletes, mental lapses by athletes—are virtually unpredictable. Yet, if a football team loses or if an athlete fails to perform "adequately," the coach involved is perceived as having "failed" also. His work and preparation for the competition are not evaluated by some impartial judge who might arrive at the conclusion that he had done an admirable job even though his athletes failed to win. The basic judgment is that, as a coach, he has failed. And the coach *feels* responsible even though the results of his decisions in many instances are known to be uncertain from the outset. Indeed, every decision that a coach makes is susceptible to Monday-morning quarterbacking. Under the circumstances, it is no accident that coaches attach enormous importance to the traits of confidence and decisiveness.

The coach's need to appear and sound confident and decisive means that he cannot always candidly admit, either to others or to himself, his areas of ignorance or inexpertness. Often this suppression of his uncertainty hinders him when he has to obtain information. He cannot explore the facts and solicit advice too avidly for fear of betraying anxiety or incapacity. Thus, despite the fact that widespread rebellions among athletes are entirely new to the sports realm, among all the coaches commenting on possible remedies for this situation, I know only *one* coach in big-time sport who has stated publicly that he does not know how to cope with this new behavior among athletes.

Other reactions may also result from the atmosphere of uncertainty in which coaches are compelled to make their decisions. The most obvious of these is an effort to control the situation so that uncertainties are minimized. This "control" may assume nonrational forms. Many coaches wear or carry special "lucky charms" or other items, or wear one jacket, one hat, or one pair of sox to every sporting event during the course of a season because they somehow associate winning with their possession of the particular item on their persons.

Coaches also seek to control uncertainties in ways that may be classified as semirational. Here, the attempt is to exercise as much control as is possible, even if the factor controlled has little input, undetermined input, or no input at all into influencing outcomes. Bed checks, uniformity of dress, "moustache" rules all may reflect in part semirational attempts by coaches to control uncertainties.

Attempts to control uncertainty may also be manifest in more rational and organized behavior—for instance, in the establishment of rules governing the recruitment and eligibility of athletes who transfer from one athletic organization to another. These rules are aimed at curtailing the type of "raiding" which made it necessary for Knute

Rockne to twice retrieve Notre Dame's legendary George Gipp—once from the University of Detroit and once from the University of Michigan —where he had been lured by alumni promises of bigger money. Agreements between official organizations governing collegiate sports and those in control of professional sports also stem in part from collegiate coaches' quest for greater security.

Theoretically, coaches may react to strain by avoiding decisions and escaping responsibility. In reality, however, this choice is a practical impossibility. For the coach, *no decision* constitutes *a decision not to act*. If this passive "decision" does not bring positive results, he is nonetheless responsible for the outcome. Hence, for the coach there can be no escape from responsibility through inaction.

But, along with liability for defeats, the coach is also free to claim or accept credit for successes though he may have had only limited control over the factors which determined victory. It is, then, generally felt that, over the long haul, a persistently successful coach is successful primarily because he is competent and efficient in his job; and that a persistently unsuccessful coach is simply incompetent and inefficient in the performance of his role responsibilities.

None are more aware of this situation involving *limited control with complete liability* than coaches themselves. And while the literature indicates that they do not shirk blame or responsibility under these circumstances, they do insist upon a right to "run their own shop": without interference of any kind. Thus, "democracy" in the management of a sports unit is unthinkable to most in the coaching profession. Any perceived "encroachment" on a coach's authority is fought adamantly. Traditionally, when athletes have failed to follow orders or when they have behaved in other ways contrary to the wishes of their coaches, they have simply been disciplined or dismissed without recourse. Administrations have allowed coaches a free hand over the years in making such decisions. Today, however, the coach's authority is being challenged by persons both inside and outside of sport. One result of this has been that coaching associations are finding themselves under pressure to fulfill an unfamiliar role—that of assessing the fairness of treatment accorded coaches whose decisions and behavior toward their athletes have been reviewed by "outsiders." Thus, after a coach was released at the University of Maryland for reasons related to his rapport, or lack of same, with his athletes, Joe Paterno, football coach at Pennsylvania State University stated

. . . I don't know who is right or who is wrong, but I think its the proper function of the Coaches Association to ask Maryland why it let Ward go . . . As an association, we ought to know what happened. If a university fired an

English Professor because his class didn't like the way he was doing things, I know darn well the American Association of University Professors would want to know what happened . . .[18]

In part, then, coaches feel that if they are to be held liable for all outcomes in the sporting realm though they have only limited control of determining factors, reciprocity demands that they must have authority to make any decision they deem necessary to success, whether such decisions appear to observers or even those affected to be directly relevant to coaching responsibilities or not. Recent challenges to their authority have heightened coaches' anxiety about the heretofore ad hoc boundaries on the coach's decision-making rights. Invariably, coaches have emerged from such confrontations appearing authoritarian, "neo-fascistic," and inflexible. The tendency of some critics to imply or to explicitly characterize this demeanor as being *solely* a manifestation of the personality structures or the political attitudes of coaches as a group is both naïve and ungenerous. Under the circumstances, it would seem that coaches would have to be masochists to continually court the very personal disaster of occupational failure while knowing full well that they not only have limited control over the total sum of factors determining their fates, but also that their decision-making authority over those factors which they *can* control is artificially limited. Many coaches view the latter limitations as arbitrary and emergent from either administrators' ignorance of the pressures inherent in the coaching role, administrative "gutlessness" in standing up for authority, or from deliberate attempts to destroy the present character of sport.

The apparent inflexibility of coaches then derives at least in part from the institutionalized demand that they be totally liable for outcomes in a situation wrought with uncertainties.

But several authors indicate that other factors may be involved which relate more directly to the personality structures of the coaches themselves rather than merely being characteristic of contemporary sports activities.

As was stated earlier, most coaches receive their academic training in physical education. In a paper, in part summarizing a study by Gerald Kenyon at the University of Wisconsin, Bruce C. Ogilvie presents some interesting findings on the orientations and perspectives of physical education majors.

. . . Male physical education majors, most of whom are prospective coaches, in contrast to other prospective teachers have a more weakly formulated, somewhat traditionalistic philosophy of education; have a slightly lower social class background; are more dogmatic in their thinking; and tend to possess different social values.

---

[18] Joe Paterno cited in Underwood, September 1, p. 25.

The suggestion here is that physical education majors have more in common with students who are not planning to teach than with those who are. This may explain in part the difficulty that coaches and other physical education-trained personnel allegedly experience in gaining the acceptance of other teachers in the educational hierarchy.

Further, recall Ogilvie and Tutko's statement from an article in *Psychology Today,* cited earlier:

. . . We know that coaches are aggressive people, self-assertive; we know that they are highly organized and ordered; . . . they will listen to others—pay little attention to what others say, but they will listen; and they have fierce psychological endurance. . . . But they are also inflexible in their profession as coaches; they dislike change and experimentation; and they are extremely conservative—politically, socially and attitudinally . . .

Information available in the literature is inconclusive as to whether the demands of the coaching role operate selectively to weed out non-authoritarian-type personalities, or whether experiences while training to become a coach or while fulfilling the coaching role condition people to react in an inflexible manner. The suspicion here is that, most likely, both selectivity and conditioning are influential in this regard, though no hard data are available to support such speculation.

COACH-ATHLETE RELATIONS

Nowhere is evidence of coaches' apparent inflexibility more conspicuous than in relationships between coaches and athletes. Autocratic rule by coaches is more typically the norm than is a pattern of interaction characterized by compromise and democratic interchange. This "dictatorial stance" is perhaps the chief source of conflict and controversy in sport today.

While the demands put upon the coaching role by the character of modern sport clearly provide at least a partial explanation of the overall inflexibility of coaches as a group, if insights are to be gained into the foundations of coach-athlete relations, one must go beyond the role demands believed by coaches to be inherent in specific sports activities. In short, we must consider the institutional functions of sport for the society in addition to the pressures upon the coaching role arising from the nature of specific sports endeavors.

It will be recalled from chapter 5 that, in general, the primary social function of sport is to disseminate and reinforce those values regulating behavior in the secular sphere of life. Reduced to its essence, this means that the institution of sport, like the institutions of the family and education, is engaged to a considerable degree in socialization and social control. As the most directly involved primary-level actor in the sports realm, the athlete is naturally a prime target of socialization and social control efforts. With regard to these functions, the role responsibilities of coaches have been characterized historically as overlapping those of parents—particularly those of father. ("Coaches . . . try to do what a lot of papas haven't done or won't do. . . .")

Beisser, in *The Madness In Sports* speculates that

. . . Based primarily upon his greater physical strength the father in ancient times was hunter, protector and the ultimate authority in his family . . . The traditional father of the Judeo-Christian family has been the strong authoritarian man, master of his home, demanding and expecting obedience from his spouse and children . . . The coming of the Industrial Revolution [meant] that . . . no longer was the man distinct because of his greater physical strength . . . [due to the impact of] machines . . .[19]

Now, since the Industrial Revolution, the roles of men and women in American society have become increasingly less differentiated. Correspondingly, this has given rise to the problem of "role confusion," especially in the case of the young male child.

A boy by the time he enters school may have already acquired a rather undifferentiated view of masculinity and femininity because of the diminishing differences in the roles of mother and father within the home. He may in fact be confused. When he enters school and finds women in the teacher's position of authority, the situation becomes even more complicated. If he identifies with [this authority figure] he assumes feminine traits. If he rejects this authority figure . . . he also rejects education . . .[20]

Sports are viewed by Beisser as representing a cultural "safety valve," an arena in which the historically traditional roles of men can be played. Herein, coaches represent and fill to some degree the functions of the traditional father. The term "the old man," once reserved exclusively for one's father, is today used frequently in reference to coaches.[21] In sport, the father figure is still "stronger" than the "sons," though this is owing more to institutionalized authority than to demonstrated physical superiority. The model of the good coach is the same as the model of the traditional "good father." "He is strong, tough, virile, deserves and expects respect, is not punitive but neither is he easy."

Though "firm discipline" has diminished significantly in the home in American society, it is still expected in sports. The errant athlete received physical punishment in the form of increased physical demands —several laps around the track, additional work on fundamentals, additional calisthenics. Because of his historically unchallenged authority as

---

[19] Arnold Beisser, *The Madness In Sports* (New York: Meredith Publishing Co., 1967), p. 193.

[20] Ibid., p. 198.

[21] Ibid., p. 200.

"father surrogate," the coach has assumed the burden of accountability for the total behavior of his "sons."

> A coach's responsibility is to teach a boy clean thinking, clean living, clean playing, how to get along with other people, to promote close friendship between boys who play and those who don't, and to teach the "Golden Rule" . . . to promote loyalty, respect, and discipline.[22]

The same societal mores which had dictated that the behavior of a child be perceived as a reflection upon the moral integrity of his parents, likewise dictated that a coach be held totally accountable for the behavior of his athletes. He has therefore demanded total authority over his charges as a reciprocal adjustment.

So it appears that the origins of the autocratic relations of the coach to his athletes are directly related to the functions of sport as a social institution. Of course, some idiosyncratic authoritarian personality traits no doubt do also play a part. But when a characteristic such as autocratic rule by coaches is found to be so generally prevalent as to cut across all the various levels of sport and sports activities as well as across class, racial, and religious lines, the more likely determining factor would appear to be some basic characteristic of sport as a social institution.

Nevertheless, a question still remains as to why coaches are so often characterized as "authoritarian" *today*. This label has not always been applied as Beisser observes: "[The coach has] historically been perceived by his athletes as the good father to the team, protecting his boys, advising them, encouraging them . . ."[23]

The contention here is that the negative portrayal of coaches as dictatorial and fascistic which has emanated from the ranks of both athletes and nonathletes alike is in large part symptomatic of strains resulting from value incongruities centering upon relations between the institutional functions of sport and demands created by relatively recent occurrences in the larger society. While these value conflicts have affected roles at all levels of sports involvement, they have had their greatest impact on the roles of coach and athlete. Unquestionably, it has been the role of athlete which has been the most affected of the two. And this in turn has put new pressures upon the coaching role. Let us now pursue the logic underlying the above contention by looking at the development of antagonistic relations between black athletes and white coaches since 1967.

Author and lecturer Louis E. Lomax once stated that the single most significant occurrence on the domestic American scene during the second half of the twentieth century has been the emergence of the

---

[22] J. K. Harper, "Turning Out Winners," *Athletic Journal* 13, no. 5, p. 21.
[23] Beisser, p. 201.

"Negro revolt."[24] While some writers date the onset of the "black civil rights movement" from the moment at which the first African slave jumped overboard from the slave ship rather than be submissively delivered into slavery, most of the public zeal of the movement has developed only since the 1950s. Perhaps the most salient feature of "the movement" over the last two decades has been the extent to which the youth of Afro-American society—particularly the students—have been involved.[25] Though the involvement of young black students was originally based upon rather naïve assumptions, 1966 marked the beginning of a more sophisticated appraisal of perceived obstacles to increasing black freedom and also more sophisticated judgments as to the methods justified in surmounting these. No longer was the achievement of greater freedom defined in terms of controlling the behavior of "racist" individuals, or as a matter of desegregating public accommodations, or of achieving enforcement of voter rights. After assessing the origins of a vast array of perceived arbitrary obstacles to the attainment of rights deemed to be guaranteed by the Constitution and demanded by the ideal values of the society, student leaders redefined the basic problem as "institutionalized racism." Perhaps the chief proponent of this definition was Stokely Carmichael, then chairman of the Student Non-Violent Coordinating Committee. In his writings and speeches, he drew upon the opinions and scholarly works of other authors to support his contention that America, as a society, behaves toward blacks in accordance with "institutionalized" racist values.

What we have discovered, in short is that all of the United States is racist to the extent and the degree that we have refused to admit . . . much less face the tragedy of race in the United States . . . The tragedy . . . that in the United States there is no American dilemma. White Americans are not torn and tortured by the conflict between their devotion to the American Creed and their actual behavior. They are upset . . . to be sure. But what troubles them is not that justice is denied but that the peace is being shattered . . . .[26]

By 1967, the concept of "institutionalized racism" had come to symbolize the by now well-established raison d'etre of the black student movement. It was not coincidental that the organized revolt of athletes in sport initially occurred at around the same time period that institutional racism became generally accepted by black students as the appropriate definition of the problem. Likewise, it was not coincidental

    [24] Louis E. Lomax, Introduction to *The Negro Revolt* (New York: Harper and Row Publishers, 1963), p. xiii.

    [25] Harry Edwards, *Black Students* (New York: Free Press, 1970), p. 3.

    [26] Stokely Carmichael and Charles V. Hamilton, *Black Power* (New York: Vintage Books, 1967), p. 5.

that the general athletic revolt had its origins in the revolt of the black athlete on the predominantly white campus. For here, the black athlete, then, much as he does today, lived a dual life. On the one hand, he is the lauded sports hero, the symbol of achievement and masculine virility in the sports situation. When not engaged in athletic participation, on the other hand, he is a black student. And the two roles seldom mesh complementarily for the Afro-American on the predominantly white campus.

Outside of the athletic arena, the life of the Black athlete on the predominantly white campus is singularly monotonous, lonely, and unrewarding. He may be a big hero on the field or on the court, reveling in the cheers and applause of fans and teammates. But outside of sport, in street clothes, he resumes his status as "just another nigger."[27]

Now, the combination of (1) the black athlete's lack of status consistency on the predominantly white campus and (2) the pressures to conform to heightened demands that all black students become actively involved in black student political activities (which attacked the whole of American social values as being racist), made the revolt of the black athlete practically inevitable. For, due to societal traditions and contemporary developments beyond his control, the black athlete was put in the position of having to choose between a rock and a hard spot. Some white coaches belatedly recognized the black athlete's dilemma, as the following observations made in 1969 by University of Washington basketball coach, Tex Winter, indicate:

. . . The Black athlete is under extreme pressure from Black students and . . . is thereby faced with a dilemma. He can allow the White athletic "Establishment" to impose . . . discipline on him, in which case he is likely to be ostracized by his peer group, or he can refuse to accept these disciplines and gratify the desires of his peer group and jeopardize his athletic career and education. Black Student groups pretend to stand for human rights, while not hesitating to deprive Black athletes of their right to compete. The pressure from his own people is just beginning on the Black athlete. . . .[28]

While one may argue with Winter's assessment as to who properly bears blame for the situation in which the black athlete finds himself, clearly there can be little debate that the dilemma exist.

In order to better understand the dynamics of the black athlete's dilemma, again recall that a major function of sport as a social institution is to socialize persons (primarily athletes) in the secular values of society. Given that sport is permeated with many symbols and beliefs that nominally signal adherence to central American values, the position

---

[27] Edwards, pp. 15–16.
[28] Tex Winter cited in John Underwood, p. 32.

of the black athlete was not an enviable one. His compliance with the role expectations of the athlete left him open to often severe criticism of being supportive of established societal practices and policies. He was seen to be at least passively in political support of "white society." Thus, the black athlete's black student peer group demanded that he, at the very least, manifest the trappings indicative of the new militancy—or else resign himself to being castigated as an "Uncle Tom." The coach, whose role dictates that he be responsible for any behavior thought to be inconsistent with the sports creed, demanded that the black athlete conform to established role expectations. The crisis for the black athlete was heightened by the fact that his peers among black students often provided his sole source of informal social relations outside of his role as athlete. White fraternities have traditionally been closed to all blacks— athletes and nonathletes alike—and massive, informal socializing between blacks and whites in the student populations of predominantly white schools has been and continues to be atypical.

Many black athletes simply adapted to the pressures arising from these conflicting role demands by adhering to traditional athletic expectations. A significant and highly vocal number, however, chose to adopt at least those accoutrements perceived by both black students and the dominant society as indicating empathy with or active involvement in the more militant aspects of the Civil Rights movement. Though many such symbols surely had no intrinsic effect upon an athlete's performance, the coaches' institutionalized responsibility for the total behavior of their charges demanded that they take action to curtail such displays. The "crunch," as it were, typically came when the athlete adopted one or all of the most virile symbols of militancy—the so-called "Afro" hairdo, a moustache, or a beard. Indicative of the pervasiveness of confrontations revolving around these symbols is the fact that in seventy-three different cases from 1967 to 1971, I was contacted by black athletes engaged in open disputes with their coaches in which main "bone of contention" was hair in the form of either "Afros," beards, moustaches, or, not infrequently, all three.

We have here then the avoidance-avoidance alternatives facing persons occupying two roles in sport and caught up in conflicting demands. Neither could ameliorate the pressures without incurring great costs. The coach could not allow the black athlete to wear the "Afro," the moustache, or the beard or sit during the playing of the national anthem because of his perceived accountability for these acts. Yet, the alternative to curtailing such behavior was not attractive either, since, if the athlete refused to alter his behavior, the coach would have to dismiss him from the squad lest his authority be perceived as having been "completely undermined." And no coach likes the prospect of dismissing athletes, given the difficulties of recruiting and the investment in training and team coordination. The black athlete could conform to the dictates and expectations of the coach and be castigated as an "Uncle Tom" by his black student peer group, or he could conform to the demands of the peer group and be dismissed from the team, thus sacrificing a great many years of training and, in many cases, opportunities to move into professional sports as well as to get an education. Most black athletes conformed to the coaches' dictates. Those who did not were dismissed. Under such circumstances, the costs to both the coach and the black athlete were considerable.

Now clearly, in a democracy, nothing is so *intrinsically* degenerate or valuable about a moustache, a beard, or a particular hair style, that the sacrifices incurred by either coaches or athletes could be rationally (that is, *instrumentally*) justified. In their attempts to ameliorate their painful cost-reward ratios, both coaches and athletes harkened back to those creedal or ideological justifications for their respective actions which were acceptable to their respective reference groups. For coaches it was not hair per se which evoked dismissals of black athletes, but the refusal of athletes to obey the coaches orders; it was the threat to authority in general; it was, in short, the violation of the "discipline" component of the dominant sports creed.

. . . I'm not just fighting the hair , , . I'm fighting for a principle. . . . If I thought that it would end with an "Afro" or a beard or a moustache, I wouldn't be so bull-headed. But if they beat you on one issue, they'll keep right on. [I] can't abandon the concepts of training, discipline, team unity and morale. . . . [Athletes] must be willing to subordinate themselves to a greater authority than themselves . . . This may not sound very democratic but I'm not running a democracy, I'm running a team.[29]

Black athletes found psychological amelioration within the context of ideological justifications also. For them, the coaches involved were racist—pure and simple.

The grounds for behavior given by both coaches and athletes, then, on the whole, represented a resort to institutionalized and acceptable justifications. With regard to the coaches' justifications, it has yet to be shown that a "domino theory" is applicable to breaches of discipline by athletes. To assert on the one hand that strict discipline is crucial to the survival of sport and to success in it, as the sports creed does, and, on the other hand, to advocate a domino theory regarding violations of discipline by athletes is to imply that sport survives because all athletes adhere "religiously" to rules of discipline. This implication simply is not true. Even some of the most successful athletes, who have become legendary in the sports lore of America, frequently and

---

[29] Dee Andros cited in Underwood, September 1, p. 23.

habitually violated the rules of discipline laid down by their coaches. Yet the sports activity survived and these athletes made enviable reputations for themselves in sport. For example, no less an athlete than the legendary George Gipp, under the stern tutelage of the great Knute Rockne, was known to have violated discipline upon several occasions. Indeed, Gipp died from pneumonia contracted during a five-day drinking bout in Chicago.[30] Also, the coaches' often-voiced contention that the principle of "subordinating self-interests to a greater cause" was violated when black athletes refused to obey orders to cut their hair or shave is weak. Perhaps no clearer example exists of *adherence* to this principle than the black athlete who sacrifices personal recognition, possible affluence, and an opportunity to achieve an education in the name of what he believes is "dignity, equality, and freedom for the black masses." The problem here seems to be not so much that the athletes failed to live up to this principle, but that they subordinated their personal interests to a "cause" which the coach, given his institutional role responsibilities, could neither condone nor tolerate. It was simply expected that, as coach, he would curtail the offending behavior.

Regarding the black athletes' justifications, the behavior of the white coaches in dismissing black athletes because of their grooming practices can by no means be assumed to have a one-to-one correlation with adherence to racist values. Overt behavior is, as has been stated, not a fully valid basis upon which to assess motivation. The interpretation here is that, on the whole, black athletes labeled coaches as racists in order to ameliorate and help resolve the dilemma of conflicting demands in which they found themselves. Once the definition of a particular coach as a racist was established, the athlete reacted to him as a racist—just as the coach, once having defined the Afro hair style as a discipline problem, reacted to it as such. It was necessary for both parties to resort to the explanations which they put forth in order to justify the respective choices which they felt compelled to make given the alternatives facing them. For the black athlete, the white coach probably became a convenient scapegoat upon which to focus his justification. There is some evidence to support this contention.

Southern black colleges have been conspicuous for their very lack of organized turmoil in the athletic realm despite the fact that the coaches at these schools adhere to the dominant sports creed, are affected by the demands of that creed upon their roles as coaches, and react in very much the same way as white coaches to "violations" by athletes. Consider, for instance, the following statements by Jake Gaither, former head football coach at Florida A. & M.:

---

[30] Wells Twonbly, "College Squeeze Is On," *San Francisco Examiner,* June 14, 1970, Section C, p. 13.

. . . you can't be democratic and run a football team. If you do, you might build character but you won't win. I say you *might* build character, because you may not either. The way I always felt, winning builds more character, because to win you have to learn what it takes, what it means to sacrifice, to be disciplined. To have a goal.

So I started weeding 'em out. We got rid of the troublemakers, and I told my coaches, "start looking 'em over more carefully, be very careful with your screening, do more counseling, be alert for this thing."

Gaither was asked about the styles of the day, the beards, the moustaches, the Afros:

I will tell you this, *Our* boys will be clean-cut. In fact, our whole conference has a regulation now against long hair and whiskers. When I recruit 'em, I tell them I want them to be clean-cut college men, to look like college men, to act like college men, that I want to be proud of them. I tell them, "Boys, you come to me when you're in trouble, when someone in your family is sick, when you need help in your classroom. You come to me. Now *I* have a favor to ask. I don't want to see long, wild-looking hair and I don't want to see any whiskers."

When you get discipline, you get rapport, and you get them both when you're honest, when you're concerned, when you care. You have to be sincere. Kids today want to get into the action, to see how far they can go. When I tell them not to, they know it's not only the football team I'm concerned about, it's their future. They know that long after they've graduated I'll be writing letters for them, helping them get jobs, trying to improve their situations. They *know* I care.[31]

Despite the "weeding out of troublemakers," no group of athletes has publicly charged Jake Gaither with being a racist or even with being an "Uncle Tom." When I visited Florida A. & M. in April of 1971, the athletes there expressed a high regard for him. The differences in black athletes' attitudes toward their respective coaches at black schools and at white schools seems to be determined by two basic factors. First, black athletes' informal social contacts outside of the athletic situation are not restricted to a black minority on the predominanly black campus. There he is part of the numerical majority. If the demands placed upon him by one "clique" of students, whether this clique be political or not, are inconsistent with his role as athlete, he can simply seek out new social contacts which are more complementary to his central source of personal identity. Such alternative contacts have seldom existed at the predominantly white school with its relatively small black population. For the black athlete at the predominantly black school then, there is an escape from incongruous role demands via alternative social contacts. Second, the rhetoric and values of the black student movement has not

---

[31] Jake Gaither cited in Underwood, September 8, p. 37.

As the view through this football mask portrays, many athletes, black and white, consider themselves unjustly "imprisoned" by coaches' restrictions on hair length and styles. (*San Jose* Mercury-News)

been amenable to allowing the black *head* coach or the coach in the *predominantly black social setting* to be used as a scapegoat. While the philosophy of the movement depicted every white person as an "institutionalized racist," hence making them legitimate objects of political attack, it decreed that "every Negro is a potential black man," thus exempting them from the type of political attack suffered by white coaches. Also, to attack the black coach at the predominantly black school would constitute a fundamental contradiction in the "Black Power" philosophy and some major demands of the black sports rebellion—most notably, the demand for more black coaches.

Another piece of evidence consistent with the interpretation that the claimed "racist behavior" of white coaches in the hair issue was primarily an ideological justification is the fact that racism was charged only when a black athlete was dismissed. When white athletes were dismissed *for the same reasons,* black students—athletes and nonathletes alike—paid little attention to the incident. And though the same justifications were forthcoming from the coaches after dismissing white athletes as were expressed when dismissing black athletes, the white athletes attributed these coaches' behavior to "fascistic or authoritarian personal political attitudes." The derivations of the expressed justifications by rebellious white athletes will be discussed in chapter 7. For the moment, I wish simply to suggest that the justifications expressed by both athletes and coaches caught in conflicting role demands are frequently more indicative of attempts to ameliorate "strains" or psychological pressures than of rationally considered analyses of their respective predicaments.

As "rebellions" among black athletes have declined from over a 180 reported in newspapers during the 1968–69 academic year to less than thirty during the first half of the 1971–72 academic year, Afros, moustaches, and even beards in some instances have become increasingly accepted as appropriate for black athletes. Evidently, at the predominantly white school, once the black athlete could diminish peer-group pressures by adopting the symbols of adherence to black student political values—or more accurately once he was *allowed* to—rebellions among black athletes diminished. Another important change has been a relatively great increase in the numbers of blacks in general student populations. Obviously coaches at all the schools where rebellions earlier took place have not now become "nonracist." Likewise, presumably, Afro hair styles are objectively no less a threat to discipline. One factor that has reduced tension has been a relaxation of the coaches' perceived role responsibility to curtail the wearing of Afros, beards, and moustaches —a relaxation due partially to the greater acceptance of these styles in the general society; modeling agencies, television advertisers, and even public agencies have all come to accept Afros on black men and women, as well as beards and moustaches on black men, as legitimate cultural fashions. This change has resulted in the opening of an avenue by which the black athlete could bring two conflicting role demands into harmony. And finally, various kinds of minority-oriented college recruitment programs have brought more black students onto predominantly white college campuses, thus giving black athletes a greater choice in terms of informal associations outside of sport.

Now all of this is not to imply that there is no racism to be confronted by the black athlete within the sports realm. On the contrary, as will be shown in the next chapter, racism is a prime factor in determining both the superiority of black athletic performances over those of whites in sports and the fact that blacks are completely denied access to some roles within the institution of sport.

Neither is the above discussion to be construed to mean that white coaches are not inclined to be racists. For if, as the Kerner Commission and many others have asserted, the United States as a society exhibits strong counter-currents of values" . . . centered around those diverse patterns which have as their common element the ascription of value and privilege to individuals on the basis of race," then this common element must be assumed to be passed down from generation to generation through the socialization processes carried out in dominant white society. It would, therefore, be logical to expect that most if not all whites socialized in this nation will harbor, either consciously or unconsciously, *some* racist values. It cannot, however, be *assumed* that all whites will act out these values in the form of discriminatory behavior toward racial minorities. There are many values in American culture which operate to suppress such urges (e.g., values on democracy, freedom, equality, humanitarianism).[32]

Similarly, it cannot be assumed, even if racial discrimination does take place, that the perpetrator always is acting out of *personal* racist motivations. On a personal level, a coach in particular often has every reason *not* to behave in a racist fashion toward the black athletes under him. It is ultimately upon them that he must depend, at least in part, for his own occupational success. Any assessment of a particular coach as a practicing, conscious racist and antiblack personality should thus be arrived at cautiously. If the characterization of a coach as racist by his black athletes or fascist by his rebelling white athletes on ideological grounds cannot be factually justified, at least it can be understood within the context of the pressures with which many of these athletes find themselves confronted today. Similarly, patterned responses by coaches to unorthodox behavior by athletes should be understood as emerging from conflicting role demands.

It is not only within the sphere of coach-athlete relations, however, that role-related hostility and associated problems emerge. Similar tensions are found in relationships between head coaches, and assistant coaches and academic faculty members. Though these areas of friction have nowhere received public exposure comparable to that focused upon coach-athlete relations, they are nonetheless prevalent and significant.

THE COACH AND THE ACADEMIC COMMUNITY

There is a potential for "natural" tensions to arise between coaching staffs and faculty members affiliated with established academic departments. Though he is a legitimate member of the faculty, the coach's role is unique in the academic community. We have already discussed the

---

[32] Robin M. Williams, Jr., *American Society* (New York: Alfred A. Knopf, 1966), pp. 413–70.

coaches' quasi-paternal responsibilities in relation to the general socialization function of sport as an institution. Although the roles of academic
faculty also encompass some socialization functions, their concern is
with socialization of a specialized kind. Here we must recall that academic education is essentially a formal extension of the informal socialization process which is carried on through the family. Formal education
presumably aims to teach the young those necessary skills and knowledge
that are beyond the capabilities of the institution of the family to teach.
Since the instruction provided by any particular member of an academic
faculty usually focuses upon a specific skill or area of knowledge, the
responsibilities attached to his position are typically explicit, the factors
to be considered in fulfilling these responsibilities are circumscribed and
clear, and his concern with the behavior of students need not go beyond
the appropriateness of their performances relative to specific academic
requirements. This is not to say that no general socialization goes on in
academic courses. On the contrary, a considerable amount of both formal
and informal training in "citizenship" is provided in the classroom. But
the emphasis is, nonetheless, on student achievement with regard to
specific skills or knowledge—mathematics, history, English, sociology,
medicine, law, and so forth. It is here that he passes or fails—regardless
of what his personal political or moral philosophy might be.

Persons in the coaching role on the other hand, are expected, as
the dominant sports creed shows, to concern themselves with a much
more general kind of socialization. The scope of the coach's role responsibilities are much more akin to those of a parent than to those of an
academic instructor. This gives him decision-making responsibilities over
a much greater (and less explicit and circumscribed) area of athlete-
student behavior.

Other differences between the roles of academic faculty members
and coaches have to do with relative visibility of role performance and
the legitimacy of the public's criticism of this performance. Historically,
academic teachers have been characterized as experts, a portrayal supported by the credentials required of occupants of such roles, the technical language associated with their fields of expertise, and depth of the
training required in order to gain access to these positions. The fulfillment of their role responsibilities have typically been carried out within
the classroom or the laboratory. Even when role-related activities have
been publicly visible—such as in the case of survey research activities
among sociologists—the public has not been readily able to assess the
quality of role performance on the basis of what they have seen or been
able to understand. Thus it has become accepted that the sole legitimate
judges of an academic teacher's performance are his peers—the community of scholars. And even after unfavorable judgments by peers it is
possible for the instructor in question to appeal to one of several profes-

sional organizations—such as the AAUP—for further review of his case.

The situation of the coach is different. Perhaps the coach's greatest critic, if not his most significant judge, is the general public, the fans. Though part of his role responsibilities as teacher-coach are fulfilled out of public view, his most significant performance of duties is carried out in full public view. Likewise, no command of technical language or highly abstract and complex knowledge is required to *evaluate* the coaches' performance—only the ability to note wins and losses. It is commonly accepted that one ultimately has only to understand the criteria for determining the victorious as opposed to the losing party in an athletic event to assess the adequacy of a coaches role performance. And the penalties incurred for perceived coaching inadequacy are harsh—even those sanctions that fall short of dismissal.

> The vicissitudes of the coaching profession are well known. The losing coach is subject to the most scurrilous insults, and he and his family may even be threatened with bodily harm . . . Hanging a losing coach in effigy has become a tradition. Success is expected of a coach. If he has a good year, he is merely performing as a good father should. . . . He receives no extra credit . . .[33]

When the coaches must also be classroom teachers, role-related tensions are likely to develop between them and the academic faculty members regarding standards for student achievement. For the academic instructor, if a particular student fails, he simply fails and that is that. For the coach-teacher, however, many of the students are typically either "his own" athletes or athletes on squads coached by his colleagues in the same department. Inadequate academic performance by one of these athlete-students thus creates a severe role conflict. As a teacher, he has a responsibility to give students grades which reflect the adequacy of their academic performances, based upon some equitably applied standard of evaluation. But as a coach he must strive to keep his athletes eligible and, in the interest of departmental harmony and reciprocity, he may well be reluctant to fail athletes under the tutelage of one or more of his colleagues. Traditionally, courses taught by coaches have been termed "mickey mouse," "gut," or given some other label that implies that a student can obtain a high grade with little effort. To the extent that "easy" grading does prevail, it would reflect the coach-teachers tendency to grade in a direction which is supportive of their own and their colleagues efforts to fulfill their prime role responsibilities—those centering around the position of coach.

Now, a lack of understanding of or appreciation for the differences in the roles of academic instructors and coach-teachers have led some authors to be quite critical of coaches. For instance, Jack Scott argues:

---

[33] Beisser, pp. 200–201.

. . . the coach has no right to require an athlete to train by a particular method, just as a professor cannot force a student to study in a particular manner. Whether it be in the classroom or in the athletic arena, unless the student specifically seeks help, the professor or the coach should render judgment only on the level of performance, not on the method of preparation for that performance. A student who gets an "A" on an examination deserves that grade . . . and an athlete who [performs well] should be able to compete . . . If a radical professor dismissed students from his sociology class because they had short hair, the administration would rebuke him immediately. The Deans of Men at most universities feel they do not have the right to regulate students personal appearance, dating habits, or off-campus drinking habits. However, administrators tolerate athletic coaches' suspending students from university [sports activities]—for having long hair . . . "poor" personal appearance, "improper" dating behavior . . . etc.[34]

Though Scott attributes the differences in behavior and treatment of students by coaches as opposed to that accorded them by academic faculty to "authoritarian" traits inherent in the personality structures of coaches, my view is that the chief factors determining such patterned behavior are to be found in the institutionalized role expectations inherent in the position of coach. Obligatory social demands, not just personality tendencies are crucial.

A statement by Ogilvie, cited earlier in this chapter, asserted that

. . . physical education trained personnel . . . are dogmatic in their thinking . . . have more in common with students planning not to teach . . . This may explain in part the difficulties that coaches . . . experience in gaining the acceptance of other teachers in the educational hierarchy . . .

Even if dogmatic and authoritarian personality traits may in part explain the apparent tendency for coaches to be poorly integrated into the faculty community, such an explanation generates questions more significant than the answer it provides. For instance, can it be assumed that "dogmatically conservative" personalities are nowhere to be found among persons who *are* integrated components in the academic faculty community? My experiences as a graduate student at Cornell University and as a professor of sociology at traditionally "radical" University of California at Berkeley seem to indicate that the answer is a resounding "no." At both Berkeley and Cornell, many instructors considered dogmatically conservative in their political opinions and authoritarian in their approaches, both to students and to their disciplines, were held in high esteem by their academic colleagues and were frequently to be found in high elective positions as faculty representatives. Similarly, what of dogmatic and authoritarian *liberals, radicals,* and *revolutionaries?* Does Ogilvie's assertion apply to them also? Well, perhaps the point is made.

---

[34] Jack Scott, *The Athlete Revolution* (New York: Free Press, 1970), pp. 39–40.

If our present sociological knowledge of the consequences of role and status consistency has any merit whatever, the case of "alienation" between coach-teacher and academic faculty is really an example of sentiments generated by divergent status and role expectations within the more general context of the academic community. Indeed, where coaches have "faculty status" it could well be that it is the coaches who are rejecting the academic faculty and not vice-versa. For as a fully integrated component of the community of scholars, the coach would in all likelihood experience a heightening of the dilemmas as to which set of role expectations should have priority—teacher or coach. By interacting primarily with other coaches, the coach can minimize strains resulting from incongruities in role expectations. Within the social circle of coaches he can find support, because each member of the group operates under more or less identical pressures—most of which stem from the coaching responsibility to win in sports, not from the teaching responsibility to perform in a scholarly fashion in the classroom.

Such selectivity in association is contrary to the long-held view that an academic community should be characterized by open and interdisciplinary exchange and interaction among faculty members. But both selectivity of background and the power of in-group reinforcements are dramatized upon those occasions when academic and coaching faculty have debated issues; there frequently has been an all but complete lack of communication. Little wonder that coaches and academic faculties pursue their own distinct responsibilities and tread their separate paths. As coach Robert Ruark put it:

. . . How do you rate [the performance of] a professor? Tough to do. A coach is rated every Saturday afternoon. Win, lose, or tie. He can work as hard as he knows how preparing . . . and then a kid has a headache or the sun gets in his eyes and its a loss. What does he do? . . . If the result is defeat, then there's dejection, . . . but if there's a heaven on earth, its in a locker room after a victory . . .[35]

THE HEAD COACH AND HIS ASSISTANTS

Because of the character of the coaching role, there is an inherent potential for strain between head coaches and their assistants. We have already observed that the head coach historically has had a paternalistic, "father surrogate" role in relation to the athlete. But this role extends beyond the direct coach-athlete relations. The sports organization as a whole is generally conceived of by coaches as being akin to a "family" with the head coach—the ubiquitous "old man"—as patriarch. The endeavors of the athletic "family" are usually portrayed in the sports creed

---

[35] In Underwood, September 8, p. 40.

as a "team effort." This "team effort" refers not just to the efforts of the athletes participating at any given time, but to the input of every person affiliated or identifying with the athletic organization. Thus, fans often state *"we* lost" when their favorite team loses. For, according to the sports creed, they are members of the family, and a loss by "their sports family" affects them deeply and personally.

The hard, autocratic stance of coaches toward their athletes may be softened somewhat by the conception of the sports unit as a family. Family members can be disappointed in one another without hating. A father can punish his son because he wants him to be better rather than because he arbitrarily wishes to hurt him. Similarly, two brothers of the same family can compete against one another with a ferocity which often times exceeds that brought to bear against strangers, but in the face of a common external threat, *"all other things being equal,"* they forget their differences and cooperate toward the accomplishment of a common end. So it is with athletes who are part of the same sports aggregation. They compete for starting assignments, star status, and so forth but when they compete against an opposing sports unit, differences in individual personal goals are at least suppressed. The characterization of sports units as families probably serves an integrative function within sports aggregations—in the coach-athlete and athlete-athlete relations—and also in reducing tension between head coaches and their assistants.

Because the head coach bears complete liability for his unit's outcomes, he has traditionally demanded and received total autonomy with regard to "running his shop." Accordingly, the authority structure in any given sports unit has always been rigid and monarchical. But, whereas the head coach has always been able to openly "discipline" his athletes for failure to follow his directives, this has never been possible with assistant coaches—short of firing them. For it has been thought that the visible disciplining of an assistant coach would essentially place him in the same status relationship with the head coach as exists between the head coach and his athletes. This would tend to undermine the perceived status and authority differences between athletes and assistant coaches. Without such perceived differentials, it is believed, athletes' respect for assistant coaches would diminish. And without the respect of his athletes, the difficulty of any coach's task becomes greatly magnified.

Assistant coaches typically harbor the same aspirations which head coaches had before obtaining their head coach positions—to wit, they aspire to become head coaches. Similarly, they have their own notions about which strategies are best, what coach-athlete relations should be like and so forth. Because these views do not always correspond to the head coaches' ideas, it is inevitable that some tension should emerge between the two.

Out of the assistant's continuing ambition to advance professionally there emerges an ongoing incongruity of interests. On the one hand, it is in the assistant coach's personal professional interests to prove his capabilities by actively devising strategies, giving advice, and otherwise demonstrating his competence. On the other hand, he must follow the directives of the head coach who wields ultimate authority over the team. If the assistant coach argues too fervently for his own suggestions, he is likely to be seen as overly ambitious, uncooperative, or even as a threat to "family" unity and morale. But if he fails to show sufficient creativity, and passively follows the head coach's directives, he may be accused of not shouldering his share of the coaching burden and thus harm his chances of being appointed eventually to a position as a head coach. Most assistant coaches relate to head coaches well within the polar boundaries of being overly aggressive or submissively passive. But, in relation to any given incident or issue, the assistant always runs the risk of erring in one direction or the other.

If participants actually do regard the athletic unit as a "team" or a family, the potential tension in this situation may be lessened or controlled. As family members, assistant coaches and head coaches can disagree without being disagreeable. Inherent deep-seated role conflicts and conflicts of interests can be "explained away" by the ideology. *Loyalty* of the assistant coach to the athletic unit becomes the norm, and supposedly precludes conscious or deliberate encroachment upon the prerogatives of the head coach. The head coach is the "quarterback" calling the signals, and for the good of the whole "team" the assistant coach should not contest his decisions.

THE BLACK ASSISTANT COACH

[White] head coaches tried to quiet the more militant black athletes by hiring black assistant coaches. It wasn't long before the black assistants realized they had been hired for something more than their coaching ability. At the NCAA convention in Washington [in the winter of 1970], a group of 14 black assistant coaches issued a statement that said, "We were hired as buffers and coaches—in that order."[36]

Since 1968, for the black assistant coach at the predominantly white school, the inherent contradictions between role responsibilities and his own personal and professional interests have been more complex than those faced by the white assistant. The nature of this heightened complexity is well illustrated by the situation of black assistants at West Coast institutions. Before 1968, there was not a single major predominantly white college or university on the West Coast which had a black assistant coach, though virtually every one of these schools depended

---

[36] Sandy Padwe, "Big-time College Football Is On The Skids," *Look*, September 22, 1970, p. 26.

heavily upon black athletic talent for sports success. But, as a result of the rebellions among black athletes and their demands that black coaches be hired "who understand our perspectives and can provide us with better counseling," almost every school involved in big-time athletics on the West Coast now has at least one black assistant coach, and many have two or more. But it is precisely the auspices under which these coaches were hired which is in part responsible for the additional problems faced by them. For not only does the black assistant coach have to contend with the usual complications of coach-teacher roles and his assistant coach role but he also has to deal with the pressures from black athletes to stand up on their behalf against the white members of the coaching staff (in many cases, against the entire athletic department).

Now, the black assistant coach at the predominantly white school has much the same aspirations and ambitions as the white assistant coach. He wants to be viewed as neither a representative of and patron for black athletes nor as the athletic department's "head nigger on nigger affairs." If this were not the case, he would perhaps be in the diplomatic corps rather than the coaching profession. As a coach, he wants above all else to be preceived as competent and efficient. He wants to have the respect of his colleagues and the athletes who train under him. But for the black coach, the struggle is particularly hard. The spurt of hiring which brought black assistant coaches into predominantly white schools for the first time *en masse* between 1968 and 1971 stimulated many blacks and whites to expect that there would be some instantaneous and appreciable changes in the athletic milieu for black athletes. But, of course, such expectations alone do not necessarily compel any desired shift in role relationships inside of the sports institution. Indeed, when the black candidate was hired as assistant coach, he assumed the same role relations with the head coach that the white assistant coach maintains. Whatever expectations black athletes may have had about the black assistant coach acting as a buffer between themselves and the head coach soon evaporated. For the black coach was a member of the "family," a "team man," as his role and the sports creed demanded.

At all but one of sixteen West Coast colleges I visited in 1970, black athletes and students privately characterized black assistant coaches working under white head coaches, and all hired since 1968, as "Uncle Toms." Furthermore some white athletes seemed also to have low regard for the black assistant coach. Judging from conversations with over a dozen black coaches at the annual meetings of the California Black Coaches Association in April of 1971, white athletes apparently feel that black coaches were hired primarily to pacify black athletes and students rather than because of actual or anticipated competence as a coach. The relationships between these coaches and white athletes, in the opinion of some black coaches, has taken on a perfunctory quality.

To compensate for the "coldness" of these relationships some coaches seem to have been overly suggestive and encouraging to white athletes, to the point of being regarded as condescending in some cases. Many black athletes, in turn, viewed the behavior of the black assistant coach toward white athletes and his deference to the white head coach as proof positive that he was simply an "Uncle Tom." Although some of the black coaches may have a generalized tendency to be condescending (or even fearful) in close social relations with whites and though some may have been hired for this reason as much as any other, the pattern of perceived "Tomism" seems adequately explained by the strong cross-pressures inevitably generated by the basic situation in which these new coaches found themselves.

Another possible source of the extraordinary problems faced by black assistant coaches lies in the very fact that a coach has a "strong patriarch" status within the athletic unit. The generalized image and social status of Afro-Americans as institutionalized in American society is not supportive of blacks in this status—especially in roles of authority over whites. The situation of black coaches hired since 1968 in professional sports differs significantly from that of their collegiate counterparts.

THE BLACK COACH IN PROFESSIONAL SPORT

It seems reasonably clear that black coaches in professional sports have been accepted in their roles to a much greater extent than their collegiate counterparts.[37] This greater acceptance seems due not to any significant differences between the personalities of collegiate and amateur athletes, but rather to inherent differences between professional and amateur sports, to differences in the auspices under which the collegiate as opposed to the professional coaches were hired, and to certain variations in the role responsibilities assumed by each.

First of all, professional sports teams are considered to be private business enterprises. The owners of these units have, in consonance with the "American business creed," the prerogative of taking whatever risks they deem appropriate, since they bear total financial liability for all outcomes. In contrast, it is. more generally recognized that the amateur or collegiate sports unit is financed largely by philanthropic donations or mandatory assessments on some public. In the case of collegiate sports, this typically means alumni and booster club contributions and mandatory student-body fees. Due to this difference, the owner of a professional sports unit has relatively greater freedom in decision making. There is

---

[37] Valuable information on this point was received in conversations between the author and Bill Russell, the first black coach hired in the National Basketball Association.

thus more latitude for innovations, including relatively radical departures from tradition. Correspondingly, it should not be surprising that the first steps toward breaking down racial segregation in sports came in the professional ranks—with Jackie Robinson's entry into professional baseball in 1947. The freedom granted the entrepreneur by the *business* creed means that the *owner* of a professional sports organization can acceptably make innovations which violate the spirit if not the letter of the *sports* creed. Thus, though the status of blacks in the general society assuredly is not conducive to their being cast in the roles of leader, patriarch, or potential "custodian of the Republic," negative reactions to blacks being cast in leadership roles in professional sports have been muted. Berny Wagner, head track coach at Oregon State University, points up the contrasting restraints under which a collegiate coach operates.

. . . Athletics at most universities are largely paid for and supported by donations from alumni and other interested private parties. The coach must be aware of where the money is coming from and must have a responsibility to the people who are financing the facilities, equipment, travel, athletic financial aid to students, etc. The privilege of having these things does not come free. The alums of another era have their own ideas about what an athlete should look like and how he should behave even if they themselves possibly did not behave this way. It is difficult, perhaps, for a man who competed some years ago when athletes wore short hair to make a substantial donation to a program in which athletes wear beards and long hair. Perhaps the time will come when alums of another era will find it difficult to support athletes with skinned heads or crew cuts . . .[38]

The professional black coaches' relatively greater acceptability was favored by the auspices under which they assumed their positions. In professional sports, though there undoubtedly were some pressures brought to bear, there were no rebellions or boycotts among black athletes such as frequently preceded the hiring of black coaches at the collegiate level. The lack of obvious coercion permitted the black coach to be hired under the presumption, at least, that he was the best man for the job. This presumption tended to dispel lingering suspicions, especially among white athletes, that the black coach might hold his position because of political pressure rather than competence.

Also, the differences in role responsibilities between the black collegiate coach and his professional counterpart made the task in professional sports less complex. For instance, the first three coaches hired in the National Basketball Association (Bill Russell with the Boston Celtics, Lenny Wilkins with the Seattle Supersonics, and Al Attles with the

---

[38] Berny Wagner cited in Jack Scott, *Athletics for Athletes* (Berkeley, Calif.: Other Ways Books, 1969), p. 20.

Golden States Warriors) were all hired as "player-coaches." As athletes, blacks have been acceptable in professional sports since 1947. Thus, by meshing the role of coach and athlete, the initial unacceptability of the Afro-American in the role of head coach was dissipated to some degree. It was not until 1971 that a black was hired as a coach in the NBA without concommitant athlete status: the hiring of Earl Lloyd as coach for the Detroit Pistons. Perhaps it is not coincidental that Lloyd was also the first black coach to become openly embroiled in an incident with a white athlete—Howard Komives—centering upon allegations that Lloyd favored black athletes over whites.[39]

A related fact is that all black coaches hired in the NBA had been performers of star or superstar status with the teams put under their direction in their coaching roles. Thus they brought to their coaching roles a good deal of idiosyncratic credit and charisma which tended to bolster the legitimacy of their appointments from the perspectives of both athletes and the general public.

And, finally, the fact that all were hired to fulfill the role of head coach alleviated the latent tensions they could have experienced as assistant coaches. As head coaches, they made their own decisions with no need to subordinate their interests to the desires of a superior authority. Therefore, many of the situations requiring that they behave in ways which black athletes could interpret as "Toming" seldom developed.

We now conclude our review of the coach. While the portrayal of the role here is by no means complete, main features significant for the present work have received consideration. The materials examined indicate that the behavior of coaches as a group is not due simply to assumed fascist, racist, or authoritarian personality structures as many critics assert. Nor on the other hand, does their behavior stem completely from attitudes of altruistic patriotism unique to the personalities of coaches as many coaches would have us believe. In short, they are neither uniquely "devilish" nor saintly. Rather, as is true with people fulfilling roles in all other spheres of societal life, much of their *patterned* behavior can be explained, or at least understood, in terms of specific role-related responsibilities. In situations where role expectations are noncontradictory and where they are congruent with prevailing values among those affected by decisions made, the coach is least encumbered in reaching his chief objective—developing a winning sports aggregation.

Let us now take a more detailed look at the two component strands of the dominant sports creed and how the coach employs these in the symbolic resolutions of patterned strains.

---

[39] "Howard Komives Apologizes," *Fremont News-Register,* January 4, 1972, p. 13.

THE COACHING ROLE AND THE UTILITY OF THE DOMINANT SPORTS CREED IN THE SYMBOLIC RESOLUTION OF STRAIN

A fundamental origin of strain in the coaching role is an inconsistency in ethical norms. In any sector of society, the institutionalization of behavior is defined by the effective establishment of obligatory social norms, supported by consensual "moral" judgments. Institutional norms can vary in many highly important ways. For present purposes the most relevant lines of variability are those summarized by Parsons in the "pattern variables."[40] The pattern variables refer to *modes of variation* in *standards* guiding the major choices implicit in all social conduct. The polar extremes of variation in such norms are: (1) universalism versus particularism; (2) ascription (qualities) versus achievement (performances); (3) affective neutrality versus affectivity; (4) specificity versus diffuseness; (5) collective interest versus self-interest. The meaning of these distinctions will become apparent as we apply them to the case of institutionalized features of sport.

To the degree that sport is an *instrumental* system of *collective* action focused on tangible *goal attainment*, it will be strongly constrained to move toward emphases on universalism, achievement, affective neutrality, specificity, and collective interest. But the total sport system also contains powerful influences which tend to produce the contrary emphases.

This general feature of inevitable "choice" and "tension" is particularly clear in the instances of two pattern variables: affectivity/neutrality and particularism/universalism. Affective neutrality does not mean *lack* of feeling; rather it means the *restrained expression* of feelings. This affective neutrality pervades the world of sport. The coach who uses his position primarily as a vehicle for expressing his own hostilities, needs for affiliation, and the like, is a "bad coach." Also, the good coach must know when to restrain any expression of feelings of anger or depression —or of great elation or affection. Similarly, the dominant standards applicable to the coach's treatment of athletes are universalistic (quality of performance) rather than particularistic (who he is; how well I like him). The coach who assigns starting roles to athletes based soley on whether he likes or dislikes them is not likely to be considered a good coach and probably will not be successful.

A third pattern variable has a prominent place in sport: collectivity orientation versus individual self-interest orientation. The sports unit rather than an individual person may be the actor that is "self-interested." Thus, a team legitimately may act in its own interests without having to

---

[40] Talcott Parsons, *The Social System* (New York: Basic Books, 1951), pp 58–67.

consider an obligation to protect or advance the interests of some more inclusive collectivity. For example, the head coach at the university has traditionally been expected to pursue the interests of the team without consideration for the larger college community.

The subordination of other concerns (including interest in the totality of an assistant's or an athlete's personal outcomes, problems, and development) to the specific criteria of coaching success unquestionably is a source of anxiety for many coaches. On the one hand, self-interested actions on the part of athletic units are tolerated and supported. "On the other hand, self-interest is considered to be an unworthy goal of action which conflicts with other ethical norms to which American society attaches great importance.[41] Since coaches, as Americans, share the values which support and define as legitimate both sides of the dilemma, the contradictions produce strain for them. Out of the coach's need to ameliorate this dilemma emerges a basic difference in emphasis and focal concern between two components of the dominant sports creed.

The instrumental strand of the sports creed largely affirms the moral priority of a self-interested orientation toward winning. To the coach torn by a conflict in normative expectations, it explains that a hard-hearted dedication to the policies and practices necessary to win in sports, far from being inconsistent with serving the general social welfare, is a prerequisite for the maintenance of the "American way of life." Likewise the instrumental strand of the creed fortifies the coach in his adherence to the *universalistic* ethic in our society.

On the one hand, it extols the virtues of hardheadedness, telling him that if he allows an athlete to participate because he likes him or because the althlete's personality will suffer if he does not participate, he is not being a good coach. On the other hand it communicates to all coaches the fact that each is on his own, that rewards and occupational advancement will come to one only as a result of his own demonstrated competence, and that each will fare as he deserves. Further, the instrumental strand of the sports creed tells the coach that if he does not demand that athletes make sacrifices in the guise of discipline, competitiveness, physical fitness, and mental fitness, he does both them and, more importantly, the society, a gross disservice.

The managerial or pattern-maintenance strand of the sports creed takes the opposite tack. It relieves the coach of the onus of a crass selfishness and self-seeking image by denying that winning is or ought to be the principal or goal of sports involvement. To the coach discomforted by moral questions which he feels may not otherwise be legitimately considered in making decisions in sport, the managerial strand of the creed states "A major part of your responsibility as a coach is to orient

---

[41] Sutton et al., p. 354.

decision making toward actions which are conducive to developing good character, an appreciation for brotherhood, loyalty, the Golden Rule, and the goodness of life in America in the athletes under your guidance. Your athletic unit is not a machine whose sole function is to crank out athletic victories. It is a family of human beings cooperating in a common purpose and it is proper for you to worry about them, their personal problems, and outcomes."

The managerial strand of the sports creed also nominally modifies the definition of personal achievement in the coaching career; as long as athletic victory is the only standard of success, the drive for success conflicts with the moral responsibilities that the managerial strand of the creed recommends. The nominal redefinition of standards for determining occupational success in the managerial strand is the view that a coach be judged not principally by his record of victories as opposed to athletic defeats, but rather by his success in developing athletic programs conducive to turning out high quality *citizens* who will have a positive influence upon the maintenance and betterment of life in the greater society.

These, then, are the two ideological strands of the sports creed which are closely related to strains in sports roles—especially in the case of the coach. At first glance, the values and norms emerging from the managerial strand of the creed may appear more appealing. No doubt the coach would prefer to see himself as presiding with wisdom, justice, and affection over a family of loyal individuals engaged in a common effort, and dedicated to service, rather than as a hard-boiled, self-oriented opportunist striving for occupational achievement. Both components of the creed, however, claim that sport serves the interest of the athlete as well as that of the general society. While the managerial strand is relatively simple and straightforward in this regard, the instrumental strand requires that some rather abstract and complex arguments be accepted. For instance, to support the idea that coaches' demands for discipline and obedience provide a service to the larger society one must be prepared to argue that imposed discipline is inevitably internalized, that it is transferable to behavior beyond the sports context, and that unquestioning obedience to established authority is desirable in society. Nevertheless the instrumental strand of the creed appears to be essential in the total ideology. In the absence of the instrumental component, the managerial part of the creed would leave the coach at sea without a compass. The moral obligations implicit in the managerial prospective are potentially numerous and conflicting. By what standards would a coach measure such diverse obligations? It is not coincidental that the managerial portion of the creed is studded with such vague concepts as "red-blooded character," "Christian principles," "loyalty," and the like. For coaches to define their responsibilities primarily in such terms would be to undertake burdensome potential anxieties. The emphasis on instrumental norms defends the coach against a multitude of troubles. The coach has strong reasons to stress any ideological explanation which defends him against far-ranging moral responsibilities and at the same time exonates him of social indifference. Within this context, the priority given the instrumental strand of the dominant American sports creed by coaches becomes quite understandable.

In sum, the instrumental strand gives a tone of practicality to the sports creed (discipline, physical fitness, mental fitness, and competitiveness), while the managerial strand provides a tone of moral appeal (character development, loyalty, altruism, religiosity, patriotism). It is in the instrumental strand that the coach finds legitimacy for the all-encompassing power and authority he exercises. This basis of legitimacy is intuitively recognized by coaches, a fact made manifest in the uniformity with which *any perceived lack of conformity by athletes or other primary actors to instrumental tenets is labeled as such* and is immediately interpreted by head coaches as a threat to their authority. On the other hand, *any such transgression of expectations relative to the managerial strand of the sports creed is not readily perceived as carrying any intrinsic threat to coaching authority.* Typically disciplinary action against the latter behavior is justified on grounds that interpret these perceived violations of managerial tenets as violations of *instrumental* creedal norms, or on grounds that *label* violations of managerial tenets in some amorphous, negative fashion.

Thus, the tendency of some athletes to adhere to "hippie" life styles—though in fact perceived as indicative of "poor character" by both coaches and the public—is labeled and punished by coaches on the grounds that such behavior constitutes a violation of *discipline*—a tenet of the instrumental strand of the creed. Likewise, assistant coaches and athletes both have been dismissed from athletic squads by head coaches and athletic directors after exhibiting behavior perceived to be in violation of norms of loyalty on grounds of exhibiting behavior "detrimental to team morale" or some other similarily amorphous justification.

The general "service-oriented" thrust of the dominant sports creed allows for the maintenance of sports involvement in a situation where uncontrollable influences and the institutionalized structure of the activity may bring to naught all efforts and preparations. Hence, an honorable defeat is never a total defeat. There is always something achieved as a result of just having been involved in sport—whether as a coach, a participant, or a fan.

The conflicts then which the coach often experiences in dealing with members of his sports unit are not merely between expediency and humane values. He feels that it is his duty to judge people fairly according to their competence (universalism). When coaches have to make hardhearted decisions, these are not without reinforcement of moral norms. The norm of affective discipline in dealing with athletes is closely tied to the norm of universalism, whereby there is a moral responsibility to judge athletes fairly according to their competence and performance. Of course, an exception in this case is the almost categorical exclusion of black athletes from central leadership and control positions. But here too the coach may find, or claim to find, justification in societal counternorms which prescribe the ascription of worth and opportunity to certain categories of people on the basis of perceived racial heritage.

Instrumental role relationships tend to be specific rather than diffuse. But in sport the limits are not easy to define or maintain. Prescribed role relationships between the position of coach and that of athlete limit responsibility on both sides, but this does not mean that informal friendliness is avoided. In fact, coaches' personal involvement with their athletes often sustain these relationships long after the formal coach-athlete role involvement has expired.

Diffuseness, affectivity, and particularism are especially prominent when the coach on recruiting ventures assumes a cheery enthusiasm and friendliness with both the prospective athlete and all associated with him; everyone associated with the athletic organization—from the secretaries in the front office, to leading members of the booster or alumni clubs, to athletes who are already part of the sports aggregation—often behave with first-name, saccharine familiarity and personal regard toward the athlete and anyone who might conceivably influence his decision to join one athletic "family" as opposed to another. Overall, it is frequently claimed and reiterated that the institution of sport itself "serves" the athlete. Thus, assumed friendliness and an emphasis on service have an obvious significance in the initial stages of a developing coach-athlete relationship. But it also gives rise to strain later, when the pseudo-Gemeinschaft meets the hard tests of win-lose criteria of performance. There have been an abundance of comments among athletes about the "shallowness" of friendships with their coaches. "Where self-oriented relationships are clothed in the forms of more intimate relationships, suspicions about sincerity can hardly be avoided."[42] Strains in this area occur on both sides of the relationship. In particular, prospective athletes who are under recruitment must assure themselves that they are not being "taken in"; coaches must avoid disillusionment and disgust over the actions of these athletes, which are often perceived to reflect indecision, immaturity, and a questioning of the coaches' integrity. Because of an awareness of the strains developed during these initial phases of contact between coaches and athletes, many coaches have harkened back to these strains as basic causes of the current rebellions among athletes.[43]

---

[42] Ibid., p. 342.
[43] See Underwood, September 1, p. 29.

Now, given the continual strains experienced, the coach has difficulty keeping a balanced moral judgment of his practices. One consequent direction of reaction is emphasis upon hardhearted pursuit of self-interest. He may become cynical, declaring in his disillusionment that "winning isn't everything, its the only thing." To the extent that reaction in this direction is conducive to ideology, it favors ideology of an "instrumental" sort, rather than that emphasizing the acceptance of moral responsibility. At the opposite extreme, the coach may attempt to invest the whole of the sports sphere with moral dignity and responsibility. The reaction of most coaches is to resort to both the managerial and instrumental components of the dominant sports creed in the resolution of strain.

SOME EXEMPLARY STRAINS IN THE COACHING ROLE AND THEIR RESOLUTION

Self-interest goals versus norms of social responsibility

The accepted standard of coaching success is the ratio of victories achieved as opposed to losses. Given this emphasis upon winning, any coach who aspires to occupational success and achievement in the coaching field must restrict consideration of all factors except those directly relevant to victory. This typically means that he must ignore or minimize interpersonal likes and dislikes, friendships, and moral considerations emerging out of informal relationships which inevitably develop between coaches and others on any athletic squad. Yet strong norms in American society dictate that a person must assume some degree of responsibility for the outcomes of others with whom he establishes close interpersonal relations—especially in situations where autocratic authority is exercised over those with whom such relations are formed. Out of this situation emerges a conflict in demands which is a source of strain for coaches.

Four features of the sports creed constitute patterned reactions to this strain. Chief among these is the emphasis upon *competition*, a theme that finds strong backing in the values of the greater society. This emphasis protects the coach from intrusions of more "moralistic" considerations upon his decision making. The creedal theme so defines competition that it enables the coach to shed moral responsibilities, and at the same time it tells him that he is performing a service for both society and the individual athlete by doing so. If an athlete for whom the coach has developed a particular fondess lacks sufficient talent to participate on the first string, the coach has a ready answer to why the athlete is not and should not be on the starting team. This answer not only serves the coach personally, but it defends him against others who might question his decision not to assign a particular athlete to a starting position. Such questioning typically comes from both athletes and their relatives, friends and other supporters who often construe the assumed friendliness of coach-athlete relations during the recruitment process as involving a moral commitment to favor the athlete in the more formal role involvement.

Due to the "fun-and-games" image of sports, however, an emphasis upon the justice of competition per se is not sufficient to completely ameliorate either the athlete's personal anxieties or the questionings of others. The nagging question still remains "Does the value commitment to competition justify the betrayal of interpersonal moral responsibilities when this competition focuses upon an endeavor as non-serious as a game?" Therefore, it becomes necessary for coaches to impute a value to competitiveness in sport which elevates it to a level of seriousness at least commensurate with the seriousness of moral responsibilities in interpersonal relations. This is accomplished by ascribing to competition in sport a value beyond the instrumental limits of the specific activity itself. In short, competition in sport is claimed to be of value in *preparing the athlete for life,* and in *providing him an opportunity for personal advancement* in the greater society. By so raising the stakes of competition, the coach is able to transcend the nonserious public image of sports activities.

The managerial creedal claim that sports builds *good character* is also of relevance here. This feature of the dominant sports creed provides a basis upon which the coach may maintain friendly relations with unsuccessful athletes and in turn legitimately expect such athletes to exhibit continued favorable attitudes toward him. Although a coach may be able to pacify his own anxieties and the questionings of others over decisions made in the interest of achieving victory, such decisions still can have strongly negative effects on relations between the coach and the unsuccessful athlete. Now clearly, no athletic unit could function well if every coaching decision selecting one player over another resulted in disruption of the latter athlete's relations with his coach. The emphasis upon character development seems to aid in preventing such occurrences. Implicit in the claim that sports participation builds good character is the injunction that losers who do their best within the rules are to be applauded for their efforts and, in turn, they are expected to be "good sports" in the face of their misfortune. A narrow conception of "character" appears inadequate to balance against the seriousness of the consequences for those whose personal aspirations and hopes are dashed by coaching decisions. The concept of character gains greater potency as a basis for reducing tensions when it is broadened beyond sportsmanship to include cleanliness, acceptable grooming, acceptable language, life styles, and other observable traits of behavior defined as indicative of good character in the larger society. The coach reacts with fervor against perceived violations of character-related expectations—whether these be primarily relevant to behavior in the sports realm or to character expectations more germane to life in the greater society. In fact, as behavior which violates traditional societal standards of "good character" has become more and more prevalent, coaches' interpretations of the character expectation have been increasingly oriented toward generalized social definitions rather than to standards restricted to the sport realm per se. In contemporary literature on sport, there appears to be little concern among coaches about any lack of sportsmanship among athletes, but great concern about violations of character expectations pertinent to behavior in the society at large. The latter violations, however, cannot be legitimately reprimanded as such by coaches. Violations of this sort can only be brought under the legitimate jurisdiction of the coach's authority by defining them as violations of "discipline." On the other hand, unsportsman-like conduct can be and is defined and reprimanded as a violation of character expectations. Here we find a major part of the answer to a question asked by many—especially athletes—in the past few years: "Why does the length of hair constitute a discipline problem when it has nothing to do with or any affect upon performance in sports?" Though the answer is complex, it is comprehensible. Out of a coach's attempts to ameliorate potential or actual problems arising from conflicts in role expectations there has emerged an additional responsibility for curtailing behavior defined as a violation of character expectations in the general society. Within the context of his formal role relationships with athletes, the only way that he can reprimand such behavior is to define it as a violation of discipline. When asked to justify this definition, coaches are typically hard put to demonstrate how such behavior is detrimental to sport or to the performance capability of the particular athlete. Not infrequently, therefore, they postulate some "domino-type" explanation which argues, essentially, that, while the specific behavior itself may have little to do with either sport or the athlete's performance it will lead to a general loss of standards. "If I thought it would end with a beard or moustache, I wouldn't be so bullheaded. But if they beat you on one issue, they'll keep right on . . . I can't abandon all my concepts of training and discipline . . ."[44]

Self-interest personal goals versus normative demand for cooperation, flexibility, and unselfishness

In sports aggregations, strains emanating from this incompatibility in value demands are ameliorated through an exaggerated emphasis upon *loyalty*. We need not repeat the earlier discussion of this emphasis relative to the role of assistant coach. An additional point, however, is

---

[44] Dee Andros cited in Underwood, p. 23.

made evident by the claim that sports participation *develops* loyalty. For this claim implies the great seriousness and value of the sacrifices demanded in the name of loyalty to the sports unit. Thus, the athlete who joins a team with the anticipation of filling a prestige position (quarterback, for instance) and is assigned to fill a less glamorous position (say defensive safety) can be assured that the sacrificing of his personal aspirations in the name of loyalty to the team has significance beyond the "fun-and-games" realm of sport. Such behavior is interpreted as a "training experience" which inculcates the athlete with the virtue of loyalty, a virtue which is believed to carry over into his interactions in the greater society.

Aggressiveness and violence versus societal and religious values prescribing altruism

As was pointed out in chapter 3, an inherent characteristic of all sports is aggressive confrontation between opponents, each having the singular goal of dominating the other. In many sports, a marked feature of such confrontation is actual physical violence (e.g., collision sports: football, ice hockey, boxing; and contact sports: basketball, baseball, and wrestling). Now in a society which has a strong value on brotherhood and humanitarianism, those engaged in pursuits which demand confrontation and violence, and which often result in serious injury and, upon occasion, death, undoubtedly experience strain. Coaches in particular are subject to such strains because it is they who devise the strategies and send the athletes into "battle."

One way of dealing with the dilemmas would be to react to the demands of sport in the same fashion that many accept the inevitabilities of war: to wit, "war is hell." While some coaches may in fact react to the above source of strain with a simple "sport is hell" attitude, it is unlikely that such a perspective is prevalent. The image of sports as "fun" activities does not support such an orientation, thus, the seriousness of sport is not perceived to rival that of war. An alternative is to assign altruistic virtues to sports involvement and to relate sport to the system of moral prescriptions upon which American society's altruistic values are founded. In so doing, the coach assures himself and others that, regardless of appearances on the field of athletic competition, athletic competition actually generates appreciation, empathy, and brotherly love and respect for others; that out of physical confrontation and the quest to dominate others emerges an abiding respect for them as fellow human beings. It is perhaps only in the realm of sport that the pursuit of confrontation and physical violence is portrayed as a panacea for the development of brotherhood. Were the implications of this believed relationship valid, then one might even expect that as a result of all the violent confrontations experienced by mankind, the entire world would today constitute one community unified under the pervasive impact of brotherly love. But while the logic of the claimed relationship between sport and altruism may escape one, the possible utility of the claim as a justification is clear.

Unquestioning obedience to authority versus values emphasizing superiority of democracy over autocracy

Coaches, we have emphasized, bear total responsibility for outcomes which they cannot hope to control. Because of the element of stark uncertainty, they would be hard put to actually justify many of the decisions which they make. Yet they have no alternative but to make such decisions. In sport, therefore, there has developed a tradition of coaches' demanding unquestioning obedience to authority. On the other hand, coaches could hardly be products of American society without internalizing to some degree values ascribing virtue to democratic processes. But the realities of sport do not allow them to subject problem situations to resolution via democratic procedures (though some coaches are experimenting in this direction in an attempt to cope with changing orientations among athletes).[45]

One patterned reaction on the part of coaches is to emphasize discipline. While they cannot see themselves instituting democracy on the athletic squad, the second best action to take under the circumstances is to emphasize the relation of sport to the development of discipline—a necessary personal characteristic to life in either a democratic or totalitarian system.

The relevance of discipline is expanded by asserting that it is carried over into activities outside of the sports realm and becomes manifest in athletes' supposed greater self-discipline and respect for rules governing social behavior.

The creedal theme of nationalism is also relevant here. Coaches are highly vulnerable to being cast in an image which would reflect unfavorably upon their beliefs in democracy. One way of countering such vulnerability is to espouse faith in and support for the "American system" and the "American way of life," to endorse unquestioningly established traditions, and to oppose any changes which are perceived to diverge from these traditions. Thus, an athlete who does not stand up for the "Star Spangled Banner" is suspended from the squad; organizations governing sport, and comprised largely of coaches, send athletes to Vietnam to let troops know that they have support at home. By such actions those in positions of control in sport possibly may counter any

---

[45] See Neil Amdur, *The Fifth Down and The Football Revolution* (New York: Coward, McCann and Geoghegan, 1971).

potential "antidemocracy" image and yet maintain their autocratically established policies and practices in the sports realm.[46]

Deliberate physical risk and endangerment versus societal value emphasis on human safety and physical security

In practically all sports—but particularly in contact and collision sports—there is some risk of injury due either to overexertion, collision, or accidental occurrences. The fact that people are maimed, injured, and sometimes even killed in sporting competition is an unintended, but institutionalized, probability. American society, on the other hand, maintains values which stress the importance of human safety and the sacredness of human life.

Coaches seem to react to this dilemma by stressing the physical fitness aspect of the sports creed. Paradoxically, among all the claims of the creed, the contention that sports, as established, develop physical fitness perhaps finds least substantiation in present knowledge. Nonetheless, the expressed belief that sports participation does in fact develop physical fitness may ameliorate the strains centered on the facts of risk and damage.

Similar implications appear in the claim that participation in sports develops fortitude. Under values prevalent in American society, anyone who "without good reason" willfully exposes himself to physical injury would be considered foolish and anyone who might direct a person under his authority to so expose himself would be viewed as less than a wholesome personality. If such exposure takes place in frivolous, fun-and-games activities, perceptions of such behavior as foolhardy would seem almost inevitable. But if exposure is defined as *demonstration of fortitude* or courage, the behavior may become not only acceptable but admirable.

In seventeen athletic events (twelve football and five basketball events) which I viewed in 1971, fortitude or courage was specifically attributed by announcers to specific athletes. In all twelve of the football and three of the basketball events, the athletes cited had engaged in behavior which predictably endangered their physical safety. In the remaining two basketball events, fortitude was attributed to one athlete who was playing despite a severe knee injury and to a second who was participating despite the fact that he had experienced a heart attack while participating in basketball during a previous season.

Intellectual achievement versus physical accomplishment

For coaches in educational institutions, particularly those fulfilling the dual role of coach-teacher, a prime source of strain is the incompatibility of demands to place emphasis upon the intellectual achievement of

---

[46] See Sutton et al., p. 381, for an account of a similar adjustment on the parts of businessmen.

all the students, and the values which dictate, on the other hand, that it is legitimate to do all that is possible to keep his athletes eligible for competition. While many coaches "pressure" other faculty members to grade athletes leniently and give high marks to athletes enrolled in their own classes, the strain of conflicting value expectations is still felt. A frequent reaction of coaches is to attribute intellectual and educational values to sports participation itself. Implicit in the coach's claim that "sports participation is conducive to intellectual achievement" is the comforting assumption that no matter how far "out of line" his actions on behalf of athletes may be in terms of usual academic procedure, he more than compensates through the dutiful fulfillment of his coaching responsibilities.

Significant here also is the claim that sports participation develops mental alertness. This reaction too stems from strain on the coaching role resulting from conflicting values on the one hand legitimizing an emphasis on intellectual development (to the point that there exists an "antiphysical" bias among academics in America) and occupation-related values demanding physical achievement on the other. Over the years, due mostly to the centrality of physical exertion and endangerment to their roles coupled with a cultural antiphysical bias, athletes have been portrayed as a group as being, for want of a better term, "dumb." The caricature of the athlete as "all brawn, no brain" is still quite pervasive. It is unlikely that any individual, whether he be a coach or not, relishes the image of presiding over a stable of mindless zombies. By claiming that sport generates mental alertness, coaches defend themselves against such a portrayal. At the same time, those pursuing their careers in educational institutions are provided additional protection against the strains emanating from their dual roles.

Now the above discussion relating to strains to specific features of the sports creed is by no means exhaustive. However, it is felt to be sufficient to establish the plausibility of our main contention here: to wit, that the patterned behavior of persons holding coaching positions can be meaningfully and objectively understood through analysis of the dominant American sports creed as a system of beliefs allowing for the symbolic resolution of psychological strains intrinsic to the coaching role. To the extent that this proposition is valid, it follows that variation in the emphasis placed upon certain values as opposed to others results primarily from the character of the role-related strains. How the role-related strains experienced by certain categories of *athletic dissenters* are resolved through adherence to the humanitarian and equalitarian sports creeds and how these strains affect the specific value emphases of these creeds will be the subjects of later chapters.

7

The athlete,
black and white

. . . Athletes are the custodians of the concepts of democracy . . .[1]

When athletic rivalries don't mean much, when loyalty to race or to a social cause is more demanding than loyalty to school or team, when the virtues of hardwork and discipline are made to appear suspect and foolish, then the coach is faced with the ultimate threat: the sport he teaches may be irrelevant . . .[2]

. . . one high school football player in California who, playing while high on amphetamines, took a handoff (or thought he did) and then made a brilliant run into the end zone. Unfortunately he was not carrying the ball, and he didn't even realize it because he was so high. The youngster has since committed suicide . . .[3]

IN AMERICA, the overwhelming majority of athletes participating in sports today are either whites or Afro-Americans. Relatively few athletes are of Asian-American, Mexican-American, Native-American (Indian) or other minority group affiliation. While several different explanations have been postulated as to why ethnic groupings other than whites and blacks are so sparsely represented, no systematic investigation as yet has shown conclusively that any single explanation provides a satisfactory answer.

---

[1] Max Rafferty cited in Von Hoffman, "College Sports," *Washington Post,* November 25, 1970, p. B1.

[2] John Underwood, "The Desperate Coach," *Sports Illustrated,* August 25, 1969, p. 75.

[3] Marshall Schwarts, "Drugs, Athletes Still A Problem," *San Francisco Chronicle,* February 15, 1972, pp. 45, 47.

It would seem, however, that *differential value orientations* and a *lack of opportunity to participate* offer the greatest promise as explanatory factors. There is no decisive evidence that capacity for physical achievement differs across ethnic categories. Even in this age where athletes of relatively large physical stature and great weight predominate, athletes of considerably smaller stature still manage to retain their positions year after year even in violently competitive collision sports such as football.

Also, Asian and South American countries yearly produce teams which fare reasonably well in international sporting competition. With the exception of a few sports not emphasized by developed countries, however, they seldom dominate in terms of overall competition. Nonetheless, the gap between developed and developing countries has been perceivably closing. The most significant factor in the increasing capability of developing countries to field winning athletes appears to be increased experience in those sports emphasized by developed countries. Therefore, it seems logical to assume that, in the United States, greater opportunity to participate in sports (and therefore to gain both experience and role models) and greater value congruence with the larger society will bring about an increased frequency of Asian-American, native-American, and Mexican-American representation.

For our purposes here, attention will be focused upon Afro-Americans and whites as the two main "ethnic" groups in American sport. The commonality in role expectations for athletes tends to make them a generally homogeneous group, much as coaches' role characteristics and responsibilities have contributed to a high degree of behavioral and attitudinal homogeneity within their ranks. However, there are some significant differences between the circumstances of male and female athletes as well as between black and white male athletes in sport. In a direct sense, these differences stem from certain institutionalized practices within the sport realm itself. But at a more fundamental level, such differences are strongly influenced by the system of values legitimizing the *ascription* of status to people in the larger society on the basis of sex and race.

Let us first examine the generic athlete role and then analyze the contrasting circumstances of black male athletes as opposed to those of their white male counterparts. Finally, we will take a brief look at the female role in American sport.

THE ATHLETE ROLE IN AMERICAN SPORT

The athlete role in sports is characterized by powerlessness in terms of decision-making authority. It will be recalled from chapter 3 that one of the institutionalized features distinguishing sport from related activities is the degree to which the formality of sport limits the decision-making perogatives of the participant. We have also seen how role responsibilities attached to the position of coach further curtail the athlete's decision-making authority. These institutionalized limitations have contributed to making the role of the athlete a curious mixture of "the best and the worst" of possible life situations. On the one hand, athletes are accorded special treatment almost everywhere; people often treat them with a deference approaching that otherwise reserved for national heroes, esteemed dignitaries, and high public officials. Their opinions are solicited on subjects which they have no special knowledge —the classic example was Joe Louis advising people to vote for a particular candidate when he himself was not voting at all.[4]

On the other hand, athletes are treated as children by those who are in the best possible position to know them well in their central life roles—coaches. From little-league sports up through the professional ranks, the athlete's role is fixated in institutionalized adolescence. George Sauer, former All-Pro flanker for the New York Jets football team who quit football partially because of the nature of the athlete's role, states

. . . It's interesting to go back and listen to the people on the high school level talk about sport programs and how they develop a kid's self-discipline and responsibility. I think the giveaway that most of this stuff being preached on the lower levels is a lie is that when you get to the college and professional levels, the coaches still treat you as an adolescent. They know damn well that you were never given a chance to become responsible or self-disciplined. Even in the pros you are told when to go to bed, when to turn your lights off, when to wake up, when to eat and what to eat. You even have to live and eat together like you were boys in camp. The bad thing about football is that it keeps you in an adolescent stage, and you are kept there by the same people who are telling you that it is teaching you to be a self-disciplined, mature and responsible person. But if you were self-disciplined, mature and responsible, they wouldn't have to treat you like a child.[5]

Athletes are not alone today in bemoaning the adolescent treatment they receive. Tommy Prothro, head coach of the Los Angeles Rams, sees little virtue in imposing some of the controls within his discretion upon the athletes under him. His first move, for instance, upon assuming his position was to abolish the traditionally hallowed curfew, the requirement that athletes be in bed by 11:00 P.M. or be fined.

These are grown men. I didn't have bed checks at UCLA, and these people are more mature than college kids. Besides, bed checks don't do any good.

---

[4] Glenn Dickey, "Can Football Players Be Treated As Adults?" *San Francisco Chronicle,* August 17, 1971, p. 54.

[5] George Sauer, "Sports of the Times: No. 83 and No. 2," *New York Times,* June 7, 1971, p. 7.

You could put a guard outside every door in the dorm and, if a man wanted to get out, he'd get out.

The system is demeaning to all. A 50-year-old coach has to spend half his Saturday nights during football season checking to make sure adult men are in bed by 11 P.M. Garbage collecting has more dignity.[6]

Now, it would seem that coaches have enough decision-making discretion to permit athletes to use their own judgment on such matters as the proper time to go to bed. If most athletes could not learn the simple lesson that keeping late hours is not conducive to high-quality performances, it is doubtful that they would be of much help to the sports unit on the field of action. Yet, the overwhelming majority of coaches stick rigorously to such traditions as curfew, the requirement that athletes eat together, and so forth. Being able to wield control even over "little things" may aid in ameliorating a coach's anxiety over the more crucial aspects of sport which he cannot control. Perhaps, then, coaches can be expected to allow athletes greater freedom on such minor issues as the most appropriate time to go to bed when the coaches feel as *uncomfortable* about having to police athletes during curfew hours as they feel *anxious* about other more significant imponderables indigenous to sport. Whether or not such flexibility would be continued, on the other hand, will depend upon the nature of subsequent outcomes. If their teams win, coaches are likely to continue their flexibility and may even be imitated by other coaches who have shunned the idea of allowing athletes greater discretion. If the athletes under these "flexible" coaches lose, however, they are likely to return to the practice of exercising total control. Such reversals of policy may reflect attempts on the parts of these coaches to allay anxieties about the limited control they wield over those factors which *do* influence athletic outcomes. Further, deviations from traditional practices may, after losses, be used by critics to bolster charges of coaching incompetence. It is quite possible that these two factors played some part in the decision of the Philadelphia head coach who rescinded a policy allowing his team to wear beards and moustaches after the squad had experienced five straight losses during the first half of the 1971 professional football season. In the case of the Prothro policy of no curfew, one astute, though sarcastic, reporter stated:

A lot of people in football will be watching the Prothro experiment very closely. The majority of pro football minds are imitative; some would not know how to blow their noses without watching their colleagues. Anything that works is immediately adopted. If the Rams win without a curfew, a lot of clubs will try that.[7]

---

[6] Tommy Prothro cited in Dickey.

[7] Glenn Dickey.

ROLE CONFLICTS

The restrictions upon the discretion allowed athletes have ramifications not only within the sport sphere. For the athlete, like most other people, fulfills a multiplicity of roles: he may be also a student, a citizen, a husband, and so forth. Not all of those roles are complementary to the central role of athlete. Scott makes the acid comment, for example that "A student who is attempting to be a serious scholar while at the same time trying to participate in athletics will find it to his advantage to be schizophrenic."[8]

Taken literally, this assertion has the unlikely implication that athletes lack the capacity to compartmentalize incongruous role demands; but the figurative thrust of his statement is well taken. The student is encouraged in inquisitiveness, debate, and thorough investigation. The role of athlete, on the other hand, demands obedience to authority. Observe how Ogilvie and Tutko outline some traits they deemed characteristic of "problem athletes."

There is the tendency to be argumentative . . . ; the athlete will use other authorities in an attempt to refute the coach's arguments . . . ; they try to catch the coach making inconsistent statements and to find flaws in his arguments.[9]

Now, undoubtedly, most athletes are able to cope successfully with student and athlete role demands. However, not all of the role incongruities experienced by the athletes are so easily solved. Some roles which make incongruous demands upon an incumbant are constant and always maintain a simultaneous significance and presence. For instance, certain ascribed roles—young person, Afro-American, male, female, and so forth—maintain a saliency throughout all spheres of life. Thus, when an Afro-American becomes an athlete, his new status and his role as an Afro-American are difficult to compartmentalize. He becomes in fact an "Afro-American athlete." When these two roles make contradictory demands, severe adjustment problems arise. Similar problems involving adaptation to role inconsistencies are faced to some degree by all athletes. A basic dilemma confronts athletes today because of incompatible demands arising from their dual roles as young people and as athletes. In his ascribed status as a young person, the athlete has traditionally enjoyed high prestige and influence in the youth culture. The athlete's status caused him no particular problem among young people so long as the values generally shared in youth culture were at least complementary, if not identical, to those characteristic of the sports realm. However, as

---

[8] Scott, p. 41.

[9] Bruce C. Ogilvie and Thomas A. Tutko, *Problem Athletes and How To Handle Them* (London: Pelham Books, 1966), p. 33.

the "apathetic generation" in the 1950s was followed by the "involved generation" in the 1960s, and then by the designation of significant numbers of young people as "hippies," "yippies," "zippies," or simply as "radicals" in the 1970s, the difficulties faced by the athlete have intensified. While not all, or perhaps not even most, of the current generation can be accurately portrayed as members of the counter-culture, a significant highly vocal segment can be so categorized. And it is this segment of the nonathlete youth culture which receives dominant coverage in the media, partly because of sensationalistic endeavors and iconoclastic behavior. To report the *conforming* behavior of nonathlete young people is generally perceived to be analogous to reporting "all the dogs that were not lost" on any given day.

The "radical" life style portrayed as being characteristic of today's young people is expressed in a tendency to question and, in many instances, to rebel against traditional societal values and the policies and practices which are supposedly legitimized by these. Under these circumstances, if the athlete is to maintain status among his peers, he must exhibit at least some of the insignia associated with a questioning or a rejection of established values. But his role in sports demands that he especially unquestioningly endorse through action and word these traditional orientations. Athletes' responses to this dilemma have been diverse. Many have simply "ignored" pressures emanating from the youth culture and have intensified their advocacy of the claimed benefits of sports as a justification for their rejection of current youth culture demands. Some have attempted to fulfill the demands of both sport and the youth culture —the result usually being a lack of complete fulfillment of the expectations attached to either role. This pattern is exemplified by the athlete who becomes disillusioned with sports participation and quits an athletic squad, only to return to sports on his own or be "talked" into returning by his coach. A classic example here is the case of Chip Oliver, former star linebacker with the Oakland Raiders, who gave up sports participation to join a hippie commune only to return a year later to attempt to make the Raider roster.

Increasingly, a third alternative appears to be chosen by athletes— dropping out of sports permanently. If there is one aspect of the "athletic rebellion" which troubles the sports establishment most, it is this apparent willingness of athletes to give up sports participation—ostensibly without remorse. The "trouble" is particularly acute in the collegiate sports establishment. Among young people, students have led the verbal and behavioral assault upon traditional values and practices. As participants in an institution through which traditional values are reinforced, persons involved most directly in sports activities have experienced diminished attention and significance. At the University of Notre Dame, where football once was the supreme campus interest, more than 700 undergraduates gave up their tickets to the 1970 Georgia Tech game to underprivileged children. According to Donald Bouffard, the university's ticket manager, "The students believe a social cause like this is more important than a football game."[10] At Princeton, several thousand freshmen and sophomores stood in line for ten to twelve hours to buy tickets for the football game against Harvard in the 1970 season. "But those who did," reported the president of the senior class, "were but a handful compared to the hordes who stood in line 24–26 hours for football tickets when this year's seniors were freshmen . . ."[11]

It was inevitable that this general skepticism about the value of sports would eventually touch collegiate athletes themselves. For the sacrifices demanded of the amateur athlete by sports are rendered acceptable and palatable in large part because he feels that the athletic experience is worthwhile, a feeling that has traditionally been validated by the prestige, status, and other nonmaterial rewards accorded him by his peers. But, if sports are viewed as being of minor relevance, then the athlete's accomplishments have little significance. Under such circumstances, few rewards accrue and the amateur athlete has little basis upon which to justify his sacrifices or to sustain his continued participation. Before accusations that sports are irrelevant had reached their present levels of apparent acceptance in the youth culture, athletes tended to react strongly against deviations from convention among their peers. As Schafer has observed:

. . . it is often suggested that athletes, partly as a result of influence from their coaches, tend to be more intolerant of "non-conventional" interests, life styles, and political views than most students. This is illustrated by increasingly frequent incidents of conflict at both the high school and college levels in which athletes have physically or verbally attacked hippies or radicals.[12]

While some coaches may, in fact, have prodded their athletes to attack "hippies" and others regarded as deviant or unconventional, such "intolerance" on the part of some athletes perhaps more nearly represents an intuitive attempt to protect their own interests. Unconventional values and political views threaten the athlete because the perceived value of his central life pursuit is predicated almost completely upon the perpetuation of *traditional* societal values. As long as those rejecting established values constituted an insignificant group whose deviate ideals could be dismissed as utopian, fanatical, or simply subversive, the athlete re-

---

[10] Donald Boufford cited in William Sievert, "Cost Burdens, Warring Student Interest Hit Intercollegiate Sports" *Chronicle of Higher Education,* January 25, 1971, p. 1.

[11] In Steven Roberts, "Students are Questioning the Role and Cost of College Athletics," *New York Times,* January 3, 1971, p. 55.

[12] W. E. Schafer, "Some Social Sources and Consequences of Interscholastic Athletics" in G. Kenyon, ed., *Sociology of Sport,* p. 35.

acted by attacking such groups upon occasion—either verbally or physically. In most situations, the athlete was able to simply ignore them. But when many of the dissenting views became visibly manifest in the concerns, life style, and political activities of large portions of the youthful generation, athletes too began to question the worth of many traditional value orientations and thereby the worth of their own pursuits. It seems probable that both the attacks by athletes on cultural and political deviants and the subsequent increasing tendency to give up sports participation stem from perceptions of (1) threats to their highly valued central life pursuits and (2) the diminished value of these pursuits, respectively.

The athlete, then, may be no more "innately intolerant" than other members of the youth culture. Significantly, there have been virtually no cases of professional athletes, who are paid for their sports involvement, attacking hippies.

So, it appears that, more than has traditionally been the case, athletes are quitting sports today because they feel these activities to be "too competitive and dehumanizing"—in line with the philosophical cliches of today's youth culture—or because they, at long last, have accepted the definition of these activities as "irrelevant" and a waste of time. But even those who continue in sports are asking questions. Jay Barry, writing in the Brown University *Alumni Monthly*, states:

. . . This is the era of the anti-hero. It is also the era when there is oft-times more scrimmaging in the dean's office than on the football field. If the coach tried the pull the old "win-one-for-the-Gipper" routine in the scintillating '70's, his athletes would probably reply "Get Serious!"[13]

It seems possible then that the willingness of many athletes today to quit sports may have little to do with any lack of "backbone" or "guts." Much of this apparent readiness to question the value of sports or to quit athletics altogether reflects the institutionalized powerlessness of athletes, the pressures of the times, and, more particularly, conflicting role demands between which there is little middle ground at present.

INSTITUTIONALIZED POWERLESSNESS

The institutionalized powerlessness associated with the role of athlete is directly relevant to a participant's outcomes on the field of action. As the least powerful component of the sports unit, the athlete has little or no input into decisions affecting most of his outcomes, down to and including his physical safety. It apparently is assumed, in both amateur and professional sports, that what is good for sport is good for the athlete.

But the fact that some sports consistently involve high injury risks casts doubt on the assumption. In football, for instance, injury is an

---

[13] Roberts, p. 55.

accepted occupational hazard. Since complete avoidance is practically impossible, the athlete's aim can only be to minimize risk. As football has become technically more efficient, as athletes have become faster and larger, the sport has prospered. But injuries have also increased. In the National Football League, for example, during the first half of the 1971 football season, 114 athletes, or one out of every ten, suffered injuries serious enough to make them miss at least one game. On the New York Jets football team alone, seventeen athletes missed at least one game during this same period due to injury.[14] Many of these injuries are accepted as unavoidable natural risks of the sport, but some are not. Some injuries apparently result from developments considered by those who exercise control in sports to be "good for the game." Seldom have athletes been allowed decision-making authority regarding the advisability of implementing such new developments. They merely live with them once they are implemented.

A case in point involves the widespread installation of synthetic turfs on playing fields for both football and baseball. This "plastic grass" has been lauded as holding the key to success in sports. While its advantages cannot be denied in noncontact sports such as track and field, in contact and collision sports such as baseball and football great doubt has emerged. Many football athletes are extremely unhappy with the plastic turf because they suspect it may be a prime contributor to increased knee and ankle injuries. The NFL Player's Association is so unhappy with the "rug" that it has undertaken to finance experimentation to test the safety of the material as a playing surface. NFL commissioner, Pete Rozelle, and the professional football team owners have not moved very rapidly to check upon the safety of the material. The possible reasons for this slowness are several. Rozelle and the owners are not the persons who have to compete on the plastic surface. And plastic has some obvious economic advantages over regular grass surfaces: low upkeep, minimal grounds crew costs, a relatively low initial outlay ($400,000), and negligible damage to the surface during bad weather.

The manufacturers too are reluctant to listen to the complaints of the athletes. Though they persuaded the owners and the commissioner of the NFL that the turf would provide an added safety factor in football, the manufacturers counter the athletes' suggestions that the plastic surface might be unsafe by arguing that there is no conclusive proof of its *lack* of safety. Herein lies a contradiction recognized by many athletes. If evidence supporting the suspicion that the synthetic turf is *less safe* than natural turf is inconclusive, then the evidence supporting the manufacturers' argument that it is *safer* than natural grass must also be inconclusive.

---

[14] Dick Shaap, on NBC T.V. report "Injuries in Professional Football," November 21, 1971.

But, until the owners and the athletic conferences and associations outlaw plastic turfs, all athletes can really do is live with them or quit sport. Both baseball and football athletes have complained not only about suspected turf-related injuries, but also of the heat radiated from the turf (actually measured at 138 degrees on warm days). Until a strike over unsafe working conditions is called or the turf is outlawed, they can only try to protect themselves as best they can—usually meaning merely more elbow and knee pads.

Other factors also peril an athlete's safety. For instance, although it is not generally known, many of the fields used in both collegiate and professional sports are not safe. All fields look smooth and pretty from the spectator seats and on a television screen. However, even some of the newest fields are dangerous. While collegiate athletes have no organized voice to speak out against such conditions, professional athletes' player associations have begun to at least express concern about them. For instance the NFL Players Association defines dangerous fields as those having brick or concrete walls near end zones, thorny bushes, baseball dugouts, poor drainage, and unpadded railings and bandstands overlooking the "braking space" behind goal posts. Evidence that danger to the athlete is posed by the features is abundant. Note the nearly incredible series of events in the case of Kermit Alexander of the Los Angeles Rams, who skidded into a big bush on the new Atlanta field and was knocked unconscious. The officials pulled him out by the heels. The NFL Players Association demanded that the bush be removed. The owners and promoters associated with the Atlanta Falcons, however, stated that the bush was decorative and too expensive to remove, at the cost of two hundred dollars. The bush is still in place. Lance Alworth, all-league receiver of the Dallas Cowboys, hit a concrete wall behind the goal posts in the new Oakland coliseum sports complex and reportedly was dizzy for three days afterwards. Despite athletes' complaints, the wall remains. Two Los Angeles Rams athletes, running pass patterns, have fallen into exposed baseball dugouts at Baltimore's Memorial Stadium. The dugouts remain as exposed as ever.

Another factor which athletes are virtually powerless to control though it affects both their physical safety and psychological well-being is methods by which sports events are covered using television.

"They roll those units right up to the bench like they owned the place," says Timmy Brown, recently of the Eagles and Colts and now a Hollywood and television actor. "In 1969 I ran out of bounds and hit a camera truck so hard I was limping for a week. We think TV should pull back and use long-range shots." Taking on the censor's role, some athletes also want tight bench shots reduced. Closeups of players who are hurt and retching or thrashing about are considered much too hard upon their watching wives, children, and parents. Then, too, there's considerable personal and professional pride involved given the image of athletes in the minds of the American public.

And what about, asks Minnesota Viking Alan Page, those commercial timeouts when you're about to score and don't want your momentum broken? Here Page brings up an old dispute in professional football, dating to a time when producers called for commercial "breaks" at will. CBS, ABC, and NBC insist that the practice ended long ago. NFL executive director, Jim Kensil, says, "We regard a team's rhythm as important. We have a continuity-of-play agreement with broadcasters that holds breaks to routine changes of ball-possession and other convenient moments." This is fine, except that Page, and others, don't quite believe it. Page asks: "How come, then, in our Green Bay game last year —at about 20 below zero—they stopped us deep in Packer territory?"

To date, only one of the athletes' complaints regarding television coverage has been heeded, that regarding benchside interviews. Athletes also view the matter of travel to games as a growing problem. In professional football, team flights number upward of 200 per season—in good and bad weather. In the NFL, expansion to twenty-six cities wasn't the athletes' idea, and, faced with plans to eventually add franchises in Montreal, Honolulu, Seattle, Toronto, Vancouver, B.C., and perhaps Memphis and Mexico City, their necks swell. "It's a circus already," growl some older athletes. "Some day, like Wichita State and Marshall University, we'll lose a plane and a whole squad."

Quietly, the NFL has established a disaster plan—one that doesn't *lift* anybody's spirits. It calls for restocking of a team from league rosters if fewer than fifteen men are lost in a crash; beyond fifteen, the stricken team's schedule is canceled.

The travel situation for both professional and amateur athletes remains poor and, in the opinion of many of them, is getting worse. Though professional football has plans for further expansion and collegiate football has already expanded its regular ten-game schedule to eleven games, the travel problems faced by football athletes are minimal compared to those faced by athletes participating in baseball and basketball. And schedules are being expanded in these sports too. Thus, in all likelihood the travel situation for the athlete in all branches of sport will indeed worsen still further.[15]

Finally, there is the problem of drug use in sports, considered by many both inside and outside of the sports realm to be the greatest hazard of all to the well-being of the athlete. As a result of the prevalence of drug use in sport, there has emerged a common joke among athletes— "It's not how you prepare for the game but who your pharmacist is."

---

[15] See Al Stump, "Ralph Nader, Where Are You" in *TV Guide* October 30, 1971, p. 14, for a brief analysis of athlete grievances in professional football.

The institutionalized legitimacy of drug use in sport poses its greatest threat to the athlete though he has the least power to curtail the practice. He is caught in a dilemma: he often feels that he must either take drugs to maintain his competitive position or be eliminated from or voluntarily drop out of athletic competition. It is likely that any solution to drug problems in sport would require that every athletic organization and association, first, admit that a problem exists as a serious threat to both athletes and sport, then endorse a policy of frequent scheduled and unscheduled tests of athletes and other sports personnel for drug use. Reluctance to take such steps may be, in part, due to the idea that any admission of widespread drug use by athletes would be inconsistent with the tenets of the sports creed; therefore, to advocate that these participants be subjected to regular and frequent tests for drugs would be almost as unthinkable and shocking as to demand that "rabbit tests" be regularly administered to nuns. Again, one encounters the real possibility that the sports creed functions as a two-edged sword where athletes are concerned: on the one hand it is the basis of his high status and position in American society; on the other the creed operates to imprison the athlete in a situation not entirely of his own making, and over which he has little control.

Let us turn our attention now to certain contrasts between the situations of black and white athletes in American sport.

THE ATHLETE IN BLACK AND WHITE

The social realities of race in the United States crucially affect the Afro-American (or black) athlete's position in sport. Together with the sports creed, these realities help to clarify some otherwise strange and puzzling facts—such as the dominant representation of blacks in some sports in contrast to virtual discriminatory exclusion from others. To understand such cryptic social facts first requires analysis of the significance of sport in black society.

Students of the Afro-American pilgrimage in America have long recognized that blacks, for the most part, face the possibility of becoming a more or less permanent lower-class stratum.[16] Wilhelm, among others, has quite vividly pointed out how the usual explanations of how European immigrants overcame difficulties and subsequently rise up the stratification scale are not applicable in the case of Afro-Americans.[17] One of the primary factors contributing to the stagnation of blacks in the strata of the social structure has been economic discrimination. In the United

[16] Hubert M. Blalock, *Toward a Theory of Minority Group Relations*, (New York: John Wiley and Sons, Inc., 1967), p. 92.

[17] Sidney M. Wilhelm, *Who Needs the Negro?* (New York: Doubleday-Anchor Books, 1971), pp. 15–47.

States, "race" has long been *the* basic factor in determining the priority of access to valued goods and services on the part of blacks. As a highly visible minority with an initially low occupational status, blacks face a competitive disadvantage as compared with other groups in the labor force. An Afro-American can expect to be hired in the least desirable position unless he possesses some compensatory resources. Blalock distinguishes two types of such resources: competitive and pressure resources.[18] On the one hand, the black person may possess certain special skills. On the other, he may be able to initiate punitive action toward a prospective employer should he fail to hire minority members, regardless of performance or cost considerations. For instance, the employer may lose minority customers or he may undergo public censure for failure to comply with fair employment laws. Accordingly, most pressure group resources possessed by blacks diminish in value once a small but highly visible token minority force has been hired, and, as a result, occupational opportunities become stabilized at a point where there are a sufficient number of such token employees to relieve pressure on the employer.

If the minority possesses competitive resources, however, *an unstable equilibrium situation is likely to prevail once the initial resistance to employment has been broken.* It is this fact which is a key to understanding the significance of sport in black society.

Perhaps the most obvious feature of sport in America is its competitiveness, not only among athletes but also among sports organizations for the services of athletes possessing demonstrated skills. The results of these skills are capable of being precisely measured—batting averages, yards gained, points scored. It is also the case that high-quality performances by athletes work to the advantage of all members of the athletic "family." Thus, though intraunit tensions and rivalries may emerge, the fact that all "family" members share in the rewards of victory tends to contribute toward muting the negative impact of these tensions and rivalries on overt group solidarity. Blalock observes that ". . . no matter how envious they might be, [athletes] must outwardly show respect for . . . the star . . ."[19]

Because of the authority relations within American sport, control being vested in the autocratic authority of the head coach, there is no major hierarchy of positions such that, if the top man is replaced, everyone moves up one notch. In effect, this means that an athlete theoretically gets ahead on the basis of his own performance. Outstanding achievement in sports leads to high prestige, increased income in some cases, and public acclaim. But such achievement does not lead to increased

---

[18] Blalock, p. 93.
[19] Ibid., p. 95.

formal power over fellow athletes since all authority is typically vested in the coaching role.

Similarly, the *quality* of one's performance is dependent only to a slight degree upon the nature of informal interpersonal relationships that develop within an athletic family, since sports activities are pursued within the context of formal rules and role relationships. The quarterback may not like the flanker, but if the play says that he must pass him the football, then pass him the football he must, unless some circumstances arise which legitimates his not doing so. And, finally, women are excluded both from sports competition with men and from instrumental positions in sports hierarchies necessitating more or less constant interaction with athletes.

Now, the socioeconomic status of Blacks in America and the above-mentioned characteristics of most sports have combined to make sports participation a particularly attractive and promising potentiality for many males in Afro-American society. One result has been the development of an extremely high value on athletic proficiency in the black subculture. This should not be surprising, in view of the lack of opportunities to obtain alternative high-prestige and reward positions in other sectors of societal life. In the role of athlete, the Afro-American can surmount many of the obstacles confronting him in any attempt to achieve social and economic mobility via other avenue.

The white phobia (which is becoming increasingly characteristic of black society as well) over the potential for interracial sexual contacts growing out of the closeness required by formal role relationships has little relevance in endeavors from which women are categorically excluded.

The fact that the entire athletic unit benefits from a high-quality performance by any one member also works in the favor of the Afro-American. For once he is part of the family, he is not dealing in the "zero-sum" game to the extent typical of competitive interaction in other realms. Thus, when the black athlete excels in his role, whites and all other team members, rather than being proportionately denied benefits, share immediately in the resulting rewards. Likewise with the factor of power. While a black athlete may increase his own prestige through an exceptional performance, he does not thereby acquire formal power or authority over his athlete peers. At no point does a black athlete's performance alter his formal power relationships with his teammates or his coaches.

A related factor has to do with the institutionalized feature of deference. In sport there has traditionally been little chance that a black athlete will assume an "uppity" demeanor toward his superiors because extreme deference to authority is institutionalized into the role of athlete. Also, the public nature of sports performances and the fact that performance can be easily and objectively appraised frees the black athlete to a greater extent than in any other realm, from his traditional vulnerability to arbitrary and biased evaluations of role performance.

In most sports, there is no need for the athlete to make extensive capital outlays for equipment, facilities, and the like in order to compete successfully. Likewise, the achievement of academic credentials, professional licenses, or certificates never enter into any evaluation of athletic performance.

The above factors in combination with the heated competition among sports organizations for top athletic talent have made participation in sports an avenue of potentially rapid socioeconomic mobility for Afro-Americans—an avenue which is virtually unrivaled today. It is this situation which accounts for the disproportionate representation of blacks in American sports. Team sports eliciting the high rewards in public acclaim, financial advancement, and prestige have been particularly attractive to blacks. Thus, as Olsen notes:

. . . The degree to which Negroes have moved into pro sports is astonishing. More than half the players in the National Basketball Association are Negroes —as were eight of the 10 starters in the last NBA All-Star Game. A quarter of the players in the National Football League are Negroes, and the 1967 NFL team was 40 per cent black. Nearly 25 per cent of all players in major league baseball are American Negroes, and here too a disproportionate number of the stars are not white. For example, of the top ten hitters in the National League for the 1967 season, only one was a Caucasian.[20]

But this extensive participation does not mean that sport now is free of discrimination. On the contrary:

. . . sport seems to mirror American life at large, in that, integration has been very slow, and where it has been rather fully achieved there remain many forms of discimination other than that of segregation.

Professional baseball is a good example of how slowly the process of integration takes place. Many herald 1947 as the year "the color line was broken" with the entrance of Jackie Robinson into major league baseball. But, ten years later there were only a dozen [black] players in the National League and as late as 1960, there were only half dozen black athletes in the American League.[21]

Black coaches have become visibly numerous in the mainstream of big-time American sport only since the onset of the revolt of the black athlete in 1967. In the professional ranks, the hiring of Bill Russell as athlete-head coach came nineteen years after the first Afro-American

---

[20] Jack Olsen, *The Black Athlete: A Shameful Story* (New York: Time, Inc., 1968), p. 170.

[21] John W. Loy and Joseph F. McElvogue, "Racial Segregation in American Sport", *International Review of Sport Sociology* 5 (1970): 15.

entered major league professional sports. Thus, blacks are over represented as athletes at most levels of sports involvement' while they have
just recently begun to appear in the coaching ranks of big-time sports.
The underlying reasons become obvious when we recall the role responsibilities attached to the position of coach. It is clear that many of
the features of sport mentioned above that hold special advantages for
the Afro-American in the role of athlete are canceled out in the case of
the autocratic patriarch role attached to the coaching position.

The disproportionate numbers and high visibility of black athletes
in sports—and the prestige, wealth, and status they receive as a result
of their proficiency—could be taken by many as evidence that Afro-
American society as a whole is advancing in terms of equality of opportunity. For Afro-Americans, it might be thought, the vehicle for advancement is sport rather than one of the avenues used historically by
the European immigrants, such as crime, political power, or the "cor-
nering" of certain occupational fields. But what is often overlooked in
this analogy is that it was necessary for European immigrants to gain
controlling influence in such areas as crime, politics, and so forth in order
to utilize these as vehicles of economic mobility. It appears that under
present social and political arrangements blacks are not likely to gain
controlling influence over sport.

BLACK ATHLETIC SUPERIORITY

The factors underlying black athletes' domination of those sports
to which they have been granted more or less "open access" and the
wider implications of this phenomena have been the focus of a tremendous amount of informal inquiry since the early 1960s. Only recently,
however, has this situation received any systematic investigation. Postulated "explanations" have ranged from Afro-Americans' supposed racially
linked, innate physical superiority, to some presumed link between superiority of athletic performance and matriarchal family structure. These
sweeping ad hoc interpretations are widely held and thus will be the
focus of examination here.

It is usually conceded today by serious analysts that the performances of black athletes are generally superior to those of white athletes.
Pascal and Rapping, for instance, state that in professional baseball,
"position by position, black players in the big leagues tend to out-perform
their White counterparts on the basis of objective measurements. This
holds for veterans and rookies alike."[22] Evidence consistent with the
contention that black athletes are superior performers in sports is abundant. Consider the following:

1. In professional basketball, three of the five athletes named to

---

[22] A. H. Pascal and L. A. Rapping, "Racial Discrimination in Professional
Baseball," Rand Corporation, January, 1970.

the 1969–70 all-NBA team were black, as were all five of the athletes named to the all-rookie team. Blacks have won the league's most-valued-player award twelve times in the past thirteen seasons.

2. In professional football, all four of the 1969 rookie of the year awards for offense and defense were won by black athletes; 165 of the first 250 athletes drafted into professional football in 1971 were black.

3. In professional baseball, black men have won the National League's MVP award sixteen times in the past twenty-two seasons.

4. Today there are 150 blacks out of 600 athletes in major-league baseball, 330 blacks out of 1,040 athletes in professional football, and 153 black athletes out of 280 in professional basketball. Of the athletes on professional sports 1969–70 all-star rosters 36 percent in baseball were black, 44 percent in football, and blacks comprised 63 percent of all-star talent in basketball. Boxing has practically become an all-black game of musical chairs in the high-prestige heavier weight divisions and championships.[23] Throughout all levels of athletic competition, a similar pattern of black domination prevails wherever blacks have access in large numbers of the various sports endeavors.

Clearly there is no doubt that black America is contributing much more than its 11 percent share of athletes and star-status performers to sports. However, there is room for considerable debate over the identity and character of the factors that have determined black athletic prowess and contributed to its perpetuation.

The first argument to be explored is the matriarchy explanation of black athletic superiority. It essentially holds that black athletic superiority is due to the development of more intensely positive relationships between athletes from matriarchal family structures and their coaches than between athletes from families where traditional father figures are present and their coaches. It is assumed that black society is characterized by the matriarchal family structure and that, therefore, more black than white athletes will be from matriarchal families. Hence, black athletes more often will have need for a substitute father figure; this need will lead to a more intense relationship between the black athlete and coach than between the coach and the white athlete; the end product will be superior performances by the black athlete.

There are a number of problems in this line of thought. First, only an estimated one-third of all black families are "matriarchal"; the norm in black society is not matriarchy but the more traditional two-parent family structure.[24] Furthermore, even when there is no person in the home fulfilling the traditional father role, the male child does not neces-

---

[23] For a complete listing of major black athletic accomplishments in the sports pursued in America, see Harry Edwards, *The Revolt of the Black Athlete* (New York: Free Press, 1970), Appendix C.

[24] Hyland Lewis and E. Herzog, "The Family: Resources for Change" in Bracey, ed., *Black Matriarchy: Myth or Reality* (Belmont, Calif.: Wadsworth Publishing Co., 1970), p. 3.

sarily lack a *father figure* in black society. Even though female-headed families are proportionately more frequent in black than in white society, there are more white families headed by females, in absolute numbers. Under these circumstances, in the competitive situation existing in American sport, one would expect to find the performances of black and white athletes more or less comparable since the favorable impact of the female-headed or "matriarchical" families would have resulted in selectively eliminating both black and white athletes from two-parent families. This is not the case. Blacks dominate sports even more today than in years past. In short, the gap between black and white athletic performances is becoming greater, overall, by any objective measure (time, distance, height, points scored, rebounds taken, yards gained, etc.) while there is no discernible evidence of increase in black "matriarchies."

Relevant also is the fact that the spectre of race diminishes the potential positive relationship between coach and athlete. The significance of racial heritage is so strong in America that, for the most part, only where the coach and the team members are *all of the same* racial category (all black or all white) are coach-athlete relations likely to be free of racial connotations and antagonisms. In the highly competitive world of sports, where failure to live up to aspirations is translated into personal inadequacy and unworthiness, blaming one's failure, in part, on the advice and training methods of a racist coach lightens the burden of guilt on the black athlete. White athletes under the supervision of a black coach often experiences a similar athlete-coach relationship. While the black athlete on the integrated team suspects racism on the part of the white coach and Uncle Tomism on the part of the black coach, the white athlete on the integrated team suspects favoritism on the part of the white coach ("To start five blacks on a basketball team at an integrated school, he must just love Negroes") and favoritism and incompetence from the black coach.

Regardless of whether an athlete is from a matriarchal family or whether he is black or white, the character of athletic competition does not readily lead to the development of actual close family-type ties either among athletes or between athletes and coaches of different races —regardless of the façade. In the world of sports as in the general society, except in those instances where they are forced into close interaction and cooperation through formal role relationships and responsibilities, blacks and whites go their separate ways.

Consider also that all-black athletic aggregations are not considered part of big-time sports. The result is that many superior Black athletes go undetected and unrecognized. Ironically, superior black athletes are recognized on a national level only after outstanding performances in *integrated* situations. Under any circumstances, the matriarchal explanation of black athletic superiority is irrelevant in both all-white and all-black athletic situations. And, finally, it has yet to be shown that an intensely positive coach-athlete relationship is a guarantee even of athletic success, much less athletic superiority.

The second explanation supposes that there are certain race-linked physical characteristics found exclusively in the black population in America. The myth of the Afro-American's racially determined, inherent physical and athletic superiority rivals the old myth of black sexual superiority. While both myths are well established in the "Negro lore" and folk beliefs of American society, in recent years the former has been subject to increasing emphasis due to the overwhelming and increasingly disproportionate representation of Blacks in high-prestige athlete positions.

But seldom has the thesis of race-linked black athletic prowess been subject to so explicit a formulation as in the January 18, 1971, issue of *Sports Illustrated*. In an article entitled "An Assessment of Black Is Best," by Martin Kane, one of the magazine's senior editors, several arguments are detailed, discussed, and affirmed by a number of medical scientists, athletic researchers, coaches, and black athletes. In essence, the article constitutes an attempt to develop a logical and scientifically defensible foundation for the assertion that black athletic superiority in sports is due to characteristics of the black population in America not generally found in the white population.

In attempting to explain Black athletic superiority, Kane invokes three major categories of factors: (1) race-linked physical and physiological characteristics, (2) race-linked psychological traits, and (3) racially specific historical occurrences. Let us consider these categories.

RACE-LINKED PHYSICAL CHARACTERISTICS

Kane's attempt to show these factors as major contributors to Black athletic superiority suffers from two basic defects—one methodological, the other arising from a dependence upon scientifically debatable assumptions and presumptions concerning differences among the "races" of men.

The methodological problem is salient in virtually every case of "scientific" evidence presented in support of a physical or physiological basis for black athletic superiority: in no case was there any indication that the data came from a random sample of the black population. The article indicates that data, for the most part, were taken from black athletes of already proven excellence or from blacks who were available due to other circumstances reflecting uncontrolled selectivity. Thus, the generalization of the research findings to the black population as a whole —even assuming the findings to be valid—constitutes an error.

Substantive considerations also cast doubt on Kane's argument, which appears within a context that assumed the biological and genetic validity of delineating human populations into "races." This approach does not give adequate consideration to the fact that human breeding populations are determined to a great extent by cultural circumstances, social and political conditions, as well as the factors of opportunity, propinquity, and convenience, and not merely by similarity in morphological characteristics. To assume the genetic validity of the concept of race implies, for example, that, as a population, Afro-Americans have bred endogamously and have maintained their original genotypical traits, except for occasional mutations. Strictly speaking, this is nonsense.

There are widely varying conceptions among human biologists and anthropologists concerning criteria for defining race and for identifying the races of man. These views range all the way from the denial that genetically discernible races exist at all to those which delineate specific "races" of man, numbering from two or three to a great many categories. Once a given biologist or anthropologist has settled upon a definition which suits him, he discovers that there is relatively little that he can do with his "races" other than list them. For, typically, there has been little success in any effort to derive consistent patterns of valid relationships between racial categories and meaningful social, intellectual, or physical capabilities. Hence, Kane treads upon ground of dubious solidity from the moment his argument assumes that proven and scientifically valid delineations of racial groupings exist at all.

With regard to physical traits supposedly characteristic of black athletes, the question can justifiably be posed, "What two outstanding black athletes look alike or are of identical build?" One of Kane's resource persons answers this question.

[Lloyd C. "Bud"] Winter makes it quite obvious that Black athletes differ from each other physically quite as much as Whites do. He notes that "Ray Norton, a sprinter, was tall and slender with scarcely discernible hips, that Bobby Poynter, a sprinter, was squat and dumpy with a sway back and a big butt, that Denis Johnson was short and wiry, that Tommy Smith was tall and wiry, and so on.[25]

Other examples are plentiful: what physical characteristics does Kareem Abdul-Jabbar have in common with Elgin Baylor, or Wilt Chamberlain with Al Attles? The point is simply that Wilt Chamberlain and Kareem Abdul-Jabbar have more in common physically with Mel Counts and Hank Finkel, two seven-foot-tall white athletes, than with most of their fellow black athletes. Even aside from these hyperbolic illustrations, what emerges from objective analysis of supposed physical differences between so-called races is the fact that for a large number of phenotypes

[25] Lloyd C. Winter cited in Martin Kane, "An Assessment of Black is Best" *Sports Illustrated*, January 18, 1971, p. 76.

there are more differences among individual members of any one racial group than between any two groups as a whole. Thus, a fabricated "average" of the differences between racial groupings may serve certain heuristic purposes but provides a woefully inadequate basis for explaining specific cases of athletic excellence or superior ability. Black athletes (and the black population as a whole) manifest a wide range of physical builds, body proportions, and other highly diverse anatomical and physiological features—as do all other racial categories, including the so-called white race.

Lack of recognition of this essential fact forces Kane into incredible qualifications when faced with exceptions which do not fit the "racial" framework. A case in point is his assertion that the physical differences between whites and blacks as racial groupings predispose blacks to dominate the sports requiring speed and strength in combination while whites, due to racially-linked physical traits, are predestined to prevail in those sporting events requiring endurance.[26] When confronted with the fact that black Africans won distance races and defeated highly touted and capable whites in the 1968 Olympic Games and that black Americans defeated white Americans, black Cubans, and black Africans among others in the games, the author makes the ridiculous post hoc assertion that "[The Kenyan] Keino and [the Ethiopian] Bikila have black skin but many white features."[27]

The attempts to argue that physiological differences underly black athletic superiority is no more convincing. For example, the author attempts to present a case for the notion that, due to an elongation of the body, black athletes are more efficient heat dissipators than are whites and thus excel over whites in sports.[28] But either tall or short individuals may have body builds which enable them to function as relatively efficient heat dissipators. The efficiency with which one's body dissipates heat is only incidentally related to the factor of height, but is directly related to the ratio of body surface to body mass. Therefore, one way to maximize heat dissipating efficiency is to present a proportionately greater amount of body surface area to the air by stretching a given body mass into an elongated shape. Another way of changing the gross mass to surface ratio is to change the overall size of the body. Hence, a decrease in size will decrease the mass (proportional to the cube root of any linear dimension) in relation to the surface area, the end result may be equivalent to that of body elongation. In this way the pygmy, simply by being small, acquires the same surface to mass ratio which is achieved by Watusi who are normal in body mass but elongated in shape.

---

[26] Ibid., p. 75.
[27] Ibid., p. 76.
[28] Ibid., p. 76.

These two groups live in close proximity in the hottest part of equatorial Africa. Thus, a small white athlete could be as efficient a heat dissipator as an elongated black athlete.

One last point: Given the complexity of the variables which determine athletic excellence, even where physical differences exist among individuals, one proceeds on dangerous grounds when he assumes that these *observable* or otherwise *discernible* differences are the major factors determining differences in demonstrated athletic excellence.

RACE-LINKED PSYCHOLOGICAL FACTORS

The belief in the existence of an invariable racial "character" was supposedly disposed of by scholars decades ago. Its persistence only indicates the difficulty with which racial sterotypes and caricatures are destroyed or altered to comply with prevailing scientific knowledge.

Kane and his resource persons, mostly coaches, create a portrait of the black athlete as happy-go-lucky and casual. Kane quotes Lloyd C. Winter, former coach of a long line of successful black track and field athletes as stating:

A limber athlete has body control, and body control is part of skill. It is obvious that many Black people have some sort of head-start motor in them, but for now I can only theorize that their great advantage is relaxation under stress. As a class, the Black athletes who have trained under me are far ahead of Whites in that one factor—relaxation under pressure. It's their secret.[29]

Some contemporary data however suggest a very different characterization of the psychological state of the black athlete under pressure.

Findings by Ogilvie and Tutko, (some of whose work was, ironically, featured in the same issue of *Sports Illustrated* in which Kane's article appeared) suggest that black athletes are significantly less relaxed than white athletes in the competitive situation. Using a test which they considered highly reliable, the authors reported the following findings:

1. On the IPAT, successful black athletes showed themselves to be significantly more serious, concerned, and "up-tight" than their white counterparts as indicated by their relative scores on the item "sober— happy go lucky." Blacks had a mean sten score of 5.1 as compared to a mean score for whites of 5.5 (statistical differences significant at the .01 level; $N = 396$ whites, 136 blacks).

2. On the IPAT item of "casual—controlled" successful black athletes scored significantly higher than white athletes, indicating a more controlled orientation. Blacks had a mean sten score of 6.6 as compared with the whites' mean score of 6.2 (significant at the .01 level).

Sociologically, one would expect this pattern of differences given

---

[29] Lloyd C. Winter cited in Kane, p. 76.

black athletes' suspicion of racism in sports and their feelings of decided disadvantage as Afro-Americans competing against whites for a finite number of highly valued positions and rewards in a white-controlled endeavor and in an admittedly racist society. Furthermore, for many black athletes, sports hold the only promise of escape from the material degradation of black society, and so to fail athletically often means total failure. Thus, the implication that black athletes are more "relaxed" than whites, because of race-linked characteristics, apparently not only lacks scientific foundation but may even be ludicrous as a commonsensical assumption.

If there is a psychological factor involved, it is quite possibly that many white athletes, some of whom may themselves be of exceptional athletic potential, *believe* blacks to be innately superior as athletes. These white athletes under such circumstances may start off at a psychological disadvantage. The "white race" thus becomes the chief victim of its own myth.

RACIALLY SPECIFIC HISTORICAL OCCURRENCES

The mythology of racial differences is further elaborated in Kane's article when he cites the remarks of Calvin Hill, Yale University graduate and a star on the Dallas Cowboys team:

I have a theory about why so many sports stars are Black. I think it boils down to the survival of the fittest. Think of what African slaves were forced to endure in this country merely to survive. Well, Black athletes are their descendants. They are the offspring of those who are physically tough enough to survive.[30]

The author also quotes Lee Evans, black Olympian and 400-meter-dash world-record holder:

We were bred for it. Certainly the Black people who survived in the slave ships must have contained a high proportion of the strongest. Then, on the plantations, a strong Black man was mated with a strong Black woman. We were simply bred for physical qualities.[31]

Continuing, Kane himself states that, "It might be that even without special breeding, the African has a superior physique."[32]

In these myth-perpetuating statements is striking confusion as to the nature of selective processes. Natural selection, or "the survival of the fittest" if you will, must have been predicated less upon strength and related physical attributes in mankind than in other forms of mammalian

---

[30] Calvin Hill, Ibid., p. 76.
[31] Lee Evans, Ibid., p. 79.
[32] Ibid., p. 79.

life and more upon social and mental capabilities. The same most certainly would have held for the slave. While some may have survived solely as a result of greater physical strength and toughness (although this is doubtful since the slave master had the gun and all the power) many undoubtedly survived because of their shrewdness. Available records of life among black slaves indicate that a slave's wits often were more important to insuring his longevity than was his physical prowess.[33] And during slavery, as is the case today, the Afro-American population was comprised of individuals who manifested greatly varying degrees and admixtures of both physical strength and intellectual abilities.

As if prototypical of older stereotypes, Kane and his informants speak as if blacks in American society have somehow remained "pure" as a racial stock, if, in fact, they ever were. Our best sociological and demographic knowledge indicates that inbreeding between whites and blacks in America has been extensive, not to speak of the influences of inbreeding with various other so-called racial groupings. Therefore, to assert that Afro-Americans are superior athletes due to the genetic makeup of the original slaves would be as naïve as the assertion that the determining factor in the demonstrated excellence of white pole vaulters from California over pole vaulters from other states is the physical strength and stamina of the whites who settled in California after surviving the historic "Donner Party" incident, and other rigors of the migrations to the coast.

Finally, an implication of this aspect of the argument is that for blacks, demonstration of physical ability alone is all that is required to become a successful athlete. Anyone who is even vaguely familiar with organized sports knows that physical ability at most will perhaps open doors, but before one reaches the level of a Bill Russell or a Gayle Sayers, there are many political, psychological, and racial hurdles to conquer.

What are other implications of explanations postulating a race-linked basis for athletic superiority? (1) Such views imply that the accomplishments of the black athlete are as natural to him as flight is to an eagle, and thus the facts of a lifetime of dedication, effort, sweat, blood, and tears are ignored. Perhaps it is coincidental, but the idea of "natural superiority" of blacks in sports would allow whites who are inclined to be racist to affirm, on the one hand, the undeniable superiority of the black athlete and, on the other, to maintain their definitions of black people in general (including athletes) as lazy, shiftless, and irresponsible. (2) The notion that black athletes are by racial heritage physically superior provides a basis for perpetuating a white monopoly on certain key positions in sports which ostensibly require greater thinking, leadership, and organizational ability—for example, quarterback in football,

---

[33] See for instance, Alice Moore Dunbar, *Masterpieces of Negro Eloquence* (New York: Bookery Publishing Company, 1914).

manager in baseball, and head coach in most sports. Thus, no matter how excellent an athlete a black player might be, a white player would always get the nod over him for these "intellectual" and control positions—since the black athlete would be assumed to excel on innate physical superiority alone. The white athlete, under these conditions, presumably would have had to work harder toward mastering any given sport and therefore he would probably know the dynamics and intricacies of the sport better than the black athlete who "naturally" sails through the requirements of the endeavor. Hence, under this reasoning, the white athlete would make the better coach, manager, quarterback, league commissioner, or even sportscaster.

A major hidden implication of Kane's argument for the black population at large—though I do not intend to impugn the author's motives—is that it opens the door for at least an informal acceptance of the idea that whites are *intellectually* superior to blacks. If blacks, whether athletes or nonathletes, give even passing credence to the possibility of inherent black physical superiority, how can they logically argue *against* the possibility of white intellectual superiority? By a tempered or even enthusiastic endorsement of a theory postulating black physical superiority, that segment of the white population which is inclined to be racist loses nothing. For it is a simple fact that a multitude of even lower order animals are physically superior in some ways not only to whites but to mankind as a species: gorillas, as were the dinosaurs, are physically superior to whites, leopards are physically superior to whites, as are bears, walruses, and elephants. So, by asserting that blacks are physically superior, even well-meaning people at best may be reinforcing some old stereotypes long held about Afro-Americans—to wit, that they are "little removed from the apes" in their overall evolutionary and cultural development.

On the other hand, intellectual capability is the highest priced commodity on the world market today. If one has the intellectual abilities, physical inferiority matters little. So, if in the affirmation of black identity Afro-Americans should accept the myth of racially innate black physical superiority in any realm, they could be inadvertently recognizing and accepting an ideology which has been used in part as justification for black slavery, segregation, and general oppression. For, in the final analysis, the argument of black physical superiority over whites is a potentially racist ideology.

In concluding his article, Kane states:

Needless to say, not all successes of the Black man in boxing or in other sports are due to physical characteristics. Motivation is a vital factor . . . But in recent years sports has opened some very special doors. Every male black child, however he might be discouraged from a career with a Wall

Street brokerage firm or other occupational choices, knows he has a sporting chance in baseball, football, boxing, basketball or track . . . The Black youngster has something real to aspire to when he picks up a bat or dribbles a basketball.[34]

Thus, the concluding statement smacks of an attempt to portray an unfortunate spectacle as a positive endeavor deserving of the efforts and energies of an entire people—the spectacle of millions of black America's most ambitious and capable youths vying against each other and a multitude of "white hopes" for a limited number of athletic positions. In the end, the overwhelming majority are doomed to be shuttled back into the ghetto either because the sports arena has room for only so many athletes, or because they are not the best among potential black athletes of star status, or simply because they cannot adjust to the political and psychological pressures of organized sports. The tragedy is that there are few alternative avenues of advancement open to them, though they may be potentially great artists, writers, physicists, or have the intellectual potential to discover a cure for sickle cell anemia or cancer. But, as long as American society demands that black youth strive first and foremost to be the world's greatest athletes, we will never be able to answer these "maybes," or to justify the tremendous expenditure of human talent in pursuit of a goal which is predestined to elude the masses of its pursuers.

OCCUPATIONAL DISCRIMINATION

Ironically, the above paragraph implies the only scientifically plausible explanation of black athletic superiority. A complex of societal conditions give rise to a heightened propensity among black males, and females to a lesser extent, to achieve success in sports. These conditions channel the aspirations of a proportionately greater number of *talented* blacks than of whites toward high-prestige sports positions. Our best evidence indicates that capacity for physical achievement, like other common human traits such as intelligence or artistic capacity, is not singularly characteristic of any one human population.[35] Thus, this capacity cuts across class, religion, and, more particularly, racial lines. For race, like class and religion, is primarily a culturally determined classification. *The simple fact of the matter is that the concept of race has no proven biological or genetic validity in terms of the determination of*

---

[34] Kane, p. 83.

[35] For a relatively tight-knit overview and evaluation of the literature on biology and race see R. H. Osborne, ed., *The Biological and Social Meaning of Race* (San Francisco: W. H. Freeman and Co., 1971); Ashley Montagu, ed., *The Concept of Race* (New York: Free Press, 1965).

socially meaningful behavior.[36] As a cultural delineation, however, it does have a social and political reality. This social and political reality of race is a fundamental basis of stratification in this society and a key means of determining the priority of who shall have access to means and therefore an opportunity to obtain valued goods and services. In American society, black people are relegated, as a consequence of the social and political realities symbolized by the phenotypical role and status signs of race, to the lowest priority in terms of having access to the full range of alternative means to obtaining values goods and services. This fact, however, does not negate the theoretically equal and proportionate distribution of talent across both black and white populations. Hence, a situation arises wherein whites, being the dominant group in the society, have greater potential access to *all* means of achieving valuables—prestige, wealth, feelings of self-adequacy, and so forth. Blacks, on the other hand, are channeled by racism and discrimination in the general society and by a heightened value on sports participation in the black subculture, into the one or two high-prestige endeavors known to be open to them—sports, and to a lesser degree, other forms of entertainment, particularly music.

Bill Russell once stated that he had to work as hard to achieve his status as the greatest basketball player of the last decade as the president of General Motors had to work to achieve his position. There are many who suggest that Russell might be correct. In short, it may take just as much talent, perseverance, dedication, and earnest effort to become a star athlete of Bill Russell's caliber as it takes to become a leading financier, business executive, attorney or doctor—though this proposition may be difficult to confirm. Few occupations demand more time and dedication than successful sports participation. A "world-class" athlete will usually have spent a good deal of his youth practicing the skills and techniques of his chosen sport. The competition for the few positions is extremely keen. Only if he is fortunate will he survive in that competition long enough to become a professional athlete or an outstanding figure in one of the amateur sports. For, as he moves up through the levels of competition, fewer and fewer slots or positions are available and the competition for these becomes more and more intense as the rewards increase.

Black society, as does the dominant white society, teaches its members to strive for that which is defined as the most desirable among potentially *achievable* goals—*among potentially achievable goals.* Since the onset of integrated, highly rewarding sports opportunities and the impact of television in communicating to all the ostensible influence (e.g., Vida Blue talking with President Nixon), glamor, affluence, and so forth,

---

[36] See Frank B. Livingston, *On the Nonexistence of Human Races,* pp. 46–59 in Montagu.

of the successful black athlete, the talents of Afro-American males (and females, again, to a lesser extent) are disproportionately concentrated toward achievement in this one area. In high-prestige occupational positions outside of the sports realm, black role models are an all but insignificant few. These are not readily visible, and they seldom have contact or communication with the masses of blacks (à la E. Franklin Frazier's *Black Bourgeoise*). Thus, given the competition among athletic organizations for top-flight athletes, it is to be expected that a high proportion of the extremely gifted black individuals would be in sports. Whites, on the other hand, because they have visible alternative role models and greater potential access to alternative high-prestige positions, distribute their talents over a broader range of endeavors. Thus, the concentration of highly gifted whites in sports is proportionately less than the number of blacks. Under such circumstances, black athletes dominate sports in terms of excellence of performance where both groups participate in numbers.

RACISM WITHIN SPORTS

It is, therefore, racism in the general society which is apparently responsible for black athletic superiority over whites. But whether one subscribes to my ideas or to Kane's, it seems that the real questions are not, "Why is the number of black athletes so disproportionately high?" and, "Why do blacks so dominate sports?" but rather, "Why is the proportion of black athletes to whites not higher yet?" and "Why do they not dominate sport to the point of white exclusion?" The answer to the latter questions revolves around the same concept as the answer to the first. Whereas the disproportionately high number of black athletes in sports at all levels and their domination of these endeavors is due to white racism in the general society, the basic factor determining that the number of blacks in sports does not soar still higher and that their dominance does not extend to the point of white exclusion is racism in the sports sphere itself. Sports organizations at all levels operate under informal quotas as to the number of blacks that are allowed to make the roster and the positions that these are allowed to hold.[37] This is particularly true in the college and professional ranks where the rewards of participation are relatively higher. Also as was mentioned earlier, certain positions in sports—such as quarterback—are the monopoly of white players. Other positions have become "black positions."

What are some of the implications of the above statements? (1) Black sports domination, far from being an indicator of Afro-American

---

[37] See Loy and J. F. McElvogue, pp. 5–24.

advancement in the general society, is perhaps one of the surest barometers of a continuing lack of equal opportunity for blacks in America. This was most certainly the case with immigrant groups arriving in the United States during the earlier periods of this century's history, especially the Jews, Italians, and the Irish who dominated such sports as boxing and football—the money sports—until alternative opportunities opened up. Furthermore, in terms of cross-cultural application of these ideas, it is to be expected that if apartheid South Africa ever integrates its athletic endeavors while maintaining segregation and intense discrimination in other societal spheres, it will not be long before sports in South Africa will be almost totally dominated by blacks. It would be "almost" rather than completely dominated because under the imagined circumstances the sports authorities in South Africa would be likely to institute discriminatory quotas on black participation, just as has been done informally in the United States, and thus avoid total innundation. (2) White-black parity in the quality of athletic performance is likely to arise only after alternative avenues for the achievement of valued goods and services are opened to Afro-Americans to the same extent that they are open to whites. (3) Opportunities in sports now channel blacks away from alternative high-prestige positions, thus lessening the pressure of competition between them and dominant group members for valued goods and services without resort to overt repression and physical coercion. As more and more black people begin to realize this covert social control function of sports in Afro-American life, the images of both sports and the sports participant in black America are likely to change. Some indications of such change are already manifest in the pressures from many sectors of black society upon black athletes to be more militant, more political, and more outspoken on all issues which affect the lives of Afro-Americans in general.

Recent studies tend to support the inference that racial discrimination is important inside of sports. In a paper entitled "Black Athletes on Intercollegiate Basketball Teams: An Empirical Test of Discrimination" presented at the 1971 meetings of the American Sociological Association, Norman R. Yetman and D. Stanley Eitzen present convincing arguments to the effect that only top-quality blacks are recruited into sports, while white athletes who may be only good or mediocre in terms of athletic skill will still be recruited.

I stated in 1968 that

. . . A black athlete generally fares well in athletic competition relative to other incoming athletes at a white-dominated college. The cards are somewhat stacked for him, however, because few black high school athletes get what are typically classified as second-and-third string athletic grants-in-aid. One simply does not find black athletes on "full-rides" at predominantly white schools riding the bench or playing second-or-third team positions. Second- and third-team athletic grants-in-aid are generally reserved for white athletes.[38]

Many individuals have concurred with the implications of this statement —to wit, that sports manifests the same racist tendencies toward discrimination that are extant in the larger society.[39]

As part of a larger study examining the social characteristics that affect the team performance of college basketball teams, Yetman and Eitzen obtained data permitting assessment of the allegation that black athletes are disproportionately overrepresented in the "star" category and underrepresented in the average or journeyman athlete category. The authors conclude that:

. . . Regardless of the control variables examined, these data have consistently shown that Black players on intercollegiate basketball teams are disproportionately in the starting roles. Several possible explanations for this phenomenon have been advanced. First, it has been suggested that Blacks are "naturally" better athletes and therefore their predominance in starting roles is explained by their innate athletic superiority. However, if this were the case, Blacks should not be systematically overrepresented in starting positions, but rather randomly distributed throughout the entire team. As Jim Bouton, a major league baseball player who has challenged the racial composition of major league teams, has written, "If 19 of the top 30 hitters are Black, then almost two-thirds of all hitters would be Black. Obviously it is not that way." The validity of Bouton's assertions have been empirically documented by Rosenblatt; and by Rapping and Pascal (cited previously). An examination based on the natural superiority of Black athletes must be rejected.

A second possible explanation is discrimination in recruiting practices. Edwards has charged that coaches, in their recruitment of Blacks, seek to obtain only those players who are almost certain to be starters. This appears to be a plausible explanation of the data described above. On the one hand, the coach may be an overt or covert bigot to whom the idea of having Black team members is repugnant but who nonetheless recruits Black "star" players only because this is certain to enhance his team's performance. In this situation the Black player who is capable but not an outstanding player is liable to be overlooked, while his White counterpart is not. Whereas this action

---

[38] Edwards, *The Revolt of the Black Athlete,* pp. 9–10.

[39] William F. Russell, "Success is a Journey," *Sports Illustrated,* June 8, 1970, pp. 81–93; Jack Olsen, *The Black Athlete* (New York: Time-Life Life Books, 1968). Charles Maher, "Athletics New World for Negro in America," six articles presented by the *Los Angeles Times-Washington Post* for syndication (March 29–April 4, 1968); "Baseball Study Finds Racial Bias," an Associated Press release reporting a study by Leonard Rapping and Anthony Pascal, reported in the *Kansas City Times,* May 15, 1968; "In Black and White," *Sports Illustrated,* February 19, 1968, p. 10; "Blacks on the Green," *Time,* February 4, 1969, p. 56; Harry Edwards, *The Revolt of the Black Athlete* (New York: Free Press, 1969); "The Angry Black Athlete," *Newsweek,* July 15, 1968, pp. 56–60; "Alienation and the Establishment," *University of Washington Daily,* March 10, 1970.

[ostensibly] represents individual discrimination on the part of the coach, institutionalized discrimination may also be operating. College coaches are sensitive to criticism, of their coaching policies by powerful alumni and booster organizations. In a situation where these groups are perceived by a White coach as highly bigoted, it is likely that his recruitment of Black players will be calculated to minimize criticism of his coaching policies. Therefore Black team members are more likely to be outstanding athletes, for the performance of average ballplayers would be inadequate to counterbalance the criticism their persence would create.[40]

Thus, to the extent that discriminatory recruitment of black athletes occurs, it also contributes to black domination of sports by eliminating less skilled black ahletes from participation.

But what of other forms of discrimination in American sport which are alleged to occur once the black athlete has been recruited. Of relevance here is the practice of "stacking." ("Stacking" is a term I coined in 1967. It refers to the practice of stacking black athletes in certain positions on athletic teams while denying them access to others. The impact of the practice has been not only to maintain a white monopoly on some positions but to limit the numbers of blacks on team rosters since each team carries only two or three athletes for any given position.) Yetman and Eitzen report "no evidence . . . of stacking" in their study of blacks in collegiate basketball. On the other hand, Loy and McElvogue report "substantial support for the hypothesis . . . that 'racial segregation [occurs] in . . . team sports by position . . .'"[41]

The hypothesis draws upon Grutsky's conceptions of formal structure of organizations and upon Blalock's propositions regarding occupational discrimination.[42]

According to Grutsky, "the formal structure of an organization consists of a set of norms which define the system's official objectives, its major offices or positions, and the primary responsibilities of the position occupants."[43] The formal structure "patterns the behavior of its constituent positions along three interdependent dimensions: (1) spatial location, (2) nature of task, and (3) frequency of interaction."[44] As far as the Loy and McElvogue study is concerned, the main import of the model is that:

---

[40] Norman R. Yetman and D. Stanley Eitzen, "Black Athletes on Intercollegiate Basketball Teams—An Empirical Test of Discrimination," paper presented at a meeting of the American Sociological Association, August 30, 1971, Denver, Colorado, pp. 10–11.

[41] Loy and McElvogue, p. 21.

[42] O. Grutsky, "The Effects of Formal Structure on Managerial Recruitment: A Study of Baseball Organization," *Sociometry* 26 (1963): 345–53; Hubert Blalock, pp. 92–100.

[43] Grutsky, p. 345.

[44] Ibid.

All else being equal, the more central one's spatial location: (1) the greater the likelihood dependent or coordinative tasks will be performed and (2) the greater the rate of interaction with the occupants of other positions. Also, the performance of dependent tasks is positively related to frequency of interaction.[45]

Loy and McElvogue, then, focused upon the concept of "centrality" in dealing with positions in team sports:

Centrality designates how close a member is to the "center" of the group's interaction network and thus refers simultaneously to the frequency with which a member participates in interaction with other members and the number and range of other members with whom he interacts and the degree to which he must coordinate his tasks and activities with other members.[46]

In *Toward a Theory of Minority Group Relations,* Blalock presented observations concerning relationships between the character of sport and the Afro-American condition in America. His analysis developed thirteen theoretical propositions concerning occupational discrimination, which can be empirically tested in other occupational settings. The analysis is an excellent example of how the critical examination of a sport situation can enhance the development of sociological theory in an area of central concern.

Blalock was, however, perhaps naïve in assuming that professional baseball is "an occupation which is remarkably free of racial discrimination."[47] Loy and McElvogue sought to test that assumption by drawing upon three of the propositions to predict where racial segregation is most likely to occur in baseball. The three propositions considered were: (1) The lower the degree of purely social interaction on the job, the lower the degree of discrimination.[48] (2) To the extent that performance is relatively independent of skill in interpersonal relations, the lower the degree of discrimination.[49] (3) To the extent that an individual's success depends primarily upon his own performance, rather than restriction of the performances of specific other individuals, the lower the discrimination by the group.[50]

The authors first condensed Blalock's three propositions into a single proposition: "Discrimination is positively related to centrality." Central positions involve frequent social interactions calling for interpersonal acceptability and require coordinative decisions that may interfere with

---

[45] Ibid., p. 346.

[46] Loy and McElvogue, p. 6.

[47] Blalock, p. 92.

[48] Ibid., proposition no. 52, p. 99.

[49] Ibid., proposition no. 51, p. 99.

[50] Ibid., proposition no. 47, p. 98.

the performance of some members.[51] These features are likely to bring forth discrimination, defined as "the unfavorable treatment of categories of persons on arbitrary grounds."[52] Discrimination takes many forms, but a major mode is that of segregation. Segregation denotes the exclusion of certain categories of persons from specific social organizations or particular positions within organizations on arbitrary grounds, that is, grounds which have no objective relation to individual skill and talent. Racial segregation, thus, should be positively related to centrality. Accordingly, Loy and McElvogue attempted to test the hypothesis, that "racial segregation in professional team sports in positively related to centrality," by examining the extent of racial segregation within major league baseball and major league football. The formal structures of positions are reasonably clear.

. . . Baseball teams have a well defined social structure consisting of the repetitive and regulated interaction among a set of nine positions combined into three major substructures or interaction units: (1) the battery, consisting of pitcher and catcher; (2) the infield, consisting of 1st base, 2nd base, shortstop and 3rd base; and (3) the outfield, consisting of leftfield, centerfield and rightfield positions.[53]

. . . Like baseball teams, football teams have well defined organizational structures. However, whereas the positions in baseball organization are determined by defensive alignment, there exists both a distinctive offensive and distinctive defensive team within modern professional football organization.[54]

In baseball, the outfield contains the most peripheral and isolated positions. Therefore the authors predicted that black athletes would be overrepresented in outfield positions and underrepresented in infield positions.[55]

In football, the most central positions are quarterback, center, right guard, and left guard, while the most central positions on the defensive team are the three linebacking positions. Loy and McElvogue predicted that black athletes in comparison to white athletes are more likely to occupy noncentral positions on both offensive and defensive teams.[56]

All professional players listed in the 1968 *Baseball Register* who had, in 1967, played fifty or more games were classified according to race and playing position. Starting players in professional football were similarily classified, from data in the official 1968 autographed *Yearbooks*

---

[51] Loy and McElvogue, p. 7.

[52] H. E. Moore, "Discrimination," in J. Gould and William Kolb, eds., *A Dictionary of the Social Sciences* (New York: Free Press, 1964), pp. 203–204.

[53] Loy and McElvogue, p. 8.

[54] Ibid., p. 8.

[55] Ibid.

[56] Ibid., p. 11.

and Zanger's *Pro Football 1968.* Differences in centrality by race were considered sufficient at the .01 level of significance to reject the null hypothesis of "no difference."[57]

The data show that only a small proportion of the black players, either in baseball or football, are in central positions. There is no evidence to suggest that differences in ability to perform in the various positions can account for the disproportionate number of blacks in non-central positions.

Rather, the evidence at hand would indicate that blacks probably must show performance superior to their white competitors before they can occupy *any* particular position. (Cumulative major-league batting averages in 1968 were higher for black than for white players at every position.) Furthermore, it is unlikely that blacks have a systematic preference for noncentral positions. More likely is the operation of a self-fulfilling belief:

. . . A black athlete assumes that he doesn't have much chance at being accepted at certain positions and thus tries out for other positions where his estimate of success is much higher.[58]

There appears to be little question, then, that racial segregation by position does exist in professional baseball and football. But the important question is what the underlying causes of this stacking of black athletes might be.

With regard to this question, Loy and McElvogue doubt that prejudice among white athletes concerning "social" mixing is of any great importance in the situation of interpersonal contact on the field. Rather, they are inclined to believe

. . . that segregation in professional sports is more a function of *management* than playing personnel. For example, there appears to be a myth among coaches that Negro players lack judgment and decision-making ability. This myth results in black athletes being excluded from positions requiring dependent or coordinative tasks. . . . In short, the central positions in major league baseball and football are typically the most responsible or so-called "brains positions." . . . [and] . . . to the degree that Negro athletes are denied access to central positions, they are also limited in obtaining positions of leadership in professional baseball [and football] . . . [in summary] . . . *Negroes, because they are not liked by the white establishment, are placed in peripheral positions; and, as a result of this placement, do not have the opportunity of high rates of interaction with teammates, and do not receive the potential positive sentiment which might accrue from such interaction.*[59]

Now, while the study just reported upon in some detail does give a strong indication that positional segregation by race exists, there are

---

[57] Ibid.

[58] Ibid., p. 14.

[59] Loy and McElvogue, pp. 18, 22.

significant questions that must be raised as to the factors alleged to underly this segregation. First, it must be said that there is no evidence that white management personnel as a group are *more* prone to segregate black athletes than are white athletes as a group. For example, Charnofsky reports that in response to the question "Is there differential treatment of players according to race or ethnicity by sports managers, participants and officials?" he received forty-two "no" answers and thirty "yes" answers—a division too marked to support the popular image of harmonious racial relations.

In response to a question dealing with choice of leisure-time partner, only one white athlete out of fifty-eight stated that he preferred to spend time with one of his black teammates—and that was a second choice.[60] Thus, to the extent that their statement has any validity at all, Loy and McElvogue's speculative assertion that "segregation in professional sports is *more* a function of management than playing personnel" should not be interpreted to mean that "playing personnel" are necessarily more liberal in behavior toward black athletes.

Let us now turn to the main questions raised by the Loy-McElvogue study. First, if "centrality of position" is the key factor in an explanation of stacking, one should find black athletes in representative abundance in those sports which are single-athlete events, for example, race-car driving, horse racing, track and field, and so forth. Second, if the relative lack of black athletes in central positions is in fact due to the alleged fact that "Negroes . . . are not *liked* by white establishment, and thus are placed in peripheral positions" one must either explain on other grounds the lack of stacking found by Yetman and Eitzen in their research on collegiate basketball teams, or one must show that the coaches and other personnel who control basketball teams "*like*" blacks more than the persons who control professional baseball and football teams. Indeed, if the personal racist attitudes of coaches and managers toward blacks are, in fact, the basic determinants of black positional segregation, one should expect to find no blacks at all in sports which have no fixed zones of role responsibility.

My own interpretation is that "centrality of position" is an *incidental* factor in the explanation of positional segregation by race in sports. The factors which should really be considered have to do with the degree of relative *outcome control* or *leadership responsibilities* institutionalized into the various positions. The factor of "centrality" itself is significant only in so far as greater outcome control and leadership responsibilities are typically vested in centrally located positions since actors holding these positions have a better perspective on the total field of activity. Thus, where leadership and outcome control role responsibilities are

[60] Harold Charnofsky, "Baseball Player Self-conception versus the Popular Image" *International Review of Sports Sociology* 3 (1968): 44–46.

TABLE 7–1

Distribution of individual white and black players by position
in major-league baseball, 1956–67

Playing position	White players	Black players	Total players	Percentage of black players	Rank order of percentage of white players
Catcher	85	5	90	05%	1
Shortstop	39	4	43	09%	2
2nd base	61	7	68	10%	3
3rd base	41	9	50	18%	4
1st base	54	13	67	19%	5
Outfield	129	61	190	32%	6
Total N	409	99	508	19%	

institutionally attached to a particular sports position, one should expect to find blacks being excluded from that position—even under circumstances where "centrality . . . leading to potential for intimacy of interpersonal contact between Blacks and White athletes" makes absolutely no sense. Let's look at some of Loy and McElvogue's findings in light of this statement.

Tables 7–1 and 7–2, from the Loy and McElvogue study, if viewed in combination, show that there is a one-to-one correspondence between the potential for occupancy of a particular position in baseball by a white athlete on the one hand, and the number of "assists" generated from that position on the other. Assists have a controlling influence on any athletic endeavor from a defensive standpoint. Thus, in those sports which have relatively fixed "zones" of defensive role responsibility allocated among the various positions—as in baseball and football—the

TABLE 7–2

Ranks for position occupancy and annual assists in professional baseball

Field position	Rank order			
	Percentage of whites*	Annual assists**	d_i	$d_i{}^2$
Catcher	1	1	0	0
Shortstop	2	2	0	0
2nd base	3	3	0	0
3rd base	4	4	0	0
1st base	5	5	0	0
Outfield	6	6	0	0

Source. —Loy and McElvogue, p. 20.

athlete who holds one of those positions most frequently involved in the action has the greatest opportunity to have a controlling influence on the outcome of the sport. Since, under most circumstances, one team or the other is going to win, such an athlete theoretically has a fifty-fifty chance of becoming a hero as a result of his performance.

Loy and McElvogue found that, in football, the position of line-backer on defense, particularly middle linebacker, is most likely to be the position which blacks are excluded from in defensive football. This is also the position most frequently involved in the action of the event, whether the opposing team's offensive attack involves a running strategy, a pass, or a run-pass combination. The linebacker, thus, is the one who has the greatest opportunity to control the action in the favor of his team. This is also true with the center and quarterback positions in football, and it is precisely at these positions where black athletes are scarcest on offense in the sport. *While beliefs about black intellectual incompetence may definitely have some influence here, other factors are certainly due consideration.*

In order to completely understand this apparent positional segrega-tion we must once more recall sports are believed to be the laboratory in which those characteristics necessary to the "perpetuation of the American way of life" are developed. One of the specific beliefs about sports is that it develops leadership ability which could prove vital to America. Remember also the fact that American society manifests a strong tendency to "ascribe . . . value and privilege to individuals based upon racial heritage." Taking all this into consideration, one should ex-pect to find whites predominating in those positions involving leader-ship and control in sports having fixed zones of role responsibility.

One not only finds a scarcity of blacks in the positions of quarter-back, catcher, center, linebacker, and so forth, but there is also a relative lack of black head coaches and managers in big-time sports. The pitch-ing position in baseball is only an apparent exception. One finds a dis-proportionate number of black pitchers in professional baseball because of the unique features of the position itself. The pitching position is in fact neither offensive *nor* defensive. An exceptionally good pitcher can be a defensive team's greatest asset. A poor opposing pitcher can be an offensive team's greatest weapon. Baseball is one of the few sports wherein *an opposing and nominally defensive* athlete initiates action for the offensive unit. Given this fact, there is high competition in big-time baseball for competent pitchers. The pitcher has one main task—to mini-mize the batting abilities of the opposing team members by throwing balls which they can hit only poorly or cannot hit at all. All other respon-sibilities arising for the pitcher emerge only when he fails to complete this task successfully—for example, covering home plate or first base.

By way of contrast, the quarterback in football is clearly offensive, and his main responsibilities are more varied than those of the pitcher. Thus, he has greater latitude in terms of "playing to his strengths." Unlike the pitcher who must throw the ball, a quarterback who is a relatively poor passer may emphasize a running attack, or throw only short passes, or he may "scramble," that is, choose to run the ball frequently himself.

This contrast between the positions of pitcher and quarterback suggests that the good pitcher may be more important to the success of a baseball team than the good quarterback is to the success of a football team. Likewise, the relative significance of the two positions to successful outcomes in the respective sports may account in large part for the fact that while quarterbacks are only infrequently changed during the course of a football event, pitchers are very readily shuttled in and out during the course of a baseball event. So in *team* sports where blacks participate in numbers and wherein winning and losing is heavily—though not totally—predicated upon the competence of a single individual occupying a *specific position* having a highly limited but critical responsibility, blacks have a greater opportunity to participate at that position. Because the perfectly pitched game is the exception and every team must score to win, even in the case of great pitching performances, persons occupying other positions on the baseball team usually have ample opportunity to contribute to a team's victory through their batting and fielding expertise. Thus, though pitching competence is critical in baseball (and therefore it is the pitcher who "wins" or "loses" the event), persons occupying other baseball positions are not totally without opportunity to be "game heroes." This is especially true of persons occupying positions in the infield—that area where the ball is likely to be hit (if it is hit at all) as a result of good pitching. And it is precisely at the infield positions, as the Loy and McElvogue study shows, that blacks are likely to be underrepresented though they are overrepresented at the pitching position.

In sports which involved a *single* participant comprising each sports unit and in sports without fixed zones of role responsibility—wherein any athlete involved in the action may exercise control or leadership at any given point during the course of an event—one still finds evidence of attempts to maintain a white predominance or presence in terms of control and leadership. For instance, in horse racing, black jockeys are practically nonexistent, though they were very prevalent in this sport prior to the turn of the century. It is not felt here to be coincidental that black jockeys disappeared from the sporting scene at about the same time that organized sports as an endeavor became a primary societal preoccupation. Likewise with auto racing. Black race-car drivers are virtually nonexistent. Now, it may be argued that blacks, due to their socioeconomic situation, do not have access to the equipment necessary to be a jockey or an auto racing driver. But this argument overlooks the fact that the overwhelming majority of white jockeys and racing-car drivers do not own their own equipment. They are hired, so to speak, to ride and drive, respectively, horses and cars owned by others. In these events, there is no "danger" of close interpersonal contact between blacks and whites but blacks are nonetheless excluded from participation altogether, as are women. The contention here is that this is due to the fact that the *only* participant's role available is seen as involving *total* outcome control of these sporting events, and it is important, in a society which is predominantly white and male dominated that a white male athlete fulfill that role. Thus, in the cases of the racing-car driver and the jockey, we are dealing with single positions encompassing assumed degrees of outcome control greater than one finds vested in single positions in any team sport; so we find virtually no blacks involved. The same is true of sports such as golf and tennis.

What about basketball, a team sport which has no fixed zones of position-related responsibilities Yetman and Eitzen, in the study discussed above, reported "no evidence of stacking," or segregation of black athletes by position. Now clearly in basketball there is no positional centrality as is the case in football and baseball because there are no fixed zones of role responsibility attached to specific positions; likewise, *total* outcome control is not vested in a single position as is the case in single participant sports such as golf because basketball is a team sport, and, therefore, blacks have not been excluded from the sport. Nevertheless, one does find an evidence of discrimination against black athletes on integrated basketball teams. Rather than stacking black athletes in positions involving relatively less control, since this is a logistical impossibility, the number of black athletes directly involved in the action at any one time is simply limited. Thus, Bill Russell observes: "In America, the practice is to put two Black athletes in the basketball game at home, put three in on the road, and put five in when you get behind . . ."[61]

While one is not likely to find black athletes stacked in one or two of the five positions in basketball (as Yetman and Eitzen's results show) one is equally unlikely to find blacks manning all five starting positions on any integrated team. Black athletes on basketball teams may be found at any position, but all positions will seldom be manned by blacks simultaneously, no matter how skilled these athletes might be. For in a racially integrated sport where any athlete in the field of action can exercise a frequent and determining control influence due to the structure of the sports endeavor, the only means of assuring that whites will have at least an opportunity to fulfill the tenets of the sports creed is to limit the

---

[61] Bill Russell cited in "Editorial," *Seattle Post-Intelligencer*, April 7, 1971, p. 8.

number of blacks who are directly involved in the action. Such limits on the number of blacks participating is significant in a nation where whites comprise the majority of the population. Because of the dynamics of fan involvement in the sport institution, it is necessary that they be able to identify closely with the sports unit. This identification is hindered in cases where an athletic unit is composed of members of one race and the population upon which it must depend for fan support is composed of another. It was this fact which motivated the management of the American Basketball Association's Dallas franchise to remove four of the ten blacks from its eleven-man 1972–73 roster. According to the team's head coach, "Whites in Dallas are simply not interested in paying to see an all Black team and the Black population alone cannot support us."

Now there is one basketball team made up of five blacks which whites literally flock to see. On the surface, the case of the Harlem Globetrotters would appear to be an exception to my contention. Upon analysis, however, this apparent "exception" proves illusionary. Whites patronize Globetrotter events, despite the fact that it is the *white athlete* who is excluded from opportunities to exercise control and leadership influence, owing to the unique status of the Globetrotter team. The Globetrotters engage in what I term "pseudosports." Other pseudosports are commercial wrestling and roller derby. These activities lack the seriousness which is a fundamental characteristic of true sports in American society. They are "put ons," staged for the purpose of pure spectator entertainment. Additionally, in the case of Globetrotter events, there is not even the pretense that athlete participation serves any of the societal or personal functions claimed for true sports in the American sports creed. Indeed, the activities of the Globetrotters are seen as reflecting the values and attitudes of *black society* as perceived by white society. The Globetrotters, then, are more actors putting on an ethnic theatrical presentation, albeit one requiring a good deal of athletic skill. The "acting" aspect of the presentation is never lost sight of by white spectators. Thus, they tolerate and even enthusiastically accept the fact that the Globetrotters always defeat their overwhelmingly white opposing teams and make them look foolishly inept in the process. Likewise, white spectators accept the total exclusion of white athletes from the Globetrotters team. For after all, these events are not serious. It's all an act, a put on which has the sole purpose of entertainment. Hence, since these events are not serious and are in conformity with white stereotypes of black cultural values, they are not taken seriously. They are not perceived as any threat to dominant societal values as these are manifest in the dominant creed and sentiments focusing upon serious sports activities.

What of track and field sports? Though most events in track and field sports are single athlete events, blacks engage primarily in those events which involve, for the most part, native ability rather than equipment, close work with coaches on technique, and so forth. Events in which blacks compete are basically track events and such endeavors as the high jump, the long jump, and the triple jump. A survey of appendix C in Edwards's *The Revolt of the Black Athlete* shows that it is in these sports events that blacks have had their greatest success in the track and field sphere. While some might argue, again, that the socioeconomic situation of Afro-Americans is not conducive to their success in field sports because of the equipment involved, it should be pointed out that few white pole vaulters own their pole-vaulting standards and other equipment; hurdling involves the use of more equipment than pole vaulting and blacks have dominated the hurdle events since the 1930s; and a sixteen-pound (steel) shot is currently cheaper than a high-quality basketball or football and blacks excel in the latter two sports. The determining factor in blacks' predominance in track events appears to be the degree of native ability required of these sports as opposed to formal training or command of technique, the fact that males are effectively segregated from females, and the fact that track and field events constitute the "showcase" endeavors of the world's greatest international sports spectacle, the Olympic Games. Where international prestige is at stake in events emphasized in America, and where some of the more deeply felt attitudes toward blacks are not violated, the United States fields its most competitive team. In those events wherein success is heavily dependent upon native talent, one cannot make up for a lagging competitive advantage by the development of new equipment and new technique alone. One must have the talent to work with. In an event such as the pole vault, on the other hand, it is generally conceded that the chief factor making for advances in vaulting records since the late 1950s has been the fiberglass pole. Advances in other field events have resulted primarily from new weight training methods and nutritional aids. So in those events where America has been able to maintain its competitive integrity by taking advantage of new techniques and equipment, whites still predominate. In those track and field events where native ability is the uppermost factor, blacks have all but taken over completely since the society could not very well exclude them and maintain any respectable international posture in sports.

In single-participant but internationally significant track and field sports, factors of control or leadership role responsibilities (which we hold are keys to understanding the segregation of blacks by position in any sport) are minimized or overridden by the excessive cost potentials for America were this country to exclude blacks from track and field competition altogether. Nevertheless, the contention still applies.

In Olympic sports such as diving and gymnastics, the United States typically fares very poorly. But though these are single participant international events, one does not find blacks involved. The main factors for consideration here appear to be (1) the amount and cost of the training equipment and facilities involved (frequently necessitating that males and females share these), (2) white attitudes about black interacting in close relationships with whites *across sexual lines*—especially where either is scantily dressed, (3) a lack of high rewards and black role models resulting in a lack of interest in such sports by the black population, and (4) a generally low popular interest in these sports.

Therefore, the exclusion of black athletes from some sports and their segregation within others by position is only incidentally related to "centrality of position," and may under many circumstances have little or nothing to do with the coach's or manager's personal attitudes toward Afro-Americans. The believed functions of sports in America, as embodied in the sports creed, demand that white males fulfill those role responsibilities involving leadership and control in our most popular team sports. From this perspective, it is not difficult to understand why in the most conservative region of the country—the South—one not only finds the greatest interest in sports but also the fewest blacks participating on integrated athletic squads, though some of the universities sponsoring these aggregations have had blacks enrolled in their student bodies since 1954. For instance, consider the composition of the athletic squads in the southeastern conference for the 1970–71 academic year. Note the "spring sports" column indicating black participation in single participant sports other than track and field and in sports which in many cases require the sharing of facilities by male and female athletes (Table 7–3).

TABLE 7–3

Blacks on the SEC's 1970–71 varsity teams

	Football	*Basketball*	*Baseball*	*Track*	*Spring sports**	*Total*
Alabama	0	1	0	0	0	1
Auburn	1	1	0	0	0	2
Florida	2	0	0	5	0	7
Georgia	0	1	0	3	0	4
Kentucky	6	1†	1	3	0	11
LSU	0	0	0	0	0	0
Mississippi	0	0	0	0	0	0
Mississippi State	2	0	0	0	0	2
Tennessee	4	1	0	7	0	12
Vanderbilt	2	0‡	0	0	0	2
Totals	17	5	1	18	0	41

Note.—The totals are based on figures supplied by the universities' athletic departments. The figures could change if some blacks fail to make the teams, or drop out of school, or if more than expected come out for the squads. It is also possible that the figures were wrong in the first place. The University of Alabama, for example, stated that two black freshman football players had been "signed," implying that they will be on the coming season's freshman team.

° Spring Sports include tennis, golf, wrestling, swimming, diving, and so forth.
† One black football player at Kentucky may also go out for basketball.
‡ Vanderbilt's black basketball player, Perry Wallace, is not included since he has already graduated. He was the first black player to complete his full four years.

In short, then, America on the whole demands that, as frequently as is possible, those "future custodians of the republic" who display their character, courage, discipline, and other such qualities on the field of athletic competition should be male and white. Perhaps this fact, as much as any other indication, illustrates the degree to which white America is really prepared to voluntarily share control and power in the greater society with women, Afro-Americans, and other minorities.

Recently there has come to light some claimed evidence that perhaps not all those factors affecting the outcomes of the black athlete in American sport are purely social in character. Data collected by Ogilvie and Tutko seem to imply that there may be psychological components which influence the disproportionate success of black athletes in sports. Though Ogilvie and Tutko appear convinced of the conclusiveness of their findings, I am rather skeptical. The reader is therefore cautioned that these data should be considered only preliminary and suggestive at best.

PSYCHOLOGICAL DETERMINANTS

Psychological components in the success or failure of an athlete have been recognized for some time.[62] The coach's awareness of psychological factors provides the motivation for the "pep talk." Not surprisingly, sports psychologists have focused much attention upon those psychological conditions that appear to be positively related to the athletes' success.

Though inconclusive, some evidence does suggest that there are some consistently discernible personality traits which distinguish successful athletes from their less successful peers.[63] In 1960, after an extensive review of athletic research, Johnson and Coffer concluded that the evidence was adequate to support the generalization that the exceptional athlete could be described as a special breed."[64] On the personality character of successful athletes, J. E. Kane, in a summary of the literature for English-speaking subjects tested using the IPAT, states that

[62] Arnold Beisser, *The Madness in Sports* (New York: Appleton-Century-Crofts, 1967), p. 153.

[63] For a review of the personality correlates of athletic success, see: Bruce C. Ogilvie, "Psychological Consistencies within the Personalities of High Level Competitors," *Journal of the American Medical Association,* (special Olympic year ed.), (September–October 1968). See also: L. Hausner, "Personality Traits of Champion and Former Champion Athletes," Research Study, University of Illinois, 1952. J. E. Kane, "Personality and physical Ability," *Proceedings of the International Congress of Sports,* Tokyo, 1964. Thomas A. Tutko and Bruce C. Ogilvie, "Comparison of Medalist and Non-Medalist Olympic Swimmers," *American Journal of Medicine* (1966). J. P. LaPlace, "Personality and Its Relation to Success in Professional Baseball," *Research Quarterly* 25 (1954): 313–19.

[64] C. Coffer and W. R. Johnson, "Personality Dynamics in Relation to Exercise and Sports," *Science and Medicine of Exercise and Sport,* ed. W. R. Johnson (New York and London: Harper Brothers, 1960).

"there is little doubt that at least a footballer-type of successful athlete exists."[65] Hausner pioneered the use of the IPAT when he compared British and American athletes against their national norms. He found that these forty-one champions exhibited consistent and statistically significant differences on many personality traits relative to the norm.[66]

Ogilvie and Tutko have been systematically collecting data on athletes for the past decade. One of their central interests has been the delineation of personality traits which are positively correlated with what they term "coachability"—the relative psychological amenability of athletes to being coached—that is, to follow orders, to accept rigorous training ordered without explanation, and so forth. Ogilvie and Tutko's basic thesis is that "coachability" is positively correlated with athletic success. The data were gathered by use of three psychological testing devices: the Edwards Personal Preference Schedule, the IPAT, and the Jackson Personality Research Form. These tests were administered to 532 athletes. Of these, 136 were black and 396 were white. The groups were roughly comparable in terms of athletic experience: each athlete involved had demonstrated outstanding athletic ability and each athlete had been drafted by a professional sports organization after his collegiate athletic career.

Since these data have as yet not been published, I had to rely upon extensive conversations with Ogilvie and Tutko in order to arrive at interpretations of their findings which were generally acceptable to them. The following discussion is largely reflective of the substance of these talks. Ogilvie and Tutko attest only to the validity of the data and have thus far publicly advanced no systematic interpretation concerning the origins of the differences.

THE IPAT: RESULTS AND SOME SPECULATIVE INTERPRETATIONS

The Cattell 16 Personality Factor Inventory has been used more widely in athletic research than any other set. Cross-cultural comparisons plus data based upon studies of age-group competitors have appeared to greatly increase the reliability of statements that can be made about the personality characters of athletes.

On the factor continuum of "reserved to outgoing," both black and white athletes scored above the norm and thus tend to be more outgoing than the average male college student. This finding generally supports

---

[65] J. E. Kane and F. W. Warburton, "Personality as It Relates to Sport and Physical Ability," *Readings in Physical Education* (London: Physical Education Association, 1966), chap. 4.

[66] L. Hausner (n. 63 above).

the results of previous studies which have found the outgoing personality trait to be characteristic of successful athletes.[67]

More important for the purposes here, however, is the fact that black athletes scored significantly higher as a group than did white athletes, a finding which would tend to belie the prevalent stereotype of black athletes as preferring to remain to themselves. This assumption of a clandestine group character among blacks has typically been used as the rationale for separating blacks from whites socially and in room assignments on athletic trips.

On the factor of "intelligence," both Black and White athletes scored below the norm for college students. This finding substantiates Slusher's report that athletes tend to score slightly lower on the intelligence factor than nonathletes.[68] Though blacks scored significantly lower than whites on the intelligence factor, Ogilvie and Tutko suggest that this result should be interpreted with caution.

They point out that, while "a lower than average intelligence may be characteristic of athletes as a group, significant intellectual differentiations among racial groupings of athletes are in all likelihood spurious." Thus, the cultural differences between blacks and whites are seen by Ogilvie and Tutko to account for significant differences between mean intelligence scores for the two groups.

On the IPAT factor continuum of "sober to happy-go-lucky," the black athletes scored significantly lower than whites. The work of Kane, Hardman, and Ogilvie indicates that one characteristic of successful athletes is that they tend to be tough-minded, no-nonsense-type persons who take a very direct approach to life.[69] These data indicate that blacks are considerably more serious than are whites. This would tend to imply not only that they are more amenable to coaching according to Ogilvie and Tutko, but also it would cast doubt upon the stereotype of the black athlete as a goof-off, one who takes very little seriously.

Given the alternative avenues for social and economic mobility open to blacks relative to those open to whites, such differentiations in seriousness are perhaps to be expected. The black athlete is also quite aware that any deviation from the rules and requirements could mean

---

[67] Kane (n. 63 above). See also: Bruce C. Ogilvie and T. A. Tutko, "What Is An Athlete," paper presented to the American Association of Physical Education, Health and Recreation, Las Vegas, Nevada, 1967, also published in the *Encyclopedia of Sports Medicine* (New York: McGraw Hill, 1967).

[68] H. S. Slusher, "Personality and Intelligence Characteristics of Selected High School Athletes and Non-athletes," *Research Quarterly* 35 (December 1964): 529–45.

[69] Kane Warburton; K. Hardman, "An Investigation into the Possible Relationships between Athletic Ability and Certain Personality Traits in Third Year Secondary School Boys," Presentation, University of Manchester, England, 1962; Bruce C. Ogilvie, "Psychological Consistencies."

his athletic career if there is a white athlete of even approximate ability who can replace him.

The factor of "trusting to suspicious" is relevant also to the determination of coachability, according to Ogilvie and Tutko. Their work shows that the more trusting an athlete is, the more coachable he is. Both black and white athletes fall below the mean for college males on suspicion. In other words, they tend to be more trusting. But, more important, blacks are significantly less trusting than are whites. It may be that black athletes are quite aware that, both in sports and in the general society, many of the obstacles to their social and economic advancement are arbitrary or based on racism, prejudice, and bigotry. Thus, on this factor, the black athlete would perhaps appear to be less coachable than his white counterpart.

On the factor of "casual to controlled," black athletes scored significantly higher than did whites. Both, however, were above the mean. According to Ogilvie and Tutko, this finding substantiates the results on the "sober to happy-go-lucky" factor. It indicates that the black athlete has strong control of his emotions, is inclined to be socially aware and careful, and evidences a greater concern for what is commonly termed "self-respect" with regard to his social reputation.

In light of the restrictiveness of athlete life, it should perhaps be expected that both black and white athletes will score higher than the mean on the factor of control. Likewise, given black athletes' knowledge of the fact that, due to the factors of visibility and racial prejudice any action perceived as a social or moral transgression on their parts is likely to be magnified, perhaps it should be expected that they would score higher on "casual to controlled" than would white athletes.

This finding would tend to contradict the stereotype of the black athlete as socially irresponsible. Both black and white athletes are more conscious of social proscriptions than are nonathlete male college students, but the black athlete is more conscious than the white. A high score on the control factor is also an important element in determining coachability. The more controlled an athlete is, the less likely he is to challenge authority.

THE JACKSON AND THE EDWARDS TESTS: RESULTS AND INTERPRETATIONS

There is a tremendous amount of overlap among the factors indexed by the Jackson and Edwards tests. For this reason they will be discussed together. It will be noted that many of the results are consistent with findings, presented above, from the IPAT.

In the autocratically controlled world of sports, high scores on the traits of "abasement and deference" are common among coachable and successful athletes. The results from the Jackson and the Edwards tests show that both black and white athlete groups scored higher on these traits than nonathlete male college students. The mean scores for the black athlete, however, were significantly higher for these traits than were those of the white athletes. Again, it is possibly the fact of different cultural experience that accounts for the differences between the black and white groups. Blacks have long understood the expediency of "playing the Negro" in circumstances where their outcomes are almost totally dependent upon the whims of others. Thus, although both black and white athletes show high scores on abasement and deference, the life experiences of the black athlete in the greater society may predispose him to produce a higher score than his white counterpart. These results would then tend to dispell the stereotype of the black athlete as flippant and contemptuous of authority.

On orderliness, the Jackson and the Edwards tests generate comparable results. But the black athlete group emerges as significantly more orderly than its white counterpart on both tests. Both groups score higher means for orderliness than the nonathlete male college population. According to Ogilvie and Tutko, this orderliness refers to such psychological traits as a preference for making plans before starting on difficult tasks or making trips; having meals organized and a definite set time for eating; for having things organized in such a manner that they run smoothly and on schedule. Other manifestations of the trait of orderliness are: self-discipline, promptness, deliberateness, and consistency of method. (These findings substantiate those obtained on the factor continuum of "reserved to controlled" from the IPAT tests.)

It may be that the substantial differences between the scores for the black and white groups are a manifestation of the black athlete's awareness that he has a great deal less latitude in terms of deviation from prescribed modes of behavior than does the white athlete. Like E. Franklin Frazier's black bourgeoisie and the Negro middle class in general, the Black athlete may be overconforming to the "rules of the game," out of an awareness of his vulnerability.

On the personality trait "exhibitionism," both black and white athletes scored below the norm for male college nonathletes. This belies a prevalent stereotype about athletes in general—namely, that they have a greater than normal propensity to show off or attract attention to themselves. This stereotype is, however, popularly projected onto the black athlete with greater severity than it is on his white counterpart. The black athlete is highly visible. Thus, any tendency to make the fancy pass, the slick dribble, or to stuff the ball through the basket in basketball, or to manifest a unique running and cutting style in football, or to exhibit "fancy footwork" or an unusual fighting style in boxing has contributed to the development of an exhibitionist image of him as an athlete in a race-conscious American society.

However, we have noted that black athletes must be better athletes than their white counterparts to compete successfully with them for athletic positions. And we have seen that proportionately more blacks are funneled in a direction conducive to the development of athletic skill, due to a lack of both role models and opportunity to advance in alternative endeavors. Both factors most likely have predisposed black athletes as a group to bring greater athletic ability to the sporting situation. Thus, black athletes in general may simply be able to do more things physically in sports than can White athletes.

Under the guise of reducing the temptation towards exhibitionism, the so-called "Lew Alcindor ruling" was instituted in collegiate basketball. Under its provisions, it became illegal to stuff the basketball through the hoop, though such maneuvers were both crowd pleasing and uplifting for team morale. But black athletes appeared to "stuff" more frequently than did white athletes. Whether this apparent higher frequency was due to the greater visibility of black athletes, to an actual greater frequency of stuffing, or both is not clear. But nonetheless, the rule was instituted.

On the factor "impulsivity" (the Jackson test) both black and white athlete groups scored lower than the mean for nonathlete male college students. But once again, black athletes scored lower than did whites. This finding on the Jackson factor of impulsivity also tends to undercut the stereotype of the black athletes as more reckless than the whites in sports competition. Even though the white athletes' scores indicate that they are more impulsive, black athletes are typically perceived as being the more reckless. These data would perhaps indicate, again, that the latter simply have greater achieved athletic ability and can thus do more things physically and with greater control in general than can the former.

On the Jackson factor "understanding" and the Edwards trait "intraception," both black and white athlete groups achieved mean scores which were below the means for nonathlete college males. It is possible, aside from effects of selectivity, that the highly controlled athletic environment is not one which encourages insight and analysis, but rather, obedience. On both traits, however, the black group scored significantly higher than the white group.

The total pattern of these findings would be expected on the assumption that the black athlete is highly aware of what is going on around him. Given the pressures uniquely experienced by the black athlete, it is essential to his survival in sports that he be able to "read the situation"; that he be able to understand not only what is given (verbal orders, gestures, etc.), but also what is given off (the overall atmosphere of a particular interactional situation).

On the Edwards variable "endurance" both black and white athletes scored higher than the college male mean. But again, the black athletes scored higher. But this too would be expected on the supposition that the black athlete has to work harder than his white competitor for a position in sports. The differences in means for athletes as opposed to nonathletes may be attributable to the direct competition inherent in the athlete's daily sports activities as opposed to the nonathletic student's involvement in less blatantly combative competition for grades in the classroom only.

Overall, then, it would appear that successful black athletes generally are more conforming in attitudes toward fulfilling their role expectations as athletes than are whites. Furthermore, we have seen that speculative explanations can be offered which are at least sociologically coherent and plausible. Nevertheless, several difficult issues remain concerning both the reliability of one of the tests and Ogilvie and Tutko's preliminary assertion that these data indicate that blacks are indeed more "coachable."

First of all, it will be noted that on the IPAT factor of "less intelligent-more intelligent," black athletes score significantly lower than do white athletes. Ogilvie and Tutko attribute this result to cultural variation more than to actual differences in innate intellectual capacity. It seems to me that this would tend to cast doubt upon the validity of the entire battery of test items in comparative research on black and white athletes. The IPAT is generally regarded among sports psychologists as the most reliable of the three tests employed by Ogilvie and Tutko; any question as to its validity thus would seem to cast doubt on the integrity of data from Jackson and the Edwards tests as well. This is not to say that the Ogilvie and Tutko findings are invalid, but only that they should be regarded as preliminary and only suggestive at best.

Of more fundamental concern here is the assertion that the delineated personality traits have a determining influence upon "coachability" and thus in turn upon the success achieved by an athlete in his sports endeavors.

It will be noted that *none* of the factors studied make any direct contribution to the development of actual physical skill or athletic ability. Rather, the degree to which an athlete possesses or lacks each of the "desired" traits is thought to render him more or less amenable to performing at a high level of efficiency under the autocratic conditions prevalent in the sporting sphere. They thus may have a significant effect as selective factors in determining which individuals will be granted an opportunity to participate in sports. Those potential athletes who are relatively nondeferential, for instance, are weeded out. Those who, for whatever reason, are prone to question authority or analyze the legitimacy of decisions or of motives underlying decisions by superiors, would likewise be weeded out.

Thus, it is quite possible that Ogilvie and Tutko's psychological indices of coachability would have more influence in determining *who will have an opportunity to participate* than in determining who will participate most successfully. The sports psychologists' interpretation of the data as correlates of athletic success is most likely an artifact of their sampling procedure. Because they tested only those athletes who were defined post hoc as successful athletes, the data do not provide scores for unsuccessful black and white athletes. A study comparing successful with unsuccessful black and white athletes would be enlightening; it is not unreasonable to suspect that some athletes may score positively in terms of their coachability, but still be unsuccessful in sports.

Second, Ogilvie and Tutko's assertion that the coachability of an athlete is directly related to his success in sports seems to reflect a belief that the coach has a decisive effect on an athlete's success. This generalization has yet to be demonstrated. We have seen in the last chapter that although overall responsibility for the outcome of a particular sports event is institutionalized into the role of the coach, the coach does not have complete control over all the factors which determine such outcomes. While a coach's handling of an athlete undoubtedly has an influence upon an athlete's performance, the exact degree and character of that influence has yet to be determined. What *is* known is that a coach can have a decisive influence in determining an athlete's *lack* of success, regardless of the athlete's skill. For instance, he may simply not allow him to participate. Coaching influence upon an athlete's *success* is much harder to establish. In the absence of empirical evidence, the data just reviewed cannot be taken to indicate any more than that the "personalities" or "attitudes" of those successful athletes tested render them especially amenable to participation in sport. This conclusion of course is hardly surprising. The finding that black athletes' personalities render them more amenable to coaching and thus to athletic participation is perhaps more interesting, but must be interpreted in the light of other considerations. In this regard, the *true* psychological character of an athlete may be of little importance relative to a coach's *perceptions* of his personality makeup. Thus the significant concern in determining the black athlete's chances of participation is not his amenability to coaching as indicated by his personality test scores but rather, the coach's *perceptions* of his amenability to coaching.

RACIAL STEREOTYPES

At a coaching conference in Fresno, California, in 1969, Tutko presented the findings detailed above. Before reading the preliminary results on each item, however, he explained the personality trait measured to the 300 coaches assembled. After each item was explained, the coaches were asked to state their expectations in terms of a dichotomous answer space—to wit, "Would you expect black or white athletes to be high or low on each of these items?" Their responses were recorded simply as *majority* and *minority* expectations since neither time nor the purposes of the conference allowed for exact counts. Table 7-4 compares coaches' expectations with the actual data results.

While the coaches' responses were undoubtedly influenced to some degree by the dichotomous outcome space imposed, the one-sided consistency of their responses does seem to show that the majority of this particular group of coaches habored preconceptions of black athletes as less coachable than white athletes. It would be reasonable to assume that coaches, like most other people, make decisions based upon their own

TABLE 7–4

A comparison of coaches' expectation and data results

Tests and variables	Majority coaches' expectations	Actual data results
IPAT:		
Reserved to out going	Blacks low	Blacks high
Less Intelligent to more intelligent	Blacks low	Blacks low
Sober to happy-go-lucky	Blacks high	Whites high
Trusting to suspicious	Blacks high	Blacks high
Casual to controlled	Blacks low	Blacks high
Jackson:		
Orderliness	Blacks low	Blacks high
Exhibitionism	Blacks high	Blacks low
Impulsivity	Blacks high	Blacks low
Understanding	Blacks low	Blacks high
Abasement	Blacks low	Blacks high
Edwards:		
Deference	Blacks low	Blacks high
Orderliness	Blacks low	Blacks high
Exhibitionism	Blacks high	Blacks low
Intraception	Blacks low	Blacks high
Abasement	Blacks low	Blacks high
Endurance	Blacks low	Blacks high

definitions of reality when they have the opportunity to do so. Thus, in circumstances where an athlete's actual personality traits differ significantly from a coach's perceptions of these, the athlete's *actual* traits become irrelevant in the coach's decision as to whether or not he should be allowed to participate in sports. It seems, then, that Ogilvie and Tutko's findings do not necessarily account even for the disproportionate *participation* of black athletes in sports, much less their disproportionate representation in "success" and "star" categories. However, these findings do suggest some avenues of further inquiry in the general area of sports psychology. Despite all of the research into personality factors associated with sports participation, many fundamental questions concerning the precise influence of psychological variables on behavior in the sports realm have yet to be answered.

The discussions above have highlighted some of the known and suspected influences differentiating the situation of the black athlete from that of his white counterpart. As is the case with other Afro-Americans, many of the black athlete's outcomes—both positive and negative—are traceable directly to the impact of either institutionalized or personal forms of racially prejudicial values. Afro-Americans are numerous relative to other minority groups and they also, unlike most other ethnic minorities, share a comon language and common cultural values with whites. These two factors have undoubtedly had some influence in blacks amenability to participation in American sports. But the overall character of the black athlete's situation is determined by discrimination in sport and the impact of racial discrimination in the larger society. Many of the black athlete rebellions and the numerous books and articles on racial discrimination in American sport have illuminated the meaning of the above statement in human terms. It is the fact of this tradition of racial discrimination in American sport that necessitates the "all other things being equal" qualification emphasized in the last chapter with regard to the possible ameliorative functions of the conceptualization of the individual sports unit as a "family." In short, this qualification points up the fact that the pervasive influences of racial discrimination often operate to heighten intrasquad antagonisms in the integrated sports situation.

In sports, where the prestige, self-esteem and, in many cases, the livelihoods of those most directly involved hinge on whether or not they make the grade on a successful team, despite the fact that everyone shares in the success of each individual team member, competition between individuals for positions on a team not infrequently generates antagonisms in informal relationships. And in a country such as the United States where prejudice, racism, and intergroup suspicion, and bigotry prevail in dangerous abundance, competition between members of differing racial groups for scarce values and a finite number of rewarding positions could further exacerbate already strained relations.

Though discrimination and stereotyping in sport has had its most devastating impact upon the black athlete, other minorities of late have become increasingly concerned over ethnic stereotyping in sport in particular. Native Americans (or Indians) have become indignant over the designation of athletic teams as "Redskins," "Indians," "Braves," and so forth. On this point Dave Bergen states:

Imagine, if you will, the University of Michigan Wolverines, say, were known instead as the University of Michigan Kikes. The football players would have little cash registers painted on the sides of their helmets. The team would win and the student body would stand up and shout in unison, "Sue. a deal!"

Preposterous. That would be brutally anti-Semitic. The people down around Los Angeles would ban Michigan from the Rose Bowl forever. A great public outcry would kick Michigan into the gutter of infamy.

There would have been some hell raised long ago, thank goodness, if, say, the University of Alabama had called its teams The Darkies, if the Alabama cheerleaders dressed like Aunt Jemima and if the fight song was an uptempo version of "Old Black Joe." Such prejudicial nonsense years ago would have gone the way of minstrel shows and Stepinfetchit.

Yet, right here in 1971, it seems perfectly acceptable that we have teams known as the Indians, the Redskins, the Redmen, the Chiefs, the Braves and the Warriors. . . . Worse than this, we sometimes call them "injuns" as a headline expedient.

There will be some who will say this is all pretty silly. It's understandable, actually. But to 750,000 American Indians, trapped in squalor on so many far-flung "reservations" and politically powerless to help themselves, it is just one more humiliation perpetrated by the white man. And the black man.

These humiliations mount. They cut deep, even when they pop up in sports. The insignia for the Cleveland Indians is a red-faced, cross-eyed Indian with a big nose. Count up all the insipid halftime shows you've seen with and Indian theme. Those aren't tributes; those are innocent little insults, and they hurt.[70]

Even the Chinese, not noted for their involvement in American sport, have been subjected to what many perceive as institutionalized racial slurs. At Pekin, Illinois, the local high school has officially dubbed its teams the "Pekin Chinks."

We now conclude this survey of the status and roles of the male athlete in American sport. The above discussion has for the most part concentrated on those influences distinguishing the situation of the black athlete from that of his white teammate. Consideration of these factors is a key to understanding many of the issues currently prevalent in the sports realm, that is, rebellions among both white and black athletes, black athletic dominance, the impact of racism in sport, positional segregation, and so forth.

Let us turn now to a brief consideration of the female athlete in American sport.

THE FEMALE ATHLETE ROLE IN SPORT

Like the factors differentiating the role of black male and white male athletes, the role of the female in sport is substantially influenced

---

[70] Dave Bergen, "Stanford Injuns?" *San Francisco Examiner*, May 4, 1971, p. 44.

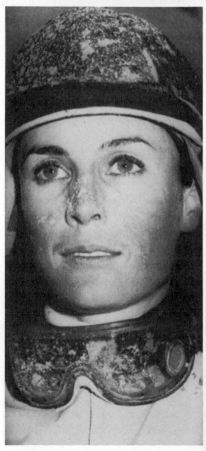

While many women still aspire to become beauty queens in the sport world, others are eschewing such traditionally female roles for roles more typically fulfilled by males. Beauty contestants (above) admire crown to be awarded to the one of them adjudged "most beautiful." Robyn Smith (right) still wears mud thrown in her face during her first race as a jockey. She had been banned from many races because she is a woman. Female footballers (opposite page) cheer teammate carrying ball in women's tackle football game. (San Jose Mercury-News)

by value orientations that are institutionalized within the fabric of American life as a whole. In a previous chapter, we stated that the values shared by the institution of sport and the larger society have functioned to covertly exclude females as potential beneficiaries of the believed rewards of sport. The aim of this section is to briefly expand upon this assertion and to explore its implications.

Exclusion and segregation by sex in sports is neither new nor a uniquely American practice. Female exclusion from sport was the rule in ancient Greece and this practice has roots deep in Western cultural traditions.[71]

Of course, females are not totally excluded from sport in America, but it is clear that they are relegated to certain types of sports and to secondary roles within the so-called major sports. In order to understand this situation, we must come to grips with the values associated with the feminine role in America and the relationship between these values and the functioning of the institution of sport.

While we may disagree as to whether it is "good" or "bad," there does appear to be general consensus that in America the status of the female is "subordinate" to that of the male. The contributory factors are numerous. Nonetheless, a relatively few appear to be of major significance.

First there is the biological universal that it is the female of the species who bears the offspring. During that extensive period in human history when infant mortality was high, when life expectancy was relatively short, and when contraceptive methods were either unknown, independable, or undesirable, it was inevitable that many women would be perpetually "incarcerated" in the domicile by a succession of pregnancies and childbirths. Under these circumstances, the more instrumental responsibilities necessary to the maintenance of life—the provision of food, shelter, protection, and so forth—became male-dominated responsibilities. Thus, differences in biologically determined capabilities contribute to our understanding of the probable bases of a division of labor by sex and the *initial* impetus for female subordination enforced by means of the male's greater physical strength. But biological considerations do not help us to understand the persistence of female subordination in the face of technological advances and the emergence of a legal-rational social order that have made differences in such traits as physical strength all but irrelevant in the determination of status. In pursuit of a more complete explanation, we must look to the values and practices differentiating social roles and statuses according to sex in the larger society.

---

[71] Elenor Metheny "Symbolic Forms of Movement: The Feminine Image in Sport" in George H. Sage, ed., *Sport and American Society* (Canada: Addison-Wesley Publishers, 1970), pp. 291–303.

In the secular sphere of American society, the male-female status differential finds expression in every institution. Certainly they are clearly manifest in the two having primary functions in socialization—the family and the educational institutions.

Within the family, males and females are prepared from birth for their traditionally separate roles in society. The female child is dressed in flowery, soft pink or yellow costumes; taught to be passive, graceful, nonaggressive. The male child is dressed in darker colors, expected to be mischievious, aggressive, and rough. For, as you know, "Boys will be boys."

Once school age is reached, these differences in socialization are intensified in the educational system. Females are, for the most part, channeled into preparation for those occupations which are basically extensions of the mother-wife role—such as nursing, secretarial and clerical jobs, social worker, and schoolteacher. Male children, on the other hand, are encouraged to pursue engineering, law, business management, political science, coaching, athletics, and so forth.

Today, it is increasingly unlikely that acceptable justifications can be brought to bear in support of either female subordination or segregation in specific kinds of endeavors. Therefore it would seem that the relegation of women to "expressive" as opposed to "instrumental" roles is predicated more on social tradition than female capability. Thanks to technology, the majority of the instrumental functions carried out by men could just as well be carried out by women. There is little reason to suspect for instance that some sex-linked factor would prevent a woman from piloting a jet airliner. (In fact, as was disclosed in 1970, stewardesses *have* been piloting jet aircraft while the male captains and co-captains have taken naps on cross-country and intercontinental flights.) Likewise, there is no rational basis to suspect that women are innately incapable of managing a bank, picking up garbage, or of functioning at least as capably as their male counterparts as statesmen and heads of state. For as the cases of Indira Ghandi, Golda Meir, and Richard M. Nixon illustrate, to perform in even the highest executive position, one need not be physically the strongest or biggest "warrior of the tribe," or even have made first team at a college that at best can be described as a fourth-rate football power.

Now it will be recalled that sport as a social institution serves to disseminate, reaffirm, and reinforce those values regulating human interaction in the secular-instrumental sphere of life. All other functions are secondary and stem from this main set of consequences—particularly that of spectator entertainment. Ultimately it is the fact of a commonality of shared values governing behavior in both the sports sphere and the instrumental sector of American life that creates the predominantly male fan enthusiasm for and identification with athletics. For this reason, as will be shown in the next chapter, foreigners and often women have a difficult time appreciating the "mania" exhibited by American men over, say, football. Since the dominant sports creed reflects secular instrumental values, it should be expected that females would be excluded from primary-level involvement (e.g. as coaches, managers, and athletes) in big-time sports. Moreover, it should not be surprising to find that where females are encouraged to participate at a primary level in sports, such sports activities are cast within the context of behavior patterns appropriate for women. A review of the work of Elenor Metheny and Marie Hart, among others, is instructive in this regard. For the most part, the work of these two scholars indicates that it is deemed inappropriate for women to engage in sports requiring bodily contact, aggressive action against an opponent, the lifting of even moderately heavy objects, or to engage in sports that require the participant to assume an awkward or "unbecoming" position.[72] On the other hand, it is quite appropriate for women to engage in sports where a physical barrier separates opponents and wherein grace and aesthetically pleasing movement are demanded. So while males are participating in football, basketball, baseball, boxing, wrestling, and otherwise preparing themselves for their destined roles as "custodians of the Republic," women are propelling themselves gracefully over the ice or through the water, or they are slapping a ball over a tennis net.

The fact of the matter is that, in America, a female's athletic competence is seen to detract from her womanliness (e.g., "she's the best athlete in the family—she can throw a ball, bat, and run like a boy"). For this reason, many females never attempt to become involved directly in the most popular sports and those who do become involved even in those sports open to women (track, swimming, ice skating, tennis, etc.) often cease participation before their prime. Most are forced by cultural definitions to choose between being an athlete (thereby facing barely hidden suspicions as to the degree of their heterosexuality) and their womanhood. Because female role responsibilities traditionally have not been of an instrumental character, females are not perceived to be legitimate recipients of sports' claimed benefits. Thus, few people in America take seriously the female who wants to become a jockey, or a professional football referee, or a baseball participant, or a major league baseball umpire or a marathoner—although she is quite acceptable as a cheerleader or pom-pom girl.

If this assertion is correct, in cultures where male and female roles are less sharply differentiated than in dominant American society, or where these roles are perhaps even reversed, there should be greater

---

[72] Ibid., pp. 282–87; Marie Hart, "On Being Female in Sport," in *Sport in the Socio-Cultural Process* (Dubuque, Iowa: W. C. Brown Publishers, 1972), p. 291.

acceptance of the female athlete. Because little research has been done on this matter, evidence is admittedly sketchy. But the information that is available does tend to support the hypothesis.

For instance, in the Soviet Union, where the roles of men and women in terms of instrumental versus expressive responsibilities outside of the home seem to be less sharply differentiated, women are more successful in sports competition. Soviet women have dominated American women in the Olympic Games in practically every event other than the sprints. Furthermore, they seem to enjoy greater status as athletes at home. There are also some clues from cultural variations within American society that suggest a positive relationship between performance and acceptability as athletes. Black society in America, which, it will be recalled, contains a greater proportion of female-headed or "matriarchal" families (estimated at one-third of all black families)[73] than dominant white society, apparently is more accepting of female athletes and offers them more opportunity to participate in sports—a fact attested to by the well-developed intercollegiate sports programs for women in predominantly Black colleges such as Tennessee A. & I., Florida A. & M., and Prairie View State. In this regard, Marie Hart, a long-time student on the subject of women in American sport and professor of health and physical education at California State University at Hayward, California, observes

There is a startling contrast between the Black and White female athlete. In the Black community it seems that a woman *can* be strong and competent in sport and still not deny her womanliness. She can even win respect and high status; Wilma Rudolph, Wyomia Tyus, Elain Brown, for example.[74]

So while the high proportion of "matriarchies" has little bearing upon the determination of black male athletic achievements, it appears that it is important to black female athletic performances as opposed to those of white females.

Though white society has also produced its female sports heroines, overrepresentation of black females and the actual number of championship performances in sporting events in which both black and white females participate in numbers are due in large part to black society's greater acceptance of the female in the athlete role. (This acceptance probably stems from the tradition in black society of a significant proportion of women fulfilling instrumental responsibilities.) In black society, women athletes tend to be perceived as legitimate participants compet-

---

[73] Hyland Lewis and E. Herzog. "The Family: Resources for Change" in J. Bracey, ed., *Black Matriarchy: Myth or Reality* (Belmont, Calif.: Wadsworth Publishing Co., 1970), p. 3.

[74] Marie Hart, "Sport: Women Sit in the Back of the Bus" *Psychology Today* (October 1971), pp. 64–65.

ing in different classes of events—in the same sense that heavyweight and flyweight male boxers are seen by the greater society as competing in different classes. Thus, a successful black female athlete is lauded as a champion in her own right. Her athletic prowess is neither evaluated in terms of male athletic accomplishments, nor is it perceived as reflecting negatively upon her femininity. On the other hand, performance by white female athletes are continually being evaluated in terms of standards set by men. The more these approximate those of males, the more the white female's "womanliness" becomes suspect. She can be "all woman" and also be involved in athletics only as a cheerleader or in some other expressive role.

Let us turn now to a summary application of the basic theoretical format of this work, namely, strain in the male athlete role and its traditional resolution through adherence to the dominant sports creed.

STRAIN AND THE MALE ATHLETE ROLE

Strains in the athlete role emerge from two basic sources: (1) conflicting demands made upon the athlete by general societal values on the one hand and values associated with his sports role on the other; and (2) inconsistencies between the role expectations and responsibilities of the athlete and those more generally associated with being young in America.

With regard to (1) of the above, athletes adjust primarily by resorting to an espousal of the managerial themes of the sports creed. Being partially insulated from the hard realities of societal life by their parents and the family institution, young people in American society have a propensity to be idealistic. "Moral ideals" define reality for them. Participation in sports activities, however, confront the athlete with a much more realistic portrayal of *how things are done* in the day-to-day functioning of the society. As a result of these revelations, athletic competition may constitute a rather traumatic experience for the athlete.

The trauma may become manifest in what Ogilvie and Tutko call a "success phobia." The athlete shows a "fear of success" in some sporting activities (particularly those involving the use of violent, aggressive tactics) while simultaneously he is incapable of accepting failure in sport.

Over the past twelve years we have found that there exist five forms of success-phobia among athletes: fear of social isolation, fear of emotional isolation, guilt with respect to self-assertion or aggression, unconscious fear of old ideals or traditions, and lastly the burden of success. Each of these fears may operate independently or conjointly with one or more of the others. Each is the result of social conditioning.[75]

---

[75] Bruce C. Ogilvie and Thomas A. Tutko, "The Unconscious Fear of Success," Department of Psychology, San Jose State College, San Jose, California, p. 3.

Other observers also point to a close relationship between the values of the greater society and some of the conflicts within the world of sports. For instance, Beisser observes

. . . In the process of growing up a child learns that under certain conditions a display of aggression has unhappy consequences.

He soon learns to think before acting and to consider the consequences first. This represents the beginning of the development of conscience and eventually is incorporated into the child's personality as a system of conscious and unconscious "shoulds" and "should nots."

He also learns that "there is a time and place for everything," and, especially if he is a boy, he is sometimes expected to be aggressive. In certain situations, such as sports, he is looked upon with disfavor if he is not aggressive or assertive enough. Unfortunately by the time he has sorted out when he is supposed to be aggressive and when he is not supposed to be, there has been some contamination of the sanction with the prohibition. The "should nots" have . . . become unconscious and generalized. In a "should-be-aggressive" situation such as, let us say, a basketball game, a player may find himself to his consternation, reacting as though it were a "should-not-be-aggressive" situation.[76]

Within the context of Sutton's strain theory, it is plausible that one factor inducing many athletes to concur with the "managerial" claims made on behalf of sport is that acceptance may aid in the ameliroation of strains generated by value incongruities and conflicts. Thus, though engaging in aggressive, violent action in sports, the athlete —according to the sports creed—is a party to activities which are conducive to the development of brotherhood, which build "good" rather than "bad" character, which reinforce traditional religious prescriptions, and which are supportive of the "American way of life."

The managerial strand also provides the athlete a means to deal with athletic failure. For, regardless of whether he is first string or fourth, the mere fact that he participates is declared to be of value to both the athlete personally and the society in general. He is believed to be learning lessons and gaining experiences that will inevitably make him more successful in adult life and a better citizen.

The second major source of strain for the athlete lies in incongruities between his role as athlete and his role as a member of the youth culture. As was stated earlier, though discipline, competitiveness, and related values are stressed "for all" in American society, involvement in sport is a major experience in which these values acquire practical significance for youth. Though competition among students for grades certainly is real and important, the athlete must make sacrifices and accept risks which are different from those expected of his nonathlete

---

[76] Arnold Beisser, *The Madness in Sports* (New York: Appleton-Century-Crofts Publishers, 1967), pp. 159–61.

counterpart. Nonetheless, these sacrifices must be viewed positively by the athlete's nonathlete peer group if they are to have any worth to him. While nonathletes may share the ideal values prescribed for behavior in the larger society, because they do not participate in sports they have greater latitude in terms of testing the boundaries of prescribed behavior than do athletes. For example, long hair and mod dress styles were worn by nonathlete students long before athletes were allowed such latitude in personal grooming, and nonathletes are much freer to publicly express deviant sexual, political, social, and religious attitudes than their athlete counterparts. Therefore, the price paid by the athlete for his status is less latitude for the expression of nonconforming behavior. That is, his boundaries of social behavior relative to those of nonathletes are not determined by what is generally "acceptable" from "impetuous youth" but more by what is "ideally" prescribed for the "good citizen."

Much as his adjustment to contradictory values of loyalty to the team on the one hand and achievement of his own individual aspirations on the other, the athlete tends *not* to rebel against the restrictions placed upon his behavior. Rather, he traditionally has resorted—by expressing concurrence with the instrumental strand of the dominant sports creed— to a heightened adherence to the values that give merit to the more or less unique sacrifices that he is compelled to make.

This chapter has presented a partial analysis of the position and role of the athlete in American sport. It has discussed some of the factors determining the complexity of the role and the relationships of its characteristics to the structure and functioning of the institution.

8

The fan

. . . There are men to whom it is a delight to collect the Olympic dust from the course . . .[1]

. . . The coach, who at the end of a victorious season, is the idol of the townfolk is likely, after a less fortunate schedule, to find himself less highly regarded by fans and even with suspicion . . .[2]

. . . Sports owes something to the public. After all, the public put us where we are now . . .[3]

. . . Sports manifests the values and ideas that have made America great and which keep her strong . . . The competitiveness, the ruggedness, the determination to succeed exemplified . . . among the early pioneers who withstood the odds, fought the Indians, braved a hostile environment and inclement weather—all this and more continues to be acted out . . . in sport.[4]

THE POTENTIAL SPORTS FAN in America is usually introduced to sport as a very young child. Many parents purchase blankets with sports scenes embroidered on them, stuffed footballs, basketballs, and baseballs, baby

---

[1] Arnold Beisser, *The Madness in Sports* (New York: Meredith Publishing Co., 1967), p. 124.

[2] "The Coach in College Athletics" in *American College Athletics,* the Carnegie Foundation for the Advancement of Teaching, Bulletin 23, p. 184.

[3] Gayle Sayers, cited in Paul Zimmerman "Pro Football's Collision at Generation Gap," *True,* September, 1971, p. 39.

[4] From pregame show "N.F.L. Today" CBS Television Network, November 21, 1971.

clothes bearing the insignia of their favorite athletic units, and so forth. Once the child is old enough to walk and to experiment with the development of his own physical capabilities, among his first "hard" toys are likely to be small replicas of sports implements—small rubber footballs, plastic bats, and baseballs. It is at this point also that the child is likely to be taken to his first sports event by his parents. Soon he begins to pay attention to sporting events on television, though he does not yet know or understand the "rules of the game." But these eventually are learned. Under the guidance and encouragement of older relatives, usually the father or some other male, young children come to know and develop an appreciation for the believed values and virtues of sport. The child may go into sport as an athlete if he possesses the physical potential and has the desire and the opportunity to exhibit the various other characteristics conducive to fulfillment of the athlete role.

The overwhelming majority of the children so socialized, however, become fans rather than athletes. And, like the athlete's role, the fan's role too has a predominantly male character. (Here again females are covertly excluded, for the most part.) Perhaps the least studied and understood role in the institution of sport is that of the "fan." The fan is not merely a passive spectator. He is involved, a vital component in the proper functioning of the institution for both the society and for individuals. The more common use of the term "fan"—which as already noted is an abbreviation of "fanatic"—as opposed to "spectator," illustrates the dynamic, active quality intrinsic to this role.

Throughout previous chapters, the societal functions of the institution of sport have been at the center of attention. The emphasis of the socialization function relative to the fan role differs, however, from the emphasis affecting the athlete role. For the athlete role, the emphasis of socialization is upon enculturation and preparation for life. The socialization relevant to the role of the fan, on the other hand, emphasizes the reinforcement of societal values and orientations already held. By involvement in sports, then, the athlete is ostensibly infused wih values necessary to function successfully in society, while in the case of the fan, values already internalized are reaffirmed and sustained.

FAN INVOLVEMENT: TWO PERSONAL FUNCTIONS

In the analytical literature dealing with sport, involvement seems to be regarded as serving two personal functions for the fan: (1) it engenders in him a feeling of belonging, and (2) it provides a socially approved outlet by which behavior and attitudes otherwise socially unacceptable can be expressed.

In *The Madness in Sports*, Beisser relates fans' enthusiasm for sport to the increased prevalence of secondary forms of social interaction, heightened affective neutrality, and general social atomization which allegedly characterize modern life in urban American society. As an exemplary case, he focuses upon the situation in the city of Los Angeles:

. . . It is not surprising that in this fluid, centerless mass the citizens seek, sometimes desperately, groups with which they can identify, so to feel that they belong . . . Los Angeles has become the center of quackery and cultism, of evangelism and prejudice, and of political extremeism, both right and left; in these spurious ways, at least, its citizens can feel that they belong to something. Sports appear to have something of the same social function . . .[5]

Now clearly, everyone needs to feel that he has ties with other human beings. In today's complex society, where family ties have become attenuated, where education, social-class mobility, and the ease of physical mobility make it difficult to maintain an image of one's present place, past roots, and future prospects in society, the need for identity may be heightened, still further. But are these aspects of the impact of urbanization sufficient to account for fan enthusiasm for sport? I contend that they are not.

A second and related point which Beisser makes is that fan enthusiasm results from the need to share strong feelings with others in the urban situation. He states that the family does not now adequately serve such a need.

. . . Everyone needs to be able to share strong feelings with others . . . The typical small American family . . . promotes such intense relationships that the family members are bound in a kind of unspoken truce to restrain their strongest feelings, and usually only impulsive moments of rage or grief break through to be expressed.[6]

Beisser further asserts

. . . Official agencies often do not serve as well as those which develop spontaneously in response to a cultural need, and of the latter the athletic team, which has developed many of the characteristics of the extended family . . . , is an impressive example. The fan in relationship to his team is like the member of a family or a tribe. He can share intense feelings in victory and defeat. He partakes of the secrets of the tribe—statistics and team information—and he can exhibit tangible evidence of belonging. He dons his tribal headdress, his Dodger cap, and joins in the ceremonies at the stadium to support the members of the tribe as they do battle. He can complain bitterly to an understanding crowd of the fallacious decision of the chief— the manager. He can complain about the errors of some team members to other tribesmen who, like him, understand.

---

[5] Beisser, p. 126.
[6] Ibid., p. 129.

The fan is united with other fans in his hatred of rival teams. Where else in American . . . encouraged to leap to his feet, at one with a sympathetic crowd, and vehemently shout, "Kill the bums!" He knows that he does not stand alone in his intense feelings—that, such feelings are shared with a host of others. Anyone who objects must take on all of them. In victory there is a boundless sharing of the joy which the fan experiences personally and collectively.[7]

William G. Thompkins likewise emphasizes the expressive uses of sport:

. . . The ability to exhibit feelings or emotions of any kind has very low priority and acceptance in a technological world . . . Modern society has gradually closed off avenues for discharge of those energies and for getting emotional assurances. But sports . . . allows those outlets . . .[8]

There are several basic problems raised by these interpretations. First, it is implicitly assumed that because urbanized society and fan enthusiasm for sport exist concomitantly, urban conditions must be responsible for fan enthusiasm. No doubt the impact of urban life frequently heightens priorities upon needs to belong and to find outlets for expression of suppressed emotions. This situation alone does not sufficiently explain, however, the fact that a significant proportion of the American public is fanatically enthusiastic about sports. For there are numerous avenues by which the assumed needs may be fulfilled. For example, many individuals can achieve a greater sense of belonging by joining a church, civic group, political party, or private club than by sitting in a stadium or gymnasium, one of perhaps thousands of nameless individuals. Also, one may find release for suppressed feelings in movie houses, the live theater, music concerts of all kinds, and in other social gatherings, not to speak of the possibility of the individual himself participating in various recreational pursuits. But although these diverse avenues are generally available, millions of people do not exhibit the intense enthusiasm over them that they expend upon sport.

Further, Beisser's and Thompkins's explanations do not account for the enthusiasm for sport exhibited in rural areas or in the society as a whole prior to the onset of widespread urbanization in America. We have already seen that the two most rurally oriented segments of the country—the South and the Midwest—manifest the highest interest in sport. Also, as was shown in chapter 2, around the turn of the century,

---

[7] Ibid., pp. 129–30.

[8] William G. Thompkins, cited in David Hendin "Footballitis: A Contagious, Incurable Disease," *Fremont News-Register,* October 29, 1971, p. 29 (from an article in *Medical Opinion,* October, 1971).

a time at which America was a society quite rural by today's standards, sports enthusiasm was quite high.[9]

Third, the explanations do not account for the predominantly male fan interest in sport. Thompkins himself observes the male-female differential and speculates about its sources.

> Men in American society do not empathize easily with the quiz shows and soap operas so popular with [their] wives . . . Therefore in a quest for healthy sublimation of human feelings, the male frequently turns increased attention to sports activities . . .[10]

Other observers have struggled with the problems of analyzing motivations for fan enthusiasm. An evocative interpretation has been offered by Schafer.

> . . . One must ask, why do [fans] give their interest and energy to athletics to the extent they do? In short, why do they get so involved in competitive contests between schools? One reason is that normative influences pull them in that direction. Put differently, it is the *thing* to support your school's football, basketball, and, where I live, track team.
>
> A second reason is that fandom, to use Gregory Stone's term, provides a sense of belonging, of identification with a collectivity larger than the family or friendship group. To the best of my knowledge, no research has been conducted on the significance of the "affiliation motive" for fandom, but it is probably considerable. . . .
>
> Third, [fans] become so strongly identified with the team because the team represents an extension of their own sense of self . . . by identifying with the team, the fan is afforded the chance to affirm his own worth and quality. But he does it at some risk. If his team wins, he feels good about himself . . . But, if his team loses, especially if it loses consistently, he too is a loser in his own eyes. Perhaps it is in this way that we can better understand why fans become so intensely concerned that their team win, and why attendance and interest fall off so markedly when a team consistently loses . . .[11]

Now, some of Schafer's assertions appear to be accurate. The fan is afforded the chance to affirm his own worth and quality through sports; he does feel good about himself when his team wins, and, similarly, he feels bad when it loses. In the former case, fan support *is* likely to be strengthened and in the latter it is likely to wane.

But other of the author's generalizations are tautological or simply of questionable validity. One plausible assertion, for example, is that fans seek to fulfill their needs to "belong and to identify with a col-

---

[9] See J. R. Betts, "The Technological Revolution and the Rise of Sport," Loy and Kenyon, *Sport, Culture and Society,* pp. 145–66.

[10] William G. Thompkins, Ibid., p. 29.

[11] W. E. Schafer, "Some Social Sources and Consequences of Interscholastic Athletics," in J. Kenyon, ed., *Sociology of Sport* (Athletic Institute, 1969), pp. 33–34.

lectivity larger than the family or friendship group" because of an "affiliative motive." But is not the proposition tautological—"people become affiliated with sport as fans because they are motivated to do so"? What we need to know is why a need to belong and identify is satisfied within the institution of sport. Schafer suggests that part of the specific appeal may be that sport affords the fan a "chance for direct involvement with sub-groups, such as friendship groups, the band, the cheerleading squad, or the concession club." But the overwhelming majority of fans never belong to or directly interact in any important way with any of these subgroups. Furthermore, more fans probably view sports events via television each year than at the scene of these sporting events.

There are difficulties also with the hypothesis that identification with the team occurs because the team represents an extension of sense of self. For a team to "become an extension of a fan's ego," it would seem that either the fan must already have established an identification with that team or else the statement is tautological. Nor does it explain people's choice of the sports realm as the institution within which to express this enthusiastic identification—as opposed to say political parties, religious groups, and so forth.

Are there other factors that could more plausibly be regarded as influences determining fan identification and personal involvement in sports? We need to know why they chose the sports realm as the focus of involvement, and the character of fan relations in general with other roles and positions within the institution of sport. Let us test this approach by attempting an explanation of the predominantly male composition of sport's fan following.

In order to explain this predominantly male enthusiasm for and identification with sport within the context of Beisser and Thompkins ideas, one must be prepared to assert either (1) that the urban environment, which has had such a great impact upon such institutions as the family and upon the character of interpersonal interaction in general, has failed to affect females; (2) or, that though both males and females have been affected in a like manner by urbanization, only the male has the developed feelings which are subsequently fulfilled within the institution of sport. Neither assertion would hold up well under sociological scrutiny.

Within the context of Schafer's ideas one would have to assume that male behavior is affected to a greater degree by an "affiliative motive" than is female behavior. This has yet to be demonstrated.

We are prepared to believe that involvement through the fan role does give rise to both a feeling of identification or belonging and to the opportunity to express suppressed emotions via a socially approved outlet.

But the explanation is too general to be helpful. Our addition is to argue that the chief specific factors determining fan enthusiasm for sport are to be found within the functions of sport as an institution. As an institution having primarily socialization and value maintenance functions, sport affords the fan an opportunity to *reaffirm the established values and beliefs defining acceptable means and solutions to central problems in the secular realm of everyday societal life.* But this fact does not stand alone; particular patterns of values are expressed through certain intrinsic features of sports activities; in combination, the two aspects explain not only fan enthusiasm but sport's predominantly male following. Sports events are *unrehearsed,* they involve *exceptional performances* in a situation characterized by a degree of *uncertainty* and a lack of total control, and they epitomize *competition for scarce values* —prestige, status, self-adequacy, and other socially relevant rewards. In his daily life pursuits, the fan also competes. In the economic realm for instance, interactions are unrehearsed; the individual cannot even hope to control all the factors which affect his outcomes; and most of all, interaction is characterized by intense competition for scarce valued goods and services. Perhaps this fact helps to explain the overwhelming representation of business men on team booster clubs and as heads of alumni groups.

Under the circumstances sketched, it is inevitable that in many instances, despite the fact that a person rigorously conforms to the "rules of the game," outcomes are going to be different from those anticipated and desired. But society could not long function if, even after substantial honest effort and frustration, people simply began to employ *any means necessary* to achieve goals, regardless of whether such means were socially approved or not. It is at this point that some possible functions of the institution of sport become relevant. Sport reaffirms the viability of the values or rules under which the fan must operate in his day-to-day instrumental pursuits—and may thereby sustain the individual's faith in and willingness to abide by those rules. The fan who identifies with a particular athletic aggregation—who joins a sports "family" so to speak—feels a genuine sense of defeat when that aggregation loses, and a true sense of personal victory and self-satisfaction when his team wins. For when he is cheering for his team, he is really cheering for himself as well. When he screams insults and abuse upon the opposition sports unit, he is verbally assaulting those forces he has confronted and that so often have combined to frustrate his own personal goal achievement efforts and his own social and psychological security. And when his team loses or does not perform up to expectations, the fan often turns his insults onto them, regardless of the quality of their past performances.

Texas Tech Coach Raps Grid Fans for Booing Quarterback

Texas Tech football coach Jim Carlen Monday rapped his own fans for booing senior quarterback Charles Napper during Saturday's 28–7 win over Texas A and M.

"If you want to boo me, that's one thing. But leave my kids alone," Carlen said. "I'm the one who went into the dressing room and saw one kid in the corner—crying his heart out."

"You seem to forget he's the same quarterback who got knocked out last year against SMU, had blood running out of his mouth, and didn't know where he was," Carlen said of Napper. "But he told me he was okay."[12]

The significant point here is that when an athlete, a coach, or an athletic unit as a whole fails to achieve, they are perceived by the fan as having failed him personally. Thus fans often say that "we" lost today or "we" beat this or that opposing team. Typically, when a team is on a losing streak, fan support drops off and hometown fans may even support visiting athletic units. But when that same team is winning, fan support picks up. There are also exceptions to these well-established tendencies, the most notable case being that of the 1969 New York Mets professional baseball team. Here, fan support remained high and is alleged to have even increased though the Mets were compiling the worse win-lose record in professional baseball history during one two-year period. (This case constitutes an exception in the annals of sport that deserves a separate analysis all of its own.) Usually fans desert losing sports units in droves. For if a team is on a losing streak, it is compounding the fan's own personal sense of frustration and failure rather than sustaining his will to continue his own life's struggles within the context of the rules, though the obstacles to goal achievement be many, frequently uncontrollable, and often unexpected. In such a situation, fans typically use the team as a scapegoat for all their frustrations.

---

[12] "Texas Tech Coach Raps Grid Fans for Booing Quarterback," *Fremont News-Register,* October 12, 1971, p. 13.

Two Detroit Coaches Quit, Blame Fans

The booing from the hometown fans cost Detroit pro sports two coaches over the weekend as Doug Barkley of the Red Wings and Bill van Breda Kolff of the Detroit Pistons handed in their surprise resignations.

Barkley, a 34-year-old veteran of the National Hockey League resigned just before the Wings took the ice at Detroit Olympia Sunday night and handed Pittsburgh a 3–1 set-back.

"I just could not live with the pressure of 15,000 fans booing and the pressure from press and television and radio," he said.

Detroit pro fans were still recovering from the surprise of the Barkley decision when Van Breda Kolff walked into the Piston's office yesterday morning and announced his resignation.[13]

A winning team reinforces the societal values upon hard work, discipline, good character, mental alertness, hard but honest competition, the "American way of life," and so forth. Its performance is evidence that the system is still capable and viable, despite occasional or even frequent contradictions.

To the extent that the above analysis is correct, it is to be expected that those individuals and social classes most directly involved with carrying out instrumental functions in society will also have the greatest interest in sport. In this regard, though women may be covertly excluded from *participation* in many sports, this would not necessarily prohibit them from expressing an *interest* in sports proportionate to that expressed by men. But the evidence is to the contrary. For example, Stone has presented data indicating that men show a greater fan interest in sport

---

[13] "Two Detroit Coaches Quit, Blame Fans," *San Francisco Chronicle,* November 2, 1971, p. 41.

than do women.[14] His work indicates that sports is a man's world and that men expressed greater interest in sports than women—about two-thirds of the men polled indicating that they talk about sports frequently or very frequently as opposed to only one-third of the women.

In terms of socioeconomic class differences in frequency of sport-related conversations, Stone states:

. . . The most interesting datum is the polarization in the lower strata between a third who rarely or never talk about sports, and about a fourth of those who talk very frequently about sports . . . [In] terms of frequent conversations, the differences among the strata are so slight as to be negligible. I think what this means is that many lower strata people are left outside the world of sport. Based upon other data, I have found that there is a general alienation of the lower stratum when using such measures as integration with the neighborhood, and a sense of belonging to the larger city. There is a general alienation and perhaps this lack of involvement as measured by frequency of sport conversation on the part of the lower stratum indicates a larger alienation than being simply alienated from the sport world . . .[15]

These data run counter to the "alienation" suppositions advanced by Beisser and Thompkins. For if urban alienation were the primary factor underlying fan enthusiasm, one should find the greatest enthusiasm among those whose achievements in the urban or metropolitan environment had been most frustrated. Stone found exactly the opposite. The latter findings, it is felt, can be explained by a different dynamic of the fans' involvement with sport.

If my hypothesis is correct, then the greater the individual's involvement in instrumental pursuits, the greater should be his interest in sport. Within the context of prescribed societal means, American males are more involved in instrumental forms of competition and goal achievement activities than are women; persons belonging to the lower class pursue fewer and a narrower scope of instrumentally relevant goals and activities than do persons belonging to the middle class; and upper-class persons pursue a broader range of such activities than do middle-class or lower-class persons. Though Stone does not interpret his data within this context—the present hypothesis appears to be consistent with both the observed male-female and interclass variance in expressed interest in sport.

It would be enlightening to compare Stone's findings with data gathered from black metropolitan communities. (Stone's data were all gathered from white populations.) My speculation is that, due to the special significance of sport in black society, the expressed differences

---

[14] G. P. Stone, "Some Meanings of American Sport: An Extended View" Kenyon, *Sociology of Sport*, p. 12.

[15] G. P. Stone, Ibid., p. 13.

among socioeconomic strata would be negligible, and that differences between black females and black males in expressed interest in sport would be less than the differences observed in Stone's sample between white males and females.

THE ALUMNI

In the realm of collegiate sports, one category of fans warrants special attention: the alumni. They typically exhibit extraordinary interest in and exercise a degree of control over collegiate sports aggregations which is seldom if ever even approached by the ordinary fan in other sectors of the sports world. In order to understand the extraordinary role of the alumni in collegiate sports one must understand the history of this involvement.

It was in the first years of the twentieth century (circa 1910) that a system of intercollegiate athletics evolved from student initiated and controlled intramural recreational pursuits. Sports for the first time were fully supported as a legitimate endeavor for educational institutions. It was not long, however, before it became clear to all concerned that intercollegiate athletics had become too complex to be left to the control and direction of students, a complexity brought about by the hiring of professional coaches, the purchase and maintenance of athletic facilities and equipment, the planning of increasingly more distant trips and more extended schedules, and the emergence of professional sports officiating.

Once training in physical education was accepted as valid academic preparation for coaches, individuals having such training quickly assumed major control over sports, with the help of alumni groups, at the institutional level and have maintained it since that time. It may be justifiably stated that college faculties and administrations lost a favorable opportunity to gain control of athletics as component activities of the educational process at the point where it became obvious that these activities had become too complex to be competently administered by student bodies whose memberships were highly transient. Rather than establish themselves as the controllers of collegiate sports programs, college faculties and administrations more or less ignored the athletic aspect of student life administratively while succumbing to demands for increased emphasis upon and funding for sports activities.

It had become apparent by World War I that independent student control of intercollegiate sports was neither practical or adequate. The scope of these programs had so increased that the details of administration were far beyond the time and abilities of students to handle and the programs frequently were out of control. Students, being a transient group, failed to provide continuity of policy and practices from year to year. Such matters as financial management, employment of personnel, and so forth, often lacked proper direction or were ignored completely. The administration and control of sports programs were at best haphazard affairs under students' administration.

This state of affairs forced educational institutions to take a stand and demand appropriate controls over college sports. Faced with this demand, students organized themselves into athletic associations similar to the athletic conferences of today. These organizations were the first steps toward the widespread formal organization of collegiate athletics in this country.

For the most part, however, these student-based associations were seen by college administrators as necessary evils to be reluctantly tolerated. Thus, they welcomed continued interest in these programs by alumni who gave the programs continuity and unity. Further, these alumni backed their administrative interests with personal financial contributions and fund-raising campaigns. The alumni typically worked more closely with the coaches and other members of athletic staffs than they did with students, other faculty, or educational administrators, who considered sports more a nuisance than an academic activity. This controlling coalition of alumni and athletic department administrations and coaching staffs still persists.

Members of alumni groups who had maintained close personal relationships with their alma maters, have typically channeled these relationships through athletics. Alumni have traditionally found sports activities to be the strongest, or a least the most universal, symbolic link between themselves and their college days. Therefore, it is a decidedly strong factor in linking them to their colleges. They enjoy the sense of expectation when they read of or witness the athletic achievements of their colleges. The entire atmosphere surrounding sports incites in them feelings of identification, pride, and vitality.

The coaches and athletic administrators work closely with the alumni because of the financial aid provided their athletic programs by alumni groups. In return, the alumni expect coaches to produce winning sports aggregations which adequately represent their alma maters and with which they can vicariously identify and loquaciously express their pride in. For it is not just the teams well-being which is at stake but their own as well.

As we shall see in the next chapter, alumni have become so entrenched in collegiate athletics that they are today indispensable in terms of their financial support, despite mandatory fees from students for the support of sports programs. And the current practice is to encourage an even greater involvement of alumni in college activities and to heighten recognition of them for their efforts.

There is an obvious danger however in the practice of allowing nonacademic or unofficial outside control over component activities of educational institutions. An educational institution runs the risk of permitting these activities to become not only noneducational but even inimical to the educational process. We shall return to this point in the next chapter.

THE SPORTS REPORTER

Unlike some collegiate alumni, not all fans have direct personal access to their chosen sports aggregations. For the overwhelming majority of fans who are relegated to the anonymity of the spectator stands, the sports reporter serves a vital function. It is through the work of the sports reporter that the fan becomes privy to the internal functioning of his sports "family" and the private personalities and concerns of various persons fulfilling primary-level roles in sport; and most of all, it is through the writings, telecasts, broadcasts and so forth of the sports reporter that the fan comes to feel that he "knows" his team or his favorite coach or athlete, their shortcomings and attributes. All this enables the fan to more closely identify his own personal daily struggles with those of his chosen athlete or team in the athletic sphere. This point is a key to understanding the dynamics of the sports reporter's *liaison role* between sports aggregations and fans.

In order for a fan to identify his own personal efforts at instrumental goal achievement within the context of approved societal rules with the struggles of his chosen athletic unit in the sports realm, both the fan's personal struggles and the struggles waged by his athletic family must be perceived by the fan as occurring within the bounds of similar if not identical cultural "rules of the game." Under these circumstances, the chief role responsibility of the sports reporter as liaison person between the athletic unit and the fan is that of casting the activities of primary-level persons in sports and of sports aggregations within the context of the societal values that the institution of sport functions to reaffirm and sustain. Out of this institutionalized responsibility attached to the position of sports reporter emerges an inherent contradiction in role demands. As a journalist, the sports reporter is bound by professional ethics to strive for objectivity. As a sports reporter, however, his role demands that he portray the activities of groups and individuals involved in sport at a primary level as conforming to the ideal values of society.

Problems emerge primarily due to the fact that in the realm of sport, as is true in every other realm of societal life, there frequently exist broad discrepancies between ideal values and actual behavior. Traditionally, however, not even publicly known discrepancies in the sports sphere have received coverage by sports reporters commensurate with the significance of these discrepancies. For instance, sports reporters undoubtedly knew of the growing drug crisis in sport and the increasing intrateam tensions centering upon racial issues long before these problems were brought into public view by rebelling athletes and others. Yet, one finds virtually no mention of racism or drug abuse in sport prior to the onset of the "athletic revolution."

Further, this apparent lack of candidness exhibited by sports reporters is tolerated not only by the public but by the journalistic profession itself. Indeed, the public often expresses outrage at the audacity of any sports reporter who *does* report on aspects of sport which reflect negatively upon the institution of sport and those involved in it. Such reporting is typically viewed by sports fans as an unwarranted attack not only upon sport, but upon the American way of life. For, as an arena wherein the viability of American secular values are reaffirmed for the public, the institution of sport has acquired a sacrosanct status. If the integrity of the institution of sport is impugned, the fan is deprived of a significant vehicle by which to sustain his own life's struggles. Significantly, fans seldom react with such vitriolic indignation when the behavior of a single athlete is questioned, though he may be extremely popular. Therefore, there was relatively little concern expressed by fans when Joe Namath was suspended from professional football because of alleged "unsavory business connections," or when Denny McLain was suspended from professional baseball for alleged "behavior unbecoming an athlete." It is only in cases where the integrity of the institution of sport as a whole is impugned that fan indignation runs high. Thus, I received a tremendous volume of hate letters, many containing death threats, between November of 1967 and January of 1971 after I accused the whole of sport of being infected with institutionalized racism. Several of the sports writers who sympathetically reported these allegations also received hate mail and telephone calls. This difference in fan reaction to accusations impugning the integrity of individual athletes or even individual athletic aggregations as opposed to those bringing into question the integrity of the entire institution of sport is determined by the character of the needs served by this institution for both the fan and the society as a whole.

The degree to which sports reporters as opposed to news journalists lack candor in reporting on sports events is tolerated by regular news journalists because it is not viewed as a threat to the integrity of the journalistic profession. Sports reporting and more "serious" journalistic endeavors are viewed both by the public and by the journalistic profession itself as having completely separate and distinct identities. The role of the news reporter demands that he adhere to rigorous ethics defining the bounds of idiosyncratic interpretation of newsworthy events. For as a person whose professional conduct may have serious consequences for the perceived integrity of the "Fourth Estate," increasingly the public's primary avenue of obtaining information about domestic and world affairs, the news reporter's role demands that he strive for objectivity. On the other hand, the sports reporter is seen as functioning primarily in the "toy department" of human affairs. The "wars" that he reports on take place in the athletic arena where the "enemy" is seldom killed. The political maneuvering that he covers is between rival athletic conferences, associations, and owners and not between individuals vying for public office, or between political parties, or heads of state. The "slaughters," the "murders," the "blitzes" that he reports are figurative rather than literal. And when he states that the Indians "bombed" the Reds, he is saying that the Cleveland Indians scored a lopsided victory over the Cincinnati Reds in professional baseball, and not that, at long last, the tensions between India and the People's Republic of China have erupted into all-out war.

Because of the lack of perceived seriousness of sports activities, its fun-and-games image, the sports reporter is permitted a great deal more latitude in terms of slanting his coverage. Objectivity beyond the accurate reporting of box scores has traditionally been at best a secondary consideration. Now, while the journalistic profession tolerates the sports reporter's lack of candidness, the sports establishment demands it. Anything reported that is likely to affect fan attendance negatively is understandably frowned upon by the sports establishment. Thus, those reporters who write stories which are seen to reflect negatively upon a particular team or upon sport as an institution are open to retaliation. And, in the case of the sports reporter, the sports establishment is quite capable of exacting punishment for perceived betrayals. This is not to say that sports reporters necessarily do not believe what they write. It should be remembered that practically all are men, and, imbued with the sports creed, they too possibly can find instrumental sustenance in that creed. So, though they are the chief disseminators of the ideology, they quite possibly also believe it.

In order to fulfill his role responsibilities, the sports reporter must have access to sports aggregations, coaches, and star athletes. This access is considered a privilege, *not* a right, and it is granted by controllers of the individual sports unit with the *understanding* that the sports reporter will use discretion in reporting what he hears and sees "backstage" in the sports sphere. He is also expected to interpret what occurs "on stage" in the best possible light. If he betrays this unspoken reciprocal agreement, he quickly finds himself persona non grata throughout the sports realm.

Schecter, You Aren't Welcome

"Mr. Schecter, you aren't welcome in our camp. So leave." And with that, Cincinnati Bengals coach Paul Brown booted writer Leonard Schecter from his news conference at the Bengals training camp here.

Schecter had written several articles on sports personalities such as the late Vince Lombardi, NFL Commissioner Pete Rozelle and Oakland Raider general manager Al Davis.

Brown said the articles were "hatchet jobs."[16]

No Desk for Writer Karras

Alex Karras, veteran defensive tackle who was cut by the National Football League Detroit Lions and is now a sports columnist for the Detroit Free Press, was barred from the Lions' press box last Sunday when Detroit beat Atlanta, 41–38. "We're still paying his salary," said Lions' publicity chief and former Free Press sports editor Lyall Smith. "He's done nothing but say derogatory things about his former team and I must assume the reason for his column is to say more derogatory things." Karras said, "My column is not to criticize the Lions. I'm simply going to tell it like it is. I have no poison pen."[17]

It is, of course, possible for sports reporters to become too accommodating and cozy with the controlling hierarchies of the sports aggregations that they cover. In a CBS radio broadcast of November 24, 1971, Nicolas von Hoffman stated

[16] "Schecter, You Aren't Welcome," *San Francisco Chronicle,* August 13, 1971, p. 41.

[17] "No Desk for Writer Karras," *San Francisco Chronicle,* October 6, 1971, p. 67.

. . . Sports reporters have traditionally enjoyed lavish treatment provided by sports organizations . . . The press parties . . . . given by these bodies are looked forward to with particular eagerness. Not infrequently, the sports reporter attending such an event can take his pick of gifts piled high on a centrally located table: toasters, coffee makers, portable or transistorized radios . . . The association of some . . . sports reporters with athletic organizations goes even beyond this, as was true in the case of the sports writer who saw nothing unethical in the fact that he received $12,000 a year as a "consultant" to a race track operation whose events he covered for a major metropolitan newspaper; or in the cases of a couple of sports writers who let the public relations departments of sports organizations write the stories appearing under their bylines. Violations of ethics have become so flagrant that some states are moving to institute controls. For instance, the Illinois State Legislature presently has before it a bill which would require all . . . media journalists, including sports reporters, to disclose publicly the amount and sources of their private holdings . . . In return for gifts, money, and so forth, sports reporters are expected to portray sports bodies in a favorable light, even if the facts are not so favorable . . .

The case of the black sports reporter is particularly problematic. For, being black, and working most often for newspapers and radio stations which serve the black communities of the nation, he is expected by his clientele to "tell it like it is" in sport. He is expected to disclose publicly any incidents of racial discrimination in particular. If he does not do so, he is accused of being an "Uncle Tom" or worse. Yet, though his clientele is black rather than white, if he is to maintain any access to those channels by which "backstage" information is gained he must meet the same expectations demanded of the white sports reporter. In this regard, the demands that many blacks make upon the black sports reporter contains an inherent contradiction. For, if he accedes to these demands, he would almost certainly be denied the very access necessary to serve the function demanded of him by vocal segments of the black community. When confronted with this dilemma, most black sports reporters chose their livelihood over becoming a "hero for a day." Many feel that their value to the black community, no matter how small, is immensely greater if they maintain a presence in and access to sport than if they were ostracized from sports completely.

Sports reporters in general are embroiled in another dilemma which has to do with the functions of sport in American society.

Aside from the money, prestige may well be the greatest incentive to professional sports participation. In amateur athletics, it certainly is a primary incentive, along with the "love of the game." Prestige typically accrues and is measured by the frequency and tone of publicity and recognition that an athlete receives in the various reporting media. Black athletes as a whole, feel that many sports reporters have not always given credit where credit is due. In a pro grid game not too long ago, a black flanker had scored on an end-around play and caught passes from his quarterback and halfback for two more scores. Next day, he was outraged to find out that most reporters covering the game had heaped praise on the white quarterback for his masterful game calling, while the flanker himself was barely mentioned in passing. Were this an isolated case, it could be dismissed as merely the complaint of a disgruntled "glory seeker." But it is not an isolated case. It reflects a state of affairs that exists at the high-school level and extends on into professional sports.

Now, as a result of this apparent racial discrimination in reporting, many of sports' critics have accused white sports reporters of acting out personal racist attitudes. While this charge indeed may be justified, it would appear that the sports reporter, even if he desired, would be hard pressed to give fair and impartial coverage, much less equal coverage, to both black and white athletes. For one thing, athletes holding particular positions in many sports are going to receive more coverage than athletes holding other positions, simply because of the differential control and leadership responsibilities attached to these positions. On the whole, the athlete manning the quarterback position in football is going to receive more publicity than the athlete manning the tackle position. The quarterback position is simply more involved at the center of action regardless of the strategy employed by a team. Since blacks are underrepresented in leadership and control positions in sports activities, it should be expected that they will receive less publicity. But the real factor to be considered here is not positional segregation, For, as has been shown, this is merely a symptom.

FAN IDENTIFICATION

It has been noted above that the demands in America for white athletes to man leadership and control positions in particular may be due to the believed service performed by sport for the society—that of developing "the future custodians of the Republic." The dynamics of the fan's relationship to sport also has an input here. Clearly, most sports fans in America are white. If our analysis of the factors determining fan enthusiasm is correct, it would appear plausible that most fans in America could more easily identify with the struggles being waged by a white athlete in the sports arena than with those being waged by a black athlete. On the one hand, the white athlete has a good deal more in common with the white sports fan culturally than does the black athlete. The general social environment of the white athlete, the obstacles to goal achievement that he must overcome are familiar to the white sports fan. On the other hand, the cultural heritage of the black athlete has traditionally been shrouded in stereotypes, myths, and misconceptions. Many of the obstacles which he must overcome to achieve desired goals in sport (or in any other realm of societal life) are not a type that easily elicits empathy from whites. Thus, when white fans identify with white athletes their preferences may be racist in effect, but the preference does not necessarily mean that white fans are motivated solely by a desire to keep blacks out.

It is at least possible that they are acting in part to maintain a situation wherein they can more readily identify with the struggles of primary-level persons engaged in sport. In short, though the *covert* effect of fan influence upon equal access to sports positions by both black and white athletes is to exclude blacks from leadership and control positions, the *overt* effort apparently is to keep whites in these positions. The sports reporter, in his role as liaison person, is expected by white fans to focus primarily upon whites in covering sports events. Thus, because of the subordinate position and status of blacks in the larger society, the role of blacks in the achievement of athletic victories may be covertly understated, or even omitted altogether—just as tackles and guards in football and outfielders in baseball will seldom receive public acclaim commensurate with their roles in achieving team victories in these sports due to the structure of these activities. No one especially dislikes tackles, guards, and outfielders. They are simply left out of media publicity, while persons manning leadership and control positions receive attention. I do not feel that it is coincidental that the values governing instrumental goal achievement in the greater society dictate that every individual be responsible for his own outcomes. According to these values, every person has an opportunity to succeed in a theoretically open marketplace of competition. Under these auspices, perhaps it is to be expected that fans should identify with the leadership and control roles in sport since, in their own life pursuits, they themselves are defined by social values as masters of their own fates. It might be asked why fans do not identify with the coach more than the athletes under these circumstances. Few fans wait outside of locker rooms to get coaches' autographs. The key consideration here is that coaches are executives. They are not the individuals most directly involved in the struggles on the fields of action. In his day-to-day pursuits, the typical fan does not have the luxury of ordering someone else into battle. It is he himself who is most directly involved in *his* struggles for valued goods and services. So in football for instance, the fan identifies with the quarterback rather than the coach, though the coach exercises greater authority.

It is this component of the dynamics underlying fan identification which I believe to be responsible in considerable measure for the low status of boxing as a spectator sport in contemporary America. Most of the legitimate contenders for the championships and the champions of the heavyweight and light-heavyweight divisions—the two most prestigious divisions—are black. As is the case in most sports, boxers today are more skilled, they are faster, and they exhibit a level of "showmanship" never before found in the sport. Yet, boxing on the whole is less popular than in the recent past. Issues of race and politics have been projected into the sport to such an extent that, unless a particular boxing match can be perceived as personifying a racial or political confrontation of some sort, it fails to draw fans. Thus, though boxing was seen as a dying sport, the Frasier-Muhammad Ali heavyweight championship match drew widespread spectator interest. It is hard to believe that it was coincidental that Frasier was accused by many blacks and by both black and white radicals of being "a great-White-hope surrogate," a representative of the establishment, an "Uncle Tom." On the other hand, these individuals looked upon Muhammad Ali as the representative of the "Third World's" struggle for justice. In short, the Frasier-Muhammad Ali boxing contest was perceived by many as a struggle between good and evil, patriots and peacenicks, whites and blacks, separatists and integrationists, and all manner of other dichotomous confrontations none of which had anything to do with the actual boxing match itself. Nonetheless, depending upon one's political perspectives, one fighter or the other became the "warrior knight" stepping forth to do battle in the name of a political cause. The promoters of boxing matches and, indeed, the boxers themselves are quite aware of this fact and will often capitalize upon it in order to increase gate receipts.

The projection of political issues in boxing matches in particular is not new—especially in matches between black and white boxers. Thus, in his *Confessions of a White Racist,* Larry L. King notes that

On the June morning of 1937 following Joe Louis's knockout of Jimmy Braddock for the world heavyweight championship, I heard an old [white] woman say in the Putnam post office, "Well, the ole nigger is champion." "Yes," her companion said, "I reckon they'll be pushing white folks off the sidewalks now."[18]

And, as Maya Angelou's observations make clear, blacks project racial connotations into boxing matches much as do whites.

"[Carnera's] got Louis against the ropes" . . . said the announcer . . . "And it looks like Louis is going down."

My people groaned. It was our people falling. It was another lynching, yet another Black man hanging on a tree. One more woman ambushed and raped. A Black boy whipped and maimed. It was hounds on the trail of a man running through slimy swamps. It was a White woman slapping her maid for being forgetful. . . . We didn't breathe; we didn't hope; we waited.

---

[18] Larry L. King, *Confessions of a White Racist* (New York: Viking Press, 1971), p. 3.

"He's off the ropes, ladies and gentlemen," shouted the announcer. . . . Carnera is on the canvas . . ."

"Champion of the World. A Black boy. Some Black mother's son. He was the strongest man in the world . . ."

It would take an hour or more for before the people [assembled at the store to hear the fight] would head for home. Those who lived too far made arrangements to stay in town. It wouldn't do for a Black man and his family to be caught on a lonely country road on a night when Joe Louis had proved that we were the strongest people in the world.[19]

Now, one might ask why it is that whites still patronize basketball, a sport that has become over 60 percent black at the professional level. This is a difficult question to answer due to the fact that there is really no way of determining the exact point at which a sport becomes so dominated by blacks as to lose its appeal to white fans. But one thing seems clear. If basketball ever becomes *all* black, whites will probably abandon it much as they have boxing.

Finally, the same factors which have rocked the traditional stability of the coaching role and the athlete role have also begun to alter the character of the sports reporters' role.

Since 1967 and the infusion of sports with issues reflecting a broad range of concerns within the larger society, it has not been sufficient for sports reporters to merely perpetuate traditional beliefs about sport and to report the box scores. In effect, the "revolution" has entered the locker room. And as Joseph Durso of the *New York Times* staff reports

. . . In the middle sits the reporter, covering the "revolution" with typewriter or microphone, hopefully with some grasp of economics, sociology, politics, and the law, to say nothing of geography. Now to get the story behind Curt Flood, the Washington Redskins, and the New York Yankees, he must match minds with Arthur J. Goldberg, Edward Bennet Williams, and John Lindsay's corporation counsel. For the latest on Joe Namath, he "covers" an orthopedic surgeon named Dr. James Nicholas or a lawyer named Mike Bite. For the inside stuff on Arnold Palmer, there is an investment counselor named Mark McCormack. And this reporter, at least, can remember spending one afternoon of spring training last year watching the St. Louis Cardinals play the New York Mets, then the next five afternoons chasing the Seattle-Milwaukee process-servers, Richie Allen's attorney, and Denny McLain's creditors . . . Sports reporters today are confronted with the fact that the dramas on the field were being crowded by dramas of finance, labor relations, and racial protest . . .

---

[19] Maya Angelou *I Know Why The Caged Bird Sings* (New York: Bantam Books, 1970), pp. 113–15.

A youthful Muhammed Ali, formerly Cassius
Clay, as Olympic heavyweight champion with
Eddie Cook (center) and Willie McClure.
(San Jose Mercury-News)

Muhammed Ali uses hand to cover name on
plaque presented him because he objected to
use of "Cassius Clay" rather than his Black
Muslim name. Mr. and Mrs. Muhammed Ali
(opposite page) after champion was deposed
for failure to submit to the military draft.
(San Jose Mercury-News)

Sport in America plays a part in our national life that is probably more important than even the social scientists believe. Sports are now more popular than politics in America, increasingly so since the spread of television. The great corporations are much more interested in paying millions for sports broadcasts than they are for all political events except for the nominations and inaugurations of Presidents, because the general public is watching and listening.[20]

Indeed, apparently the public does pay more attention to and gets more worked up about sports than domestic politics, except perhaps presidential elections. For sport in American society, we have said, constitutes for the fan a quasi religion. Viewed from this perspective, perhaps it is to be expected that the public should turn its attention more and more toward sport in search of confirmation, as conditions in the secular spheres of societal life appear increasingly less stable and as the traditional values governing goal achievement in the environing society seem less viable.

Pseudo-Marxian perspectives on the functions of sport in American society are not new. For instance, in 1926, in an article entitled "Killers of Thought," Upton Sinclair argued that

. . . just as in ancient Rome gladiatorial combats were provided for the purpose of diverting the minds of the populace from the loss of their ancient liberties, so the masters of modern America provide gigantic struggles [in sport] . . .

Capitalists control the colleges. Theirs is the task to keep students from thinking. So they make college a noisy, competitive place, where thinking cannot go on; they pay two or four or six thousand dollars for the cost of a gigantic arena; they pay for expert trainers for the gladiators and for rubbers and stretcher-bearers and surgeons and undertakers and other attendants of the spectacle; and they fit college youth perfectly for that world of competitive commercialism which the alumni have created and which they intend to maintain. Boys who have taken part in commercialized college athletics are ready for the million betrayals of the general welfare which organized class privilege commits in our society . . . And professors who have sat in silence while commercialized athletics destroys the idealism and humanism of the American colleges—these gentlemen will be ready to sit in silence while organized class privilege wipes out the last pretenses of a republic in our country . . .[21]

For the American fan then, sport, whether by deliberate design or social happenstance, has achieved a stature not wholly unlike that enjoyed by traditional religions. Sport also has other features in common with religions.

---

[20] Joseph Durso, "Sportswriting—and the All American Dollar," *Saturday Review*, October, 1971, pp. 66–73.

[21] Upton Sinclair, "Killers of Thought" *Forum* 76 (December 1926): 838–43.

Sport has a body of formally stated beliefs, accepted on faith by great masses of people across America's socioeconomic strata, from the president of the United States down to the most humble bootblack. These beliefs are stated primarily in the form of perceived attributes of sports and are widely disseminated.

It is not infrequently that former or presently active athletes are called upon to give a "what sports have done for me" testimonial or otherwise bear witness to the expressed virtues of sport involvement.

The responsibility for maintaining and perpetuating the sanctity of sport is vested for the most part with men. For, as is the case with traditional religious orders in America, the woman is relegated to a position secondary to that of men.

Sport also has its "saints"—those departed souls who in their lives exemplified and made manifest the prescriptions of the dogma of sport. Such individuals as Knute Rocke, the late Notre Dame football coach, and one of his star athletes, George Gipp; Almos Alonzo Stagg, Jim Thorpe, Babe Ruth, Vince Lombardi, and others are examples of men who achieved virtual immortality and sainthood in the world of sport, and have been duly enshrined in one sports "hall of fame" or another.

Sports also has its ruling patriarchs, a prestigious group of coaches, managers, and sportsmen who exercise controlling influence over national sports organizations. These are also the individuals who are imitated and looked to by younger coaches for guidance and direction. Men such as Paul "Bear" Bryant, George Halas, John Wooden, and Red Auerbach typify the caliber of person who abides in the upper echelons of sport's prestige, status and honor structures. It is individuals of this type who are likely candidates to pass into the realm of sainthood and immortality in the world of sport.

Sports has its "gods"—star and superstar athletes who, though powerless to alter their own situations, wield great influence and charisma over the masses of fans.

Sport has its high councils, controlled or greatly influenced by patriarchs who make and interpret the rules of sports involvement. Such organizations as the NCAA, the AAU and the United States Olympic Committee are examples of sports' high councils.

Sport has its scribes—the hundreds of sports reporters, sports telecasters and sports broadcasters whose primary duties are to record the ongoing history of sports and to disseminate its dogma and word of its day-to-day glory among the people.

Sport has its "seekers of the kingdom," its true believers, devotees and converts. In short, sport has its fanatics, a following partially made up of special groups such as college alumni and ex-athletes. But, mostly, these fans emerge from among the ranks of the general public. All of these various elements among the flock attend and view sport events hoping not only to share vicariously in the thrill of victory but to find reaffirmation of the values which give meaning to their own personal struggles.

Sport has its shrines—the national halls of fame and thousands of trophy rooms and cases gracing practically every sports organization's headquarters, regardless of its level of sports involvement.

Sport also has its "houses of worship" spread across the land where millions congregate to bear witness to the manifestation of their faith. These are, of course, the thousands of stadia, gyms, swimming pools, tennis courts, and other sports facilities. These are sometimes huge, ornate, multimillion-dollar facilities. The Astrodome, for instance, probably surpasses or at least rivals any structure ever built by the pharaohs or under the aegis of one or the other of the great religions. But regardless of their size or value, these are meticulously cared for and otherwise given the attention becoming a house of worship. Many are maintained by full-time staffs of workers whose only task is to perpetually clean and groom the facilities in preparation for sporting events.

Sport has its "symbols of the faith"—the trophies; game balls; the bats, gloves, baseballs, and so forth, that "won" this or that game; the clothing, shoes, headgear or socks of immortal personages of sports. Thousands of believers marvel or shout in triumphant joy at the mere sight of this or that torphy or plaque. And, perhaps the greatest thrill of all is experienced by the fan who retrieves a ball actually used in an official sporting event. Sport involves "feeling," ritual, and the celebration of human achievement. It provides fans with a set of organized principles which give meaning to their secular strivings and sufferings. And beliefs about sport support social values and norms.

And finally there is one other feature apparently characteristic of both traditional religions and the "secular religion" of sport.

Roger Bastide writes in *Daedalus*:

The Christian symbolism of color is very rich. Medieval painting makes full use of it. Some colors are, however, more pertinent to discussion than others. The color yellow, or at least a dull shade of yellow, has come to signify treason. When Westerners think of Asiatics, they unconsciously transpose this significance to them, converting it into a trait of ethnic psychology. Consequently, they treat Asiatics as persons in whom they cannot have confidence. They can, of course, give excellent reasons in defense of their behavior: the closed or uncommunicative character of the Japanese, the smiling impassiveness of the Chinese, or some historic case of treason—but these are all reasons invented after the fact. If Westerners could have prevented themselves from being influenced by a symbolism centuries old, they could just as easily have found reasons to justify an impression of the yellow race as loyal and affectionate.

But the greatest Christian-two-part division is that of white and black. White is used to express the pure, while black expresses the diabolical. The conflict between Christ and Satan, the spiritual and the carnal, good and evil came finally to be expressed by the conflict between white and black, which underlines and synthesizes all the others. Even the blind, who know only night, think of a swarm of angels or of devils in association with white and black— for example, "a black soul," "the blackness of an action," "a dark deed," "the innocent whiteness of the lily," "the candor of a child," "to bleach someone of a crime." These are not merely adjectives and nouns. Whiteness brings to mind the light ascension into the bright realm, the immaculateness of virgin snow, the white dove of the Holy Spirit, and the transparency of limpid air; blackness suggests the infernal streams of the bowels of the earth, the pit of hell, the devil's color . . .

Although Christ transcends all questions of race or ethnology, it must not be forgotten that God incarnated himself in a man of the Jewish race. The Aryans and the Gentiles—even the most anti-Semitic—worship their God in a Jewish body. But this Jewish body was not white enough for them. The entire history of Western painting bears witness to the deliberate whitening or bleaching effort that changed Christ from a Semitic to an Aryan person. The dark hair that Christ was thought to have had came to be rendered as very light-colored, and his big dark eyes as blue. It was necessary that this man, the incarnation of God, be as far removed as possible from everything that could suggest darkness or blackness, even indirectly. His hair and his beard were given the color of sunshine, the brightness of the light above, while his eyes retained the color of the sky from which he descended and to which he returned.[22]

Now, while its origins may be debatable, it cannot be denied that the dichotomous imagery projected onto the colors black and white, and discussed by Bastide above, is somewhat prevalent in American society. In America, this imagery is manifest in many cultural traditions and especially in the lexicon of the society. One need not think very long or very hard to recall some of these: the white dove of peace, the black raven associated with the works of Edgar Allen Poe; the black lie which breaks up life-long friendships and families, the white lie which does no harm and frequently has a beneficient affect upon human relationships; the white wedding gown, the black funeral garb; the white angel food cake, the dark devil's food cake; "the good guys" wear white hats, the "bad guys are dressed in black; when someone does something that pleases a person, he is frequently told "That's damn white of you."

If Bastide's assertions are correct, and if American society is as obsessed with the alleged virtues of "whiteness," as Western civilization

---

[22] Roger Bastide, "Color, Racism, and Christianity," *Daedalus: The Journal of the American Academy of Arts and Sciences* (Spring 1967), pp. 314–15.

as a whole (and I believe there is ample evidence that it is), then there is little ground for the expectation that this society, which does not tolerate an image of its sacred God cast in a Semitic body, would be strongly predisposed to tolerate black heroes and "gods" in its secular religion of sport. The speculation here is that this fact contributes to determining the positional segregation of blacks in some American sports and their almost total exclusion from most single-participant sports.

Relevant to this last point is the fact that here may be a paradoxical dilemma for black people resulting from the black athlete's success in sport. Given the functions of sport for the fan and American society, the black athlete's highly visible success in sports endeavors could have the affect of stimulating black society's hopes for eventually competing successfully as equals throughout the secular instrumental sphere of life. However, far from being an omen of positive change in the area of interracial relations, the very fact of the black athlete's superior performance is itself—as we have seen—evidence of continued if not heightened black oppression. In recognition of this fact, anyone who would alter the societal complexities generating black athletic superiority must consider the relative value to black society of (1) destroying the myth that black athletic success is indicative of a general improvement in the life circumstances of all blacks as opposed to (2) allowing the myth to continue, thus allowing blacks in America to sustain a questionable hope while simultaneously deriving a sense of pride by vicariously identifying with the successes of the black athletic champion who defeats the white athlete (or some other person perceived as a symbol of the oppressive white society) in the sports arena. The choice is not an easy one. There is no objective way of determining if the black pride derived from black athletes defeating white athletes in sports offsets the impact of the frustrations emergent from the black community's internalization of the societal values propagated through sport—values which for blacks are only marginally appropriate and creditable due to the mitigating factor of white racism and historical disadvantages.

It is my judgment, however, that the pride derived by black society from the black athlete's domination of whites in certain sports is an "empty" and "phony" pride—as empty and phony as the assumption by nations that superiority on the athletic field can be creditably interpreted as indicative of superiority in political philosophy and social policies and practices. It is because nations hold this illogical and rather warped view of the relations between sport and political philosophy that many have fought the admission of South Africa and Southern Rhodesia to the Olympic Games.) For though the perceived relationship is a falacious one, people behave *as if* it were real. Nevertheless, after Kareem Abdul-Jabbar has annihilated his white counterparts in basketball, after black track and field athletes have dominated whites, and after black boxers, baseball athletes, and football participants have dominated their sports, racism and oppression are still the predominant facts of black life in white America. Similarly, no matter how many times the Americans "beat" the Russians in international sports events, the ubiquitous spectre of a nuclear holocaust and a dozen costly "limited" wars still persist. Thus, when the black athlete puts life, limb, and health on the line in sports, he becomes a *key* factor in a social *sedative process* whereby America dulls black consciousness and awareness of the totality of the impact of white racism and oppression.

Finally, a brief word about the character of relations between the role of fan and that of cheerleader is in order. As a result of the black athletic revolt, "lily-white" corps of cheerleaders have become less and less prevalent at schools fielding integrated athletic units. But the black athletes' demands that black females be allowed access to cheerleading positions and the subsequent accession to these demands have given rise to some unexpected difficulties. While the expressive activities of cheerleaders undoubtedly affect athletes actually engaged in sports events, the main and more direct thrust of cheerleading duties is aimed at the fans. And herein lies the source of difficulties that are apparently becoming more and more widespread.

In visits to five college campuses during the 1971–72 academic year, I found that strained relations existed between fans and cheerleaders. In each case, the cheerleading corps was more than half black. This numerical majority of black cheerleaders over white had resulted in each case in the development of routines and cheers which had distinctly Afro-American style. Frequently, the rhythms of the cheers were taken from the latest "soul song" hits, the steps of the cheering routines were taken from new black dances, as were the body movements.

The difficulty is that, apparently, neither white cheerleaders nor white fans (always in the majority at sports events where two predominantly white schools are involved) find such cheerleading activities stimulating. At one school, a white cheerleader remarked "I just can't catch on to the 'boogie-woogie' cheers. And just about the time that I think I'm beginning to pick up on one, they [the black cheerleaders] are doing something else." At another school, a white cheerleader stated, "The fans boo us. They don't want African cheers; they want good old traditional American cheers. They can't follow that stuff—and neither can I." The black cheerleaders in each case rejected these statements as racist and accused both white fans and white cheerleaders of trying to "force white ways on blacks."

At yet another school where black cheerleaders outnumber whites, the entire situation had developed into something of a minor scandal. The antagonisms between black and white members of the cheerleading corps had become so intense that the two white cheerleaders seldom took part in routines at all during athletic contests. At four football games that I attended, the four black cheerleaders were able to elicit only boos from the predominantly white audience.

I suspect that the breakdown in fan-cheerleader relations under these circumstances is not wholly a reflection of racist attitudes among fans—though antiblack prejudicial attitudes certainly play a part. More likely, white fans' inability to identify with cheerleading routines choreographed within a black cultural context simply heightened some already existing anxieties about black women and thus blossomed into resentment. At the three schools where the fans had actually booed cheerleaders, the three football teams involved also appeared to be heading for losing seasons, and this probably did not aid cheerleaders in their attempts to elicit fan enthusiasm. At one of these three schools—whose football team and cheerleader corps were both 60 percent black—the alumni association actually hired a white former athlete to lead cheers for the home team. By use of spectacular entrances at sporting events (once he was escorted onto the football field at game time by city police cars and motorcycles with sirens blaring and at another time he was flown onto the field at half time in a private helicopter), this paid cheerleader effectively subverted any legitimacy which the regular, predominantly black cheerleading corps may have retained.

The lesson here then appears to be that a predominance of black cheerleaders performing routines derived largely from black cultural styles in a situation where the overwhelming majority of fans are white heightens into interracially sex-centered tensions and creates intercultural incongruities that destroy the traditional fan-cheerleader relationship. And while those fan-cheerleader clashes that I have witnessed have for the most part been dismissed by both black fans and black cheerleaders as merely manifestations of white America's racist inclinations, I wonder what the fan response—particularly the response of the black female fan —would be at, say, Grambling College, to a cheerleading corps which was predominantly white and which performed routines in a style to which black fans were unaccustomed to responding.

STRAINS AND FAN ENTHUSIASM

As was stated in chapter 5, fans are involved in sport at a secondary level. As such, the sports creed does not function for them in the same manner that it functions for primary-level actors—particularly the athletes. Yet, fan involvement in and enthusiasm for sports is still affected by relationship between strains experienced by them and the major themes of the sports creed. Unlike the coach and the athlete, who engage in sports activities as the central activities of their lives, strains experienced by fans do not emerge initially from within the sports realm. But fans do experience strains emergent from their own instrumental activi-

Black cheerleaders prepare to do routine while white cheerleaders look on. Friction between black cheerleaders and white cheerleaders and fans has increased as blacks have come to dominate some groups. While white cheerleaders want no part of "African" and "boogie-woogie" cheers, black cheerleaders characterize what they call "that little honkie hop that whites do" as "soulless" and mechanical. (Photo by Rich Blomberg)

ties and occupational pursuits outside of the sports sphere. They too are subject to strains resulting from uncertainty, conflicting value demands. uncontrollable influences, and so forth. "In most societies, discrepancies between expectations and concrete outcomes have [always] plagued [people] . . . It appears that we never reap exactly as we sow; the flourishing of the wicked [who violate society's values and ethical norms] and the blighting of the good [who abide by these values and norms] have long constituted problems for religious questioning."[23] But particularly in a society *emphasizing* achieved rather than ascribed status, the intervention of unforeseeable and uncontrollable factors which cause achievement to fall short of expectations and effort generate tremendous

[23] Sutton et al., p. 334.

strains for those involved. It is from the amelioration of these strains through secondary level involvement in sport than fan enthusiasm emerges.

Let us begin our summary discussion relating strain to fan enthusiasm by looking at two features of sport which may contribute *initially* to determining fan attentiveness. These features of sport are the exceptional character of the physical demands that it makes upon athletes, and its institutionalized "confrontation" structure. These two features combine to generate what Dunning calls "tension-excitement."

All known human societies have activities and institutions which perform the function of generating tension-excitement. Today, they form an important counter to the routines of "ordinary" life.[24]

Dunning's idea of sport's function in generating tension-excitement is a variation of Thompkins' and of Beisser's theories and has much the same limitations. Nonetheless, "tension-excitement" generated by sport probably does serve the initial sport function of gaining public attention—much the same as an impending fistfight does. But it is not sufficient to generate the ongoing enthusiasm which the designation "fan" denotes.

In their day-to-day instrumental functioning, most of society's members adhere to the generalized "cultural blueprints" or normative rules defining acceptable conduct and regulating human interaction oriented toward the achievement of valued goods and services. Inevitably, however, most people experience discrepancies between legitimate expectations as to the end products of their efforts and the actual concrete results. If such outcomes persist or if they occur over pivotal expectations, many of society's members could be tempted to "innovate" (Merton's terminology)—that is, to violate the rules regulating conduct and strive to achieve desired ends by whatever means are necessary. But again, most of society's members have internalized and deem legitimate the prescribed means of achieving instrumental goals. Herein lies a crucial source of strain. Despite the magnitude of their efforts and the fact of their adherence to prescribed rules of conduct, achievement all too frequently falls short of expectations. But innovative rule-breaking behavior is typically not regarded as an acceptable alternative to establish means as these are defined by prevailing norms and values.

The dominant sports creed has its roots in central components of the American cultural heritage. As such, the values propagated in the sports realm generally mirror those regulating behavior in the larger society. Under these circumstances, the sports institution functions as a "value receptacle" for the society in general, and the activities pursued in this institution become microlevel demonstrations of the viability of

---

[24] Eric Dunning "Notes on Some Conceptual and Theoretical Problems in Sociology of Sport," *International Review of Sport Sociology* (Warsaw: Polish Publishers, 1967), p. 148.

"blueprints" prescribed for successful conduct in the larger society. The fact that the values popularly said to be operative in sport may in fact have a negative, little, or no known or proven relationship to the outcomes experienced within this realm is irrelevant. The significant point is that primary-level actors' adherence to generally prescribed societal values is *believed* by fans to be pivotal influences in determining positive outcomes in sport. To the extent that fans perceive such values to be operative *as a matter of faith,* the American sports creed constitutes a system of "cultural fictions."

In *American Society,* Williams defines a "cultural fiction" as existing . . . whenever there is a cultural description, explanation, or normative prescription that is both *generally accepted as a norm* and *is typically followed* in conduct but is at the same time markedly at variance with subjective conceptions or inclinations of participants in the pattern, or with certain objective scientific knowledge . . . [Cultural fictions] are not "mere forms" but actually define the individuals conception of proper and desirable behavior; the individual "really feels" and "wants to act" as the convention dictates he should. [Thus, conventional norms] supported by such psychological involvement are not fictional except in the sense that *all* norms and values are fictional because they are validated by consensus and practice rather than by realities independent of the social system . . . To the degree that [cultural fictions] serve to limit and define spontaneous personal responses, they facilitate social interaction . . .

If cultural definitions are to be socially effective, . . . they must be invested with some kind of reality . . . and the pressure to accept fully the definitions and prescriptions become the more intense the greater the stress and the higher the ranking of the values involved in any particular case . . . Thus [cultural conventions] can be arranged on a continuum from those practiced by individuals who accept them as necessary or expedient fictions ["Crime does not pay"] . . . over to the abiding beliefs and values not regarded in any way as fictional [Christ was born of a virgin], though objectively the latter might very well be fictional in fact. It is in this sense that, within the context of scientific analysis cultural conventions believed to be and acted upon "as if real and absolute" by society's members can justifiably be termed *fictional.*[25]

It is the common belief in cultural conventions as "real" which make them effective in the regulation of conduct and interaction. Thus, in the sports realm, when we see verbal assent to the creedal belief that sport develops altruism existing alongside violence, aggressiveness, and efforts to dominate others, the "fictional appearance of the creedal belief may not be apprehended by the persons" who believe it.[26]

Applied more specifically to the realm of sport and the fan's involvement in it, Williams' analysis of the dynamics of cultural fictions

---

[25] Williams, 391–95.
[26] Ibid., pp. 394–95.

provide greater insight into the phenomenon of fan enthusiasm. The institution of sport becomes a "staging area" where microlevel demonstrations of the viability of prescriptions for conduct and interaction in the greater society occur. Because fans *believe* these sports (i.e., football, basketball, baseball, and so forth) to be governed by the same values prescribing acceptable conduct for themselves in the larger society, these sports become microcosmic illustrations that this system of values continue to be effective in efforts toward goal achievement. Thus, persons (1) who are involved in a continual struggle for goal achievement in the greater society (particularly that of an instrumental sort) within established societal rules governing such efforts, and (2) who inevitably experience disappointments in terms of concrete gains falling short of expectations given the efforts put forth and the sacrifices made, but (3) who cannot resort to innovative behavior because of having internalized established "blueprints" for conduct, can find solace as sports fans. The ameliorative affect offered to society's members by the institution of sport is the primary determiner of fan enthusiasm. It also determines the fact of sports primarily male, middle-class appeal.[27] For it is primarily within the male role that responsibilities for instrumental goal achievement are vested, and the middle-class constitutes the "mainstream" of American societal life. We have noted that these considerations perhaps explain Stone's findings that women and lower-class individuals were less "fanatical" about sports than were men in general and the middle class, respectively.[28] Of significance here also is the work of John Robinson on time expenditure on sports in ten countries, which shows that, in the United States, middle-class people tend to expend more time viewing football while lower-class people expend a greater amount of time viewing baseball.[29] Though Robinson does not offer any interpretation of the finding, the differences most likely result from differences in the degree of active involvement in the mainstream of American life. Baseball is a more "passive" activity than is football. Middle-class persons, more actively striving toward instrumental goal achievement possibly have a greater tendency to empathize with the aggressive activities of football. Just the opposite conceivably would be the case for lower-class persons—most of who do not function in the mainstream of American life. If the above speculations are correct, the more aggressive the sport (not counting pseudosports such as commercial wrestling and roller derby) the greater should be the proportion of middle-class to lower-class clientele. Although no data are available that would conclusively

---

[27] See Gregory P. Stone, "Some Means of American Sport: An Extended View," in Gerald S. Kenyon, *Sociology of Sport,* pp. 5–16.

[28] See chapter 9 of the present work and Stone's article cited above.

[29] John Robinson, "Time Expenditure On Sports Across Ten Countries," *The International Review of Sport Sociology* (Warsaw: Polish Publishers, 1967), p. 79.

substantiate this proposition, it does seem a plausible implication of middle-class involvement with football as opposed to baseball. Hence, the claim that "baseball is too slow" may in fact be the reason why football has overtaken it in terms of fan attention. As the United States has become more "middle class," both in orientation and in fact, there may have emerged a propensity for more fans to develop an enthusiasm for more active, aggressive sports. Thus, "progress" in the form of a higher mean socioeconomic level of existence may erode baseball's fan appeal or force such a radical change in the structure of the sport that it will lose much of its present character.

Parenthetically, there appears to be a tendency in American society for fans who have previously established no identity with either athletic unit in a sports event to identify with the unit rated as the underdog. While this tendency may result in part from a general humanitarian idealism in America, the chief determining factor may quite possibly be that fans themselves do not have "favorite" ratings in their own life's strivings. If anything, the odds are against any specific individual gaining desired achievement of scarce valued goods and services—even in a theoretically open system of competition. Therefore, it is at least plausible, given the functions of sport for the fan, that there would be a greater likelihood of his identifying with the "underdog" than the favorite in sports events wherein he has established no previous identification with either of the athletic units.

The institution of sport, we suggest, then, serves a pattern—or value—maintenance function for the general society, and thus sustains the fan's belief in the viability of social values through his involvement. Though the act of becoming a fan and fan enthusiasm can be accounted for in part by the above argument, the determination of *which* athletic unit active in a given sports activity a fan *will* choose to identify with seems a matter of idiosyncratic choice within culturally set alternatives— analogous to tastes in clothing color, art, music, and so forth. Nonetheless, it is undoubtedly true that fans experience elation and confidence when the team with which they have identified achieve victory, and disappointment and depression when these sports aggregations lose. For the fan, his chosen team or athlete represents himself in his own struggles in the greater society within the context of prescribed societal values. Opponents in sports events represent the forces and obstacles confronting the fan and hindering achievement in his own life's struggles. If the team with which the fan has chosen to identify continues to lose, he not unfrequently turns against it, venting not only his frustration over the team's failure to realize hopes and expectations, but his own personal failures as well. Within this context, fans' shouts of "kill the umpire," their commands to "murder" the opposing quarterback and so forth become understandable.

This analysis has significance beyond the level of the individual fan's responses to lack of athletic success by "his" team. In the areas of intergroup and intercultural relations, it could very well apply also. Hence, far from generating a spirit of friendly intergroup or intercultural relations, athletic confrontations between sports aggregations having fan followings that maintain ongoing antagonisms toward each other may serve to precipitate violent outbreaks. As has been stated, it is an institutionalized feature of sport that one opponent should win—a tie is a disappointment. Given the significance of sport for fans and the above analysis of the dynamics of the individual fan's involvement in sport, fights after sporting events between fans from opposing black and white high schools are perhaps to be expected, as one should expect the "soccer riots" which have taken place in Europe and South America. In this regard, Scott observes

. . . outbreaks of violence and mass rioting at sporting events are all too common phenomena throughout the world. Race riots, from the national rioting after Jack Johnson, the first black heavyweight champion, beat Jim Jeffries in Reno, Nevada, on July 4, 1910, to the 1962 riot in Washington, D.C. following the city's high school football championship game, a riot in which 512 people were injured, have occurred with saddening regularity in America. Today, the situation has deteriorated to such an extent that nearly every major city in the United States prohibits evening athletic contests for high school teams. And sporting riots are in no way a uniquely American phenomena. The frequent mass rioting at soccer matches in South America and Europe often involve a level of violence seldom seen in America; Europeans call it soccer-mania. The violence surrounding England's soccer matches apparently is not limited to the stadium. A report prepared by seven British doctors reveals, there is some evidence that hooliganism may invade the home after the match. . . . Some wives apparently live in dread of Saturdays and wait apprehensively to see what mood their husbands will return home in after the football match. If the local side loses, a wife may fear her husband will return home the worse for drink and give her a thrashing to get rid of the anger he feels about the lost game . . .[30]

For the fan, it seems, outcomes on the athletic field are inextricably intertwined with outcomes in his own life. The sense of failure which he experiences in the "real world" and which occurs despite the fact that he abides by all the "rules of the game" is compounded by his team's failure in sports; and, more significantly, a suspicion which he dares not admit to himself or others has received greater affirmation: to wit, that the cherished values and beliefs which essentially define life in the United States, which he has internalized, and which govern his life's activities are invalid in so far as they are *not* productive of expected outcomes.

---

[30] Jack Scott, *The Athletic Revolution* (New York: Free Press, 1970), p. 174.

9

The economics of sport

CLEARLY SPORT RESTS on an economic foundation. Yet the sports creed has little to say about the economic side of the sports world. Any tendency of the creed to focus public attention on the economics of sport is reduced by two main conditions. First, the overwhelming majority of athletic units in America receive substantial financial support from taxes or fees assessed against the public or from private donations. Practically all interscholastic sports programs (e.g., high-school, junior high-school, and grammar-school programs), intercollegiate programs, and advanced amateur sports programs—including the United States olympic sports program—receive the bulk of their fiscal support from one or both of these sources. And this condition holds for most sports programs in both public *and* private institutions and organizations. Even professional sports are in part indirectly supported by public funds through the tax bonds used to build the multimillion dollar sports complexes necessary to make professional athletics a viable economic concern, and, to no mean degree, through exemptions from government antitrust regulations. In view of the dominant sports creed's support of a traditional conception of the "American way of life," it is at least plausible that the creed's neglect of the economics of sport occurs because the fiscal functioning of the institution of sport itself does not coincide with traditional American emphasis upon free enterprise and open competition in the marketplace. In short, sports in America more nearly approximates "socialism" than the "classical capitalism" historically expoused by the society in general. Under such circumstances, expressed beliefs comprising the dominant sports creed could not very well advocate the virtues of public subsidy.

Second, the fan's relationship within the institution of sport is quite different from the relationship which the consumer has traditionally maintained with business in America. For the fan is simultaneously a consumer of the intangible product of sports endeavors (i.e., entertainment and the amelioration of uncertainties concerning the success potentials of his own secular instrumental efforts), and a vital component in determining the *character* of that product through his support of and identification with the team. To a significant degree, the fan, once he identifies with a particular sports aggregation, becomes in a sense a consumer on the one hand and a partial "producer" of the intangible product which he consumes on the other. This situation would mean that if classical free-enterprise economics were in fact practiced among sports units, they would be competing not only for the fan's sports dollar but for his identification, for his feelings of belonging to the sports "family." It is not entirely clear that the latter can be voluntarily given as a result of rational judgments as to the quality of the expected product—as the case of the New York Mets professional baseball team illustrates.

The omission of creedal statements focusing upon the economics of sport notwithstanding, in the literature on sports one finds a tremendous *concern about* money. In the professional ranks, the emphasis is upon making a profit. In the amateur ranks, the chief economic concern is to break even in terms of debts incurred in maintaining a sports program. And in one way or another, it is the fan who ultimately pays for sports in America.

Because the dynamics of the economic operations of sports are different in professional as opposed to amateur sports, these two levels will be considered separately.

PROFESSIONAL SPORTS

Paradoxically, the image of professional sports as a highly visible and lucrative business in America coexists with the public image of sport and sports participation as primarily fun and games. Due partially to the impact of radio and the automobile after World War I and of television and the jet airplane after World War II, professional sports evolved from a few baseball and football franchises struggling for public attention and "passing the hat" at Sunday sporting events, into the primary entertainment interest in America today. Professional sport, since its inception, has undergone an expansion of revolutionary proportions, and, as Durso states:

. . . The prime mover in it all is, for want of a better term, money. The problem is not just to chronicle where it comes from and where is goes, but what it buys, whom it corrupts, and why it works. It is there, from the $2.50 grandstand seat to the million-dollar basketball bonus, to the $70-million paid by TV for four seasons of baseball, to the $50-billion poured into gambling each year, most of it illegally. It is why sports teams sprout like supermarkets, why leagues split into "conferences" and conferences into "divisions." It is why the National Hockey League started the Sixties with a half a dozen teams and the Seventies with fourteen(with Vancouver in the "East" and Philadelphia in the "West"). It is why the National Basketball Association multiplied to seventeen teams, the American Basketball Association from none to eleven; why the sixteen baseball teams in the big leagues went to twenty-four; why the football teams, which took shape in places like the empty lot behind Hagemeister's Brewrey in Green Bay, spawned twenty-six franchises in six divisions, in two merged leagues on all three TV networks—and why nobody bothers to pass the hat on Sunday afternoons . . .[1]

While it is clear that professional sports have evolved into big-time business enterprise, just how big that business is remains a matter of perspective. If one includes all money transactions determined by the existence of professional sports, the business emerges as a multibillion dollar endeavor. The Chamber of Commerce of Atlanta, Georgia, for instance, states flatly that professional sports have meant over 200 million dollars to that city alone in the past half-dozen years. Says a Chamber spokesman: ". . . When you add up the money spent for tickets, for food, for lodging and for other sports related expenses, the 200 million dollar figure is probably low . . ."[2]

Since the Atlanta Falcons professional football team and the Braves professional baseball team first came to Georgia in 1966 over eleven million sports fans have attended their sports events. The Braves alone grossed forty-five to fifty million dollars since coming to Atlanta. The income from professional sports evidently is seen as somehow offsetting the public cost of having the teams in Atlanta. However, upon close examination, one finds that this cost includes a "sweetheart contract" for Atlanta Stadium which gives these professional sports aggregations use of the facility at extremely favorable rates. Costs also have included moving expenses for the Braves from Milwaukee—including fees for moving the franchise. Though the owner of the Atlanta Hawks professional basketball team is building his own coliseum, the taxpayers had to guarantee the payments on the loan. And the Atlanta Falcons football team leases Atlanta Stadium directly from the management of the Braves baseball team, thus avoiding what undoubtedly would be higher lease rates imposed by the public Stadium Authority. These costs would tend to diminish the 200 million dollar "face value" of professional athletics to the city of Atlanta. Even the Chamber of Commerce admits that "there is

---

[1] Joseph Durso, "Sportswriting and the All-American Dollar," *Saturday Review,* October 9, 1971, p. 67.

[2] *Fremont News-Register,* October 27, 1971, p. 18.

slow headway in paying for things." And finally, despite the availability of efficient transportation, the majority of the fans providing the funds through ticket sales to repay the public debts incurred undoubtedly live within the seventy-five mile "blackout" radius for televised professional home games. This means that since home games can be seen free on television outside of that circle, many of the fans whose tax money financed professional sports are also forced to pay again in order to see what their money has bought. In a losing sports season, the end result for the public could be a net financial loss since gate receipts typically drop drastically under these circumstances.

Financial transactions which are peripheral to sports cannot really be considered in any equation determining the size of the professional sports business. Little of the billions expended on gambling, sports toys, and so forth is actually channeled back into sports industry. How big then is professional sports as an industry in America? According to a United Press International survey carried out by its member reporters in every city having a major league sports team, a generous estimate of the total financial value of the professional sports industry in 1971 was 360 million dollars.[3] The report states that apparently the boom of the 1960s, during which football expanded from twelve to twenty-six teams and baseball expanded from sixteen to twenty-four, is over. Although franchised sports such as football, baseball, basketball, and hockey grossed an estimated 360 million dollars in 1970, businessmen are taking a closer look at their sports investments. For in terms of alternative investment opportunities in the larger economic system, professional sports constitutes both a small business and yields a relatively meager investment return.

The following summarizes the conclusions reached after the extensive UPI survey of professional sports franchises across the nation:

1. In terms of "big business," franchised sports with its 360 million dollars gross ranks far below the giants of American industry. The world's largest corporation—General Motors—could take one year's gross sales and operate the NFL for over 200 years at current rates. Even the Macy's department stores rank above sports, with an 800 million dollar annual gross.

2. While sports must be classified as a high-risk investment, it can be profitable, and more people are making money in sports today than are losing it. All twenty-six pro football teams and the majority of the National League baseball teams and the National Hockey League teams are operating at above the break-even level.

3. As an investment, sports may in many cases pay a lower return than a normal business. But there are many side benefits and compensa-

---

[3] *San Francisco Chronicle,* October 12, 1971, p. 46.

tions such as the glamor of running a pro team and the tax benefits such as "amortizing the players as depreciable property."

In determining how big the sports franchise business is, estimates have to be combined with the few public financial statements available.

Those estimates indicated these gross incomes: baseball $160 million dollars; football 110 million dollars; basketball 55 million dollars; hockey 43 million dollars.

Taken as a whole, the figures are impressive. Yet, according to *Fortune Magazine*'s listing for 1969, some 500 individual industrial concerns had higher gross sales than the 1970 total for all of major league baseball's twenty-four teams combined.

No individual sports franchise ranks as a really big business. It takes about five to six million dollars to operate a major-league baseball team for a year and from 3.5–4 million dollars to run a football team. Basketball can operate on between one and two million dollars per team, hockey for 1.5–1.8 million dollars.[4]

Other sources tend to verify the UPI survey results showing that professional sports is a relatively small economic enterprise. Roger Noll, an economist with the Brookings Institute who has of late become known as the Ralph Nader of professional sports, states ". . . Professional sports is not very big as an industry . . . It's something like half the size of canned soup, just a small industry . . ."[5]

As a business endeavor, professional sports still constitutes entertainment, albeit of a unique sort. Basically, this means that the financial solvency of the industry is determined by the availability of the recreation dollar, the amount of spendable income that members of the public have over and above that required to fulfill financial obligations. In times of inflation and a "tight economy," all entertainment industries find the going rough.

In order to maintain a desired profit margin, professional sports have resorted to two tactics—both of which serve to *stifle* intraindustry economic competition. The first of these is the merger; the second is the "reserve-type" clause.

League mergers are made possible by the exemption of professional sports from federal antitrust legislation. This exemption, for instance, in the cases of professional baseball and football, is justified on the grounds that professional sports has only "bottom-rung" economic stature as an industry in the *overall* business structure of society. Under such circumstances, it has been judged logical to exempt these activities from antitrust legislation since it was assumed that open competition between teams for top athletic talent and the public's recreational dollar

---

[4] Ibid., p. 46.
[5] Ibid., p. 46.

would undoubtedly drive the less competitive aggregations out and eventually destroy the industry completely. However, there is growing concern over the legitimacy of professional sports' antitrust exemptions.

This concern came to the fore in the early 1970s when the NBA and ABA commissioners proposed to Congress that the two leagues be granted exemption from antitrust legislation and allowed to merge. Before Senator Sam J. Ervin, who chaired the hearings on the merger, the commissioners of the two leagues urged approval of legislation exempting them from prosecution under the antitrust laws when the merger is completed.

The ABA commissioner, Jack Dolph, and the NBA commissioner, Walter Kennedy, said if the merger did not go through professional basketball would soon kill itself with staggering contracts to untested rookies.

Dolph cited one player who got a $900,000 five-year no-cut contract, a $50,000 bonus, three Cadillacs, a $2,000 per year housing allowance and a $10,000-a-year job in the club's public-relations department for his mother.

Ervin was unimpressed. He stated

. . . Personally, I believe that if a basketball player is good enough, he should be paid the highest that bidders for his services are willing to pay . . . I do not believe that contracts for player services will rise indefinitely beyond what a team can pay . . .

. . . The professional sports industry is about the size of the pork and beans industry. But the pork and beans industry is subject to anti-trust laws. So we have the ridiculous situation that people who deal in pork and beans are subject to anti-trust laws while people who deal in human beings are not. Congress approved the football and baseball mergers—these were railroaded through Congress. But it'll never happen again. We have had enough Lockheeds for this year . . . [6]

Despite Ervin's objections, however, professional basketball may yet manage to curtail the cost generated by the existence of two leagues. This could be done by one of the leagues—probably the less-established ABA—voluntarily dissolving as a corporate structure under a claim of financial hardship. The NBA would then be free to buy up the more promising franchises of the defunct ABA. If congressional objections to a merger continue, this may be the tack taken by the two leagues to reduce competition for highly talented athletes.

Another way in which professional sport reduces competition is via "reserve-type" clauses. Though the nature of the reserve-type clause varies from sport to sport, all such contract clauses operate to restrict athlete's freedom of choice of a team, thereby restricting their bargain-

---

[6] *Fremont News-Register,* October 13, 1971, p. 21.

Kareem Abdul-Jabbar signed a contract in excess of $1 million to play with the NBA Milwaukee Bucks. Because of its competition with the ABA for big-name athletes, the NBA considered the signing of Abdul-Jabbar a major victory. (UPI)

ing power. All organizations engaging in professional team sports have such clauses in their contracts. These clauses do not, however, prevent these sports organizations from trading or otherwise disposing of athletes as property without the athlete's approval or consent. The logic underlying the legality of the reserve-type clause was recently challenged and upheld in court. Nonetheless, the validity of the arguments offered in support of these clauses continues to be questioned. The case of Curt Flood is demonstrative of this point.

Curt Flood, formerly of the Saint Louis Cardinals, was traded to the Philadelphia Phillies, without consulting him and without his consent —practices perfectly legal under professional baseball's "reserve clause." Rather than go quietly, Flood fought the trade and took professional baseball to court. He contended that the reserve clause relegated professional baseball athletes to the status of slaves and chattel. Flood contended that in his case moving to Philadelphia would necessitate his abandoning his Saint Louis business interests and the possible uprooting of his family. Further, he stated that since he was obligated under the reserve clause to perform for the team to which he was traded or to retire from baseball, the clause was in violation of federal antitrust legislation.

Economists and others have often criticized the reserve-type clause. Some contend it is a device for collusively lowering the salaries of baseball players (and by the same token increasing the profits of the club owners). The owners on the other hand have traditionally argued that the reserve clause is essential in helping to equalize team strengths, an objective that is of relevance to the survival of the league. Are there compelling reasons to accept or reject the club owners' argument?

The owners argue that, without the reserve-type clause, the richest club would outcompete poorer clubs for talent and, hence, unbalance the league, or that intense competition for athletes would cause the economic collapse of the league. There are several difficulties in these arguments. First, there are economic limits on the willingness of the richest club to purchase all or most of the best athletes. The addition of high-quality athletes eventually will begin to only marginally contribute to club success in winning games; furthermore, at some point, attendance capacity will not increase sufficiently to justify the purchase price of additional high quality talent. In fact, the reserve-type clause by itself is by no means a sufficient condition for preventing one club (the richest club) from dominating a league. Between 1946 and 1964, the New York Yankees won fifteen of nineteen American league pennants, and from 1959 to 1969, the Boston Celtics dominated professional basketball.

In addition, there is reason to suspect that clubs will be *more* unbalanced with the reserve clause than without it. Under present arrangements, clubs can trade or sell athletes independently of the athletes' desire to remain in one location, while economic incentives for athletes to be reallocated among clubs are not eliminated by the reserve-type clause. The effect of the clause, therefore, is only to shift the moving decision from the athlete to the club owner; it does not eliminate the incentive for movement to occur.

In professional football too, one finds evidence that the owners' arguments for the reserve-type clause (termed the "option clause" in professional football) are at best debatable. The NFL Player Association characterized the "option clause" as the central issue facing it during the 1972–73 football season.

The professional athlete draft serves also to curtail the prospective athlete's bargaining power—ostensibly under the guise of preserving the competitive balance among league teams. It would seem however that the draft too is less creditable as a mechanism for maintaining

---

NFLPA to Explore Anti-Trust Action

Miami—The National Football League Players Association told its attorneys yesterday to explore the possibility of taking anti-trust action in the courts against the NFL's option clause.

But NFLPA executive director Ed Garvey said no action would be taken until the attorneys report back on their study of the clause, which binds a player to his team for one year after his contract expires.

"The option clause has to be the dominant issue confronting the association at this point, along with injury grievances and player safety," Garvey said.[7]

---

intraleague competitive quality than the league and the owners would have the public believe.

The essence of sport is that the thought that any team can beat any other team on a given day. It keeps Pete Rozelle and his hordes of PR men busy maintaining the fiction that this is so in pro football, where the best teams win and the worst teams lose a disparate amount of the time. Still, the idea prevails. So, the draft is necessary to preserve equality. But does it? Answer this: Do you believe it coincidence that Dallas is in championship games year after year; that the Raiders have lost only 12 games in the last five years; that Kansas City has not had a losing season since 1963?

In theory, the worst teams use their high draft positions to build themselves into the best, and occasionally it happens: Dick Nolan has done it with the 49ers. *But it doesn't happen often, because the people behind the desks in pro football front offices are not equal. Some are very sharp, and some work for the New York Giants.* . . .

All but three teams—Kansas City, Oakland and Cincinnati—belong to scouting co-operatives, and thus get the same information. But some teams, Dallas being the most obvious consistently have better drafts with the same information . . .

In the old days, teams used to select players on the basis of magazine and newspaper reports; the Giants once picked Rosey Grier because he made a Negro All-American team picked by a Pittsburgh newspaper. But while others have improved their scouting and drafting techniques since, the Giants have not. They specialize in drafting a player No. 1 and then moving him to a different position, at which he fails.

---

[7] Les Kjos, "NFLPA to Explore Anti-trust Action," *San Francisco Chronicle,* January 31, 1972, p. 46.

Or, take the San Diego Chargers, who approach the draft so whimsically others look at their selections and wonder what the Chargers could have been thinking. There has been no clear answer yet.

Which is a major reason why some teams finish at or near the top each year and others at or near the bottom, and why the draft can never change that.[8]

Given the evidence, it is more likely that the primary function of the professional football draft, for instance, is to curtail the athlete's bargaining power and "competitive balance" is of secondary concern at best.

In denying Flood's suit for an injunction on the use of baseball's reserve clause and for $100,000 in damages for alleged violation of his occupational rights, Judge Irving Ben Cooper told Flood:

The plaintiff's $90,000 a year salary does not support the spirit of his assertion that the reserve clause relegates him to a condition of involuntary servitude. For if it did, he would be the highest paid slave in history.

In a later hearing before the United States Supreme Court, Justice Harry A. Blackmun agreed with Flood's contentions but, in reading the five to three decision against Flood, he sidestepped any responsibility for correcting the situation. "If there is any illogic and inconsistency in all of this, it is an illogic and inconsistency of long-standing that is to be remedied by the Congress and not by this Court."

Thus it seems that the length of time an injustice has persisted has become the key factor in determining the jurisdiction of this nation's court of last resort. Under such an assumption, the court never would have reversed the "separate-but-equal" ruling that had legalized for over fifty years racially segregated educational facilities—to mention just one of the "long-standing inconsistencies" on which the court *has* ruled.

Although the court ruled against Flood, it seems that Flood's efforts may yet bring some restatement of baseball's clause. Even the judges presiding over the case felt that some rephrasing of the reserve clause was needed in order that it might accommodate at least some of the interests of the athletes in question.

The special exemptions and economic privileges granted professional sports are paid for indirectly by the sports fan. Partial exemption from the limitations of open market competition leaves professional sports organization relatively free to charge whatever "the traffic will bear" for tickets. According to economist Noll, regarding the proposed basketball merger:

If owners were philanthropists and wanted to make cost and no more, teams like the Knicks, the Bucks and the Lakers, which have the highest prices

---

[8] Glenn Dickey, "Some Teams Are More Equal Than Others," *San Francisco Chronicle,* January 31, 1972.

and highest attendances in pro basketball, would lower prices. There is no reason to believe that ticket prices and other policies of the team will change because of the merger.

In other words, they charge what the traffic will bear, because it is the only game in town. Anti-trust exemptions and exclusive territorial rights should be abolished in all sports and replaced with a system of supply and demand.[9]

In a more immediate and direct sense, some of the costs of professional sport's antitrust exemptions and other economic privileges are borne by professional athletes. And other factors contribute further to the professional athlete's vulnerability, especially in team sports. First, professional sports place upon the athlete all of the role expectations faced by the amateur participant. All discretionary power is still vested in the role of coach; athlete behavior is still strictly scrutinized both inside and outside of the sports realm; and the sports creed applies to the athletic pursuits of the professional athlete just as it does to the endeavors of his amateur counterpart. In addition, professional sports aggregations are business enterprises in which athletes (employees) are formally classified as "property," a designation which has been legally upheld in the courts. The institutionalized powerlessness attached to the athlete role, combined with professional sports' special economic privileges and unique employer-employee relationship, has had serious consequences for the athlete. One such consquence has been that athletes are weakly organized as an occupational group, and those unions that do exist have traditionally functioned more as social clubs and athlete-oriented "fraternities" than as mutual-aid or bargaining agents organized to help settle the occupation-related grievances of their members. If the actual functions of athletic unions are evaluated in terms of what is expected of unions and associations organized on behalf of other occupational groups, these professional athletes' associations appear lacking indeed.

Now, the popular literature is replete with examples of how professional sports have provided athletes with opportunities to enhance their economic positions. In fact, one of the chief incentives for many amateur athletes to continue in amateur team sports, despite institutionalized adolescence and the pressures stemming from conflicting role demands, is the ever-present hope of a professional sports career. And if one is to believe the popular literature on professional sport, opportunities abound. Annually, a great deal is made in the press over the five-, six-, and seven-digit bonuses and salaries paid unproven rookies. Even single-athlete sports ostensibly offer the perservering and talented athlete affluence. Thus, Durso notes:

---

[9] *The San Francisco Chronicle* (n. 3 above), p. 46.

"Once upon a time," commented James Roach, the sports editor of *The New York Times,* who on many days of the year might be taken for the financial editor, "I wrote about horse races for *The Times,* and when I learned what leading jockeys were paid, I decided that if I ever had a male child, I'd start him on big black cigars at an early age and stunt his growth and make a jockey of him and retire early.

Now I'm not so sure. I think maybe I'd give the male offspring plenty of vitamins and fresh vegetables and other nourishing food and buy him a 7-iron at the age of six and, in time, make a professional golfer of him."

Mr. Roach's conviction was strengthened when he calculated that the second-ranking money-winner in golf on July 2, 1970, was a twenty-eight-year-old Californian with the unfamiliar name of Dick Lotz. He had earned $107,000 by then and still had twenty-two tournaments to go, seventeen of which listed prize money in excess of $100,000 each. His conviction was cemented a year later, when the leading money-winner by the middle summer was a chubby thirty-one-year-old Mexican-American from Texas named Lee Trevino. He had earned more than $209,000 by then, including a sweep of the United States, Canadian, and British Open tournaments within a month's time.

"In the old days," Trevino remembered, "I had trouble finding people who could afford to pay me for a golf lesson. Now everybody wants to take lessons from me. Five years ago, I didn't own a car. Now I got five cars. I used to live in a trailer. Now I live in a five-bedroom house. I didn't have a phone. Now I got a phone and the number's unlisted. Boy, that's progress.[10]

An investigation of professional sport, however, tends to indicate that plans to engage in sports as a life's occupation constitutes a relatively poor occupational choice for even those aspirant athletes of outstanding potential.

In the first place, only a few athletes out of the multitude of aspirants ever get an opportunity to participate in big-time sports. Moreover, the overwhelming majority of single-athlete sports that ostensibly offer opportunities for financial advancement typically pay little or nothing at all to athletes who are not among the top twenty or so competitors in the sport, although admittedly the latter may do quite well financially. But such athletes must earn enough to pay all expenses and still have take-home pay. In this sense, gross earnings figures are deceptive in individual participant sports.

In addition, in those professional sports such as baseball, football, and basketball which do pay a minimum living wage, financial security in the traditional sense is practically nonexistent; that is, meager provisions for retirement or, in some sports, no retirement provisions at all; no promotions or scheduled salary increases as one gains more experience in his occupational role in the industry. In fact, the longer an athlete stays in the sports industry, the more vulnerable he becomes to being

---

[10] Durso, p. 67.

dismissed (or having his salary cut). And, as already noted, the unions for athletes—the so-called "player associations"—have typically existed more as social clubs than as bargaining and grievance agencies for their members. Finally, legally stifled economic competition limits still further the professional athlete's economic alternatives.

Dave Meggyesy, in *Out of Their League,* describes the findings of a disgruntled pair of Saint Louis Cardinal professional football players regarding the renumeration for athletes as opposed to that of owners:

. . . When Parrish and Gibbons met with members of the Cardinals, they brought out some rather startling facts. Perhaps the most amazing statistic was this: during the period 1956–1967, the profits of the National Football League owners had increased 4300 percent but the player salaries had gone up only 73.6 percent. If you subtract rises in the cost of living during those years, our actual salary increase amounted to only 48.4 percent.[11]

Further, John Mackey, president of the Professional Football Player's Association, calls attention to the lack of fringe benefits for professional football participants:

. . . People fail to realize that the average professional life of a pro football player is 4.4 years . . . and since he has invested at minimum 10 years preparing for his risky vocation, he surely deserves some strong long range job security. People fail to realize we don't have widows benefits, that some players were killed playing football and their survivors get nothing. We have no benefits for permanent partial disability. We have ex-players now with plastic knees, withered arms, nerve endings pulled away from their spines because of football injuries, and they don't get anything . . .[12]

So while a few of the salaries earned by some professional athletes do appear to be substantial and more than adequate, spread out over a life time or viewed in terms of *net* rather than *gross* income, many athlete's might even incur losses as a result of their athletic involvement, especially if one takes into account time expended on training, the risks and costs of injury, and the opportunities lost to investigate potential alternative occupational interests. (For the black professional athlete such losses are less severe, of course, since he has a much narrower range of high-prestige occupational choices from the outset.) Traditionally, if an athlete does not like the economic auspices under which American professional sports are operated, in lieu of better unions, he has a choice between discontinuing his sports career (since he can't join any other club due to professional sports antitrust exemption) or going to Canada, if his sports competence happened to be in football.

[11] Dave Meggyesy, *Out of Their League* (Ramparts Press 1970), p. 37 (publisher's galleys).

[12] John Mackey, "Annual Football Roundup: The Year of the Strike," *Ebony Magazine* 26, no. 1 (November 1970): 144.

Dave Meggyesy sits before poster of John Carlos and Tommie Smith as he works on his book Out of Their League. (*Photo by Micki Scott*)

Increasingly, however, professional athletes are organizing themselves into collective bargaining associations and strengthening those
unions which already exist. As a result, in professional football, for
instance, there was an athletes' strike in 1970 and numerous "holdouts"
in 1971. Likewise, there was an athletes' strike in professional baseball
which delayed the start of the 1972 season.

Even those professional athletes participating in tennis have begun
to organize against the prestigious International Lawn Tennis Federa-
tion and have demanded $500.00 a week minimum salary for their serv-
ices. Race-car drivers and golfers too are beginning to move toward
the development of athlete-controlled unions.

There is also some movement among collegiate athletes to break
the long existing "sweetheart" agreement between professional sports
and collegiate athletics. This agreement saves professional football and
basketball owners literally millions of dollars, and at the same time it
allows college athletic departments to have professionalized intercollegiate athletic teams without having to pay their "employees" competitive wages. Athletes have the choice of playing for the slave wages of
an athletic "scholarship" for four years, giving up sports, or (as a few
highly talented high-school athletes such as Cookie Gilchrist have done)
leaving for Canada or some other foreign country where they are eligible to play as professionals. Most of them, of course, choose to take the
athletic "scholarships"; consequently, there are many muscular young
men on our college campuses who have no real interest in being there
except for athletics.

The National Collegiate Athletic Association's explanation in support of this agreement is that the ineligibility of a collegiate athlete for
participation in professional athletics assures him of an opportunity to
obtain a college education. Perhaps this is an honest explanation, but
many feel otherwise.

. . . Colleges and professional sports leagues have worked together—"con-
spired" might be closer—to restrict the freedom of young athletes. The draft
rule has benefited the NBA and NFL. It has benefited the colleges.

It is much more questionable how much it benefited those few athletes
who could—or who could have—received large bonuses or contracts to turn
professional when they were sophomores or juniors in college. Or, for some,
right out of high school.

The significant point is that supremely gifted young athletes did not
have a choice . . .

One highly placed pro basketball official said, "The original concept was
that the player who decided to enter college presumably wanted an education.
And the draft was instituted to prevent his being lured off campus by recruiter-
salesmen. . ."

The official line of the pros comes under suspicion by studies made which show that, for example, only about one-half of all pro basketball and football players receive degrees with their classes . . .[13]

AMATEUR SPORTS

If the economic operations of professional sports can be accurately characterized as more precarious than in past years, financial situation of amateur sports (especially interscholastic and collegiate programs) must, by comparison, be labeled a fiscal disaster.

While antitrust exemptions, mergers, and reserve-type clauses have enabled professional sport to keep its "fiscal head" above the water line, collegiate sport has enjoyed no such advantages. The financial crisis in collegiate sport stems from three factors: (1) tight money and increasing cost of maintaining an intercollegiate sports program; (2) waning support from the campus community; and (3) and some alienation among traditional supporters due to the campus turmoil of the late sixties. And finally, there is the threat that the increasing propensity among athletes to quit sports will have an indirect impact in terms of diminishing the quality of athletic events from the fan's viewpoint.

The present financial crisis in collegiate sport revolves primarily around the cost of maintaining a major sports program. In one sense, the present monetary problems are the culmination of fiscal policies and practices established in collegiate sports decades ago, in the 1920s and 1930s during "Sports' Golden Era." During this period, when sport experienced its first phase of rapid growth, it became standard procedure for colleges and universities to upgrade and expand their athletic programs in order to make more money; then to build bigger stadia and gymnasium facilities in order to accommodate the increased attendance; and finally, the debts incurred in building these facilities necessitated still more upgrading of athletic programs in order to attract more fans and more alumni donations.[14] The result was a spiral of expansion leading to debt leading to expansion leading to debt, and so forth, until today collegiate sport is a multimillion dollar fiscal problem. In the last decade alone, collegiate athletic budgets have increased 108 percent, only 35 percent of which can be attributed to cost-of-living rises.[15] Two-thirds of all collegiate athletic programs are operating at a loss and each year the debt increases. Figures released by the NCAA indicate that just ten years ago the total athletic budget for all schools over 4,000 students was just over sixty million dollars; by 1965, the cumulative budget had

---

[13] Ira Berkow, "Pro Drafts: Who Benefits?" *San Francisco Chronicle,* April 4, 1971, Section C, p. 6.

[14] John Tunis, *$port$* (New York: John Day Publishers, 1928), p. 294.

[15] Pat Ryan, "A Grim Run for Fiscal Daylight," *Sports Illustrated,* January 1, 1971, p. 19.

zoomed to 115 million dollars; the budget for the 1971–72 academic year is 195 million dollars. It is not uncommon for some schools to spend a million or two million dollars on their athletic programs alone.

For instance, the budget for all· sports at the University of California at Berkeley for the 1970–71 academic year was just over a million and a half dollars. The University of Michigan spent $2,077,600.

Unquestionably the most financially solvent collegiate sports activity is football. Yet NCAA figures show that, whereas in 1960 the average major college spent $330,000 to field a football team, by 1969 this average had risen to $668,000. In the 1960s, collegiate football managed to stay generally abreast of escalating cost of upping ticket prices and cashing in on the funds to be gotten through television contracts. But now expenses are rising ahead of revenues. NCAA figures reveal that football revenues rose 12 percent in the 1968–69 academic year, but football expenses increased 19 percent. Many athletic directors admit that ticket prices cannot be raised anymore and stadium expansion—with construction prices being what they are—in all likelihood would worsen rather than ameliorate the problem. A case in point is that of Ohio State University which found that to enclose the open end of its stadium would cost more than the entire stadium itself did when it was first built.

According to a survey made by the University of Missouri, the average NCAA member school spent $548,000 on sports programs in 1969. But the extremes are more revealing than the mean.

The fifty or so schools (like Ohio State or Notre Dame or Texas) that have the biggest football operations average about 1.3 million dollars in outlays, with about $670,000 of it devoted to football.

Schools with modest but vigorous football programs (like Delaware) average $250,000, with about $85,000 going to football.

The largest group of all, schools that are not big time in either football or basketball, average less than $100,000 a year in athletic expenditures.

But in the first group, the big football schools, income from football accounts for 68 percent of a total revenue of 1.3 million dollars. In the second group, income averages $185,000 well below the break-even point, and football provides only about 34 percent of that. And in the nonfootball or small-football schools, total athletic income averages about $30,000.

Football, then, justifies its expense (large squads, numerous scholarships, large and well-paid coaching staffs, costly recruiting, complex plant maintenance, and large bills for travel, training table, and promotion) by its special ability to produce income.[16]

Table 9–1 shows that the dollar costs of collegiate sports have

---

[16] Leonard Koppet, "Colleges Question Old Views on Sports," *New York Times,* January 11, 1971, p. 70.

about doubled in the last ten years, as have revenues. But this has not occurred in a balanced manner. A relatively small number of schools, committed to big-time football and/or basketball, are taking in more dollars while the majority, with modest or low-key athletic programs, face a growing gap between revenues and expenses.

TABLE 9-1

Athletic expenditures and revenues* (in thousands of dollars)

	1960		*1969*	
	Expenses	*Revenues*	*Expenses*	*Revenues*
Total, average:				
Group A	635	672	1,322	1,397
Group B	90	77	274	185
Group C	47	17	102	37
Group D	128	62	196	69
Group E	25	10	54	22
Football, average:				
Group A	330	498	668	960
Group B	40	26	85	45
Group C	15	7	24	8

Source.—University of Missouri Sports Cost-Income Study.
Note.—Group A = 118 schools with "major" football programs; Group B = 157 schools with full-scale football (but not "major"); Group C = 170 schools with varsity football on a distinctly smaller scale; Group D = 40 schools with no football but "major" basketball; Group E = 170 schools with no football and no "major" basketball.
* The proportion of all revenues that can be attributed directly to football is as follows: 1960: Group A, 72%; Group B, 40%; Group C, 44%; 1969: Group A, 68%; Group B, 34%; Group C, 33%.

The University of Missouri study shows that athletic income matches athletic costs only at colleges with large-scale football programs, and that expenditures have tended to increase faster than income for colleges as a whole (Tables 9–1, 9–2).

In general, four sources account for roughly three-quarters of all income to college athletic departments: ticket sales, 48 percent; guarantee received as the visiting team, 11 percent; student fees, 10 percent; and television and bowl-game receipts shared by members of various conferences, 4 percent.

Let us now consider some of the factors which have contributed to the financial crisis in collegiate sports. As was stated, only 35 percent, or roughly one-third, of cost increase can be attributed to cost-of-living rises. Though no data are available on the magnitude of the relative contribution to the crisis made by each of the other factors considered below, undoubtedly their cumulative impact accounts for a great deal of collegiate sports' fiscal problems.

In terms of rising cost, equipment expenditures have risen 33–40 percent. Recruiting expenses for each of the top fifty schools in football alone exceed $50,000 per year. In 1960, the training table at Pennsylvania State University cost $18,000; now the cost exceeds $35,000. Coaches' salaries too have increased with the cost of living. When the University of Oklahoma was rated the nation's greatest collegiate football power during the 1950s, Bud Wilkinson made $20,000 a year. In

TABLE 9-2

Breakdown of athletic expenditures—1969 (in thousands of dollars)

	Football	*Basketball*	*Other teams*	*All else*
Group A	674 (51%)	132 (10%)	158 (12%)	357 (27%)
Group B	104 (42%)	57 (23%)	37 (15%)	49 (20%)
Group C	26.5 (26%)	12 (12%)	27.5 (27%)	36 (35%)
Group D	. . . . . .	100 (51%)	47 (24%)	49 (25%)
Group E	. . . . . .	17 (31%)	24 (45%)	13 (24%)

Note.—See table 9–1 for source and explanation of terms.

salary alone in 1970, Darrell Royal made $35,000 (not counting gifts from alumni and others or income from other sources).

On day-to-day "housekeeping" expenditures, Pat Ryan of *Sports Illustrated* gives the following examples:

. . . One Big Ten team is spending $19,000 a year on telephone and telegraph, but that is paltry compared with the sum run up at a Southern power that requests anonymity. Its coaches spend $28,000 telephoning and another $15,000 on postage. "We have no reason to refuse to let you use the name," an official said, "except that we are spending so much money it would shock people. They would think we are spending a lot more than everybody else. If every other athletic budget could be published, we'd be happy to publish ours, because we know we'd be pretty much in line . . ."[17]

A major factor in the collegiate sport financial crisis has been grants-in-aid provided athletes in exchange for their services. Again Ryan comments on the problem.

. . . The number of athletes receiving scholarships is higher than ever before, but more significant is the fact that tuition in most schools has doubled in 10 years, and in some cases has tripled. At Northwestern, for instance, tuition in 1960 was $1,000 a year; it will be $2,700 next year. Athletic directors can only wince when projections are made of the tuition fees of the future. By 1980, Northwestern estimates, its students may be paying $8,000 a year for their education. Ten years ago grants-in-aid cost the Ohio State athletic departments

[17] Pat Ryan, p. 20.

$198,000. Now Woody Hayes gets a bill for $407,000. At Kansas one tuition-and-fee hike increased grants-in-aid $40,000 overnight.[18]

Another factor contributing to the crisis has been the fact that many campuses have experienced a waning interest in sports and a heightening of criticism of the legitimacy of intercollegiate athletics in the educational milieu and the cost of maintaining these programs. We have already discussed the value discrepancy between some parts of today's campus youth culture and the beliefs attesting to the intangible attributes of sport. In the collegiate situation, one serious result of such incongruities has been that, increasingly, student governments and student bodies are urging or voting outright to limit or to cut off completely the flow of funds going to athletic departments from mandatory student body fees. Such action has taken place at UCLA, California State University at San Francisco, California State University at San Jose, Florida State University, University of Miami (Coral Gables, Florida), Holy Cross, and La Salle College, to name just a few.

Athletic departments could once rely on university regents and alumni contributions to aid their sagging budgets—student funds or no. But as of 1971, these sources too are drying up. This is in part due to the general economic climate; in large part, however, it is due to alumni dissatisfaction with student behavior on college campuses. The University of Buffalo for instance saw gifts to the athletic program drop from $74,000 to $1,500 in one year. Although the economy is certainly "tight," it has not worsened at a rate sufficient to explain that magnitude of decrease. Perhaps it is significant that the year prior to the drop in alumni donations the university had experienced some of the most heated student turmoil in its history.

Increasing numbers of universities are on very tight budgets for academic pursuits; some of them are shutting down entire departments, cutting back on full-time faculty or simply not filling vacated faculty positions, and freezing salaries in an attempt to maintain some semblance of fiscal integrity. Under these circumstances, athletic deficits are becoming harder and harder for university trustees and regents to justify. At present, however, 400 of 655 NCAA member schools operate at a deficit, and the prognosis is that these will go even more into debt unless these schools' chief administrators order a de-emphasis of sport or abandon it completely.

What kind of action has traditionally worked in dealing with financial crises in collegiate sports? The traditional formula for financial solvency has been that winning athletic aggregations stimulate alumni contributions and fan enthusiasm—especially among students. Winning also usually has had a favorable effect upon legislatures that vote ap-

---

[18] Ibid., p. 20.

propriations to public institutions. Winning has had a similar effect upon general support from greater local communities. But today, new attitudes on the parts of alumni and local communities about students, and the general fact of soaring athletic costs have all but wiped out the credibility of this aspect of the traditional formula.

Another component of the traditional formula for fiscal solvency has been the use of publicity. No academic achievement can match even a mediocre football season for making people aware of the name of a school and some of its characteristics. While a "jock factory" will not fool anyone for long about its academic standards, many a university that *does* have a worthwhile academic program has become better known, and faster, because of its well-publicized athletes. Prestige and money often accompany sports success simply because of publicity for the school. The classic case here is the University of Notre Dame.

During the 1960s, television was the savior of collegiate sports. The American Broadcasting Company television network (ABC) paid 12.1 million dollars per year for the rights to NCAA member-school football games alone. But due to its own rising costs, ABC, by 1968, was sustaining a 1.8 million dollar net loss per year in this effort. After the end of the 1970 collegiate football season, Chuck Howard, vice-president in charge of sports at ABC, stated quite frankly, "The NCAA will either have to lower its price demands or become more lenient in its selection of games to be televised." It did both.[19]

It seems, therefore, that the traditional formula of a winning record coupled with maximum public exposure is no longer as valid as it once was as a means of solving fiscal problems.

What *are* schools doing today to deal with fiscal problems? An increasing number of colleges and universities are dropping sports requiring high budgets. Hardest hit, of course, has been football, though it is also the most lucrative sport. In the last ten years, forty-two schools have dropped intercollegiate football, and at least twenty-five more have indicated an intention to do so.

A case in point is that of the University of California at Santa Barbara, a school having a moderate athletic program, which announced on December 9, 1971, its intention to drop intercollegiate football.

The University of San Francisco and the "Galloping Gaels" of Saint Mary's College have followed Santa Barbara in abandoning football for economic reasons.

Ironically many of those schools choosing to maintain big-time sports programs have sought a solution to fiscal problems through a continuation of the very policy which brought the problems on in the first place—to wit, the expansion of their athletic programs. In this regard,

---

[19] Ibid., p. 19.

UC Santa Barbara Quits Football

The University of California at Santa Barbara dropped out of intercollegiate football today because of financial losses.

Chancellor Vernon I. Beadle said a series of studies indicated football was not financially feasible.

Beadle issued a statement saying: "It is clear from these studies that the football program as presently constituted has consistently produced the greatest financial loss among all sports despite scheduling and other efforts undertaken to provide additional income and interest. It is also quite clear that except for a comparatively small number of extremely loyal and dedicated townspeople and students, that football at UCSB lacks any broad range of support."

The school has a student body of 13,000 but attendance at recent football games has been below 5,000 which a spokesman said was not enough to meet expenses.[20]

the scheduling of an eleventh football game was hailed as a panacea. But the result, even after one year, was predictable—an increase in fiscal problems for most schools. If a school has trouble breaking even with a ten-game schedule, eleven, twelve, or even thirteen games would merely increase the headache in that proportion.

Other suggestions which have been made include eliminating off-season practice such as "spring ball" in football; putting territorial limits on recruiting and limiting the number of assistant coaches a school can hire; and eliminating tutoring programs and cutting the allowable size of traveling squads. In football there has been talk of eliminating "two-platoon" systems, but there is little agreement on how much money would be saved through using this tactic.

It appears that, regardless of the attempted solutions, the fiscal future of intercollegiate sport looks bleak for all but a relatively few big colleges and universities. With the likelihood of extinction facing them, some athletic departments have resorted to desperate means to obtain financial support. California State University at San Jose is a striking case. At this school, a financial crisis in the athletic department (re-

---

[20] Ibid., p. 19.

sulting partially from a cut in funds by an antagonistic student government), coupled with the fact that control of the athletic program was significantly influenced by alumni and others outside of the educational institution, led to the establishment of a practice which impugned the integrity of the entire college. Because the college's administrative officials had no control over the operation of the sports program, it was not until considerable damage had been done that they realized what had been happening. The situation at what was then San Jose State College (now California State University at San Jose) stems in part out of America's first organized athletic revolt among black athletes in 1967. There were essentially two issues in the revolt.

The first was the treatment of black athletes, the second was the use of the so-called "California State College Two-Percent Plan." After three days of public hearings, the athletic department candidly admitted a need for changes in its policies and practices toward black athletes. But its stand on the school's use of the "Two-Percent Plan" was quite different.

Under the provisions of the "California State Master Plan for State Colleges," any state college can admit a number of underqualified students. The number of such students admitted, however, was not to exceed two percent of the school's total student enrollment. Originally the two-percent plan was aimed at insuring that minorities and other underprivileged categories of students would not be denied access to California's "free" education merely because they did not have access to better schools. However, through a "gentlemen's agreement" with local state college administrations, athletic staffs have been allowed to use the two-percent plan to bring highly talented athletes into California's state colleges when such athletes were for academic reasons ineligible for admission to other colleges or universities.

The use of the two-percent plan in this fashion was justified by the noncompetitive sports budgets of the state colleges relative to those of other institutions. The plan was thus used as a balancing mechanism to make up for the financial deficiencies of state college athletic programs.[21]

As a result of the San Jose State College athletic staff's use of the two-percent plan, as of September, 1967, there were only seventy-two black students at the school in a total enrollment of 24,000 students.

---

[21] (Parenthetically, the NCAA sets limits on the amount of financial aid that can be granted to athletes by its member institutions. The fact is, however, that corruption is widespread among big-time athletic institutions, with the result being that the richer schools can offer talented athletes more than the less endowed state colleges and universities. For this reason, schools such as San Jose State are at a decided financial disadvantage with other institutions. The former simply cannot match the latter in terms of providing illegal funds and under-the-table payments to its athletes.)

Over fifty of the seventy-two students were either athletes or former athletes finishing their degrees. There were only eight black female students on campus.

When black students and athletes demanded that the college's administration curtail the use of the two-percent plan by the athletic staff and use it instead to bring underprivileged blacks and other minorities into the school, the athletic department objected strenuously on the grounds that such a change would mean the destruction of the school's big-time sports program.

Working through the college's president (at that time, Robert Clark), a plan was eventually developed whereby the two-percent plan would be used by the athletic department and minority students would be admitted on an unlimited basis with the provision that they would spend the last year of their high school matriculation and their first year of college attendance in remedial preparatory programs of study.

With the settlement of this issue and the athletic staff's agreement to correct its treatment of black athletes, a campus crisis was averted. Clark, however, came under tremendous fire from the conservative California state government, particularly from the state superintendent of schools, Max Rafferty, for his handling of the situation. The pressure upon Clark was heightened by the criticism of San Jose State College alumni who staunchly supported the athletic staff. Clark later resigned his post at San Jose State to become president of the University of Oregon. One of the most powerful inducements to his resignation was the expectation that he would be fired as a result of his handling of the conflict between the black athletes and the athletic department.

Before his resignation, however, Clark made provisions for the appointment of an athletic counselor to handle problems arising from coach-athlete difficulties. This counselor was to keep particularly close watch over the relations between coaches and black athletes. It fell to his successor, Acting President Hobart W. Burns, to implement the counselor plan.

Burn's appointee, after a great deal of pressure was brought to bear by the black student and faculty communities, was Kenneth Noel, an instructor in the school's Department of Sociology and a former San Jose State athlete who had helped to organize the 1967 revolt and who knew the San Jose State athletic situation intimately. It was Noel who first discovered the problem giving rise to a second athlete–athletic staff confrontation at San Jose State College.

As black and other minority students were brought in San Jose State under the newly instituted unlimited enrollment plan, various financial-aid programs were developed to meet the needs of these students. Some members of the San Jose State athletic staff objected to these programs, arguing that they constituted a misuse of public funds. But another reason behind their objections was that if blacks (in particular) could receive financial aid to pursue their educational careers without an obligation to participate in athletics, it would not be long before some black athletes would choose to drop out of athletics rather than tolerate the known or suspected inequities in the school's athletic program. Though the athletic staff objected, there was little that they could do to stop financial aid to black students. These funds were administered in the form of Educational Opportunity Grants (EOG) to students on the basis of financial need.

The second confrontation between black athletes and the San Jose State athletic staff was brought about when Ken Noel discovered that the athletic staff had devised a system to support intercollegiate athletic programs with federal funds earmarked for underprivileged students. So prevalent was the use of such funds by the athletic department that in the 1969–70 academic year, EOG funds provided more support for athletes participating in track and field and basketball than did athletic department funds. In short, what the athletic department could not stop, it joined and used for its own purposes.

The situation came to light when a black athlete supported by EOG funds was told that he could no longer participate in track and field because he was missing too many of his preparatory classes due to athletic trips and training demands. The track and field coach at San Jose State sent the captain of the team to discuss the matter with Ken Noel and the directors of the EOP (Educational Opportunity Program).

When the track and field team captain, himself a black athlete and world record holder in the 100 meters, was told that the decision to restrict his failing teammate was irrevocable, he became angry and denounced the entire EOP operation and its administrators. It was then pointed out that the team captain had also entered San Jose State under the provisions of the EOP and was still receiving support from it. At this point the athlete's anger flared. He denounced the EOP administrators as liars and went home, returning with a copy of his grant-in-aid contract in his hand.

The contract essentially stated that he was on full athletic support from athletic department funds. Ken Noel and the EOP financial counselling officer, William Carter, then showed the athlete how much money he was getting per month from the EOG and the cashed check numbers. The athlete was astonished. The track and field team captain and Ken Noel and Bill Carter proceeded to the office of the president of the college to detail to him the highly questionable use of government funds by the athletic department. The system was intricate and clever.

The athletic department would locate talented black athletes who had experienced difficulties in gaining admittance to a four-year college. The coach of the sport in which the athlete participated would then guarantee him a full athletic grant-in-aid to San Jose State. This coach would have the athlete get in touch with the EOP program directors and apply for admittance under its provisions.

Through an athletic department liaison person in the college's financial aids department, all EOG checks for the athlete would be held rather than given to the athlete. When the athlete arrived on campus, he would be sent to the financial-aids department where he would be required to endorse the check face down and give it back to the athletic department liaison or a secretary operating on his behalf. The individual presenting the check always kept a hand on it to prevent the unsuspecting athlete from turning the check over and thus discovering its origin. Several black athletes were tersely reprimanded for attempting to view the face of the check that they were signing. They either endorsed it face down or not at all. Refusal to sign would mean, of course, that they would receive no support. The athletes therefore signed.

After the endorsed check was cashed by the Athletic Department, a second check would be made out to the athlete and given to him. The funds backing this check came from a combination of athletic department funds, provided through alumni donations and associated mandatory student-body fees and a portion of the athlete's own EOG monies. The athletic department thus gained more funds for support of its sports program than it would ordinarily have access to.

In the case of the track and field team captain's "athletic grant-in-aid" the system worked in the following manner: The amount of funds guaranteed in the athlete's grant-in-aid contract with the school was $1,200. This is the manner in which that $1,200 a year contract was fulfilled:

Athlete's EOG grant	$1,200
Funds granted in ASB support to athletic department for athlete	600
Funds due athlete from Athletic Department	600
Total	$2,400

The Athletic Department took the EOG check which had been blindly endorsed by the athlete and cashed it. They then took half of those funds, two-thirds of the ASB funds, and one-third of its own departmental funds and presented the athlete with his $1,200 package.

Athlete's EOG grant	$1,200 less $	600
ASB funds for athlete	600 less	200
Athletic Department funds	600 less	400
Total		$1,200

The Athletic Department thus cut its athlete personnel cost in half. As Bob Bronson, then director of intercollegiate sports at San Jose State stated, "Using the EOG program, we can get two athletes for the price of one." Another justification for the use of EOG funds was that "The use of these funds allows the black athlete to provide support for one of his black brothers." This was, however, proven to be highly spurious rationalizing, since the percentage of black athletes at San Jose State College had remained relatively constant since 1964, three years before the EOG program was established.

Acting President Hobart W. Burns was, of course, disconcerted by these disclosures, particularly since the situation possibly involved what might be defined as the fraudulent misuse of federal government funds. Under the provisions of the EOP program, only the student to whom funds are granted may cash the EOG check. Not even EOP administrators can issue or cash these. Such checks are legally handled through the financial-aids departments of participating educational institutions. Thus, the necessity for the Athletic Department to establish a liaison in the school's financial-aids office.

Second, the contracts offered to EOP athletes were signed by the athletes, Bob Bronson (the athletic director), and the coaches of the sports in which the prospective collegiate athlete would compete. However, the athletic director and the various coaches have no authority to make contracts with athletes obligating the college to support them in return for their athletic services.

Third, the status of the proportion of the $2,400 due the athlete but withheld from him by the Athletic Department, $1,200, was unclear. There was no account of the disposition of the $1,200 by the Athletic Department. One thing, however, was certain—the athlete had $600 in EOG monies due him which had been taken by the Athletic Department.

A fourth problem had to do with the violation of NCAA financial aid regulations. The athletes involved in the Athletic Department—EOG combination clearly could not have received all of the $2,400 due each of them. If they had, both these athletes and San Jose State College could have been declared ineligible to compete in NCAA postseason events or in some other way penalized. However, when they did not receive all of the $2,400, half of the monies due them were being withheld, possibly illegally, by the Athletic Department. If the Athletic Department had simply given them the $1,200 EOG grant monies, it would not have been fulfilling its contract with the athletes to provide an athletic grant-in-aid.

Complicating the situation still further was the fact that many of the athletes who were unknowingly drawing EOG funds had planned to use these funds to complete their educations after their eligibility for athletic support was exhausted. However, since EOG funds can be provided for a student for only four years, some of these athletes had used up a significant proportion of their anticipated government support unknowingly.

The hardship upon these athletes is particularly severe at San Jose State since it takes the average student six and a half years to complete his undergraduate career. The average among black athletes is seven and a half years, and many never complete their degrees at all.

Burns immediately ordered a full investigation into the situation. He issued the following memo:

April 20th 1970

To: Mr. William Carter, Black EOP
    Mr. Robert Martin, Dean of Students
    Mr. Bruce Ogolvie, Faculty Athletic Representative
    Mr. Donald Ryan, Financial Aids Officer
    Mr. Wayne Williams, Controller
    Mr. Ken Noel, Special Athletic Counselor

Re: Appointment to Special Administrative Committee on Financial Aids to Students Participating in Intercollegiate Athletics.

Gentlemen:

By use of this memorandum let me appoint you to membership, under the chairmanship of Mr. Williams, to review policies and procedures—in general and in specific—in the awarding of athletic scholarships.

There is some feeling that, on the one hand, recipients of such grants are not entirely aware of what is expected of them and, on the other hand, that what is expected is based on incomplete or inadequate information. In any event, for at least two years now I have had reports that there are problems, perhaps serious, in this area and, without the assignment of fault, I am concerned that this committee undertake a thorough review and audit of all policies, procedures, records, disbursements, or whatever is necessary for the College to have a clear picture of the present situation. If that situation, on analysis, needs revision then I trust the committee will make specific suggestions for emendations.

While I hope the committee will undertake a thorough review let me ask that it be careful in attending to the facts and that its conclusions flow from the facts.

In this context this memorandum authorizes the committee, in the name of and on request by Chairman Williams, to talk with anyone or view any document or record which may assist the committee in completing its task.

I hesitate to put a suggested date of report in this memo; hasty review may generate an incomplete review; so let me ask you to undertake and complete this as soon as possible consistent with the time needed to do a thorough, impartial, objective and defensible report.

Sincerely yours,
Hobart W. Burns.

In pursuance to the requests of Acting President Burns, College Controller Wayne E. Williams issued the following announcement:

Memo To: Mr. Stanley Benz, Executive Assistant to the President
              Mr. William F. Carter, EOP for Black Studies
              Mr. Kenneth Noel, Black Studies
              Mr. Bruce Ogolvie, Psychology Department
              Mr. Don Ryan, Director, Financial Aids
From: Wayne E. Williams, Controller
Subject: Student Financial Aid-Athletic Department
The President has asked that I chair a committee of the above members to start an immediate investigation of the practices followed in granting student athletic grants in San Jose State College Athletic Department.
This group will cover the following:
1. A review of the Athletic Grants for the Fall and Spring Semesters 1969–1970.
2. Funding for these Grants.
3. Records maintained by the Athletic Department to support individual grants.
4. Records maintained in Associate Student Office.
5. Records maintained by Student Financial Aids, Business Office.
If your schedule would permit, please meet with me at 9:00 A.M., Tuesday, April 21, 1970 in Mr. Glen Guttormsen's office, Room 258 Administration Building.

When the investigation was finally begun, the Athletic Department and its alumni supporters strongly objected to what they considered an intolerable intrusion into athletic affairs. Nonetheless, the investigation was initiated and completed.

In the meantime, student demonstrations over the invasion of Cambodia on April 30, 1970 had resulted in the temporary resignation of Acting President Hobart W. Burns. Fearing that the findings of the investigation into the athletic funding situation would add further to the campus turmoil, Controller Williams sent the following memo to his committee of investigators:

May 14, 1970
To: Mr. William Carter, Black EOP
     Mr. Robert Martin, Dean of Students
     Mr. Kenneth Noel, Black Studies
     Mr. Bruce Ogolvie, Faculty Athletic Representative
     Mr. Donald Ryan, Financial Aids Officer
Subject: Student Financial Aid-Athletic Department
Gentlemen:
Attached is a rough draft of a report to the President on the above subject. I would appreciate your review. I will call a meeting the first part of next week to discuss this report and obtain your reaction and comments.

With the current situation on campus, i.e., the loss of Presidential representation, it would be unwise, in my judgment, to forward this report until an Acting President is appointed.

So that we do not add to the existing turmoil on campus, I would appreciate each of you keeping this in confidence and not discussing any part of this report until we can have our committee meeting and decide the prudent approach.

Sincerely,

Wayne E. Williams, Chairman

Administration Building-Room 255

San Jose State College

San Jose, California

It was discovered that the Athletic Department and its supporters outside of the college had learned of the contents of the investigative committee's reports and immediately embarked upon efforts to suppress its public disclosure completely.

Because it was commonly believed that the now resigned Acting President Burns would be the State College trustees' next choice to fill the presidency at San Jose State, he retracted his resignation and once again assumed the duties of Acting President. At this point the investigating committee presented its findings to him. They were essentially the following: (1) that the Athletic Department had in fact been using federal EOG funds to support its sports program; (2) that the Athletic Department had in fact forced athletes to endorse EOG checks face down; (3) that members of the Athletic Department staff had signed athletes to athletic contracts in an unauthorized fashion; (4) that the Athletic Department had retained significant proportions of funds earmarked for use by student-athletes without the athletes' permission or knowledge; (5) that the Athletic Department had not kept the college's financial aids department adequately informed as to the disposition of its funds; (6) and finally, the investigating committee found that the Athletic Department had encouraged some of its athletes to apply for government loans. The checks for these loans were sent to the athletic liaison person in the financial aids department and dispersed in a fashion similar to the EOG funds.

By the time that Burns received the findings, he had also learned of the pressures against him emanating from the Athletic Department and the alumni. He, therefore, decided to "take the findings under advisement" until after he was appointed to the position of permanent President. At this, several members of the investigating committee expressed disappointment—particularly Bill Carter, the official from the EOP program, and Ken Noel, the athletic counsel. They feared that the findings would be suppressed, and the situation would go uncorrected. Their fears were justified. Nothing has been said of or done about correcting the use of EOG funds to support the intercollegiate athletic program.

There have been other consequences of the investigation, however. Burns did not receive his expected appointment to the position of permanent President, but rather, was installed in the position of academic vice-president, a position having no authority over or responsibility for the athletic sphere of San Jose State activities.

Ken Noel, the newly appointed athletic counselor, was summarily fired from his counseling job with the explanation that such action was required by a shortage of funds. Further, the former liaison person in the financial aids office has, since the suppression of the investigation, been appointed assistant athletic director in charge of athletic grants-in-aid.

On Thursday, August 20, 1970 after verifying a report that S.J.S. might be using federal funds to support its athletic program, the *San Jose Mercury* carried the following page-one headline: "Federal Subsidy to S.J.S. Athletes: $75,012 Paid Out in the Last Three Years."

When asked by newspaper reporters to comment on the situation, Academic Vice-President Burns—the man who, as acting president, was so outraged over the alleged situation that he appointed a committee to investigate it—stated:

> The situation is not as bad as it may seem. To call it a program of federal subsidies to athletes is not entirely accurate. Rather, we view it as a program of subsidies to students who are also athletes.
>
> If we had a regulation that we're not permitted to use any E.O.G. funds for athletes, that would be discriminatory, wouldn't it?
>
> It would also be a violation of the economic code.

In this statement, Burns apparently overlooked the possible legal ramifications of the situation, as well as the ethical and moral implications of the Athletic Department's activities.

The power flow in the situation just discussed presents an interesting illustration of how outside control over collegiate athletic programs serve to threaten the integrity of an academic institution: (1) athletic Department makes arrangement with financial-aids liaison; (2) athletic Department instructs athlete how to get his "athletic grant-in-aid;" (3) financial aids liaison administers various funds per agreement with Athletic Department; (4) disgruntled athletes expose situation to athletic counselor and EOG financial-aids officer; (5) athletic counselor takes situation to acting president; (6) acting-president alerts college controller and mandates him to establish investigative committee; (7) college controller establishes committee, carries out investigation, and informs athletic counselor and EOG official of findings; (8) Athletic Department discovers nature of findings and informs alumni association;

(9) there is an interchange of ideas and information among coaches, alumni, and government officials; (10) acting president is passed over for position of permanent president and re-installed as academic vice-president; athletic counselor is fired; EOG financial-aids officer is notified of his impending dismissal. Findings of investigation are suppressed until made public by former athletic counselor. The now academic vice-president is suddenly supportive of Athletic Department practices, though it is commonly believed that he considers the EOG–Athletic Department situation as a prime factor preventing his appointment to the position of president.

As of June 1972, the situation at San Jose still persisted though slightly changed in some minimal ways, that is, athletes are no longer required to sign checks face down. Thus, it seems that not even the president of San Jose State had control over the school's Athletic Department, its policies or its practices. And when the athletic program at San Jose State is evaluated in terms of the emphasis put upon sports at the universities of Southern California, Alabama, Syracuse, and other institutions, San Jose State is a relatively second-rate institution in terms of its emphasis upon athletics, a "jock sweatshop" rather than a "jock factory." Little wonder that faculties and administrations appear to have little control over the collegiate sports programs at colleges and universities engaged in truly big-time athletics.

Though no one a San Jose State College was ever indicted for misuse of federal funds, some administrators and coaches at the University of Montana were not as fortunate. On July 19, 1972, the Justice Department secured indictments charging thirty-two counts of conspiracy and fraudulent use of federal funds against one of the school's vice-president, the school's athletic director, two assistant football coaches, and the athletic department's business manager. Named as coconspirators but not indicted were the University of Montana's basketball coach, its track coach, and the university business manager. Those involved were accused of misusing over $200,000 in federal funds to aid in financing the school's athletic program though these funds were earmarked by HEW for student financial-aid programs similar to the EOG program at San Jose State.

The degree to which the San Jose State and University of Montana situations constitute examples of widespread practices in the collegiate sport sphere has yet to be determined. Nonetheless, an investigation into the possibility of similar financial arrangements at other schools is clearly needed.

The San Jose State case illustrates another reason why coaches and athletic administrators are so conscious of the desires of alumni groups. Such groups provide them a direct channel of influence with high-level political or other officials whose aid may be of value in thwarting attempts by academic administrators and faculties to control athletic programs. For the same alumni who finance athletic programs frequently contribute also to the political campaigns of elected officials.

An understanding of established power relationships such as those discussed above must be a key component in any plan to alter the current situation in collegiate sports wherein neither students, academic faculties, administrations, nor the athletes themselves have control over collegiate athletics proportionate to their stakes and interests in these activities. In private schools, the equivalent of state government officials who exercise considerable influence over college faculties and administrations are these schools' boards of trustees, and the power flow is essentially the same. These boards of trustees, always conscious of the badly needed financial support furnished by members of the alumni group, are usually amenable to influencing college affairs on behalf of the athletic departments.

The degree to which the control of collegiate sports has become solidly vested and entrenched with booster-type organizations and alumni–athletic staff coalitions established outside of the academic community constitutes one of the serious problems facing higher education today. Such outside control contributes to supporting most coaches' policy of operating athletic programs as they see fit and their position that any attempt by students, athletes, academic faculty members, or administrative officials to supervise or exercise more than a minimal degree of control over sports constitute an unwarranted intrusion. The outside control of collegiate sports contributes to bringing about rebellions among athletes. Lacking impartial avenues of redress for their grievances, some athletes rebel against the policies and practices of their coaches and other officials of athletic departments.

And perhaps most important of all, we have seen illustrative evidence that such outside control of collegiate sports has been a contributing factor in casting doubt on the integrity of institutions of higher education.

HIGH-LEVEL AMATEUR SPORTS

Big-time amateur sports outside of the collegiate sphere are also beginning to experience an intensification of preliminary shock waves that signal what I believe to be an impending economic crisis of both national and international consequence. Since the banishment of the legendary Jim Thorpe from amateur athletics for life as a result of his participation in a "professional" baseball game, the question of "amateurism" has been a fundamental issue in both national and international sports. Until recently, it was primarily among the ranks of those who control big-time, noncollegiate amateur sports that the debate over the propriety of amateurism was waged. The opposing arguments usually focused upon the wisdom of the "Free World's" commitment to amateurism while Communist countries, most notably the Soviet Union, were subsidizing their athletes. The freedom from the need to pursue a livelihood simultaneously while training for sports events, or so the anti-amateurism forces have argued, is a determining factor in the athletic success of these countries in such sports spectaculars as the Olympic Games. The pro-amateurism forces, whose chief advocate has been Avery Brundage, for many years president of the International Olympic Committee, have usually based their argument on less pragmatic concerns—to wit, "amateurism is the purest form of sport expression and should be maintained as an ideal—especially in the Olympic Games."

But of late, amateur athletes themselves have become party to the debate, and the basis for their argument is highly practical indeed—their believed personal right to a livelihood and to openly and honestly take advantage of the economic opportunities opened to them by their athletic accomplishments. Increasingly, from the perspectives of many amateur athletes residing in the so-called Free World, it is no longer acceptable that *they* should not be allowed to capitalize on their sports success due to some purported "ideal" held by those who control amateur sports. They see no reason why an amateur should also be a pauper. Many believe it to be primarily the noble ideal of "amateurism" that stands in the way of amateur athletes receiving financial renumeration for their efforts. Scott, for instance, gives precedence to the ideals of "crusty old amateur officials" and the self-interested complaints of "those athletes who are unwilling or unable to train more than a few hours each week" as the chief factors working against amateur athletes who seek to capitalize financially on their athletic success.[22] The contention here is that these factors—an adherence to the ideal of amateurism by officials and the complaints of some athletes—are secondary at best in the *perpetuation* of "amateurism" though the existence of an "amateur ideal" may have been the *initial* factor behind the establishment of a high value on amateurism. The real factor to be considered today in this regard is the character of the values governing interactions in the economic sphere in the Western world in general and the United States in particular. Let us first look at the evidence counter to Scott's arguments before developing this last assertion.

It may be true that allowing amateur athletes to capitalize on their

---

[22] Jack Scott, *The Athletic Revolution* (New York: Free Press, 1971), footnote, p. 101.

sports success would enable the more successful athletes to train more than the less successful athletes (who would still have to work for a livelihood). But the economic history of Western nations would suggest that this problem could not fully explain the dogmatic concern of the amateur sports establishment with the maintenance of amateurism. For the main historical tendency has been to open all and any avenues promising of economic productivity. The income of professional athletes from commercial endorsements is indicative of the potentially lucrative rewards awaiting amateur athletes and the businesses which would use their names, faces, and testimonials in advertisements. It is unlikely that the complaints of a few or even many unsuccessful athletes who felt that they would be put at a competitive disadvantage would be enough to stifle development of such a promising economic relationship.

Also, the image of those who control amateur sports as "idealists" seems, at best, out of character. Such a wily old industrialist as Avery Brundage, perhaps the chief spokesman for amateurism in international sports, can hardly be termed a paragon of idealism. And we can ask why, in both the national and international spheres of amateur sports, the ideal of amateurism is applied *only* to the *athlete*. In collegiate football for example, coaches receive very large salaries. The new coach at Texas A. & M., for instance, reportedly received a "salary plus benefits" contract in excess of one million dollars spread out over a ten year period. And while his athletes would be immediately banned from amateur competition for even lending their names to commercial advertisements, Ara Parseghian, head football coach at Notre Dame, has for a number of years done Ford Motor Company advertisements on television wearing a Notre Dame jacket. Athletic directors, trainers, team doctors, sports announcers, promoters, equipment companies, are all permitted to capitalize financially upon their particular skills and assets in the sports realm. But the athlete must remain an amateur.

International sport also furnishes much evidence contradicting the notion that an idealistic commitment to amateurism is the primary obstacle to amateur athletes seeking to capitalize on their athletic success. National and international Olympic and amateur sports officials benefit economically from their association with sport through income tax deductions where applicable, and through salaries, expense accounts, and business contacts made through travels ostensibly for purposes related to their sports responsibilities. Further, the displays, symbols, and insignia which are part of international sports events in particular are highly commercialized. The commercialism occurring at the Winter Olympics in Sapporo, Japan, in 1972 constitutes a case in point. NBC news reporter Lou Cioffi reported on January 31, 1972, that everything from "official Olympic ski suits, hats, sweaters, and boots to flags were being sold at a profit by the Olympic Organizing Committee in Japan." In fact, the Japan Olympic Organizing Committee put the Olympic symbol itself on sale. For a fee of 15,000 dollars any business organization was granted permission to use the Olympic symbol (five interlocked rings) in the commercial advertising of its products. This is how, for instance, this foot powder or that breakfast cereal comes to be the "official foot powder" or the "official breakfast cereal" of the United States Olympic team or of the Olympic Games. At the same time, Karl Schrantz, Austrian ski champion, was banned from Olympic competition for having allowed use of his name and picture in commercial endorsements of ski equipment. This type of contradiction is not unusual. It is characteristic of both the summer and winter Olympics as well as some national amateur sports.

Further, the same national and international amateur sports officials who have traditionally banned "Free World" athletes from amateur competition, sometimes on only the flimsiest evidence of commercialism, have openly tolerated the commonly known fact that Communist countries subsidize their athletes.

Under the circumstances, an idealistic value on amateurism is untenable as an explanation of why sports officials refuse to allow Western countries' amateur athletes to capitalize on their athletic success. A more defensible explanation must be sought in the contrasting values governing interaction in the economic spheres of life in the "Free World" and in Communist countries.

In Communist countries such as the USSR, East Germany, and Hungary there is little danger that the granting of living subsidies will escalate into demands for still higher payments on the parts of either individual athletes or organized athletic unions. Both the rigid system of political control and the philosophy governing behavior in the economic realm—epitomized by the slogan "to each according to his need, from each according to his ability"—militate against such a potentiality. Recall our hypothesis that a control function of sport is to reaffirm the established values of a society. Thus, it is at least possible that these countries subsidize their "amateur" athletes not because they are more immoral or more political in their approach to international sports than "Free World" countries, but because the values defining acceptable behavior in the economic sphere allows them to legitimately bring severe social and political pressures to bear on any athlete that attempts to capitalize on his or her sports stardom for personal financial gain. It may well be *this* fact which makes the Communist governments' subsidies to amateur athletes palatable to such hard-line "amateurists" as Avery Brundage. And it is also this fact which suggests that the "idealistic" insistence upon amateurism among Free World athletes, particularly those of the United States, may be seen as a "sham," a "front," calculated to preserve the economic viability of amateur sports as we know them today.

In the industrialized non-Communist countries, the striving on the part of each party to an economic transaction to secure for himself the greatest economic advantage is not only legitimate, it is expected and approved. This has led to a fear among amateur athletic officials, at both the national and international levels in amateur sports, of any move to permit either direct payments to athletes or to allow them to profit from their athletic fame by commercial endorsements. Any "commercialism" is looked upon as the opening of a Pandora's box of woes.

The specific fear with regard to permitting the payment of a minimum year-round living subsidy to amateur athletes appears to be that the steadily increasing cost of living and inflation, among other factors, would result in the unionization of amateur athletes and yearly or semiregular bouts of economic bargaining between athletes and officials sports bodies—the National and International Olympic Committees, college and university athletic departments, the AAU, the NCAA, and so forth. It is felt that if such widespread bargaining came about, amateur sports could not long survive. For even with athletes who are not paid, amateur sports from Olympic activities and collegiate sports through high school and junior high school athletics are faced with a financial crisis.

"Commercialism" in the form of permitting athletes to receive pay for endorsing products is seen as a threat not only to amateur sports but to professional sports as well. Suppose that an amateur athlete can make $40,000–$50,000 a year endorsing commercial products (as Karl Schranz is reputed to have grossed endorsing ski equipment in 1971). Unless he simply loved to compete, the chances are that, when an athlete had amassed a satisfactory amount of capital, he would (1) not wish to continue in amateur sports, perhaps wishing to pursue business interests instead, or (2) not compete in professional sports without a salary sufficient to cover not only his competitive value as a professional athlete, but to compensate also for the time he spends away from his established business. Under either circumstance, both professional and amateur sports could experience a drop in quality of competition—since it would be primarily the less talented athlete who would remain in sports aside from the few who are devoted to participation for its intrinsic satisfactions. Today, sport is practically without a competitor for the special talents of athletes. No other industry would pay a yearly salary for a person's skill in running or dribbling a basketball or kicking a football. But if commercialism became an acceptable part of sports careers at *all* levels, an athlete would constantly have to evaluate the relative financial rewards to be gained from one more year of competition as opposed to retiring from sport and pursuing his business interests.

Given greater economic opportunity in business, undoubtedly many would retire at the amateur level rather than put up with the uncertainty, danger of physical injury, and insecurity of a professional sports career.

A third fear is that the establishment of commercialism in amateur sport would *lead to* subsidizing less successful athletes and conversely that the subsidizing of all amateur athletes would lead to commercialism on the part of the more successful athletes. The argument is that if all athletes were subsidized at a standard rate, in a society where self-interested economic activity is the rule, it would be perfectly legitimate for the more successful athlete to seek greater compensation for his efforts. Correspondingly, if the more successful athletes were allowed to capitalize upon their athletic reputations, one could hardly argue against some form of financial renumeration for the less skilled athletes for their efforts. On these assumptions, therefore, it appears that any program to establish financial compensation to amateur athletes portends increased economic problems, if not disaster, for amateur and, indirectly, professional sports. Given the functions of sport for society, the supporters and spokesman of the present system regard such potentialities as something to be avoided at all costs.

Given the divergence of values governing economic affairs in Communist versus non-Communist societies, international sports officials could not very well ban athletes from the former countries. Athletes from Communist countries, therefore, compete annually as amateurs in good standing in both national and international sports events while Free World amateur athletes found guilty of "capitalizing" on their sports prowess in any way are often suspended and their performances, even those of record caliber, disallowed and stricken from the books.

This ostensible double standard for defining who is an amateur is justified by sports officials and the sports media in several ways. The ideal of amateurism is postulated as a sacrosanct virtue. This has been traditionally accepted as a valid explanation of why American amateurs, for instance, have not received year-round financial compensation for their athletic efforts that is at least sufficient to sustain the necessities of life—despite all the evidence that the "ideal" is applied *only to Free World amateur athletes*.

Also, the media and sports officials have appealed to ethnocentric and anti-Communist sentiments of Free World societies by characterizing the communist countries as immoral and politically opportunistic because they *do* subsidize their amateur athletes. And of course, a frequent reaction is "If the Communists do it that way, it *must* be immoral."

And finally, the media and the sports establishment continue to perpetuate the image of sports as fun and games: endeavors whose worth is predicated solely upon the value and satisfaction they hold for the individual participant; a sphere or life where competitive *success* is secondary, wherein "it is not whether you win or lose but how you played the game" that counts. Thus, amateur sport and play are portrayed as synonymous activities—and who would argue that anyone should be paid for *playing?* Of course, any athlete is aware that fun and enjoyment typically is of secondary concern in sport from high school through the professional ranks. Yet, the myths of the amateur ideal, the fun-and-games character of sport, and the intrinsic immorality of compensating amateur athletes financially continue to be believed.

The contention here is that just as the Communist countries are not necessarily immoral and politically opportunistic because they compensate their amateur athletes financially, Free World sports officials are not necessarily hard-hearted and unconcerned about the welfare of amateur athletes simply because they refuse to allow similar compensation. These officials *and* the officials of Communist countries are more likely attempting to maintain the quality and caliber of international competition—at least in part—because of its positive significance to all the nations concerned. Periodic strikes and boycotts of international sports events by Free World athletes *over economic issues* presumably would serve little political purpose to any country. Such self-interested economic behavior on the parts of athletes could not be glorified within the context of communist ideology, and it represents a clear danger to international sports competition—especially if it occurred just prior to scheduled competition between national teams or just before the Olympic games. The sports media, too, could only be negatively affected by such an occurrence.

I feel that there is a partial solution to the dilemma that confronts amateur sports as a result of increasing pressures from athletes for compensation for commercialism in the face of the realities of the economics of sport. The proposal is a compromise which would, of course, be totally satisfactory to none of the parties to the dispute. The plan would essentially involve the granting of a nontaxable allowance on an amateur athlete's future income. For each year that he makes the roster of an amateur athletic aggregation, the athlete would be allowed an income-tax deduction on one year's income after his amateur career is completed. Perhaps the minimal subsistence income as set by the federal government and prevailing during the years in which the athlete competed could be used as the ceiling for standard "amateur athletic deductions." Safeguards against abuse could also be built in. For instance, once an athlete took a deduction he could no longer participate in amateur sports. He would thus have both an incentive for remaining active in amateur sports as long as possible, and at the same time he would be directly receiving financial compensation of a sort for his athletic efforts.

From the perspective of amateur sports, a good deal of the pressure for amateur athlete subsidies potentially could be relieved through such a plan. Also, a heightening of the economic crisis in sports could be avoided, since sports organizations would not bear the additional economic burden of compensating amateur athletes. And finally, through such a plan, those sports officials who have steadfastly propagated the ideal of amateurism could "save face" since no amateur athlete would stand to gain financially from such a plan until his participation in amateur sport had ended. Thus the cultural fiction of amateurism would survive.

This seems a very appropriate solution to the problem given the existing stalemate. A similar economic mechanism called "income-tax averaging" has been used by writers and artists for years in the United States. There appears to be little reason why it could not be extended to cover amateur athletes—especially those with little or no future in professional sports such as track and field participants, swimmers, gymnasts, and so forth.

Of course, this approach would by no means solve all of the economic problems facing big-time international amateur sports—especially those of the Olympic variety. A striking example is presented by the economic problems facing the state of Colorado as a result of its winning the bid for the 1976 Winter Olympics. Here is an account by Sam Brown, Jr.:[23]

To promote Denver, Denver representatives had made trips at public expense to Mexico City, Spain, Yugoslavia and Switzerland, among other places, long before the Amsterdam IOC meeting. The committee had been able to prepare an impressive report for the IOC.

Richard O'Reilly, reporter for the "Rocky Mountain News," wrote in a six-part series on the Olympics published April 4–9, 1971:

By May 1970 [the Denver Organizing Committee] had compressed its bid into a fancy two-volume color picture book edition complete with slipcase and a half-hour movie for presentation to the IOC at Amsterdam.

The bid book was and is a magnificent piece of salesmanship. From the heavy coat of snow air-brushed by an artist onto a photo of Mt. Sniktau, to cover potentially embarrassing bare spots, to the statement that construction of an Olympic speed skating rink "will begin in 1970," the books contain a series of misrepresentations.

Denver promised 100,000 beds for tourists when only about 35,000 will be available, Norman C. Brown, DOC public affairs manager, admitted.

And it promised a 45-minute drive from the Olympic village to Mr.

---

[23] "Snow Job in Colorado," *New Republic*, January 29, 1972, pp. 15–19.

Sniktau, but didn't mention that was possible by shutting off all traffic in I–70 and running six lanes of buses up the mountains, Brown acknowledged.

Denver promised to stage Nordic ski events requiring snow-covered countryside in a rapidly growing mountain residential area with a 4 percent chance of having enough natural snow.

And Denver promised to hold Alpine ski races on a mountain which probably wouldn't be developed except for the Olympics.

By this impressive if dishonest salesmanship, Denver beat Sion, Switzerland, by a 39–30 vote of the IOC as the chosen location for the 1976 Winter Olympics.

The only return the state will get is increased tax revenues, which is not expected to cover the costs. In fact, no government has ever made money on the Olympics, and even the DOC admits it is unlikely Colorado and Denver will. The Squaw Valley Winter Olympics in 1960 has, to date, cost the taxpayers more than 13 times the original estimate, a total of $13.5 million. The area has never become self-supporting, and when recently put up for sale by the state, only one bid was received—$25,000. H. D. Thoreau, chief organizer of the Olympics there, has said that if the California legislature had known the full cost from the beginning, "the games would not have been held in California."

The Grenoble Winter Olympics in 1968 cost $250 million, of which $50 million was paid by taxpayers. The city is still heavily in debt for it, and local property taxes have risen by an incredible 125 percent.

These figures, of course, do not reflect hidden costs such as highways and streets, policing, water and sewage extension, solid waste disposal, military equipment and personnel on loan, use of public lands, governmental agencies and services, uncontrolled growth costs to communities, and, of course, such items as loan of Public Service Company helicopters for visiting dignitaries. (This latter cost is presumably adequately covered by a recently granted rate increase.)

(On November 7, 1972, Denver citizens voted not to provide the funds necessary for holding the games in that city, thereby becoming the first city in history to reject the awarding of the games.)

INTERSCHOLASTIC SPORTS

Interscholastic sports have also felt the economic pinch. In many cities across America, there is evident an increasing tendency to rethink the priority of athletics in light of monetary shortages in such vital areas of academic concern as teachers' salaries, funds for classroom construction, and equipment. One city, Philadelphia, made headlines nationally when it dropped the funding of interscholastic sports completely. It was apparently felt that the continued financial support of these activities, when concerns more basic to the academic process were going unfunded, was unjustifiable. (Cut also were two other extra-curricular activities—art and music.) There have been sporadic efforts to revive sports in Philadelphia schools. For instance, Leonard Tose, owner of the Philadelphia Eagles professional football team, gave the school district what has been variously reported at $55,000 and $76,000 from proceeds of exhibition games. But whatever the size of the gift, it was inadequate. The school board thanked him kindly, but noted that, under the financial circumstances, it could not assure him that the money would be used to reinstate interscholastic football in Philadelphia. Superintendent of the district Mark Shedd stated: "Ours is not a 350,000 dollar problem [the cost of maintaining varsity sports] . . . but a 35 million dollar problem [the cost of running the school district] . . ."[24]

Philadelphia's problem is becoming an increasingly familiar one. Across the country—in Cincinnati, in the affluent suburbs of Detroit, in Los Angeles—similar crises have developed. In San Francisco for the first time there will be no junior high-school sports competition. In Oakland, California, after it was announced that the public school football program was in jeopardy, enough money was donated or raised at a celebrity banquet to maintain the sport, but it is decidedly an austerity operation—old uniforms and no nonleague games. Such makeshift efforts apparently cannot serve for Philadelphia, and unless something unforeseen develops, it will maintain its status as the first major city in the country to totally eliminate high-school athletics.

The key problem is illustrated by the following. Although the nation spent a record 85 billion dollars on private and public schools in 1971, the 9.7 percent increases in funding over the 1970 budget was barely enough to keep abreast of (1) inflation, (2) a 1 percent increase of 500,000 students, and (3) wage increases for teachers and others that went into effect before President Nixon's price and wage freeze. At the interscholastic level then, sport is not threatened by high-powered recruiting, elaborate facilities, or high coaching salaries. There is simply not enough money available, even to properly carry out what have long been regarded as legitimate and necessary academic functions. As Superintendent Shedd remarked, unless something radical is done to deal effectively with the financial crisis in the frequently criticized public school systems of the nation, "in the words of a famous American, there won't be any urban public schools to kick around anymore."

THE FUTURE OF SPORTS

What does the financial crisis portend for the future of sports in America? It must be recognized that any factor which negatively affects the functioning, structure, or prevalence of sport on any one level affects

---

[24] Mark Shedd cited in Ron Fimrite, "We Expect Them to Storm the Gates," *Sports Illustrated*, September 6, 1971, p. 21.

sport on all levels—professional, collegiate, advanced amateur, and interscholastic. This is primarily because the various levels are components in an interdependent system. High schools provide training in basic skills and familiarize athletes with the rules of sports. In doing so, they serve as unofficial "farm clubs" for colleges. Colleges and universities prepare athletes for professional sports in much the same way.

Similarly, the high-school athlete is rendered more amenable to the autocratic coaching practices characteristic of all levels of sport by the potential opportunity to pursue a collegiate sports career. The promise of a professional sports career has a similar affect upon the collegiate athlete. In short, any widespread financial crisis at any level in sport would affect the customary abundance of trained athlete personnel, and if any level (high school, collegiate, or professional) collapsed or de-emphasized sport, athlete control and discipline problems would likely emerge.

Thus far, no data are available on the effects of the collapse of interscholastic sports in some large urban school systems. If the trend continues, however, it may not be long before the results will be reflected in even more intense competition among colleges and universities for a reduced number of superior high school athletic stars and, ultimately, in a reduction in the overall quality of both collegiate and professional sports.

If present fiscal trends continue in collegiate sports, many colleges now existing on the margins of financial solvency will join the growing ranks of institutions that have dropped either single sports activities or entire programs. Thus, while the greatest long-range threat to sport in America may be that of changing values and perspectives among significant segments of the society, the most immediate threat is economic. Despite the importance of inflation and rising costs, the greatest difficulty seems to originate in the functioning of sports organizations themselves. As Pat Ryan notes:

> It has been explained by Oregon State Athletic Director Jim Barratt as "keeping up with the Joneses." He says, "If our major opponent hires another football assistant coach, we try to match them. If our major opponent has more football scholarships than we have, we try to catch up. If our major opponent has an athletic dormitory, we get out the hammer and nails. If our major opponent shops for artificial turf, we start organizing a fund-raising campaign. This goes on and on. If we don't work through the NCAA for a solution of limitations, many of our coaches will be out selling insurance within five years."[25]

To date, the NCAA has offered no viable solution to the economic problems. It seems therefore that sport, for all but a relatively few colleges, may join "panty raids" as hallowed collegiate traditions doomed to

---

[25] Pat Ryan, p. 19.

extinction by contemporary pressures and concerns. High-school sports, too, seem severely threatened. And although professional sports have been protected somewhat under its exemptions from antitrust legislation and reserve-type clauses, inevitably it too must be negatively affected by the increasing tendency of athletes to unionize and by the crises affecting collegiate and interscholastic sports.

What all these difficulties suggest is that American sport, at the apex of its development and popularity, already may have begun to move down the road to widespread de-emphasis as an institution. Beleaguered on the one hand by a growing dissatisfaction with its structure and functioning, and on the other by seemingly insurmountable fiscal problems, it appears highly unlikely that sport will survive even the 1970s in its present guise. On the horizon there appears to be a sort of polarization developing: ever higher-priced, big-time athletics pursued in the professional ranks and by increasingly fewer colleges; little sport at all in high schools—especially large urban high schools such as those in Philadelphia, New York, and Oakland, California (which have turned out the likes of Elgin Baylor, Wilt Chamberlain, Kareem Abdul-Jabbar, and Bill Russell); and no sports, coupled with the development of truly amateur intramural recreational endeavors, at most colleges and universities.

Parenthetically, the de-emphasis of sport as an institution would in all likelihood have its most devastating effects upon black society in America because of the significance of sport to Afro-Americans.

10

An assessment of the sports creed

The Great Sports Myth . . . is a fiction sustained and built up by . . . the news-gatherers [and other] professional sports uplifters . . . who tell us that competitive sport is health-giving, character-building, brain-making and so forth . . . They imply more or less directly that its exponents are heroes, possessed of none but the highest of moral qualities; tempered and steeled in the great white heat of competition; purified and made holy by their devotion to . . . sport. Thanks to [coaches and sportswriters], there has grown up in the public mind an exaggerated and sentimental notion of the moral value of great, competitive sport spectacles. . . .

Why not stop talking about the noble purposes which sports fulfill and take them for what they are? . . . In short let us cease the elevation of [sport] to the level of a religion . . .[1]

John Tunis, *1928*

THROUGHOUT THE PREVIOUS chapters of part two, much of the discussion has either implicitly or explicitly focused upon the ideological character of the creedal claims made on behalf of sport. In this regard, it must be stated that probably the vast majority of *all* social beliefs are to some degree ideological in both substantive content and emphasis. Often they are normative—expressive of virtues or what *should* be; or they express desires, wishes, needs, or hopes. Also, social beliefs may supply "meanings" or "explanations" for what *is*. Therefore most social beliefs are not *true* or *untrue* in the simple sense of "empirical" or "scientific" fact. Rather they are largely symbolic—they "express" or "stand for"

---

[1] John Tunis, *$port$* (New York: John Day Publishers, 1928), p. 24 and also in *Harpers*, "The Great God Football," 157 (November 1928): 742–52.

something other than a sheer empirical description of a state of affairs. It follows, then, that merely to *debunk* such ideologies or systems of social beliefs—though easily accomplished—does not get us very far analytically or in terms of generating understanding. Indeed, the fundamentally "functional" approach of the present work to the institution of sport has been one that *attributes consequences to beliefs without much consideration of the correspondence between these beliefs and "objective reality."* Given this approach to understanding sport, however, it is felt that some space must be devoted to explicitly assessing the status of the dominant sports creed as basically a system of ideological beliefs or statements. Thus the goal here is not to debunk, but to provide evidence as to the soundness of the approach to sport employed here by portraying in summary form the overall status of the dominant sports creed.

While information is readily available for some of the statements constituting components of the dominant sports creed, little or no information has been compiled on other categories. For some claims there are no investigations or documented observations. Similarly, some claims are so general and vague as not to be amenable to objective evaluation. But this characteristic should be expected in any ideological system. Any set of unqualified claims referring to empirical conditions must be somewhat vague and general in terms of its applicability to specific circumstances and in the degree to which its focal variables are clearly defined. Were this not the case, creeds or ideologies would continually run the risk of being disproven. Hence, though the statement "Being a Christian makes one a better athlete" at least implies a testable proposition, because there are no clear, explicit consensual statements in the creed which operationally define the concept "Christian," the precise meaning of "better athlete," or the conditions under which being a "Christian" would make one a "better athlete," the statement cannot be conclusively proven true or false. If creedal concepts were, as a rule, rigorously defined and the applicability of creedal claims to specific circumstances clearly delineated, the creed would in all likelihood lose its evocative power. The fact of this vagueness itself belies to some degree the certainty of expressed creedal claims as to the realities of sport in America.

As a format for assessing the ideological status of the dominant sports creed, each specific claim is listed and discussed under the general theme of which it is a component element.

CHARACTER

1. Sports participation develops "good character"

Though the exact definition of "good character" is nowhere to be found in the literature on sport, there does exist some information which suggests the possibility that persons manifesting personality traits deemed unacceptable or undesirable are selectively excluded from sports participation, and that sports competition itself may in fact be detrimental to the development of what are commonly believed to be desirable character traits. We have discussed some of this information in earlier chapters—particularly data presented by Ogilvie and Tutko.[2]

My observations tend to support the above authors' claim that a severe selection process may exclude persons manifesting perceived undesirable character traits from athletic participation. It is unlikely that a coach would knowingly recruit any athlete who was perceived to have exhibited generally "bad character." It is widely recognized in sports circles that coaches' recommendations as to an athlete's overall character and "attitude" typically has as much bearing upon whether the athlete is recruited into collegiate sports (or is drafted into professional sports) as the athlete's demonstrated physical abilities. Similarly, it is not uncommon for athletes perceived to have "bad" or even "questionable" character to be temporarily suspended or banned from sports participation entirely. However, the extreme emphasis on winning in sport has led to widespread cheating and recruiting violations in some colleges and universities and a commensurate de-emphasis on such "good character" traits as sportsmanship. In light of the above, the judgment here is that available information is inconclusive on the claim that sports "builds character." On the other hand, existing data are not sufficient to warrant the assertion that sports participation is detrimental to the development of "good character" (though Ogilvie and Tutko suspect that it might be). *Inconclusive*

2. Sports participation develops a value on loyalty

Ogilvie and Tutko's assertion that a distinctive kind of selectivity operates to weed out individuals perceived as possessing intolerable character traits would also hold for those whose behavior is viewed as being indicative of disloyalty. We have seen earlier how both coaches and athletes who allegedly committed disloyal acts were suspended or dismissed from athletic units. It seems clear that disloyalty to the sports "family" by primary-level actors is not tolerated. It would likewise seem inconceivable that such individuals would be deliberately recruited to fill primary-level positions. Undoubtedly, rather stringent selectivity occurs with regard to loyalty also.

The selectivity, however, must be imperfect, for in the absence of overt acts which may be interpreted as showing disloyalty, it is difficult to know whether the individual places a high value on loyalty. For instance, frequently in the sports creed it is implied that loyalty was

---

[2] Bruce C. Ogilvie, and Thomas A. Tutko, "Sports: If You Want to Build Character, Try Something Else," *Psychology Today* (October, 1971), p. 61.

manifest in an athlete's willingness to speak well of his team and team-mates (even in the face of humiliating defeat) and to protect the image of the team. But as with some other proposed signs of loyalty, there is no conclusive evidence which shows that the willingness of an athlete to speak well of his team and so forth emanates solely from a sense of loyalty.

Much the same holds for the idea that a secondary-level involve-ment in sports (e.g., as a fan) generates loyalty to the nation, to a college, or to a local community. The literature on sports shows that loyalty to sports organizations—to the extent that this is accurately reflected in attendance figures and a willingness on the parts of local voters to sup-port bond issues for new sports facilities—is closely associated with those organizations' anticipated or actual records of success in their various athletic endeavors. In these terms, the loyalty of fans—whether of students or the general citizenry—typically wanes and ebbs according to the losing or winning records of the athletic aggregations with which they identify.

But under any circumstances, there has yet to be presented any evidence which either negates or substantiates the idea that loyalty to sports organizations is transferable from the sports arena to other secular social structures and relationships—whether the social structure is the nation, a local community, or a college.

Obviously, no firm judgment can be made as to the objective status of this claim because of an almost complete lack of evidence. *No evi-dence pro or con.*

3. Sports participation generates altruism

We have already seen that it is quite possible that sports competi-tion, far from generating an altruistic attitude toward others, may, in fact, contribute to intensifying already existing animosities. The concep-tion of the sports aggregation as a "family" has the function of sup-pressing the intensity of rivalries and self-interested behavior that emerges from role relations within the athletic unit.

Further, as Ogilvie and Tutko state:

. . . Most athletes indicate low interest in receiving support and concern from others, low need to take care of others, and low need for affiliation. Such a per-sonality seems necessary to achieve victory over others. There is some question whether these trends are temporary character trait—changing when the athlete gets out of sport—or permanent ones. Using men coaches and women physical educators as reference groups, we would predict that these character trends remain highly stable . . .[3]

Our judgment is that any evaluation of the creedal claim that sports participation generates altruism must be inconclusive in light of current knowledge. *Inconclusive.*

---

[3] Ibid., pp. 61–62.

DISCIPLINE

4. Sports participation generates a value on social and/or self-control

In terms of the claimed contributions of sports participation to the development of self-control (or self-discipline) and an appreciation for social control, findings are mixed. We have seen that the observed tendency of some athletes to attack those whose behavior violates established norms may be as much a result of these athletes' intuitive perceptions of threats to their own personal interests as a manifestation of their respect for established norms per se. There is theoretical evidence nonetheless which suggests that sports may serve a social control function in educational institutions as well as in the general society. Some sociological and psychological studies suggest that in order to achieve higher proficiency in sports, the athlete must have internalized the social values of high mobility aspirations in the existing social structure, deferred gratification, a value on hard goal-oriented work, and high achievement motivation.[4]

Though these values are prescribed as desirable regardless of one's goals in life, the educational institution provides practically the only arena wherein they assume any degree of immediate significance for young people, and in this arena sport has become the prime vehicle by which this significance is made manifest.[5]

Athletics may thus serve to channel the time and energy of young people involved in it, through one capacity or another, away from unacceptable or delinquent activities which may be all the more tempting due to the lack of a wide range of explicitly prescribed roles and positions for youth in American society generally.

Further, Cohen, Ferdinand, Parsons, and others have contended that antisocial, undesirable, or delinquent behavior sometimes results from the motivation of young males to assert masculinity to themselves and their peers through daring, adventuresome, or illegal acts. It is argued that this is particularly true of boys from middle-class homes, for whom conformity is linked to the mother.[6]

Ferdinand in particular points out that sports, as an institutionalized display of force, skill, strength, speed and competitiveness, represents a visible, socially acceptable means of public and private behavior

[4] W. E. Schafer, "Some Social Sources and Consequences of Interscholastic Athletics: The Case of Participation and Delinquency," *The International Review of Sport Sociology* (Warsaw: Polish Publishers, 1969), vol. 4, p. 69.

[5] David Matza, "Position and Behavior Patterns in Youth" in R. E. L. Faris, ed., *Handbook of Modern Sociology* (Chicago: Rand McNally, Inc., 1964), p. 207.

[6] Albert K. Cohen, *Delinquent Boys* (New York: Free Press, 1961), pp. 157–69. Talcott Parsons, "Certain Primary Sources and Patterns of Aggression in the Social Structure of the Western World," *American Sociological Review* (May 1947), pp. 167–81. T. N. Ferdinand, *Typologies of Delinquency* (New York: Random House, 1966), chap. 4.

demonstrative of masculine prowess and competence and at the same time, it provides a vehicle of actualization of middle and higher class values.

We have seen how sport may serve a safety-valve function with regard to potentially explosive competition between blacks and whites for scarce values. Similarly, fans do seem to be channeled toward continued adherence to established norms through their involvement in sport. None of the above information, however, suggests that sport generates an appreciation for the necessity of social control or the strict adherence to social rules.

Other than the observation that athletes are seldom allowed an opportunity to exercise *self*-discipline or *self*-control in the athletic sphere itself, little information is available on the extent to which sports generate self-discipline. Nonetheless, if athletes' behavior with regard to academic responsibilities can be taken as indicative of the degree of self-discipline achieved, a study undertaken at the University of Kansas may be enlightening. Seeking methods of reducing the football budget, coach Wade Stinson at the University of Kansas was surprised not only by the amount of money expended on athlete tutoring but also by the pattern of these expenditures. He states:

. . .There is no more reason why an athlete should be provided with free tutoring than a nonathlete should; the trouble with tutoring is that it becomes a crutch to the athlete. Instead of starting out on the first day of classes and keeping up his work, he waits until shortly before exams and then yells for tutoring. A study of the Jayhawk annual budget bears this out. The books have sometimes shown less than $50 spent in tutoring fees between September and December. But between Jan. 1 and March 1, which includes the period of semester exams, tutoring jumps to $5,000.[7]

Even here, however, it is not conclusively clear that sports participation in an of itself either contributes to or detracts from the development of self-discipline.

The above discussion suggests that existing evidence regarding the status of the present creedal claim is inconclusive. *Inconclusive.*

COMPETITION

5. Sports participation develops fortitude

Observation of sports tends to indicate that the requirements of participation in sports may selectively screen out individuals not possessing a certain minimal degree of fortitude, rather than it being a case of sports actually *generating* courage in athletes.

---

[7] Wade Stenson in Pat Ryan "A Grim Run for Fiscal Daylight," *Sports Illustrated*, February 1, 1971, p. 19.

Perseverance and self-confidence are strongly related to individual histories of past success resulting in self-gratification and a positive self-image. Under circumstances where an individual's life may be characterized by a pattern of failures in activities of significance to him, he is not likely to have developed self-confidence comparable to that of the individual who has met with success. If these failures and his consciousness of them predominate in the individual's life, he may be inclined to turn to innovative means of attaining some degree of "success" outside of accepted traditional definitions. In either event, such a person would likely be screened out of participation in sports by failing to measure up in one aspect of an activity or another.

Successful participation in sports may, however, serve to sustain or heighten an already developed self-confidence and a value upon perseverance, but likewise, failure in sports may serve to diminish or preclude the development of these if sports are central to the failing individual's sense of self-worth and identity.

Thus, in lieu of hard quantitative data, available evidence indicates that athletics do not necessarily generate fortitude, but they may provide a situation wherein an individual can gain positive experiences that may sustain or heighten existing self-confidence and reinforce an already positive self-image. But athletics may also provide the situation wherein the individual experiences failure, and, as a result, his courage and self-confidence may be diminished or its development may even be precluded.

Under any circumstances, there are not sufficient data to substantiate or refute the claim that sport develops fortitude. *No evidence pro or con.*

6. Sports participation prepares the athlete for life

Evidence in the literature on this highly diffuse claim is scant and what little that does exist is theoretical and inconclusive.

For the participant, sports is more than merely the act of participation in the actual sporting event itself. The athlete's involvement in sport is his chief source of identity in most cases. It is the central activity in his life. Thus, whereas, for the fan, sports may be a peripheral supportive interest (related through a common value system to daily concerns), for the athlete, sports are the central aspect of life. This typically holds whether the athlete is an amateur or a professional.

Hence, participation in sports may no more "prepare" the athlete for life than the experiences of coaching prepare a coach for life, than the work experiences of a corporation executive prepare him for life, or than the research and teaching experiences of a sociologist prepare him for life. In each of these situations the experiences of the individuals mentioned constitute *serious and significant elements of life,* not isolated, compartmentalized, playlike, or casual interests. For each of these individuals, a significant proportion of the sense of self-worth and identity is linked to achievement and success in their chosen endeavors. So it is also for the athlete. Sports for him *is* life—ongoing and important. As such, his ability to stand back and observe it objectively and disinterestedly as a "drama of life" in microcosm, as a rehearsal for life, is precluded, or at least postponed, until after his participation days are over.

At such time as he *may* be able to observe athletics in retrospect as a drama of life on a small scale, the lessons of life remembered may not be the lessons learned. Time and the human psyche have a way of ordering past events and rendering them amenable to interpretations consistent with current attitudes, values, and personal circumstances.

The former athlete, then, may in fact look back over fifteen years and bear witness to the creedal contention that the factors determining victory in this athletic event or that was the discipline and competitiveness of his team, its clean living and the early hours its members kept, and, further, that his continued adherence to these "rules of the game" had brought him success in his current life endeavors. But he is likely to have forgotten or repressed the instances wherein his team was competitive and disciplined, lived cleanly, and kept early hours only to emerge from sporting activities as losers, perhaps due to the fact that the opposing team was more talented, or due to the poor or discriminatory officiating or some other factor beyond direct individual control.

So, though spectators, sports writers, and coaches may interpret occurrences during the course of athletic events as lessons having a significant learning impact upon the athletes involved and of direct relevance to their future successful involvement in the greater society—all beliefs consistent with the dominant sports creed—this interpretation need not, of course, inevitably be correct. There are no systematically gathered data on the frequency with which former athletes have difficulty achieving success and obtaining meaning from new activities after their participation days are over. Schafer reports, however, that

. . . athletes whose sense of identity and self-worth is entirely linked to athletic achievement often experience an identity crisis when the athletic career has ended, and it becomes necessary to move on to something else. How often athletes have difficulty getting new meaning from activities other than sports is not known, but countless examples can be cited of men who have never successfully made the transition, and, as a result, linger on as marginal men in the world athletics, have family or personal problems, or fail to adjust to a new work role. Research is clearly needed on this general question, as well as on the type of athletes, in terms of personality, background, and nature of the athletic career, who are most vulnerable to such identity crises.[8]

---

[8] W. E. Schafer, "Some Social Sources and Consequences of Interscholastic Athletics" in Gerald Kenyon, ed., *The Sociology of Sport* (Athletic Institute, 1969), p. 35.

The works of Biddoulph and French would tend to buttress Schafer's assertions. Biddoulph observed that:

. . . Unnatural popularity which many athletes enjoy is often a disintegrating influence rather than a stabilizing influence upon their personalities and is, therefore, an inaccurate gauge of their adjustment.[9]

French suggested that since high status in athletics cannot be achieved by all who participate, for many, participation in sports could have a psychologically debilitating effect.[10]

A review of evidence and informed opinions does not allow any conclusive evaluation of the claim that sports participation prepares an athlete for life. It does suggest that there may be many cases in which participation is detrimental to his adjustment in the greater society. *Inconclusive.*

7. Sports provide opportunities for individual advancement

We have seen earlier how sport does, in fact, offer opportunities for socioeconomic mobility, but that mobility is not an inevitable product of athletic competition, even for very gifted athletes. Of the thousands of aspirants to collegiate and professional athlete roles, relatively few ever gain opportunities for advancement through direct economic renumeration for athletic services rendered, or through educational achievement. In some cases, athletic participation may actually retard such advancement. Once more, the judgment here is that, all considered, evidence is inconclusive. *Inconclusive.*

PHYSICAL FITNESS

8. Sports participation generates physical fitness

Part of the basis for the popular conceptions that sports participation generates physical fitness is the widespread confusion as to what constitutes *physical exercise* as opposed to sports or athletics. One of the chief differences is that sport, by its very nature, demands physical extention frequently beyond the bounds of mere exercise. It has been known for quite some time that regular physical exercise enables one to stay physically fit and to sustain the average individual in his daily activities. But if one wishes to participate successfully in sports, he must go far beyond the simple expedient of regular exercise. He must engage in intense and frequent physical drills geared toward developing those physical qualities most necessary to success in his particular sports endeavor.

---

[9] L. G. Biddoulph, "Athletic Achievement and Personal and Social Adjustment in High School Boys," *Research Quarterly* 25 (1954): 1–12.

[10] M. French, "Personality Differences Among Athletes" (Master's thesis, Dept. of Psychology, San Jose State College, San Jose, Calif.), p. 24.

This simple fact is partially a result of specialization, organization, and more systematic approaches to training in sports—all of which have served to heighten competition and place greater physical demands upon the athlete.

For instance, Johnny Weissmuller's training program consisted of swimming and more swimming. But, Weismuller, even in his prime, could not keep up with individuals who *failed* to qualify for some all-conference college swimming teams in the 1960s and 1970s. This is a result of today's intensive exercise programs for swimmers—first initiated by Robert Kiphuth at Yale. Since such exercises have become common-place, swimming records have dropped. It has been found that in swimming, as it is carried on today, one cannot develop the level of fitness necessary to win races merely exercising by practicing swimming.

The principle holds true for other sports as well. Coaches have learned that, given the level of competitiveness and physical fitness required in sports today, practicing or competing in the sport without substantial physical training beforehand is more conducive to physical disability than to the achievement of peak fitness. Both the practice session and the actual sports competition typically lack exercises of sufficient intensity and frequency to adequately condition the athlete's body for the demands of competition.

Intensity of exercise is associated with the development of strength and power and is regulated by the amount of resistance to be overcome. In many sports little strength can be developed because the resistance to be overcome is relatively moderate. For instance, in baseball the batter must overcome only the inertia of the bat during a swing at a ball. But an athlete could practice swinging all day and not add much power to his swing. In fact he may injure his back, arm, or some other portion of his body used to put power into a swing. Thus, it is not surprising that athletes like Mickey Mantle, Ted Williams, and others report that in their playing days they exercised regularly with weights.

Other athletes are faced with similar situations. It takes strength and power to be a successful badminton, tennis, handball, or basketball competitor. Yet the movements required in these sports are not intense enough to develop necessary power.

Frequency of exercise is closely associated with endurance and is regulated by the length of the interval between actions and by the number of these actions. Many sports have relatively low frequencies of action for the individual performer. But an athlete must be able to react at top efficiency each time an occurrence on the sporting field necessitates physical action on his part. Thus, to excel in sports and to reduce his chances of injury, the athlete needs a level of endurance which the sports themselves are incapable of developing.

But even given proper conditioning, there is a great deal of evidence that the demands of sports as activities in and of themselves are not conducive to physical fitness. For instance, sports participation typically demands that an athlete push himself to the limits of fatigue. Vince Lombardi has stated:

> Fatigue makes cowards of us all. You don't get in shape the day of the game. Who wins and who loses is determined in the final analysis by who is in the best physical condition. And that is a matter of hard physical training.[11]

Clearly the athletically unfit are selectively screened from sports, since being "unfit," by definition, either lessens their probability of making the grade or increases the probability of injury. In short, if an average individual seeks *physical fitness*, he would best turn to frequent exercise and not to participation in sports.

Today, both collegiate and professional athletes are listed as "high risk" by many life and health insurance companies. Race-car drivers are of particular interest here. In the last eleven years, twelve professional drivers have been killed on race tracks around the world, an average of more than one per year. Scores of both big-time and small-time drivers are injured and maimed yearly. We have already discussed injuries in the collision sport of football. However, one need not be involved in big-time sport to incur injury.

A study of 750,000 little-league baseball athletes showed that only 2 percent needed immediate medical attention. Scrapes and bruises were the most common injuries. Yet the injuries which most physicians worry about—the ones which have the higher probability of becoming permanent disabilities—were found to have been incurred extensively in one sample of this larger group. These are injuries to the epiphysis, the end of a long bone in the arm, legs, fingers, and toes.

An examination of eighty California pitchers—ages nine through fourteen—who had pitched an average of three years in organized baseball, revealed that every single one had developed some kind of epiphyseal abnormality in his throwing arm.[12] "Delayed-effect" injuries also occur in other sports. Young football athletes imitate professional stars, for example, in "spearing"—blocking or tackling head first. There is no formal rule against spearing in college football (and even if there were it would be virtually impossible to enforce), but, theoretically, it is frowned upon. Among professional football athletes, spearing is a routine weapon. It has led to severe head and spinal injuries and even death at all levels of football participation.

Finally, many sports emphasized for young people cannot be practically pursued in later adult years. Some sports such as football are

---

[11] Taken from a CBS television interview with Lombardi in August, 1969.

[12] Charles Mangel, "How Good Are Organized Sports for Your Child—Physical Fitness?" *Look*, June 1, 1971, p. 61.

totally out of the question. In fact, meeting the demands of participation at the higher levels of football and boxing competition in particular may be detrimental to physical fitness in later adult years. The classical examples here are the 290-pound former professional football tackle who retires from sport, whereupon his weight becomes an immediate problem rather than an attribute; and the boxer who begins to hear bells and roaring sounds and to "see double" years after he retires from the ring.

In sum then, it appears that sports participation in and of itself is not conducive to physical fitness, and may be actually detrimental to it. *Unsubstantiated.*

MENTAL FITNESS

9. Sports participation generates mental alertness

Despite the above claim, the paucity of information on the psychological effects of sports participation is actually startling. We know essentially nothing about this aspect of sport's claimed benefits. *No evidence pro or con.*

10. Sports participation is supportive of educational achievement

Evidence in support of this claim is inconclusive and much of it tends to suffer from rather severe defects in methodological design which are typically reflected in the lack of control and/or awareness of potentially intervening variables. For instance, most of the studies surveyed which alleged that sports participation is conducive to educational achievement did not control for differing entrance standards for athletes and nonathletes or for differing academic concentrations and treatment (by professors of athletes and nonathletes (e.g., more lenient grading of athletes). While differential grading is a very difficult factor to control for, it nonetheless must be taken into consideration. The following two studies illustrate the latter point.

Schafer and Armer examined the records of 585 boys in two midwestern high schools over a three-year period. Schafer and Rehberg also studied the records of 785 boys in six Pennsylvania high schools for a three-year period. The grades of athletes averaged between "B" and "C" while those of nonathletes averaged below "C". When athletes and nonathletes with comparable IQs were paired, the athletes were shown to have slightly better grades than their nonathlete counterparts. Further, both studies showed that the greater the number of sports in which a particular athlete took part, the higher his grades were compared to those of his nonathlete peer.

Of the students not planning to go to college, the athletes performed far better than nonathletes. "In short," said the sociologists, "the boys who would usually have the most trouble are precisely the ones who seem to benefit most from taking part in sports." Nearly five times as many nonathletes as athletes became dropouts, and a greater percentage of athletes were planning on at last two years of college.[13]

These researchers could not determine the precise reasons for the differences in educational achievement. The studies did not control for the influence of varying socioeconomic and class backgrounds. Similarly, they did not consider differing student curricula compositions and grading standards in the schools studied. Further, there is the problem of utilizing grades as a valid index of the degree of intellectual proficiency achieved during the educational process. Grades given athletes are known to be influenced in many cases by coaches persuading other teachers to behave leniently toward athletes in order that they can stay eligible for competition. We have already discussed the fact that coaches themselves sometimes give athletes grades that do not reflect their educational achievement.

Evidence pertaining to this claim is therefore inconclusive. *Inconclusive.*

OTHER CLAIMED ATTRIBUTES

11. Religiosity

There simply is no objective evidence pro or con. *No evidence pro or con.*

12. Nationalism

Again there have been no evaluations of the degree to which sports participation is conducive to the generation of patriotism or national pride, though the work of Morton (*Soviet Sport*), Kolatch (*Sport, Politics and Ideology in China*), and Ballantine (*The Nazi Olympics*), tend to indicate that other nations have attempted to use it in this way. *Inconclusive.*

Let us now summarize in table form our assessment of these claims (table 10–1).

Now while this entire chapter may appear to be an exercise in building and destroying a "straw man," I felt it necessary to establish that the claims made on behalf of sport do not have a sufficient basis in current knowledge to justify the dogmatic certainty with which they are expressed. It may be argued that in situations where sports are "properly conducted" there is greater conformity between the realities of life in the sports sphere and the tenets of the sports creed. But to make such

---

[13] In Judith Randal and James Welsh, "A For Athlete" *Parade Magazine* (November 1970), p. 7.

TABLE 10-1

An assessment of the sports creed as ideology

Creedal claims relating sports participation to:	Substantiated	Unsubstantiated	Inconclusive	No evidence pro or con
1. Character development			X	
2. Loyalty				X
3. Altruism			X	
4. Social and/or self-control (discipline)			X	
5. Fortitude				X
6. Preparation for life			X	
7. Providing opportunities for advancement			X	
8. Physical fitness	X			
9. Mental alertness				X
10. Educational achievement			X	
11. Religiosity				X
12. Nationalism			X	

an assertion is also to imply that our most notable sports are *not* "properly conducted." *Under the circumstances, since the effort here has been to generate an understanding of sport in America as it exists, hypothetical assertions as to the possibilities of sports if they were conducted differently become irrelevant for our purposes.* Further, it has yet to be demonstrated that sports could maintain their present character were they conducted differently. Thus, a question which is central to the future of sport in America as we have come to know it is "can the dynamics and internal relationships of the institution of sport be altered to accommodate contemporary social, economic, and political realities without seriously changing the traditional character of sports activities?" Part III focuses upon this question.

part three

Sport in society

IN PART 3, my purpose is to determine the extent to which the various creeds focusing upon sports have their roots in the American cultural heritage and to assess the future of current sports activities and sport as an institution in an environment having as its most ubiquitous feature the phenomena of rapid social change. Toward these ends, chapter 11 concentrates upon the origins of the values comprising the dominant sports creed, the humanitarian creed, and the equalitarian creed. Chapter 12 discusses some major factors influencing social change in the larger social system and their potential impact upon the institution of sport.

11

Sports-related beliefs and American culture

Whether an ideology or creed is devoted to conservative rationalization of the existing society or stoutly demands revolutionary [or radical change], it is always grounded in the culture of the society in which it appears.[1]

THE VALUES EMPHASIZED in the dominant American sports creed are by now so obviously dependent upon the American cultural heritage that this relationship need not be explored in detail here. Rather, the effort will be to present a broad outline of the creed's general character and how this is derived from main features of American cultural traditions. As important, is the task of relating emphasized creedal values to the American cultural values that currently are perfunctorily recognized in sport but which either (1) do not receive general emphasis or (2) which are discriminantly applied in the day-to-day functioning of the institution. For it is precisely those values which can be categorized under (1) or (2) that have provided the foundations for the two counter-ideologies.

THE DOMINANT CREED

Generally speaking "the effect of the cultural heritage is to define the range of values which an ideology may legitimately express."[2] Thus, despite conflicts, the dominant American sports creed, the humanitarian counter-creed, and the equalitarian counter-creed, all share three features:

---

[1] Francis X. Sutton et al., *The American Business Creed* (Cambridge, Mass.: Harvard University Press, 1956), p. 274.

[2] Ibid., p. 279.

(1) all three creeds can correctly claim legitimacy in the American cultural heritage, though clearly each emphasizes a different aspect of that
heritage; (2) each is de facto ideological in character—that is, each is
expressed with the primary aim of influencing the actions and opinions
of some audience rather than promoting understanding; and (3) implicit
in each creed is the view that organized physical activity is a desirable
and wholesome pursuit which can and should be controlled to serve the
needs of both the participant and the society at large.

The overriding value orientation salient throughout the institution
of sport and the dominant sports creed is that of the "individual achievement through competition." This orientation gives sport in America a
demeanor of practicality and gives cohesion to the specific values, activities, and role relationships of the institution.

. . . American society is marked by a central stress upon personal
achievement, especially secular occupational achievement. The "success story"
and the respect accorded to the self-made man are distinctly American if anything is. . . . [America is] a society in which ascribed status in the form of
fixed, hereditary social status has been minimized. It has endorsed Horatio
Alger and has glorified the rail-splitter who becomes president . . . [Quoting
Robert K. Merton: Even the school boy knows that Lincoln was thrifty, hard-
working, . . . ambitious, . . . and eminently successful in climbing the lad-
der of opportunity from the lower-most rung of laborer to the respectable heights
of merchant and lawyer.] . . . The comparatively striking feature of American culture is its tendency to identify standards of personal excellence with
competitive occupational achievement.[3]

Now, the origins of American society's emphasis upon individual
achievement has been the subject of scholarly analysis for decades. Research upon this question has typically focused upon the developments
within the economic institution and harkened back to Max Weber's work
postulating a relationship between the emergence of capitalism and the
Protestant ethic in Western civilization. Thus:

. . . At the core of the Calvinistic Puritan tradition as it worked itself
out in social life were the linked values of *austerity, individualism,* and devotion
to *occupations as* "[divine] *callings.*" The dramatic pathos of predestination and
the reaction against the sacramental church implied a sharp isolation of the
individual in his chances of salvation. From this a complex edifice of individualism was built up . . . This austere selflessness [prescribed by the
Protestant ethic] could be achieved in a strictly limited number of ways . . .
Devotion to an occupation, not primarily as a means of earthly reward, but for
itself as a "calling" fitted admirably the pattern set by religious postulates . . .
Whereas elsewhere in Western Civilization, the [Puritan heritage] had to compete with ideologies which approved class distinctions . . . in the United
States it had a relatively clear sweep of the field . . . [Thus] Troeltsch has

---

[3] Robin M. Williams, Jr., *American Society* (New York: Alfred A. Knopf,
1970), pp. 454–55.

argued that Puritanism [has a greater significance] in the Anglo-American tradition than elsewhere in the Western world . . .[4]

In light of the above characterizations and of the demonstrated tendency of sport to reflect the values of dominant American society, it might seem plausible to attribute sport's emphasis upon "achievement through competition" to the pervasive influences of the Protestant ethic. However, there is a danger of serious oversimplification in such a facile interpretation. For there are strong indications that the predominant emphasis upon this orientation in sport does not stem solely from Protestant religious traditions. Cross-national comparisons show too many exceptions to permit the categorical stipulation of such a relationship. As Luchen notes:

. . . The [postulation] of a strong relationship between Protestantism and [the achievement orientation in sport] is theoretically insufficient . . . As is the case with postulating an [argument] relating [this orientation] and the development of sport to industrialization, there are too many exceptions . . . The high achievement in sport by the Russians, the Poles, the Japanese, the Mandan Indians, the Sikhs, and the Watusi of Africa cannot be related to Protestantism, though in Japanese Zen-Buddhism there are parallels . . .[5]

Further, Luchen observes:

. . . In Russia [an emphasis upon achievement] is expressed in the norm that societal status should depend only upon achievement . . . The Sikhs and the Watusi are both minorities in their environments. In order to [counter their ascribed status] they have to achieve more than the other members of the societies they live in. The Japanese and the Mandan Indians live in cultures which place heavy emphasis upon [individual] achievement . . .[6]

The tendency to oversimplify and exaggerate the relationship between Protestantism and the individual achievement orientation is widely prevalent even with regard to the economic system itself. Sutton et al. state that "the Puritan tradition . . . was to *give a religious sanction to individualism and occupational effort as values . . .*"[7] The implicit message is that Protestantism did not *create* the orientation toward individual achievement, but rather provided religious reinforcement.

For present purposes, we take the "achievement orientation" and not the Protestant ethic per se (though the latter undoubtedly heightens and legitimizes the achievement value) as the "independent variable" from the culture which determines the overall character of American sport. On the other hand, some part of the Protestant tradition in America

---

[4] Sutton et al., pp. 277–78.

[5] Gunther Luchen, "The Interdependence of Sport and Culture," *International Review of Sports Sociology* (Warsaw: Polish Publishers, 1967), p. 133.

[6] Ibid., p. 133.

[7] Sutton et al., p. 277.

may, quite possibly, be directly responsible for giving substance to the emphasis upon some specific individual achievements, for example, self-discipline, clean living (good character), mental alertness, and so forth.

Now, given sport's emphasis upon achievement, it should be expected that the institution would have a predominantly middle-class orientation. Again, Luchen observes that

The greatest emphasis on achievement and thus the highest [involvement rate] in sport is to be found in the middle-class. It is considerably less in the lower-class where routine responsibility [is prevalent]. The notion that there is no way to gain higher status [fatalism] accounts for the high regard for games of chance or those sports where one may just have a "lucky punch" as in boxing . . .[8]

This feature of sport—the relationship between the structure of a particular sport and its class appeal—in combination with the fact that America appears to be moving increasingly toward becoming a middle-class dominated society also may, along with considerations of race, influence the declining popularity of such sports as boxing. Loy has related the different types of sports, and passive and active involvement in these, to the different modes of adaptation exhibited by members of various social classes.[9] His data show that the middle class is more inclined toward involvement in *active* sports than are lower-class persons. This commonality of emphasis on achievement in the middle class and in the sports sphere appears to be an important foundation of fan enthusiasm in America.

As the achievement value has come to influence more and more the overall character of sport, however, other value orientations extant within American culture have been relegated to the background. The counter-ideologies which are today challenging established sport focus upon these neglected values and beliefs. Hence, it is largely on the matter of *value emphasis* that the ideologies differ. Each has roots in the American cultural heritage, though many people adhering to the established sports creed frequently portray counter-creeds as foreign in origin. (This perception of counter-ideologies has a specific ideological function that will be discussed later.)

THE HUMANITARIAN CREED

What is termed here the "humanitarian counter-creed" finds acceptance primarily among white, educated, middle-class young persons either affiliated with universities or active with some professional sports or-

---

[8] Luchen, p. 135.

[9] John Loy, "Sport and Social Structure," paper presented at the AAHPER Convention, Chicago, 1966.

ganization. They may be younger members of university faculties, active or former collegiate athletes, or professional athletes. For the most part, coaches eschew the ideology, though there are a few who openly advocate implementation of some of its demands. The humanitarian counter-creed is presented most completely in *The Athletic Revolution,* by Jack Scott, perhaps the ideology's staunchest and most dedicated advocate. Scott typifies the adherents to the creed: he is a Ph.D. from the University of California at Berkeley, a former athlete, and a political activist with a sincere concern about contemporary social issues. Though Scott and those who support him have often been accused of propagating and disseminating an un-American ideology, upon analysis the general orientation and specific values of the humanitarian counter-creed are revealed to be as American as cherry pie.

The humanitarian counter-creed is, for the most part, still in its formulative stages. As the ideological foundation of a new movement in sport, it lacks the stability of the dominant sports creed and manifests a dynamic quality which has led to almost continuous adjustments and refinements in its tenets. For instance, in the initial stages of the counter-culture movement, the humanitarian creed (1) placed a great emphasis upon values demanding altruism and interpersonal and communal moral responsibility, while it was openly hostile toward values legitimizing behavior perceived as aggressive or violent; (2) advocated absolute democracy in sports while attacking the current autocratic authority structure in sports as inhumane and undesirable; and (3) advocated a system of sports participation which would be open to all regardless of sex, innate physical capabilities, political philosophy, or life style—while it castigated the current system wherein, for instance, less than 2 percent of America's collegiate youth ever have the opportunity to participate in collegiate athletics and only a negligible number of women ever participate in sports at any level. Likewise, the competitiveness and hard work required of sport were decried as dehumanizing.

Today however, the humanitarian creed seems to be moving slightly away from the extremes of these value positions. Jack Scott summarizes the current humanitarian creed in the following fashion:

> The [humanitarian creed] says there is nothing wrong with the essence of competitive sport. It says that agonistic struggle in sport . . . is a healthy, valuable human activity. [But] there is a vital interplay between competition and cooperation in healthy sports activity. Competitive sport is in trouble when the balance is tipped toward competition, as it is today, or toward cooperation as the counter-culture would prefer. . .
>
> There is nothing wrong or dehumanizing about a person taking pride in accomplishment. But his quest for excellence should not be accomplished at the expense of himself or others. When a humanistic process replaces the present dehumanizing system the sport experience will be [all the] richer. . . pro-

ponents of the [humanitarian creed] understand the need for hardwork . . . A counter-culture long distance runner will not have a peak experience . . . if he gets fatigue cramps after the first mile [of the race].

The [humanitarian creed] sees nothing wrong with team spirit as long as it develops from a genuine spirit of community rather than from authoritarian intimidation.

Perhaps the most fundamental aspect of the [humanitarian creed] is how the competitor sees his opponent . . . The Champion athlete will share his knowledge and skill with lesser athletes in hope they will rise to his level. His pride in victory comes when he struggles courageously in the fact of real challenge.

The [humanitarian ethic] assumes women will have access to the competitive sport experience. Allowing women to compete against men however does not provide women with an equal opportunity. [They] should be provided with separate institutional and economic support."

That a . . . humane ethic such as this is characterized as "radical" should tell us something about the nature of American society.[10]

In the fall of 1972, Scott was appointed chairman of the Department of Physical Education and Intercollegiate Athletics at Oberlin College—ironically, the school at which John Heisman, for whom the college football trophy is named, served as the first head football coach. In this position, Scott will have the opportunity to implement his ideas. Many people are watching his efforts closely—though of course with differing hopes and expectations. It is quite likely that many involved in established sport view Scott's efforts with a jaundiced eye. Other, more beneficient, observers wish him luck and see his Oberlin sojourn as a pilot effort in instituting changes felt to be long overdue.

Because of sport's interdependence with the larger society and the fact that sport at Oberlin does not exist in a vacuum bust must function within the context of the sports institution, I suspect that Scott's task will be far more difficult than generally thought. Two real dangers face the Oberlin athletic department: isolation within the sport realm or *cooptation* by it. The successful establishment at Oberlin of a functioning model for bringing about and institutionalizing change in the structure and relationships inside of sport based upon the humanitarian sports creed seems quite remote under the circumstances. But, then too, so do all such attempts to alter tradition.

Nonetheless, as the most articulate advocate of the humanitarian creed, Scott will undoubtedly have some effect in shifting the value emphasis of the humanitarian movement. But it is much too early to assess what the total impact will be. For the most part, adherents to the humanitarian creed still espouse the creed's initial values placing emphasis upon democracy in sport and a greater commitment to sport's moral value strand and its believed humanitarian potentialities.

---

[10] Jack Scott, "Sport: Scott's Radical Ethic," *Intellectual Digest* (July 1972), pp. 49–50.

Tommie Smith and Jack Scott. Scott, now chairman of the Department of Physical
Education and Intercollegiate Athletics at Oberlin College, appointed Smith head
track coach and assistant athletic director as one part of his efforts to institutionalize
the "Athletic Revolution. He has also made Cass Jackson, a widely sought after black
football coach, the head football coach at Oberlin making this school perhaps the
only predominantly white four-year college with a black head football coach.
(Photo by Micki Scott)

There is little question that this creed has a genuine basis in the American cultural heritage. Williams lists as pervasive value orientations in America the very features which form the philosophical foundations of the humanitarian counter-creed: "a moral orientation, humanitarian mores, equality, freedom, and democracy."[11] Were this not the case, it would not find nearly as much favor in this society as it has. It is this cultural legitimacy which enables the humanitarian creed to serve as the guiding philosophy of a discernible "social movement" in sport. There is no central organization guiding the behavior of rebelling athletes or ordering confrontations with coaches. And even were such an organization to be formed, it is questionable whether it could successfully operate in such a unitary or "totalitarian" manner. The nearest thing to an organized body of athletes who subscribe to the humanitarian creed is the so-called "Woodstock Nation of Athletes." This group—if in fact it can be called that—holds no meetings, has no membership rolls, no leader, no official staff, sends out no communiqués, and has no headquarters. In fact, it constitutes more an expression of esprit de corps printed on sweat shirts than an organized group.

Those adhering to the humanitarian counter-ideology make use of culturally significant symbols in much the same way as those espousing the established sports creed do. While coaches are berating the athletic dissenters as "hippies," and "freethinkers," the dissenters castigate coaches as fascist, latent homosexuals, and authoritarian personalities. While coaches demand conservative grooming practices and life styles, the dissenters emphasize a tolerance of *any* life style or grooming habits that an individual may chose to adopt. While coaches are enforcing respect for flag and country, the dissenters are emphasizing a kind of international cosmopolitanism.

Again, it is a matter of *emphasis* that separates the two ideologies and not the factors of support in cultural traditions. (Value orientations common to American society support *both* discipline and democracy, *both* nationalism and international understanding and tolerance.) Adherents to the two creeds nonetheless perceive themselves at loggerheads with one another.

The crux of this ideological struggle thus has little to do with the values expressed per se, but a great deal to do with changes in the structure and functioning of the institution of sport as these will predictably emerge from any radical change in value emphasis. Coaches and others, intuitively, if not consciously, recoil when confronted with the implication of the value orientations postulated for sport in the humanitarian creed. For the type of activities emerging from implementation of this philosophy as it now prevails would in all likelihood bear little

---

[11] See Williams, pp. 424–60.

resemblance to the aggressive, competitive, and often violent sports we know today, and would have a great deal of resemblance to recreational pursuits. The covert effect would still be to destroy contemporary sports. While some of the changes in sport advocated by Scott (for instance, a balanced emphasis upon competition and cooperation) would enable the institution to alter its processes without radically changing the structure of its component activities, the tenets of Scott's modified humanitarian creed appear no more likely to be implemented than the more radical beliefs he originally advocated. For the values currently dominant within sport reflect the value emphases of the society at large. And so long as there is such strong and widespread emphasis upon achievement, success, and competitiveness in American society, these value orientations will predominate in sport as well, while other values and interests are covertly de-emphasized. For, as has been reiterated throughout this work, the fact of a shared value emphasis between the institution of sport and the larger society is pivotal in shaping fan enthusiasm, the character of the coaching and athlete roles, as well as the overall relationships between sport and society.

THE EQUALITARIAN CREED

We have said that the equalitarian counter-creed also has strong foundations in the American cultural heritage. It is among blacks that the equalitarian value orientation is almost singularly emphasized. This equalitarianism is a response both to the long history of discriminatory treatment of minorities in the general society and also to discriminatory application of the value itself (which is otherwise stressed in the established sports creed) in the sports sphere. Like the white adherents to the humanitarian counter-creed, Blacks who espouse the equalitarian creed are typically middle class in orientation (if not in fact), educated, active or former collegiate athletes, or professional athletes. The equalitarian counter-creed finds its most complete expression in Edwards's *The Revolt of the Black Athlete.*

Unlike the humanitarian creed, the equalitarian ideology does not advocate broad sweeping changes in the overall structure and functioning of sport, but rather a change in a single, specific area of its functioning. In essence, dissenting blacks have demanded equal status and opportunity with whites in sports. Thus, though the change demanded is not sweeping, it is one which goes to the core of the institution of sport in America. Under the circumstances, if the equalitarian creed espoused by blacks were implemented, the contrasting opportunities that would be available to blacks in sports as opposed to those in other spheres of American life would in all likelihood result in a tremendous influx of highly talented and competent black athletes, coaches, administrators, and other athletic personnel. The consequence would be a corresponding decrease in the proportion of white athletes, coaches, and others in sports. This shift would so entirely alter the relationship of sport to its predominantly white fans in America—though it is unlikely that the structure or overall value orientation extant within the institution (achievement orientation) would change—that fan support would probably decrease drastically as has been the case in boxing, and sport would go on the decline just as surely as if it had been in fact altered in structure. There probably are only a few coaches who have rationally analyzed the demands of rebelling black athletes and the implication of the equalitarian creed. But the presence in the cultural "blueprint" of beliefs legitimizing the ascription of opportunity, privilege, and status on the basis of race has provided them with a ready answer, to wit, "America is not ready" for black head coaches, black professional sports managers, or all-black athletic units.

Two facts stand out in this review of the two counter-creeds in sports: (1) there is nothing "new" about the values espoused; and (2) the values espoused are "radical" not because they advocate foreign values but because they advocate an *emphasis* upon certain American values which contrast markedly with those emphasized in the established dominant sports creed, and which could potentially alter in some significant way the contemporary character of sports in America.

REACTION OF THE SPORTS ESTABLISHMENT

The reaction of the sports establishment in America to the counter-creeds has been three-pronged. First, those feeling threatened by the counter-creeds have attempted to label the origins of these ideologies as "foreign" and to link their adherents to common negative symbols. Thus, an editorial in the *NCAA News* (December 1969, pp. 2–3) linked my activities to "hardcore revolutionary forces" seeking to destroy the United States government.

. . . The evidence is clear that there is operating in this country a hardcore revolutionary force designed to destory the present governmental and educational system in the United States. It divides into a number of different groups, and representatives of this movement have direct communication with communist-oriented revolutionary groups in other nations . . .

Intercollegiate athletics is a prime vehicle for them because of the publicity value inherent in sports and the fact that the Negro or Black athlete involved in a mild disorder will be a subject of newsprint.

As an antidote to feelings of insecurity generated by the iconoclastic activities and views of athletic dissenters, the labeling of counter-creeds as "foreign" provides the sports establishment with feelings of superiority.

"If social critics and their disturbing ideas can be tagged as alien they are also automatically tagged inferior. For no matter how 'good' or 'right' the ideas may sound 'in theory,' the fact remains that it is the United States which has the most motor cars, has won the most wars, [and which put the first men on the moon]."[12]

The humanitarian creed, too, has been attacked as "foreign." Both the humanitarian and equalitarian creeds are vulnerable to such attacks: neither places any particular emphasis upon nationalism, neither explicitly espouses an adherence to traditional American religious prescriptions, and both creeds are antagonistic to some traditional value emphases common to both sports and the general society.

In a second main line of response, many adhering to the established sports creed have lumped together the adherents of the two counter-creeds. Though there certainly are some grounds for cooperation between black and white rebelling athletes, there is nowhere near the monolithic, single-minded cooperation between them that establishment protagonists imply. On the contrary, there are some reasons why they should be perceived as potential antagonists. Given the facts of black life in white America, the consequences of an implementation of the current value emphasis espoused through the humanitarian creed would probably not be welcomed by either black athletes or black society at large. For the humanitarian creed does not deal in any way with the basic problem faced by blacks throughout the society: a lack of *power*. So, though democracy is a laudable value, sheer majority "rule by the people" could nonetheless result in continued black powerlessness in a situation where whites constitute a majority in sports. The chief reality of black life has been racism: to wit, as a rule whites in America have actively supported or passively accepted a system of discrimination against blacks. The chief problem of blacks in America is that they lack sufficient power to keep racism from being expressed in discriminatory or other forms of categorically abusive behavior. And the humanitarian creed does not deal with this fact.

Second, though the humanitarian creed contains an emphasis upon human equality, there is no guarantee that lip service to the value will be sufficient to curtail racism. As Williams shows in *American Society*, the persistence of racist values alongside more democratic and humanistic values in American society has been almost uncanny. One specific change in sport currently advocated in the humanitarian creed is directly related to this point: the advocacy of the admission of women to traditionally male-dominated sports competition and the establishment of coeducational sports activities on a nationwide scale. The opening of sports to women, especially the development of coeducational sports, under a

---

[12] Sutton et al., pp. 381–82.

system emphasizing humanitarian values (or under the present athletic system) would inevitably result in heightened discrimination against blacks unless racism in America were eliminated. The inclusion of women in sports would destroy one of the primary features of sport that has made it accessible to blacks, namely, no women, and therefore no white sex phobia focusing upon a concern over black male–white female sexual contacts evolving out of relationships established through involvement in sport.

Finally, a precipitous change in the structure and functioning of sport (whether this be brought about through economic crisis or by way of the forced implementation of "radical" ideological orientations) without certain concommitant changes in the environing society could destroy sport and thus eliminate one of the two avenues by which blacks secure visible achievement. Even if more "humanitarian" activities replace sports as we know them today, from the perspectives of many blacks, Afro-Americans could still be the losers. In this regard it is significant that black athletic dissenters have not demanded overall change in the institution of sport, only an equitable opportunity to achieve at all levels throughout the *existing system*. It would therefore appear that there are at least as many points of potential antagonism between adherents to the humanitarian and the equalitarian creeds as there are grounds for cooperative effort. Nevertheless, they do share one primary *strategic* political tie: significant numbers of both groups are alienated from established sport—though each for its own reasons. But the existence of a mutual adversary should not be construed as a commonality of goals. In any event, Scott's Oberlin project notwithstanding, it would appear that the demands of each group in the immediate future will receive only token satisfaction—a black assistant coach here, a more liberal grooming policy there. (Though I have my own political perspectives on whether or not the destruction of established sports would be a "good" or "bad" political occurrence for blacks given the probable social control functions of sport, to interject these here would be to intrude upon the intent and character of the present work.)

Finally, the third prong of the sports establishment's response to the two counter-creeds has been to use their adherents as scapegoats upon which to vent feelings resulting from frustrations due to strains intrinsic to certain sports roles.

The dominant sports creed provides coaches, for instance, with accepted reasons for attacks upon perceived adherents to the counter-creeds. Representatives of the counter-creeds thus can become "appropriate" targets of discharge for emotions generated by strains emergent from their role.

1. Sports dissenters constitute convenient personifications of the obscure forces which cause outcomes to fall short of expectations. In

sport, where the emphasis is upon practicality and instrumental rationalism, the prevailing assumption tends to be that every occurrence has a knowable cause. When outcomes fall short of expectations in day-to-day interactions, therefore, it is "normal" for coaches to look for the *cause* or the *person* or *persons* responsible. Athletic dissenters are the best available candidates for personifying the dimly understood impersonal relationships in sport which frequently combine to result in a lack of team harmony and even athletic failure. Dissenters are *human beings* perceived as exercising some degree of control and influence over factors affecting coaches' outcomes. This means that coaches, theoretically at least, can potentially *neutralize* the influence of the dissenters. If the failure of outcomes to approximate expectations was laid to impersonal forces intrinsic to the institution of sport or to supernatural forces, coaches could not even hope to exercise neutralizing control.

Also, the actions and advocacies of dissenters can be more readily related to negative outcomes in sports than can impersonal forces operative in the sports realm. For dissenters have, in fact, advocated certain changes in the structure and functioning of sport which would disrupt established policies and practices. They have also frequently intervened in the affairs of sports aggregations in ways that were unpleasant for coaches and disturbing to established routines, for example, advocating boycotts, rebellions against coaching authority, and so forth. But, though the character of the institution of sport and the nature of coaches' role responsibilities predispose members of the sports establishment to blame athletic dissenters for problems, there still remains a question of the exact degree to which dissenters are *actually* responsible for *creating* such problems. My own view is that they have for the most part merely capitalized on problems already in existence and provided athletes and others with alternative ideologies through which iconoclastic behavior could be rationalized. Thus, coaches have attributed much more influence and power to dissenters than they actually have at their disposal. The *real* culprit in creating athletic turmoil is most likely strain emerging from incompatibilities between the functioning of sport and contemporary trends in values and societal processes.

2. Sports dissenters are convenient candidates for attack because of their supposed freedom from responsibility and accountability relative to that demanded of coaches. The accountability to which the coach is subjected under the impersonal, precise standards of the scoreboard and the overall victory-defeat ratio is firm and exacting. But, in a familiar kind of psychological dynamic, coaches have exalted the burden of accountability into a virtue, and feel that their voluntary submission to its demands makes them morally superior to those who are not subject to the disciplining influences of accountability.

Now, the most vocal bastions of athletic dissent in America are to be found on college campuses. The dissenters are for the most part college students and young radical professors. Since these persons appear strikingly exempt from the accountability imposed on the coaching role, coaches can scorn the "irresponsibility" of students and the "impracticality" of professors who suggest or advocate changes in the sports sphere. College professors, in contrast to coaches, have the option of merely adhering to bureaucratic prescriptions for performance, they are seldom held responsible for tangible and specific results—especially those highly influenced by the actions of others. (Significantly, the two individuals perhaps most frequently accused of directly instigating athletic rebellions on a nationwide level are myself and Jack Scott. We are both on college faculties. But we exercise nothing like the direct controlling influence over athletes that the sports establishment has attributed to us.)

3. The scorn which coaches exhibit toward athletic dissenters is reinforced by their own ambivalence over the aggressive exploitation of personal friendship. We have seen that in the coaches' relationships with athletes there is a good deal of tension generated over the sincerity of personal friendships. The dissenter is made by coaches to symbolize a pattern of insincere and selfish "camaraderie" for which the coaching role itself provides strong temptations. After all, the person encouraging athletic dissent and the coach have many things in common: in order to have any degree of success in the achievement of their respective goals, each must become proficient in "winning friends and influencing people." Both strive to convince the athlete that their one consideration is what is "best" for him. This frequently requires an assumed friendliness or a "front" which camouflages the self-interested behavior of both the coach and the person advocating dissent. In a society which places great stock on sincerity in affective relationships, both coaches and athletic dissenters are vulnerable to the charge of seeking friendships among athletes to exploit them. Thus, the mutual animosity between coaches and those advocating dissent may partially represent a projection of some of the things which each dislikes about the demands of his own role. In sum, the common assertion that advocates of counter-creeds are part of some monolithic conspiracy and directly responsible for the turmoil in sports would appear to be highly exaggerated if not totally inaccurate.

But aside from the question of the degree of overall influence on sport by those who express and advocate athletic dissent, it nonetheless seems that sport may be headed for some changes which it may not survive in its present form. Whether sport does survive as presently structured depends primarily upon two factors: (1) the rate and direction of changes in the value emphasis extant in American society and (2) the capacity of athletic dissenters to solve an age-old problem facing insurrectionist movements—how to broaden their base of popular appeal while simultaneously avoiding cooptation by the established system.

Depending upon which segment of American society one looks at, an argument can be made for either an increasing rate of value change toward radicalism (as in the case of the young minority group persons, college students, and some women) or an increasing rate of change toward conservatism (as in the case of so-called middle Americans and noncollege young people). So, overall, any assessment as to the potential direction of value change must be theoretically based since, empirically, it has not yet been established that a single pervasive orientational change characterizes the whole of American society.

Scott's statement (quoted above) modifying the previous extremes of the humanitarian creed constitutes primarily an attempt to broaden the base of the movement's popular appeal. How much success will be forthcoming remains to be seen. The greatest threat to the continued viability of the black athletic rebellion is cooptation—a process already well underway as manifest in the widespread hiring of black assistant coaches. For the most part, these coaches have failed to effect any significant changes in the outcomes of black athletes. Further, there appears to be a pattern emerging that indicates these assistant coach positions to be "dead-end" jobs. At a number of schools where coaching staffs have been dismissed after losing seasons, the black assistants involved have been retained. These assistant coaches interpret this to mean that, from the perspective of their athletic departments, they have no coaching responsibilities and therefore are not held responsible for coaching outcomes. They see themselves as having been hired primarily to pacify black athletes. Such a role provides little opportunity for occupational advancement. In fact, the more accomplished they are in their roles as "head niggers in charge of nigger affairs," the greater the likelihood that they will remain in that position. And this appears to be precisely what is occurring.

Because the values emphasized by the equalitarian creed are meaningful primarily for blacks (since other minorities are scarce in American sport) the chances are very slim that the popular base of the revolt of the black athlete can be effectively broadened to include whites inside of the sports sphere. And, since whites constitute the majority in athletics, this fact becomes crucial in any evaluation of the potentials for the equalitarian creedal orientation becoming a major value emphasis in American sport. Therefore, if one were inclined to speculate as to the chances of relative success for each of the two counter-creeds, it seems most likely that the humanitarian creed would have the edge in this regard. However, aside from the impact of overt social movements inside of the sport realm, there are other influences affecting change in the larger society that will necessarily affect the structure and functioning of the institution of sport as well. These factors are the concern of chapter 12.

12

Sport and social change

THE ANALYSIS of sport presented in this work justifies two general conclusions: (1) that the patterned behavior and the expressed beliefs of persons fulfilling various roles within the institution of sport are importantly determined by and can be generally understood within the context of enduring values indigenous to American society; and (2) that conflicts and incongruities between societal values and between discrepant role demands generate adaptational problems for incumbents in sports roles, resulting in their placing a heightened emphasis upon some values while covertly minimizing or only perfunctorily recognizing the significance of others. Thus, what is termed here the dominant "American sports creed" emerges as being solidly based in the American cultural heritage, but representing a special set of emphases within that heritage. The sports creed recognizes the values emphasized in counter-creeds but places relatively less emphasis upon these. For the most part, those values in the sports creed which have received greatest emphasis have been those classified here as belonging to the "instrumental strand" (e.g., competition, discipline, physical fitness, and mental fitness). The orientation of those in positions of authority and power in sport is manifest more in a tendency toward "hardheaded practicality" rather than theorizing or moralizing. Among coaches in particular, this tendency toward practicality gains a great deal of reinforcement from the strains of adjusting to a rapidly changing society. The questioning of traditional value emphases and relationships in sports by critics has led to vociferous counter-attacks and a kind of "antiintellectualism" among coaches. Col-

lege professors, students, and others who dissent from established policies and practicies in sport are termed freethinkers, fuzzy-headed intel-
lectuals, and accused of undermining traditional American institutions
and the "American way of life," of being guided by alien influences, and
of being unpatriotic and disloyal.

The period since 1967 is not the first era to be characterized by
severe criticisms of the functioning of sports in America. During the
early 1930s, sport came under heavy attack, and again it was from the
academic community that the most caustic criticism emerged.

After having struggled for the first thirty years of the twentieth
century to achieve some degree of legitimacy in the educational institution, many coaches and administrators found both the legitimacy and the
expressed redeeming qualities of their trade under severe attack. And
the recruiting scandals in colleges, the exorbitant financial expenditures
by athletic departments for equipment, facilities, and travel expenses,
and the embarrassing drunken brawls which were rampant at college
sporting events from 1930 to 1938, rendered athletics even less defensible in the minds of its critics.[1]

In response to the clear threats to the perpetuation of sports activities, the *Athletic Journal* printed the following announcement in an
editorial statement:

The Athletic Journal will gladly publish the results of any valid study
which shows the redeeming qualities of athletics . . . The athletic coaches
are on the firing line, consequently, we should not hesitate to justify the programs which are serving the needs of so many twentieth century children.[2]

The fact that sport not only survived this first massive assault with
its characteristic features virtually unaltered, but has since actually
prospered and developed leads many of the more optimistic coaches to
see the present crisis in sport as a "passing" fad—as part of an inevitable
cycle of occurrences evident in the history of sport. George Halas,
founder and owner of the Chicago Bears, has seen the leading sport in
America today, football, grow from its "rockpile days" to the complex
sophisticated activity that it is now. He has seen not only football but
also sport in general weather all kinds of crises. Of the present crisis
in athletics he states:

No, I don't see any trend in all this. I don't think it is a sign of the times.
I think [the dissent against sport] involves just a case of players who made
wrong moves . . . and got publicity.

---

[1] For an indication of the severity of the social problems arising out of sports
see *Athletic Journal* (September 1933–June 1934), esp. vol. 14, no. 2, p. 20.

[2] Ibid., p. 21.

But then he adds a statement which betrays his air of confidence in the future as a front: "But I've got to admit, in all my fifty years in sports, I don't remember anything ever happening like this before . . ."[3]

Though it is unlikely, Halas could be correct in his "theory" that the present crisis constitutes no more of a threat to sport than past crises did. Another coach with a long history of involvement in sports states outright what Halas only implies. Paul Brown says:

> We've had people come and go in the past. The only thing is that they didn't get the notoriety these guys are getting now. Then nobody sat down and wrote books. . . . These guys today will be quickly forgotten [sport will] go on.[4]

But some fundamental considerations are omitted in the implied thrusts of both Halas and Brown's statements. I believe that the two coaches are correct in their opinion that a key difference between the crisis in sports today and those of the past is the degree of publicity focused upon athletic dissenters. But one cannot dismiss the impact of this publicity itself. The volume of publicity about dissent in sports has both resulted from and been a prime influence in opening an increasingly greater market for books and other written works whose flavor is diametrically opposite that of the traditional, "what sports have done for me and America" ghostwritten autobiographies and sports columns. In short, the onset of truly mass communication in the United States since the 1930s has resulted in an information explosion that has had a tremendous impact in broadening Americans' perceptions of and interests in events occurring around them. Under the impact of this information explosion, many old "truths" have frequently emerged less hallowed and somewhat more tarnished than past generations ever could have thought possible. Television, books, telephones, radio, mass rallies made possible by the jet plane and the automobile, newspapers, and magazines are not merely vehicles which have allowed the dissemination of an increased volume of information at an increased rate. The volume and rate of information dispersion has itself had an enormous impact upon society's members, especially in terms of their perceptions of the world and their definitions of reality.

Under the circumstances, it could just well be that the greater public exposure granted the ideas of today's athletic dissenters are indicative of major societal changes already underway. Therefore, the more significant question is perhaps not, "Will sports survive the present crisis despite the notoriety and publicity granted the ideas of athletic dissenters and the overall impact of mass communication?" but, "Has sport

---

[3] George Halas in Paul Zimmerman, "Pro Football's Collision at Generation Gap," *True*, September, 1971, p. 41.

[4] Paul Brown, Ibid., p. 42.

Chip Oliver (left) and Dave Meggyesy, two former star football players who wrote widely read books and brought the "Athletic Revolution" into the ranks of professional football. (Photo by Micki Scott)

managed to survive earlier crises in large part because of a *lack* of massive publicity regarding dissenting views on sport? My contention is that the answer to the latter question must be largely affirmative. And, given the present circumstances of mass communication, it is my guess that the crisis in sports today is only the initial manifestation of value changes that promise ultimately to alter the character of sport in America in significant ways.

THE NATURE OF CURRENT DISSENT

Today not only is there an increase in the amount of publicity or notoriety granted athletic dissenters but there are changes in the sources of dissent and in the character of dissent. In the past, the chief critics of sport's traditional functioning have been for the most part a few middle-aged journalists and social reformers, and faculty members and academic administrators, repulsed and dismayed over the corruption in sports and the perceived failure of coaches and others to operate organized sports in a way that was conducive to realizing the goals of the sports creed. But the critics of the 1930s and other eras on the whole did not criticize or dispute the claimed *potentialities* of sport (though there is at least one notable exception, namely, John Tunis). In one of the most thorough studies of intercollegiate athletics ever carried out—the work of Tunis notwithstanding—the question was never considered as to whether or not organized sport as then established should have been abolished or *radically* altered in form and function. The introduction to the massive two-volume study by the Carnegie Foundation for the Advancement of Teaching stated:

. . . The competitions and contests, the delight in bodily activity, the loyalties, and the honor that form a part of that vast organism called college athletics are the reflections in our college life of characteristics that are common to the youth of the world. In the pages that follow, these and other less pleasing phenomena of college athletics will be examined in the hope that those aspects which are good may in course of time achieve an unassailable predominance over those which are less worthy to survive. There can be no question of abolishing college athletics, nor should there be. What can be looked for is a gradual establishment through concrete action of a few general principles, to which all men would agree in the abstract. But even this slow change will be impossible without the sanction of an enlightened college and public opinion . . .[5]

Today the situation is quite different. For not only do dissenters receive greater public exposure, but they are younger people ("under thirty"), more numerous, and they are demanding changes in athletics at all levels that would effectively alter the institution of sport as we know it today. Paul Zimmerman sums up the impact of these facts in professional football as manifest in the contrasting views of two athletes —Alex Karras a thirty-six-year-old, thirteen-year veteran of the game and Dave Meggysey, a twenty-eight-year-old, seven-year veteran who quit the game for ideological reasons.

. . . Alex Karras, defensive tackle for the Detroit Lions, is a 36-year-old veteran of the football wars. In his 13 years as a pro he has had his ups and downs with the game's hierarchy, yet takes a tolerant view of the game and the men who run it.

"Some of the things Meggysey said are true, I'm sure," says Karras, "but I think he took them too personally. Yet that's that way things are. You have to accept them. Sure, there are things about the game I don't like—the commissioner, for one—but there are enough good things to counterbalance the bad."

The younger players, however, might not be as ready as Karras to accept the things they don't like.

"It's amazing," says Jack Scott, "but schools in the Northern California area—schools with a rich athletic tradition—are having trouble getting kids to turn out for football. They're having trouble fielding a team. Even at the high-school level football seems to be going through a boxing syndrome—only the most desperate are taking part."

What all this means, of course is that football—particularly pro football, a near-holy pastime—is being tampered with. Revolution is a strong word much misused these days, but the fact is that athletes simply aren't accepting the kind of thing they swallowed without question only a decade ago. The violent world of pro football is starting to produce agnostics, and the irony is that the Players' Association has never been stronger, that player contract benefits have never been more solid. Yet the structure of pro football may be

[5] See Carnegie Foundation for the Advancement of Teaching, *Athletics In American Colleges and Universities,* Volumes 23 and 24, 1928–29.

undergoing a philosophical housecleaning, the result of which will be a game vastly different than the one millions of fans follow avidly on television and in stadiums throughout the country.[6]

That it is the young who are dissenting is significant because no one is going to pay to see George Halas and Paul Brown compete in football or to watch Avery Brundage run in track. That the very values emphasized and the orientation underlying the structure of sport are being questioned is significant because, "Only those orientations that are strongly invested with attention and effort escape the museum of [acknowledged] cultural fictions."[7] The younger generation of today controls the society tomorrow. Their increasing tendency to perceive sports as irrelevant and, in many cases, as a malignancy in the social body provides little basis for the faith many older persons express in the future of sport.

The societal environment in which sports exist in America today is radically different from that of the 1930s or even a decade ago. Essentially what is happening in sport is only secondarily related to the agitation of a Jack Scott or a Harry Edwards or any other of the dissenters often attacked by the sports establishment as *responsible* for sports' troubles. What is happening in sports today results from the impact of the twentieth century, with its affluence, its speed, its mass communications—all of which have combined to create a much smaller world and new definitions of reality. As tradition has become less and less relevant to contemporary perceptions of reality, tremendous strains have resulted. These strains themselves are manifestations of social change—a change which is rapidly approaching "critical mass" wherein not only is an adjustment in institutional processes demanded, but an alteration in institutional foundations and structural relationships as well. As early as 1956, Sutton et al., noted:

. . . . [Present] institutional changes are the conspicuous and tangible results of deeply rooted and pervasive changes in American society: changes that involve important shifts in values. These shifts represent the working out of a set of values well grounded in our heritage—activism, universalism, and social responsibility . . . [In contrast to an all pervasive orientation toward individual achievement].[8]

To the extent that the current revolt in athletics is a manifestation of developmental trends cited by Sutton almost two decades ago, it would appear that the revolt is not a passing fad. The specific issues of

---

[6] In Zimmerman, p. 44.

[7] Robin M. Williams *American Society* (New York: Alfred A. Knopf, 1970), p. 436.

[8] In Sutton et al., p. 397.

the revolt may change (e.g., hair length, grooming practices, and so forth), but the fundamental conflict between those value emphases vested by societal tradition in the institution of sport and those value emphases dictated by the younger generation's perceptions of contemporary reality will in all likelihood remain. It would thus seem that, through token concessions, those attempting to save sport as we know it today may be able to buy time, but it would also appear that many of our most popular sports activities are likely to undergo substantial changes in character and some may even follow the path of another once widespread pastime—pitching horseshoes. In a general sense, the life style, technology, and other changes emergent during the course of the twentieth century are responsible for the demise of pitching horseshoes. The continually emerging changes in the main aspects of life in America will ultimately also affect our value orientations to the degree that even our most cherished current practices could become passé and irrelevant.

VALUE CHANGES

Throughout this work, the persistence and stability of the value emphases within the institution of sport have been demonstrated. It has also been pointed out that while the value emphases of sport constitute the primary source of sports' appeal, these value orientations are also key factors to be considered in understanding such recent phenomena as the perceived inflexibility of coaches, athlete rebellions, and so forth. It could very well be that these problems and conflicts are precursors of more far-reaching and fundamental alterations which lie in wait in the not too distant future.

By definition, an institution manifests some stability or continuity. To a greater extent than is the case with most institutions (excepting, perhaps, religion) the institution of sport has been obliged—because of its societal functions—to narrowly constrain both the structure of its component activities and the degree to which the values regulating human behavior within its sphere could legitimately vary from emphasized societal ideals. While these features have traditionally provided the institution of sport and its component activities and relationships with a stability of character, in times of incipient change such stabilizing influences could lead to inflexibility, or inability to alter internal structures and processes to accommodate external realities. In short, when an institution makes for itself a Procrustean bed, it is preparing the way for its own destruction by the on-moving and dynamic agents of social change. Such destruction may come about as a result of internal disruption or external neglect. The former is already underway in sport and the forerunners of the latter—though now quite minimal—have also emerged; for example, a wanning interest among student bodies in sports activities, or the difficulties some coaches are experiencing in recruiting athletes from high-school student populations. As objective conditions of social life in America undergo rapid change, traditional value orientations are bound to be affected, and opposing value orientations invariably come to the fore. If the institution is sufficiently inflexible, there ensues a period in which confusion reigns as to which value orientation —the new or the traditional—is more legitimate. If the forces opposing tradition continue to grow, those in control of established sport must either make concessions—that is attempt the readjustment of the institution themselves—or they must face conflict and confrontation with the parties of opposition. If only minor concessions are made (e.g., to longer hair styles, hiring *acceptable* black *assistant* coaches) conflict and confrontation is inevitable. This appears to be the course that the athletic establishement in America has chosen. Such occurrences as the defeat of the Curt Flood case against the reserve clause in baseball, the dismissal of dissenting and nonconforming athletes and coaches, and the labeling of those advocating change in sport as "agents of foreign revolutionary powers" may prolong the stability of the sports institution in the short run. But, in the long run, these actions in opposition to change could give rise to changes of a less gradual, deliberate sort and, in the process, result in even greater disruption and destruction than that presently feared by the sports establishment.

How much "adjustment" can be made in the structure and functioning of sport? That is, how incongruous can the actual operation of sport become in relation to the dominant creedal values emphasized before changes in the very character of sports are required? This question focuses on the scope of the institution of sport as a "value receptacle." In this regard, there are limits on the capacity of sport as now established to mirror values. Beyond these limits, change must occur in both the structure and functioning of the institution of sport and the activities which comprise its focal concerns. As a societal institution, sport in America not only reflects the values, but its character and the structure of its component activities are also determined *by* those values. Thus, for example, for interactions within an institution of sport to manifest an emphasis on individual "competitiveness," the social system of which that institution is a component must place high value upon a commitment to achievement through individual-centered competition. To the extent that activities carried out within the context of an institution are so far a variance with prevailing societal value "blueprints" as not to command personal commitment and involvement by large numbers of people, these activities and the institution itself must be either altered in character to more closely conform to prevailing values or become irrelevant and ultimately extinct.

All institutions are therefore vulnerable to the pervasive affects of value changes among significant segments of the society. For, by definition, institutions are based upon traditional values and norms. A conflict thus arises when current value trends conflict with those which have traditionally prevailed.

Now the institution of sport is particularly vulnerable to value changes. As an institution, sport is today caught on the margins of a value change situation wherein large numbers of people are clinging to traditional values and significant numbers are espousing values which often conflict with those traditionally prescribed. There is also a great segment of the population which seems to be increasingly questioning both the old and the new values.

Under these circumstances, the beliefs associated with sports involvement and scientifically definable as "cultural fictions" have been publically acknowledged by significant segments of the population as *cultural fictions in fact*. In this regard, Williams states:

. . . [The widespread acknowledgements of] cultural fictions often represent more subtle processes of "loss of conviction," expressed in the language of psychology as withdrawal of affect or loss identification and involvement . . .[9]

It is at the point that this "loss of conviction" begins to manifest itself that one finds widespread sentiments holding that even such sports spectaculars as the Super Bowl in football and the World Series in baseball have become "dull," "lackluster," or "unexciting."

Now, "value orientations retain effective regulatory power only to the extent that they are defended when attacked, used as referents for concrete actions, and affirmed in social interaction . . ."[10] It follows then, that to the extent that significant numbers of people do not defend, refer to, or affirm the system of beliefs espoused in the institution of sport, these beliefs become irrelevant in terms of serving a function for such persons. To the extent that such perceptions of sport-related beliefs become prevalent in society, sports activities become irrelevant also, unless the values propagated are altered to conform to the values espoused by those who no longer view sports as relevant. Herein lies the crux of the chief dilemma faced by sport today. Though the economic situation poses the most immediate threat, the long-range threat is much less obvious. Sport in America is, in effect, being challenged to alter its structure and functioning. But this is not as simply and easily accomplished as many of the advocates of change in sport believe it to be. In fact, without some massive change in the value prescriptions of American society as a whole—and not merely among some significant segments thereof—the institution of sport cannot alter its structure and functioning and still survive. Even assuming that new values could be immediately substituted for the traditional ones, the "sports" which would emerge from such a fundamental change would in all likelihood manifest few

---

[9] Ibid., p. 395.
[10] Ibid., p. 395.

of the characteristics we have come to associate with sports today. But, in point of fact, such fundamental changes are seldom immediate (excepting, of course, in situations where revolution alters the structure and functioning of the entire social order), and it is doubtful that coaches could institute changes in the general structure and functioning of the institution of sport even if they were inclined to do so. Part of the reason underlying many athletic dissenters' assumption that coaches *can* alter the character of sports at will has to do with the misconception that coaches as a group are simply "bad men" who have deliberately structured sports to meet their own selfish ends. While such a conception of coaches has obvious ideological utility for athletic dissenters, the characterization is nonetheless naïve, simplistic, and fallacious. As we have seen, coaches say what they say and behave as they do more as a result of their institutionalized role responsibilities and the relations between the institution of sport and the general society than as a result of any group—specific personality characteristics. Given these constraints which set limits upon the alternative choices open to coaches in terms of fulfilling their role functions in sport, to go beyond the limits set would undoubtedly result in the demise of the very activities that such action by coaches would be aimed at salvaging.

Whereas the present structure and functioning of sports antagonizes significant numbers of people adhering to and placing emphasis upon values which conflict with those emphasized in and espoused through sport, to the extent that any change toward accommodating the new values emphasis occurs, those individuals who concur with the traditional value emphasis and who presently identify with sport will be antagonized and alienated from sports activities. So even if they were inclined to initiate sweeping changes in sport, coaches have tremendous incentive *not* to do so: (1) the changes demanded would alter radically, if not totally destroy, the very activities which coaches' accommodating behavior would be geared to salvage; (2) those fans who now identify with athletic units would be alienated and would thus cease to support, financially and otherwise, these aggregations and sports in general; and (3) coaches' own internalized values, which affect every aspect of their functioning in society including their occupational achievement aspirations, would constitute monumental obstacles to fundamental changes in sport—even if such changes were acknowledged as necessary and "right." Most coaches would probably drop out of coaching if such changes could be and were forced. So if changes were immediately instituted, sports as we know them today would probably become extinct.

But on the other hand, the future of established sports also seems bleak if it continues to adhere to tradition, since the chief source of dissent from sport is found among the young, particularly the white, middle-class young. Here we have a category of people who have seldom, if ever, known material want, who have for the most part been insulated from the more mundane struggles of day-to-day existence, and many of whom have come to view the sphere of organized sport as crass, vulgar, and oppressive in its functioning. As part of the white youth culture, the perspectives and attitudes of this segment of the youth population carry tremendous influence and significance. It is the middle-class youth who for the most part populate the nation's college campuses. It is from among their ranks that most of the nation's athletes come. Under these circumstances, the perspectives of the middle-class nonathletes of the youth culture was bound to have impact upon the athletes given the relationship between the institutions of sport and education in American society. As the perception of sport as "irrelevant" pervaded the youth culture to a greater and greater extent, it was inevitable that athletes would eventually internalize the definitions of sport espoused by their nonathletic peers. Athletes then begin to question, rebel, and/or drop out of sports completely. If these definitions of the significance and character of sport persist among members of the youth culture into their adult years, sport as we know it today is likely to decline for want of attention and interest.

TWO PROBLEMS

The speed at which sport is moving toward change could be further increased by two problems discussed earlier: the economic crisis in athletics and the drug problem. As yet, no real promise of a possible solution to the economic problem has appeared which would save any but a handful of sports aggregations. The eleven-game schedule in college football, more television exposure for all sports, expansion of athletic schedules in basketball and baseball, making freshmen eligible for varsity competition, and the formation of new conferences and leagues have failed to ameliorate the financial problems of most collegiate athletic departments. The only sure "solution" thus far has been to either de-emphasize sports or drop them completely. The tendency today for athletes, fans, and the United States Congress to balk at the idea of mergers in professional sports seems to portend an ominous future for these activities also.

Perhaps the most promising step for dealing with the economic crisis in sport is that which sport officialdom is most reluctant to take—off-track betting, or OTB. State-run off-track betting on all sports has been proposed numerous times, but has always been rejected. Those advocating OTB have generally based their arguments on the supposed economic advantages to be gained. If the state legalized off-track betting on all sports activities, it could cut substantially into the estimated billions of dollars gambled away by the American public each year illegally, and share the proceeds with sports bodies. If the winnings from legal sports gambling were ruled "tax-free" income, tremendous incentive to engage in legitimate sports gambling would be created, thus destroying illegal gambling activities—or so the argument goes. It is further argued that, since sports gambling is extremely prevalent in America today, any question as to the morality of gambling on sports events is irrelevant. The only question is "Will the state control and share in the economic benefits of this gambling or will it continue to allow these benefits to be siphoned off by illegal bookmaking activities and small-time office pools?" In short, as one advocate of OTB has stated "Americans are going to bet anyway. If there were only two Americans left on the face of the earth, one would bet the other on who would die first."

The arguments posed against OTB have been several. First there is the fear that the legalization of OTB will encourage gambling and contribute to increasing its prevalence. Thus, few of the politicians who would have to vote in favor of state controlled gambling on sports events have been willing to take a strong affirmative public stand in this regard. Gambling is still considered sinful and immoral in many areas of the nation, so any elected official advocating legalized OTB runs the risk of courting political disaster despite the fact that the activity is thriving illegally.

Second, there is the question of controlling corruption. Memories of the "point-shaving" scandals which almost destroyed collegiate basketball in recent decades are still fresh. How would such potentialities as point shaving be controlled if gambling were legalized? In fact, would athletes be allowed to bet at all—either on other teams or for or against their own teams? The NFL Players Association has come out against OTB because of the heightened pressures that it would put on athletes. Even the best athletes occasionally drop well-thrown passes in the end-zone, muff "gut lay-ups" in basketball, get caught off base in baseball, and so forth. If OTB were legalized, there would always be the suspicion that an athlete, especially an exceptional one, had deliberately fouled up on such occasions. The legitimacy of the expectation that even the greatest athletes will occasionally make a disastrous, but human, mistake would be severely curtailed. In short, legalized OTB on all sports would add the element of direct "economic interest" to fan involvement. The legalization of OTB could turn fan attention from consideration of strategies, hard work, character, discipline and so forth on the part of a sports aggregation to a more intense concern about luck and the likelihood of bad breaks—not to speak of the deliberate "throwing" of an athletic event. This change in the average fan's relationship to the sports aggregation from one predicated upon a belief in a rationalism and achievement toward one based upon fatalism and luck could transform the entire atmosphere of the sports realm and undermine the established relationship between the institution of sport and the larger society.

Nonetheless, it should be expected that coming decades will bring the legalization of OTB. The economic crises faced today by the nation's educational institutions and by the sports world, coupled with a growing dissatisfaction with sky-rocketing property and sales taxes will likely make OTB inevitable. And just as inevitably, there will emerge with legalized OTB increased allegations of corruption—especially in amateur sports where economic corruption is made all the more tempting by the demands placed upon the athlete who wishes to maintain his amateur status.

With regard to the drug problem in sport, it is only a matter of time before there is a case of an athlete dropping dead or of unsavory drug-induced behavior *on the athletic field*. Regardless of official denials, the drug problem is immense and it is growing. According to the president of the German Olympic Organizing Committee, the number-one problem faced by Olympic officials at the 1972 Summer Games was the drug problem. Aside from the likelihood of unfortunate incidents on the athletic field stemming from drug abuse among athletes, there is another way that this problem poses a direct health threat to sports participants. We have noted that injury is an accepted risk in many sports. The hazards of injury are increased immeasurably, however, when the physician treating a particular athlete does not know the athlete's drug-use history. It has long been recognized that combining drugs is dangerous. Unless the drug problem in sport is brought out into the open and steps are taken to deal with it effectively, sports participation is going to become even more dangerous then it presently is. It would be naïve to lay the whole of the drug problem to the current emphasis on winning in sport. "We are a drug-oriented society" William Cambell, chairman of the California Subcommittee on Drug Abuse and Alcoholism, states.

In horse racing, when a horse is found to have been administered drugs, the owner and trainer of the animal are fined or suspended or both. It is unlikely that such a fining or suspending of owners, coaches, and team physicians when athletes are found to use drugs will work in sports in which the primary actors are human beings. Drugs are simply too readily available to athletes via sources outside of sport. The only method of control that promises to be reasonably effective is that of regularly and irregularly administered tests for drug abuse. An effective system of monitoring and of imposing sanctions, however, remains to be devised and implemented.

CONCLUSION

This then is American sport. Whether the present structure and functioning of sport is "bad" or "good" or "right" or "wrong," or whether the changes that apparently await it in the future are desirable or to be regretted have concerned me, but have not been my central focus here. The effort has been to present an honest and comprehensive portrait of sport in America. As to further specific value judgments, the reader must decide.

If the reader has concluded that there *is* something "wrong" in sport, one further conclusion is inescapable: from its racial problems to drug abuse, from its economic crisis to female segregation, what is "wrong" with sport in America reflects America itself—particularly the relationships between contemporary social, political, and economic realities and this nation's value priorities, its attitudes and its perspectives. Sport, as one of the less flexible components of a dynamic social system, has been moved by imperceptible steps and under the influence of external factors beyond its control to the point where significant changes in its structure and functioning are demanded if it is to survive under any guise at all. The degree of flexibility of sport as an institution, then, will perhaps be the ultimate factor in determining its future.

It is hoped that this work has shed new light upon what is perhaps the least researched and most poorly understood institution in American society. I have stuck my academic neck out in many instances, and in some instances, quite far out. And while undoubtedly many of the arguments made here will be contested and some perhaps refuted by later investigations, at least some new questions have been raised and some old questions have been addressed from a new perspective. The implications of this work for the discipline of sociology are potentially numerous. For instance, it provides a basis for critical appraisal of the diagnoses of those authors who have viewed involvement in sports as a potential substitute for work as modern nations, it is assumed, enter a period of increasing leisure. A striking example is provided by Wohl:

. . . The perspective of an increase in leisure time opens up before us a new road . . . There is no need to doubt that mankind will make the proper use of this surplus time in order to take part in sport. Already at present, as was revealed by research, sports . . . [have] come to the forefront as regards leisure time pursuits. Thus, there exist foundations to assume that together with a further increase in leisure time, such activity will occupy [a greater and greater amount of time], provided that the growing amount of free time will be accompanied also by an increase in the means, needed to indulge in sport, such as equipment, sports facilities, instructors, etc.

There is no doubt that the invaluable features of sport as entertainment and a spectacle as well as its educational significance will help to put all these aspirations into practice. The development trend of competitive sport points, on the other hand, to the fact that such a popularization of sport will certainly bring about a perfection of the human body, will make it stronger, agile and nimble, capable of quick reaction and the ability rapidly to regain the lost equilibrium. This will, undoubtedly, be one of the most lofty gifts of the leisure time epoch. . . .[11]

Aside from the questionable acceptance of the physical fitness value of sports participation, there are deeper problems in these views. If the analysis of the present study is correct, it is unlikely that in the future there will develop any massive leisure-time involvement in sports as we know these activities today. Given a shared value emphasis between the institution of sport and the rest of society, a change in the character of societal life will be reflected in a change within the institution of sport. Change from a work-oriented to a leisure-oriented society would necessitate commensurate changes in value orientations and emphases. Observations of the unemployed (of all ages and classes) and retired elderly persons in America point up two basis problems which will face society's members if mass leisure is achieved *without* concomitant changes in values emphasized: boredom and loss of self-esteem. Boredom is generated by the urge to do something meaningful when there is nothing meaningful to do within the context of internalized definitions. Loss of self-esteem is perhaps the most prevalent consequence of unemployment in a situation where one has internalized a strong achievement orientation that is institutionally connected to occupational roles. In short, a culture cannot teach its members that "anyone who does not work is a bum," and simultaneously promise fewer and fewer jobs in the face of increasing population size and greater leisure.

One hypothesis of this work has been that an important source of fan enthusiasm is the fact that values emphasized in sport are shared by the fan in his own instrumental endeavors. A leisure-oriented society probably would significantly diminish enthusiasm because fans would not be inclined to identify with the type of activity we call sports today.

Sport has been frequently hailed as a catalyst by which national integration and international cooperation might be significantly improved. Perhaps the most frequently cited event in support of the latter has been the so-called "ping-pong diplomacy" between the United States and the Peoples Republic of China. The approach of the present work suggests that, as an integrating influence, sport would have its greatest impact *within* social units already fairly well integrated or *between* social units which have already established cooperative ties or a relationship based upon some foundation of shared values. Where hostility rages openly or lies just beneath the surface, intergroup confrontations in the sports arena may well serve as a focus for heightening conflict or as mere substitute "battles" through which opposing participants and fans alike may express existing hostility toward each other. Under these

[11] Andrzej Wohl, "The Problem of Leisure in Our Time," *The International Review of Sports Sociology* (Warsaw: Polish Publishers, 1967), p. 121.

circumstances, it would seem unlikely that sport has any real potential for *bringing hostile groups closer together.* On the contrary, it could very well intensify existing intergroup antagonisms, as the so-called soccer war between Honduras and El Salvador in 1968 illustrates.

So it would seem that the so-called "ping-pong diplomacy" was in fact more a reflection of Premier Chou En-lai's subtle sense of humor than an act validating the assumed capacity of sport to ameriorate intergroup antagonisms.

Another point is relevant here. Recalling the discussion above on the impact of the information explosion in terms of reducing the perceived validity of traditional "truths," international sports events and many domestic sports spectaculars may have to be discontinued in the not too distant future because of increasing political factionalism within societies. In an earlier chapter it was stated that, to the extent that beliefs focusing upon sport (the sports creed) reflect traditionally emphasized values and orientations, sport becomes conservatively political. Under the impact of the information explosion, many people have come to dissent from such values and orientations, athletes among them. Much of the ceremony and pomp which surrounds sport spectaculars at least implies generalized traditional political orientations. It could come to pass that athletes and others occupying sports roles will reject the implied political thrust of such ceremonies and seek to substitute gestures and ceremonies perceived to be more in line with their own personal political views. The public exposure given these sports events would provide added incentive for dissenters from traditional political views to demonstrate their own political attitudes. Forerunners of such expressive events possibly may be the Smith-Carlos incident and the demonstrations staged by the Czechoslovakian gymnasts at the 1968 Olympic Games, the Mathews-Collett incident at the 1972 games, the suit filed by the University of Michigan Marching Band to force permission from the Rose Bowl Committee for an "anti-Vietnam war" halftime program, and other similar acts of dissidence staged by athletes and others during the course of sports events since 1967. To what extent various nations will attempt to maintain the traditional de facto political aspects of sports events in the face of disaffection remains to be seen. In international sports, at least, it seems likely that the playing of national anthems, the hoisting of national flags, and similar accoutrements will have to be ended just to buy time. In the future, the alternative may be to cease holding the sports events themselves.

THE FUTURE: TOWARD A SOCIOLOGY OF SPORTS

As to the future of the "Sociology of Sport" as a subdiscipline within the field of sociology, I believe that it promises to be extraordinarily productive. The institution of sport provides a "natural" laboratory for sociological inquiry of significance far beyond the realm of sport itself. In sport, the presence of the social scientist does not contaminate or interfere with the character of the phenomena being studied. The spectator is a natural part of the sporting event. Thus, for the price of a ticket, the sociologist who has done his homework and knows what to look for, can gain access to a mirror reflecting the past traditions, the present turmoil, and, to a great extent, the future destiny of society. Whether one's concern is with specific areas such as interracial relations or male-female role relationships, or with more general areas of scientific inquiry such as social organization and social change, sport offers a virtually unexplored avenue for generating new knowledge and gaining better insights into old problems. In the not-too-distant future, therefore, it would not be surprising if among sociologists there emerged a new appreciation for the old sports refrain "Take Me Out to the Ball Game."

Appendixes

Appendix A

Methodology

The purpose of Appendix A is to present the methods by which the data used in this study were gathered and subsequently developed into a description that has been termed the "American Sports Creed."

The assumed virtues of sport depicted in this work are so familiar and so widely believed that it may seem unnecessary to use any formal procedures to reveal the substantive content of those virtues. However, if a research effort is to be even remotely defensible as objective or "scientific," it is never sufficient for a researcher to rely solely upon his own a priori perceptions or assumptions about the data he uses—no matter how "generally known" these data might be.

Furthermore, for the purposes of this study, it was as important to know the attitudes and beliefs of individuals fulfilling specific roles within the institution of sport as it was to have such knowledge about the general population.

And finally, only by a formal analysis of the literature relating to sport can one hope to delineate the diverse and sometimes conflicting perspectives on athletics, as well as certain consistencies. As we have seen, there is no single monolithic attitude toward sport in America. Rather, there are three main bodies of belief—the American Sports Creed, the Humanitarian Sports Creed, and the Equalitarian Sports Creed—as well as other less significant systems of beliefs about sport. (Members of the Nation of Islam, or Black Muslims, denounce all sport as evil and without redeeming virtue. For this reason Muhammad Ali was suspended from the religious group because of his insistence upon pursuing his heavyweight boxing career. See "On Sport and Play" in Elijah Muhammad, *Message to the Black Man,* Muhammad Mosque No. 2, Chicago, 1965, pp. 246–247.)

In the introduction to Part II, it was made clear that in order to obtain a representative picture of the *dominant* belief system relating to sport, the attitudes and beliefs of persons directly involved in professional positions in sport should be sampled. This sampling of professional attitudes was taken from *Athletic Journal,* America's first professional journal in the sports realm. (For considerations influencing the choice of *Athletic Journal* as the source of data on professional attitudes and expressed beliefs about sport, see pages 146–48 in the text.)

To develop the categories necessary to classify the numerous statements of diverse attitudes and beliefs about sport, the first formidable task was to carefully read randomly selected *Athletic Journal* volumes. Reading was continued until, in the author's judgment, a consistent pattern of expressed attitudes had crystalized. As it turned out, seven volumes were read, cover to cover, before this point was reached. During this reading, each virtue ascribed to sport was listed upon first being encountered and, in turn, every subsequent encounter was duly noted.

Once the boundaries of the data to be analyzed had been established to a rudimentary degree, the next tasks were (1) determining the sampling procedure used in surveying the journal volumes, (2) operationalizing the categories in order that expressed statements could be reliably and consistently coded, and (3) devising some means of determining the reliability of the coding process.

The task of arriving at a suitable sampling procedure was undertaken first. Because no single library to which the author had access had all published issues of *Athletic Journal,* it was necessary to use the facilities at three educational institutions—Bancroft Library at the University of California; San Jose State, the University of California at Berkeley; and Stanford University. It was thus possible to secure for analysis Volume II (September 1930 to June 1931) through Volume 49 (September, 1968 to June 1969).

The major sample population was comprised of entire journal issues rather than articles, since the preliminary reading had indicated that not every article contained materials relevant to the task at hand. But each issue did contain some references to, opinions of, or beliefs about what is termed here the sports creed. It was therefore decided that every third issue would be analyzed from each volume, making the sample population 130 issues out of a total population of 390.

In order to determine the issue with which the sampling would start, a table of random numbers was used. By chance the number 32 was chosen. Starting with the thirty-second issue available, every third issue became part of the sample. This procedure was to be continued until each of the thirty-nine available volumes had been thoroughly read.

The task of operationalizing the categories derived from the pre-liminary reading also constituted a formidable task. While the categories were clearly separate, such separation was not always the most obvious characteristic of the statements *as these were expressed*. Consider for instance the following statement:

The ability to adjust to adverse conditions in life . . . the value of physical fitness, the importance of self-sacrifice and loyalty . . . all this is . . . com-petitive athletics' contribution to the education and development of young Americans. (*Athletic Journal*, Editorial, Volume 37, March 1957, p. 18).

This one statement was coded under no less than five different categories.

1. *Prepares an individual for life in a competitive society.* (The ability to adjust to adverse conditions . . . .)
2. *Promotes Altruism.* (. . . the importance of self-self sacrifice.)
3. *Conducive to development and/or maintenance of physical fitness* (. . . the value of physical fitness . . .)
4. *Supportive of loyalty* (. . . the importance of . . . loyalty)
5. *Supportive of the educational process* (. . . all this is . . . com-petitive athletics' contribution to the educational and development of young Americans).

It was not infrequent that such multiple codings were employed to re-cord an expressed relationship between sport and several positive out-comes.

The most important criterion for classifying a sentence in whole or part under one category or another, then, was the specific expression of a relationship between sport and one of the central concepts used in developing the categories. Rather wide latitude was used in interpreting the strength of the cause-effect relationship between sport and the posi-tive outcomes denoted by central concepts. For instance, the following two statements were both coded under the category *Facilitates self and/or social control*, though there is admittedly a vast difference in the strength of the expressed cause-effect relationship between sport and each outcome:

. . . Participation in sport . . . supplies a desirable outlet for surplus energy common to youth (Gordon R. Fisher, "School Athletics Become Increasingly Valuable," *Athletic Journal*, Vol. 13, No. 8, p. 16). Participation in sport will develop (in the individual) a willingness to abide by rules of (social conduct) . . . (Gordon R. Fisher, *ibid.*, p. 16)

Because such central concepts as "character" and "physical fitness" were not always expressed in an explicit cause-effect relationship with sport involvement, it was necessary to employ a second criterion in the coding process. Essentially, this involved the development of supplementary descriptive guidelines detailing the broader limits of each category. These guidelines allowed for the coding of statements according to the context within which each appeared. Thus, though the concept "social control" was seldom mentioned explicitly in the literature, a great many statements were judged to postulate a cause-effect relationship between sports involvement and the facilitation of social control because the context within which they were presented fell within the limits of the guidelines determining which statements could be coded as such.

The basic *units of analysis* thus were the *sentence* and the *phrase* explicitly expressing relationships between sport and the development of certain positive outcomes (character development, physical fitness, mental fitness, etc.). However, without supplementary consideration of the *context unit*—usually in the form of a paragraph—much data would have been lost or it would have been necessary to develop an unmanageably large number of categories. The guidelines detailed the criteria for deciding whether the context of a statement justified its being coded under one category or another. Oftentimes in the main text of the present study, entire paragraphs and even larger passages are presented in support of the author's assertions concerning the substance of the dominant sports creed because a presentation of both the unit of analysis and the context unit was deemed necessary to the explication of such assertions.

Having decided upon the sampling procedure and the coding categories, the author carried out the content analysis of the sample drawn and coded the results.

The content analysis resulted initially in 21 sentence classifications, one of which was labeled "miscellaneous." To check the accuracy of the coding process for the 20 substantive classifications, a sample of 10 statements was drawn from each category and randomly arranged into a list totaling 200 items. The list was submitted to three graduate students who were writing their Master's and Ph.D. theses on sports—two at San Jose State College and one at the University of California at Berkeley. Bruce Averoy, a white student, was at the time an M.A. degree candidate in sociology at San Jose State College and had worked closely with the present author in organizing the 1968 Olympic protest movement. His thesis proposal focused upon the social psychology of sport in America as did that of William Carter, a black student and a candidate for the Master of Arts degree in psychology at San Jose State. Ken Noel, the third student coder is a black student and a Ph.D. candidate at the University of California at Berkeley. His area of academic interest is the structure and functions of sport as a social institution. He was chiefly responsible for much of the organization and strategy employed in the Olympic protest movement of 1968.

Prior to presenting the students with a sample of statements to be coded independently by each of them, two discussion sessions were held to familiarize them with the criteria for coding each category of statement. Each student was provided with a sheet outlining the concept that was key to each category and presenting the contextual guidelines which they were to use in interpreting statements which mentioned no specific concept such as character, social control, nationalism, and so forth. After each student coder had satisfied himself and the author that he was sufficiently familiar with the coding procedure to undertake the task at hand, each was given his list of 200 statements which he was to code independently and return to the author.

By comparing the results of the student's work with the author's coding of these same sentences, a type of reliability index was developed for each category employed in the coding process. For instance, each student independently coded the same 10 statements that the author had previously coded under the category "character development." If all 30 of their codings had been perfectly consistent with the coding results arrived at by the author, the coding procedure for this category would have been assumed to be 100% reliable. However, only 27 were consistent, and thus the coding procedure for this category was deemed to be 90% reliable.

The results of the content analysis and the author's interpretations of these data were recorded in a preliminary manuscript draft and submitted to Professors Gordon F. Streib, Robin M. Williams, Jr., and William F. Whyte of Cornell University for their suggestions and criticisms. After much correspondence and one meeting, it was mutually decided that the data as then structured represented more nearly what Dr. Streib called a "laundry list" of significant but unordered beliefs than a systematically related set of tenets in a sports creed. Professor Streib in particular suggested that the treatment of the data might be improved by strengthening the author's explicit theoretical format and by a more specific statement of the continuity of values hypothesized to exist between the institution of sport and the greater society.

A thorough review of such works as Robin M. William's *American Society*, Chapters X and XI, and Francis X. Sutton et al., *The American Business Creed* showed that, if the values found within the institution of sport were to be systematically discussed within the context of the value orientations of the larger society, a great deal more research would be required. For one thing the values represented in a single professional journal were simply insufficient to serve as the sole basis for such a statement of relationships. Furthermore, almost two-thirds of the journal issues sampled were written prior to 1955. Given the fact that a good deal of change has taken place in sport—technologically, politically, and structurally—even since 1960, additional and more recent data were obviously called for.

Using the same categories and coding procedures employed in

gathering data from the *Athletic Journal* sample, three additional data sources were analyzed.

The first additional source was the Institute for the Study of Sport and Society, directed by Dr. Jack Scott. As part of its activities, this organization maintains a continuing file on socially relevant occurrences in organized athletics. Part of the input into this file is collected by regular volunteer staff members at the institute but the overwhelming majority of it is gathered by a professional magazine and newspaper clipping service. In all, over 1100 articles from these files were read and relevant aspects of their contents coded for inclusion in the present study. Sample articles were also photocopied to be used as illustrative materials throughout this work.

The institute also maintains a file on all available official and legal documents and rulings having a bearing upon some level of sports activity. Most of these materials comprise decisions made by the various courts and, to a greater degree, by the governing bodies of sports (such as the National Collegiate Athletic Association and the National Football League). To a limited extent, these materials were found to be useful.

A second source of additional materials was the body of data collected by Eldon E. Snyder of Bowling Green University on the use of dressing room slogans as a means of socialization. In the spring of 1969, Mr. Snyder with the cooperation of the Ohio Association for Health, Physical Education and Recreation drew a systematic sample of 270 high schools (one-third of the schools affiliated with this organization). A questionnaire was sent to the basketball coach and two basketball team members from each of the 270 schools. One open-ended item on the questionnaire asked for a listing of slogans put up in the dressing room facilities provided for each team involved in the study. Of those contacted 65 percent of the coaches responded as did 50 percent of the athletes. These responses showed that 71 percent of the coaches and 61 percent of the athletes indicated that the slogans or statements listed were put on dressing room walls and bulletin boards by coaches. Clearly, the slogans gathered through this study represent a valuable source of data for the purposes here.

The final source of more up-to-date information was the author's own file of magazine articles, newspaper clippings and other literature pertinent to the task here. From these materials, some 557 articles were read and analyzed. Of these, over half (293) were discarded since they were duplicates of articles found in the files of the Institute for the Study of Sport and Society.

Despite the relatively wide range of sources tapped, the data analyzed here cannot be said to represent a statistical sample of the information available. The author is satisfied however that the creedal statements derived and presented are representative of the core of publically expressed beliefs held by those directly involved in organized sports at all levels in American society.

As a result of the analysis of data derived from the three additional sources, two major adjustments were made in order that this study would more accurately reflect the overall and continuing character of the sports creed in America. A number of preliminary categories developed during the examination of *Athletic Journal* were eliminated because these were, in the author's opinion, not significantly evident consistently throughout all the data analyzed. The substantive content of a category of statements labeled "miscellaneous" was also dropped once it became clear after analysis of auxiliary materials that these represented, for the most part, "unique" idiosyncratic sentiments.

The number of categories derived from the analysis of all the above-mentioned sources was finally reduced from 21 to 12. Using the work of Williams and Sutton as theoretical guides, these 12 specific categories were organized under 7 central themes of what is termed the "American Sports Creed":

   I. *Character:* general statements pertaining to (1) character development and relating sports to such traits as clean living, proper grooming, "red-bloodedness," etc.; statements specifically relating sport to the development of (2) loyalty and (3) altruism (brotherhood, unselfishness, or self-sacrifice).

  II. *Discipline:* statements relating sport to the development of (4) social and or self-control.

 III. *Competition:* statements and slogans relating sport specifically to (5) the development of fortitude and more generally to (6) preparation for life and (7) providing opportunities for advancement for the individual.

 IV. *Physical Fitness:* (8) statements and slogans relating sport to the achievement of physical health.

  V. *Mental Fitness:* statements relating sports to the development of (9) mental alertness and to (10) educational achievement.

 VI. *Religiosity:* (11) expressions relating sports achievement to traditional American Christianity.

VII. *Nationalism:* (12) statements relating sports involvement to the development of patriotism.

Presented below are (*a*) the operational definitions and guidelines governing the inclusion of statements from all data sources, under each of the 12 categories, and (*b*) the reliability index (expressed in percentages) for each category based upon the student coders' work (on data from *Athletic Journal* only).

1. *Character.* 90% consistent with author's coding. Statements

coded under this category are those specifically and explicitly referring to some relationship between character formation and sports involvement; or they may pertain more generally to such traits as "clean living," "red-bloodedness," or to an appearance and social disposition which is deemed appropriate, in conformity with social expectations, or otherwise desirable.

2. *Loyalty.* 83% consistent with author's coding. Statements coded under this category may be those specifically positing a relationship between sports involvement and the development or reinforcement of a value on loyalty.

3. *Altruism.* 90% consistent with author's codings. Statements coded under this category may be those expressing a relationship between sports involvement and the development of values emphasizing self-sacrifice, brotherhood, the diminution of racial or ethnic prejudices, or the lessening of intergroup antagonisms and, conversely, the heightening of intergroup understanding and empathy.

4. *Social and/or self control.* 83% consistent with author's coding. Statements coded under this category may be those specifically expressing a relation between sports involvement and social control or self-control or those that can be judged by context to posit a relationship between such involvement and the formation of a respect for established authority, an inclination to conform to established rules, norms, or laws regulating social behavior.

5. *Fortitude.* 97% consistent with author's codings. Statements coded under this category may be those specifically positing a relationship between sports involvement and the development or reinforcement of "guts," courage, perseverence, or self-confidence.

6. *Preparation for life.* 77% consistent with author's codings. Statements coded under this category may be those that either explicitly state or suggest that sports events constitute a microcosm of competitive life in the greater society, that the sports arena is a laboratory where potential life circumstances can be experienced and confronted by those involved in sports, or that sports is essential to the preparation of youth for their roles in American society.

7. *Opportunities for individual advancement (social status mobility).* 100% consistency with author's coding. Statements coded under this category may be those that explicitly state or suggest a relationship between sports involvement and the realization of opportunities for the achievement of increased social status, positive social recognition, or vertical class mobility.

8. *Physical fitness.* 97% consistent with author's codings. Statements coded under this category may be those that explicitly express or suggest a relationship between sports involvement and the development or maintenance of physical fitness, physical health, or physical well being.

9. *Mental alertness.* 80% consistent with author's coding. Statements coded under this category may be those which explicitly state or suggest a relationship between sport and the maintenance of "healthy mental attitude" or a constant and rati nally optimistic awareness of one's potential and alternatives in any goal-directed activity.

10. *Educational achievement.* 97% consistent with author's codings. Statements coded under this category may specifically express or suggest a relationship between sports involvement and the achievement of a "well-rounded," "complete," or wholesome education; improved educational achievement in non-athletic courses; or the educational value of sport as a physical and mental activity.

11. *Religiosity.* 97% consistent with the author's codings. Statements coded under this category may be those either explicitly or implicity positing a relationship between sports involvement and the development, reinforcement, or re-affirmation of traditional Christian religious beliefs.

12. *Nationalism.* 83% consistency with the author's codings. Statements coded under this category may explicitly assert or suggest a relationship between sports involvement and the development or reinforcement of patriotism (including national pride, commitment to "the American way of life" and the "American system" or American social traditions, reverence for the flag and other societally relevant symbols, support of established or traditional American policy in the political and military arenas, and so forth).

Appendix B

Definitions of personality traits

FROM IPAT

Reserved. Detached, critical, cool. The person who scores low tends to be stiff, cool, skeptical, and aloof. He likes things rather than people, working alone, and avoiding compromises of viewpoints. He is likely to be precise and "rigid" in his way of doing things and in personal standards, and in many occupations these are desirable traits. He may tend at times to be critical, obstructive, or hard.

Outgoing. Warmhearted, easygoing, participating. The person who scores high tends to be good natured, easygoing, emotionally expressing (hence naturally affectothmia), ready to cooperate, attentive to people, softhearted, kindly, adaptable. He likes occupations dealing with people and socially impressive situations. He readily forms active groups. He is generous in personal relations, less afraid of criticism, better able to remember names of people.

Less Intelligent. Concrete-thinking (lower scholastic mental capacity). The person scoring low tends to be slow to learn and grasp, dull, given to concrete and literal interpretation. His dullness may be simply a reflection of low intelligence or it may represent poor functioning due to psychopathology.

More Intelligent. Abstract-thinking, bright (higher scholastic mental capacity). The person who scores high tends to be quick to grasp ideas, a fast learner, intelligent. There is some correlation with level of culture, and some with alertness. High scores contraindicate deterioration of mental functions in pathological conditions.

Sober. Prudent, serious, taciturn. The person who scores low tends to be restrained, reticent, introspective. He is sometimes dour, pessimistic, unduly deliberate, and considered smug and primly correct by observers. He tends to be a sober, dependable person.

Happy-go-Lucky. Impulsively lively, gay, enthusiastic. The person who scores high on this trait tends to be cheerful, active, frank, expressive, effervescent, carefree. He is frequently chosen as an elected leader. He may be impulsive and mercurial.

Trusting. Adaptable, free of jealousy, easy to get on with. The person who scores low tends to be free of jealous tendencies, adaptable, cheerful, uncompetitive, concerned about other people, a good team worker.

Suspicious. Self-opinionated, hard to fool. The person who scores high tends to be mistrusting and doubtful. He is often involved in his own ego, is self-opinionated, and interested in internal, mental life. He is usually deliberate in his actions, unconcerned about other people, a poor team member.

Casual. Careless of protocol, follows own urges. The person who scores low will not be bothered with will control and regard for social demands. He is not overly considerate, careful, or painstaking. He may feel maladjusted and many maladjustments (especially the affective, but not the paranoid) show.

Controlled. Socially precise, following self-image. The person who scores high tends to have strong control of his emotions and general behavior, is inclined to be socially aware and careful, and evidences what is commonly termed "self-respect" and regard for social reputation. He sometimes tends, however, to be obstinate. Effective leaders, and some paranoids, are high.

FROM JACKSON PERSONALITY RESEARCH FORM*

Description of High Scorer	*Defining Trait Adjectives*
Orderliness. Concerned with keeping personal effects and surroundings neat and organized; dislikes clutter, confusion, lack of organization; interested in developing methods for keeping materials methodically organized.	neat, organized, tidy, systematic, well ordered, disciplined, prompt, consistent, orderly, clean, methodical, scheduled, planful, unvarying, deliberate.
Impulsivity. Tends to act on the "spur of the moment" and without deliberation; gives vent readily to feelings and wishes; speaks freely; may be volatile in emotional expression.	hasty, rash, uninhibited, spontaneous, reckless, irrepressible, quick-thinking, mercurial, impatient, incautious, hurried, impulsive, foolhardy, excitable, impetuous.
Understanding. Wants to understand many areas of knowledge; values synthesis of ideas, verifiable generalization. Logical thoughts, particularly when directed at satisfying curiosity.	inquiring, curious, analytical, exploring, reflective, incisive, investigative, probing, scrutinizing, inquisitive.

* See Edwards' factor definitions for descriptions of traits of abasement and exhibitionism.

FROM EDWARDS' PERSONAL PREFERENCE SCHEDULE

Deference. To get suggestions from others, to find out what others think, to follow instructions and do what is expected, to praise others, to tell others that they have done a good job, to accept the leadership of others, to read about great men, to conform to custom and avoid the unconventional, to let others make decisions.

Orderliness. To have written work neat and organized, to make plans before starting on a difficult task, to have things organized, to keep things neat and orderly, to make advance plans when taking a trip, to organize details of work, to keep letters and files according to some system, to have meals organized and a definite time for eating to have things arranged so that they run smoothly without change.

Exhibition. To say witty and clever things, to tell amusing jokes and stories, to talk about personal adventures and experiences, to have others notice and comment upon one's appearance, to say things just to see what effect it will have on others, to talk about personal achievements, to be the center of attention, to use words that others do not know the meaning of, to ask questions others cannot answer.

Introspection. To analyze one's motives and feelings, to observe others, to understand how others feel about problems, to put oneself in another's place, to judge people by why they do things rather than by what they do, to analyze the behavior of others, to analyze the motives of others, to predict how others will act.

Abasement. To feel guilty when one does something wrong, to accept blame when things do not go right, to feel that personal pain and misery suffered does more good than harm, to feel the need for punishment for wrong doing, to feel better when giving in and avoiding a fight than when having one's own way, to feel the need for confession of errors, to feel depressed by inability to handle situations, to feel timid in the presence of superiors, to feel inferior to others in most respects.

Endurance. To keep at a job until it is finished, to complete any job undertaken, to work hard at a task, to keep at a puzzle or problem until it is solved, to work at a single job before taking on others, to stay up late working in order to get a job done, to put in long hours of work without distraction, to stick at a problem even though it may seem as if no progress is being made, to avoid being interrupted while at work.

Bibilography

Amdur, Neil. *The Fifth Down and the Football Revolution,* New York: Coward, McCann and Geoghegan, 1971.

Beisse, Arnold. *The Madness in Sports,* New York: Appleton-Century-Crofts Publishing Co., 1966.

Bendix, R. *Max Weber, An Intellectual Portrait,* New York: Doubleday, 1962.

Berne, Eric. *Games People Play,* New York: Grove Press, 1964.

Biddoulph, L. G. "Athletic Achievement and Personal and Social Adjustment in High School Boys," *Research Quarterly,* Vol. 25, 1954.

San Francisco Chronicle. "Biennial Sex Tests for Girl Athletes," July 13, 1971.

Blalock, Hubert M. *Toward a Theory of Minority Group Relations,* New York: John Wiley and Sons, Inc., 1967.

Blau, Peter M. and Scott, W. R. *Formal Organizations,* San Francisco: Chandler, 1962.

Bouton, Jim. *Ball Four,* New York: World Publishing Co., 1970.

Bowen, W. P. "The Evaluation of Athletic Evils," *American Physical Education Review,* Vol. 14, No. 3, March 1909.

Boyle, Robert H. *Sport: Mirror of American Life,* Boston: Little Brown, 1963.

Brown, Sam. "Snow Job in Colorado," *The New Republic,* Jan. 29, 1972.

Bucher, Charles A. *Foundations of Physical Education,* St. Louis: The C. V. Mosby Co., 1968.

Caillois, Roger. *Man Play and Games* (translated by Meyer Barash), New York: Free Press, 1961.

Coffer, C., Johnson, W. R. "Personality Dynamics in Relation to Exercise and

Sports," *Science and Medicine of Exercise and Sport,* Edited by W. R. Johnson, New York and London: Harper Bros., 1960.

Cohen, Albert K. *Delinquent Boys,* New York: Free Press, 1961.

Coleman, James S. *The Adolescent Society,* New York: Free Press of Glencoe, Inc., 1961.

————. *Adolescents and the Schools,* New York: Basic Books, Inc., 1965.

Dickey, Glenn. "Can Football Players be Treated as Adults," *San Francisco Chronicle,* Aug. 17, 1971.

Dunning, Eric. "Notes on Some Conceptual and Theoretical Problems in the Sociology of Sport," *The International Review of Sport Sociology,* Warsaw, Vol. 3, 1967.

Durant, John and Bettman, Otto. *Pictorial History of American Sports,* New York: A. S. Barnes and Co., 1952.

Durso, J. "Sportswriting—and the All-American Dollar," *Saturday Review,* October 1971.

Edwards, Harry. *Black Students,* New York: Free Press, 1970.

————. *The Revolt of the Black Athlete,* New York: Free Press, 1969.

————. "The Myth of the Racially Superior Athlete," *Intellectual Digest,* March 1972; "Desegregating Sexist Sport," *Intellectual Digest,* Nov. 1972. "Munich Now, Montreal Next," *Intellectual Digest,* Dec. 1972.

Eidsmoe, Russell M. "The Facts about the Academic Performance of High School Athletes." *Journal of Health, Physical Education and Recreation,* Vol. 32, Nov. 1961.

Erikson, Erik. *Childhood and Society,* New York: W. W. Norton & Co., 1950.

Fisher, George J. "Athletics and the Youth of the Nation," *Proceedings: The National Collegiate Athletic Association,* 1927.

Fisher, Gordon R. "School Athletics Became Increasingly Valuable," *Athletic Journal,* Vol. 13, No. 8, April 1934.

Frazier, E. Franklin. *The Negro in The United States,* Chicago: University of Chicago Press, 1949.

French, Lee. *Personality Differences Among Athletes and Between Athletes and Non-athletes* (thesis), San Jose State College, San Jose, California, Jan. 1970.

Freud, Sigmund. "Group Psychology and The Analysis of Ego," *International Psychoanalytic Library,* New York: Liveright Publishing Corporation, Vol. 6, 1951.

Goffman, Erving. *Encounters,* Indianapolis: Bobbs-Merrill, 1961.

————. *The Presentation of Self in Everyday Life,* New York: Doubleday and Co., 1959.

Hackensmith, C. W. *History of Physical Education,* New York: Harper and Row, 1966.

Hart, Marie. "On Being Female in Sport" in Hart, Marie, (ed.) *Sport in the Sociocultural Process,* Dubuque, Iowa: W. C. Brown, Pub. 1972.

————. "Women Sit in the Back of the Bus," *Psychology Today,* October, 1971.

Hausner, L. "Personality Traits of Champion and Former Champion Athletes," University of Illinois, Department of Psychology, 1952.

Henderson, Edwin B. *The Negro in Sports,* Washington, D.C.: The Associated Publishers, Inc., 1949.

Hoch, Paul. *Rip Off the Big Game,* New York: Doubleday Anchor Books, 1972.

Huizinga, John. *Homo Ludens: A Study of the Play Element in Culture,* Boston: Beacon Press, 1938.

Hussey, M. M. "Character Education in Athletics," *The American Educational Review,* Vol. 33, Nov. 1938.

Kane, J. E. "Personality and Physical Ability" in *Proceedings: International Congress of Sports,* Tokyo, 1964.

————. and Warburton, F. W., "Personality As It Relates To Sport and Physical Ability," *Readings in Physical Education,* The Physical Education Association, London, 1966.

Kane, Martin. "An Assessment of Black Is Best," *Sports Illustrated,* Jan. 18, 1971.

Kenyon, G. S. "Sport Involvement: A Conceptual Goal and Some Consequences thereof," *Sociology of Sport,* Gerald S. Kenyon, (ed.), The Athletic Institute, 1969.

Kolatch, J. *Sport Politics and Ideology in China,* New York: Jonathan David, Publisher, 1972.

Koppet, L. "Colleges Question Old Views on Sports," *The New York Times,* Jan. 11, 1971.

Komarovsky, Mirra. *The Unemployed Man and His Family,* New York: Dryden Press, 1940.

Kramer, Jerry. *Instant Replay: The Green Bay Diary of Jerry Kramer,* New York: Signet, The American Library, 1968.

Krout, John A. *Annals of American Sport,* New Haven: Yale University Press, 1929.

Loy, John W. and Kenyon, G. S. *Sport, Culture and Society,* New York: The MacMillan Co., 1969.

Loy, John W. and McElvogue, J. F. "Racial Segregation in American Sport," *The International Review of Sport Sociology,* Vol. 5, 1970.

Le Bon, Gustave. *The Crowd,* London: Owen Press, 1917.

Lewis, Hyland and Herzog, E. "The Family: Resources for Change" in Bracy (ed.) *Black Matriarchy: Myth a Reality,* Belmont, California: Wadsworth Publishing Co., 1970.

Lomax, L. E. *The Negro Revolt,* New York: Harper and Row, Publishers, 1963, 1971.

Los Angeles Times. "Gridders Visit Vietnam," May 30, 1971.

McIntosh, Mary. "The Homosexual Role," in Skolnick and Skolnick, *The Family in Transition,* Boston: Little, Brown and Co., 1971.

McIntosh, Peter C. *Sport in Society,* London: C. A. Warrs, 1963.

Mangel, Charles. "How Good are Organized Sports for Your Child's Physical Fitness," *Look,* June 1, 1971.

Mead, G. H. *Self and Society,* Chicago: University of Chicago Press, 1934.

Meggysey, Dave. *Out of Their League,* Ramparts Press, 1970.

Metheny, Elenor. "Symbolic Forms of Movement: The Feminine Image in

Sport," in Sage, George, H. (ed.), *Sport and American Society,* Canada: Addison-Wesley Publishers, 1970.

Miller, Arthur. *Death of a Salesman,* New York: Viking Press, 1958.

Miller, Norman P. and Robinson, Duane M. *The Leisure Age,* Belmont, California: Wadsworth Publishing Co., 1963.

Montague, Ashley (ed.) *The Concept of Race,* New York: Free Press, 1965.

Moore, R. A. *Sports and Mental Health,* Springfield, Illinois: Charles C Thomas, Pub., 1966.

Morton, Henry W. *Soviet Sport,* New York: Collier, 1963.

Myrdal, Gunnar. *The American Dilemma,* Boston: Beacon Press, 1956.

Natan, A. *Sport and Society,* London: Bowes and Bowes, 1958.

Newsweek. "Are Sports Good for the Soul?" Jan. 11, 1971.

Nixon, Richard M., and sport. "Lombardi Memorial Planned," *San Francisco Chronicle,* June 10, 1971; "Nixon at Hall of Fame Inductions," *San Francisco Chronicle,* July 10, 1971; "Nixon Greets A's," *San Francisco Chronicle,* Aug. 18, 1971.

Ogilvie, Bruce and Tutko, Thomas A. *Problem Athletes and How to Handle Them,* London: Pelham Books, 1966.

———. "Sports Don't Build Character," *San Francisco Chronicle,* Sept. 23, 1971; *Psychology Today,* Oct. 1971.

———. "The Mental Ramblings of Psychologists Researching in the Area of Sports Motivation," Department of Psychology, San Jose State College, 1967.

———. "Self Perception as Compared with Measured Personality of Male Physical Educators," presented at the Second International Congress of Sport Sociologists, Oct. 1968.

———. "Psychological Consistencies Within the Personalities of High Level Competitors," *Journal of the American Medical Association,* Oct. 1968.

———. "The Unconscious Fear of Success" (unpublished), Department of Psychology, San Jose State College.

Olsen, Jack. *The Black Athlete: A Shameful Story,* in *Sports Illustrated,* Aug. 8, 1968.

Osborne, R. H. (ed.) *The Biological and Social Meaning of Race,* San Francisco: W. H. Freeman and Co., 1971.

Padwe, Sandy. "Midget League Sports Rapped," *The Philadelphia Inquirer,* Feb. 14, 1971.

———. "Sports and Politics Must be Separate—At Least Some Politics, That is," *The Philadelphia Inquirer,* Dec. 14, 1971.

———. "Big Time College Football on the Skids," *Look Magazine,* Sept. 22, 1970.

Pascal, A. H. and Rapping, L. A. "Racial Discrimination in Professional Baseball," The Rand Corporation, 1970.

Peking Review. "Ni Chih-Chin: The Man Who Set the World Record in the Men's High Jump," No. 7, Feb. 12, 1971.

Richmond, Charles A. "Personality of Coaches," *Association of American Colleges,* Bulletin 12, May 1926.

Robeson, Paul. (on his life and accomplishments), "Paul Robeson: The Great Forerunner," in *Freedomways Magazine,* Special Issue, Vol. II, No. 1, first quarter, 1971.

————. *Here I Stand,* Boston: Beacon Press, 1971.

Roberts, Steven. "Students are Questioning the Role and Cost of College Athletics, *The New York Times,* Jan. 3, 1971.

Rodgers, F. R. "Olympics for Girls," *School and Society,* Vol. 30, Aug. 10, 1929.

Rose, Arnold. *The Negro in America,* Boston: Beacon Press, 1944.

Russell, William F. *Go Up For Glory,* New York: Coward McCann, Inc., 1966.

Ryan, Pat. "A Grim Run for Fiscal Daylight," *Sports Illustrated,* Jan. 1, 1971.

Saasta, Tom. "Athletics: A Question of Values," University of Southern California *Daily Trojan,* Sept. 27, 1971, p. 4.

Saturday Review. "Education in America," Oct. 16, 1971.

Savage, Howard J. "The Coach in College Athletics," of *American College Athletics,* New York: The Carnegie Foundation for the Advancement of Teaching, Bulletin 23, 1929.

Savage, Howard J., et al. "The Growth of American Collegiate Athletics," in *American College Athletics,* New York: The Carnegie Foundation for the Advancement of Teaching, Bulletin No. 25, April 1930.

Schafer, Walter E. "Some Sources and Consequences of Interscholastic Athletics," in the *Sociology of Sport,* Gerald S. Kenyon, (ed.), The Athletic Institute, 1969.

Schneider, Ralph. "We Expect Them to Storm the Gates," in *Sports Illustrated,* Sept. 6, 1971.

Scott, Jack. *Athletics for Athletes,* Berkeley and Hayward, California: An Otherways Book, 1969.

————. *The Athletic Revolution,* New York: Free Press, 1970.

————. "Scott's Radical Ethic," *Intellectual Digest,* July 1972.

Sievert, William. "Cost Burdens, Wanning Student Interests Hit Inter Collegiate Sports," *The Chronicle of Higher Education,* Jan. 25, 1971.

Slavson, S. R. *Recreation and the Total Personality,* New York: The Association Press,1948.

Slusther, H. S. "Personality and Intelligence Characteristics of Selected High School Athletes and non-Athletes," in *Research Quarterly,* Vol. 35, Dec. 1964.

Snyder, Eldon E. "Athletic Dressing Room Slogans as Folklore: A Means of Socialization," presented at The Sociology of Sport Section, American Sociological Association, Aug. 30, 1971.

Solomon, George. "High School Coach Finds Winning Isn't Everything" in *Sports Focus,* (NEA Release), May 5, 1971.

Spencer, H. *The Principles of Psychology,* New York: D. Appleton and Co., 1873, cited by H. C. Lehman and P. A. Witty, *The Psychology of Play Activities,* New York: A. S. Barnes, 1927, p. 73.

Stone, G. P. "Some Meanings of American Sport" in Kenyon, G. S., *The Sociology of Sport,* The Athletic Institute, 1969.

————. *Games, Sport, and Power,* New York: Dutton, 1972.

Stump, Al. "Ralph Nader, Where Are You?" *TV Guide,* Oct. 30, 1971.

Sumner, W. G. *Folkways,* Boston: Ginn and Co., 1906.

Sutton, Francis X., et al. *The American Business Creed,* Cambridge: Harvard University Press, 1956, 1961.

Thompson, Richard. *Race and Sport,* London Institute of Race Relations, New York: Oxford University Press, 1964.

Tornawsky, Pat. "Women Vs. the Myth," *Runners' World,* March 1971.

Tunis, John R. *$port$,* New Haven: The Quinn and Boden Co., 1928.

Twombly, Wells. "College Squeeze Is On," *San Francisco Chronicle,* June 14, 1970.

Underwood, John. "The Desperate Coach," *Sports Illustrated,* Vol. 31, Nos. 9–11, Sept. 1969.

Veblen, Thorsten. *Theory of the Leisure Class,* New York: The Modern Library, 1934.

Von Hoffman, N. "College Sports," *Washington Post,* Nov. 25, 1970.

Weiss, Paul. *Sport: A Philosophical Inquiry,* Carbondale and Edwardsville: Southern Illinois University Press, 1969.

Wilhelm, Sidney. *Who Needs the Negro?* New York: Doubleday Anchor Books, 1971.

Williams, Robin M., Jr. *American Society: A Sociological Interpretation,* New York: Alfred A. Knopf, 1966, 1968.

Wolf, David. *Foul!,* Canada: Holt, Rinehart, and Winston, 1972.

Wolff, H. *The Sociology of Georg Simmel,* New York: The Free Press, 1964.

Indexes

Name index

Subject index